D0457000

SPORTS MARKETING

SPORTS MARKETING

It's Not Just a Game Anymore

PHIL SCHAAF

Prometheus Books
59 John Glenn Drive
Amherst, New York 14228-2197

Photograph of Candlestick Park on front cover used by permission of the San Francisco Giants and Major League Baseball

Published 1995 by Prometheus Books

 Inquiries should be addressed to Prometheus Books, 59 John Glenn Drive, Amherst, New York 14228–2197, 716–691–0133. FAX: 716–691–0137.

99 98 97 96 95   5 4 3 2 1

Library of Congress Cataloging-in-Publication Data

Schaaf, Phil, 1964–
Sports marketing : it's not just a game anymore. / Phil Schaaf.
p. cm.
Includes bibliographical references and index.
ISBN 1-57392-019-3 (alk. paper)
1. Sports—United States—Marketing. I. Title.
GV716.S32 1995
338.4'3796—dc20   95-20147
CIP

Printed in the United States of America on acid-free paper

This book is dedicated to the Public Libraries,
the places that made this book possible.

And to the efforts (especially Jean's) contributing to the rehabilitation of the greatest guy in the world, Raymond Joseph Schaaf Sr.

Contents

Acknowledgments

Mom and Dad. The satellite office, R.J. and Janice, Trey and Chase. Dave and Sis. Lisa Larkin for hardware and software consultation services. The Larsons, Ratays, and Sweeneys.

Ted Walsh, Bronco Hinek, the Bernies, Dave Rahn, Bobby Monica, Michael Zagaris, Andy Kuno, Harris Barton, the Rices, the Wilsons, and S. Young.

Steven L. Mitchell, Chris Arcara, Mike Powers, Jody Kaplowitz, Jonathan Kurtz, and the entire Prometheus staff.

Larry Jabbonsky, Dan Schoenberg, Rob Correa, Robin Carr-Locke, Irene Firmat, James Emmerson, Catherine McLandress, Linda Zider, Art Morley, John Carthum, Damon Skyta, Robert Reed, Ray Fosse, Rick Bishop, Julie Dittmar, David Stepp, Kerry Crough, Pete Boss, Tom Golubic, Bow Rodgers, Fernanda Carapinha Erlanger, Phil Erlanger, Barb Frank, Jeff Atkinson, Chris Friden, Steve Whyte, Dave Guingona, Gary Radnich, Pete Boss, Kerry Crough, Lisa Marie Smith, Laura Mancl, Marlene Korim, Laura Shooter, Sue Mezzin, Elizabeth Cattaner, Larry Maxwell, Ron Barr, Beth Anderson, Patty Stanton, Ron Owens, Shaun Minton, Eileen Murphy, Dale Fuller, Scott Sowry, Kelly Forden, Mike Waite, Reg Smith, John Durham, Dave Feldman, Jeanie Surowski Fred Fried, and Larry Wenner.

Marty Connell, Rob Simonds, Mel, Mike Gainza, Joe Carroll, Gene Bratcher, Jeff Medeiros, Paul and Mari Hays, Rich Risner, Jim Flaharty,

Keith Bullen, Matthew Mangiantini, Stanton Young, J.J. Cox, Madeleine Schriger, Chris Stadler, Zack Rye, Brendan O'Donnell, Marcus Notti, Luke Weidner, Kalib Friden, and Max McKone.

John Nagle, Czechs, Perc, Santo Domingos, Pete King, Vardannis, Mark Longstaff, Jen Huggans, Soz, Osgoods, Underwoods, Mike Keady, Tori Keady (sorry about your purse), Ramsey Masri, Adam Schor, Doc Reeder, Dwight Bandak, Kims, Adairs, Shooters, Brahneys, Eisenstats, Zaharias, Fitchens, Pardinis, Coxs, Vas, Plumbs, Larkins, Mangiantinis, Cowans, Thomases, Schrigers, O'Donnells, Sechler's, Shooters, Simonds, Gavin Christensen, Pete Hopkins, Taylors, Youngs, Weidners, Miccos, Simonds, Ryes, D.R., Stadlers, Jack Baker, Tom McInerny, Shepards, Mallinckrodts, Protivas Gainzas, Hunters, Barnes, Flahartys, Owens, Petries, Hunters, Keenans, Habelts, "Latz", Burkes, Kim Whitcomb, Arthurs, and the Sanfords.

Jimi Hendrix, Pete Townshend, Joe Louis, Andechs, Jimmy Buffett, Duck Lake, Krems, *The Last Shot, Hoop Dreams,* Copernicus, Kornblatts, Jake Scott, the memory of William Slottman, and to anyone who has had a sense of humor and/or resisted ignorance and bias.

Introduction

There is a famous story that circulates in the Marketing Department at Great Western Bank in Los Angeles. Several years ago, a man walked into their Bellflower branch (Los Angeles), and asked to see the manager. The manager came out and the customer informed him that he had his last paycheck in hand and that he wanted to deposit it into a new Great Western checking account.

> "That's fine," commented the manager, "but you look rather young to retire and never work again."
>
> "Well," replied the customer, "I just won the lottery, and I want to bring all of my money to Great Western Bank."
>
> The manager smiled and asked, "You must have passed six other banks on your way to this one. Why do you want to deposit your money at Great Western?"
>
> "I've been a Lakers fan my entire life," stated the new millionaire. "Great Western sponsors the team, puts their name on the building they play in, so that's where I'm bringing my money!"

* * *

At the 1972 Summer Olympic Games, athletes were assisted by Olympic hostesses who helped with their arrangements and administrative needs. Among other tasks, the hostesses gave the athletes some free Adidas shoes for their use in training and/or competition. The athletes, especially the ones from the Eastern Bloc, were thrilled to receive their free shoes. At the time, *no* amateur athlete received any endorsement money for shoe contracts, and they were all happy to benefit from any corporate largesse.

Four years later, at the Montreal Games, the athletes received similar boxes from the hostesses, but they were a little heavier. Along with the shoes, the Adidas boxes included some expense money, up to $10,000. The word was that if an athlete wore the shoes, *and* won a medal, there would be some reward money packaged in future boxes. This black-market endorsement pool was an effort to target the athletes (especially the American athletes) and their television markets in a tacit, but effective, manner.

The archaic state of amateur athletics in the seventies did discriminate against the competitors and encouraged this informal endorsement payment. But the value of product usage was not lost on Adidas, or the athletes. Adidas hedged its bet as best it could to ensure that its products were worn on the world's stage. The best way to do that, of course, is through financial incentive. Years later, the unfair situation, for both the athletes and sponsors, formally changed and the ridiculous restrictions were lifted so that formal endorsement agreements could be developed, signed, and integrated at a consumer market level.

* * *

In the late 1980s, a Nabisco executive gave a newspaper interview where he discussed his sponsorship with a prominent local baseball team. In the article, he identified his luxury box access as a tremendous advantage in entertaining key customers. "The luxury suite," he stated, "allows me to entertain customers, especially the decision makers, at the highest level."

Two weeks later, the baseball team won the pennant and was on the way to the World Series when the Nabisco executive received a phone call from one of his most important supermarket buyers. "Look," the customer said, "if you want to sell me some product, I need to be entertained at the highest level. . . . How about some series tickets?" The buyer apparently read the article, and decided he knew a way to get a good ticket.

* * *

This book will not exclusively discuss extraordinary circumstances in sports advertising. Rather, it will explain the ways that companies use sporting events to reach their customers. The multibillion-dollar sports revenue cycle is dependent upon the successful relationship between sponsors, fans, and event promoters. Sporting events, and their participants, are sold as consumer products to sports fans in the form of tickets and viewership. Perhaps more importantly, they are also integrated into sophisticated consumer product marketing campaigns (such as the annual Bud Bowl*), which influence consumer behavior for the sponsoring companies. Also, promotional development and consumer integration binds sports properties and corporate investment.

Some investments and payoffs of sports marketing:

• NBC paid $401 million to broadcast the 1992 Summer Olympics in Barcelona. The network lost millions, especially on their pay-per-view venture, "TripleCast." When NBC had a chance to bid for the 1996 Summer Games in Atlanta, it bid $456 million. NBC is certain that the investment will complement its current sports offerings, which includes properties such as the NFL, professional golf, and the NBA. NBC is also certain that it will turn a profit. How?

• Quaker Oats pays Michael Jordan millions of dollars to be an international spokesman for Gatorade®. In what manner can Gatorade® measure the value of its investment? Among many things, Jordan's product endorsement has helped Gatorade® expand its distribution, a key goal, from ten to twenty-eight countries. Long after Jordan has retired, these valuable relationships will have evolved, a potentially priceless result of its investment in Jordan.

• CBS paid $1.7 billion for the seven-year rights to broadcast the NCAA championships. Fox paid the NFL $1.58 billion for four years of televising privileges.

• Cadillac states that its Senior PGA Tour sponsorship has brought its dealers over $250 million in sales since 1990.[1]

• The 1995 NCAA Final Four basketball championship generated $30.8 million of economic activity in the Seattle metropolitan area.[2]

---

*The Anheuser-Busch promotional tie-in with football's Super Bowl.

Thirty-five thousand visitors came over the course of seven to ten days and cheered UCLA, Oklahoma State, Arkansas, and North Carolina in the quest for the national championship. The millions of dollars these fans spent with Seattle's merchants indicates why cities, states, and countries aggressively compete for events and teams.

• The Dallas Mavericks signed rookie sensation Jason Kidd to a contract worth more than $40 million. Kidd responded by winning Rookie of the Year honors. He should have won "employee of the year" as well. Television ratings rose 90 percent, and attendance almost 40 percent.

• Pepsi-Cola will pay a reported $68 million to codevelop an arena in Denver, Colorado, to house the Nuggets and a future NHL team.[3] Pepsi's name will adorn the facility and supply concessions featuring Pizza Hut, KFC, Taco Bell, and other PepsiCo products.

• Oksana Baiul went from being an orphan from Dneprpetrovsk in the Ukraine, to a figure-skating gold medalist in the 1994 Olympics. Her reward is an annual income approaching $3 million.[4] The price she pays is a grueling ninety-day tour of seventy-five shows in seventy-one cities.

• In 1994, $2.7 billion worth of basketball shoes were sold. To contrast that category, $100 million worth of popular sports sandals were sold in the same year.[5]

• The 1995 PGA, LPGA, and Senior PGA Tours will stage 123 events and compete for almost $115 million. Sponsorships and television rights contracts are two main sources of Tour income. Star Bank of Dayton, Ohio, is one such sponsor. Star Bank will pay $1.125 million for a three-year contract to be the title sponsor of the Children's Medical Center/Star Bank LPGA Classic.[6]

• The Boston Garden cost $4 million to construct (in eleven months) by the time it opened in November 1928. Seating over fourteen thousand for both basketball and hockey, the Garden hosted many classic sporting events in its sixty-seven years. Deemed too old, outdated, and inefficient in its revenue potential, the Garden was replaced by the FleetCenter, which took twenty-nine months to build at a cost of $160 million. The FleetCenter will have air conditioning, no obstructed views, sixty-eight more luxury suites, thousands more of the regular seats, and even the old parquet floor. Even though the new facility may have many more amenities and a sponsor, it won't have the history and the appeal of the venerable old Garden.

• According to the *Hot Dog Fact File,* over 20,000,000 hot dogs are eaten at baseball games every summer. In 1993, 1.8 million hot dogs were eaten at Colorado Rockies baseball games alone.

• Sports Bars can sell seventy-five kegs of beer (15,000 glasses) during one football broadcast.

• Fans annually wager an estimated $38 billion in illegal bets.

• Television and video are such fixtures in the home that the replacement market for remote control devices is a $350 million annual business. Universal Electronics, a major manufacturer of an all-in-one remote device just introduced a "Sports Clicker®," a remote control apparatus featuring your favorite NFL team's logo. Universal supported the product introduction with a $3 million fourth-quarter (1994) print and media campaign.[7]

• In 1969, 53 percent of advertising expenses went to the three major networks and print magazines such as *Life.* By 1992, that figure dropped to 25 percent, as budget allocations emphasized more event promotions—the byproduct of evolving contemporary sponsorship.

The above information is a random sample of the issues that shape the sports business industry. While there are many financial and sociological consequences affected by athletics, the cultural merit of sports entertainment will not be judged. Instead, the financial context and impact of the relationship between fans, athletes, and sponsors will be analyzed.

1

Defining Sports Marketing

> Every time I call it a game, you call it a business. And every time I call it a business, you call it a game.
>
> —O. W. Shaddock, *North Dallas Forty*

The fictional O. W. Shaddock is not attempting to explain or confuse the relationship between athletic competition and business in this dialogue. He merely points out that sports has significant financial implications, with or without the consent of each participant. Shaddock knew that the humble origins of sporting contests were not influenced by broadcast considerations, concession sales, labor (dis)agreements, salary caps, category exclusive sponsorships, complicated licensing rights contracts, ambush marketing tactics, and consumer retail promotional considerations. Today, however, these issues are intimately involved with the actual competition, and even a throwback like O. W. Shaddock would not hesitate to say that the financial power of sports entertainment makes it a successful business enterprise for the participants, promoters, and sponsors.

The appeal and wealth of sports is at an all-time high. The industry employs over 4.5 million people and generates enough international commerce to be the twenty-second largest industry in the world.[1] Five of the top ten most watched television shows in United States history are sporting events (four Super Bowls and the Harding-Kerrigan

Olympic figure skating competition).[2] The Atlanta Committee for the Olympic Games sold the 1996 domestic (U.S.) Olympic broadcast rights to NBC for $456 million.[3] The NFL, NBA, and Major League Baseball annually sell a combined $9 billion worth in internationally licensed merchandise such as hats, shirts, and related items. Superstars like Michael Jordan, Carl Lewis, and Arnold Palmer both perform and endorse products around the world.

In the context of sports marketing, the "product" is either the entertainment of competition, or a product/service that is associated with the excitement of an event, or both. The term "sports marketing" applies to both the T-shirt vendor at the United Center selling Blackhawk and Bulls merchandise and to the marketing director of the New York Yankees. Ski and boat show organizers, player agents, and the corporate representatives who purchase sponsorship opportunities all make vital contributions that define this growing industry. *For the purposes of this book, sports marketing is simply any sales or publicity-related activity associated with an organized sporting event (or events), its personalities, or the celebrity lifestyle of its participants.*

Sports as a Consumer Decision

Sports entertainment is a multibillion-dollar consumer decision. In 1993, America's spectator sports ticket purchases totaled $6 billion (excluding pay-per-view, and radio/television fees).[4] To take advantage of these captive audiences, 4,500 different companies invested $3.7 billion in 1993 ($4.25 billion in 1994 and projected at $4.7 billion for 1995) event sponsorship opportunities.[5]

The proven ability of sports to influence consumer behavior off the field of play drives the chameleon forces of "sponsorship," the powerful turnkey that identifies sports entertainment properties with products and services around the world. Sponsors choose from hundreds of events and sponsorship packages to identify with their existing markets and expand into others. The widespread popularity of athletic competition helps companies successfully sell breakfast cereal, soda pop, checking accounts, automobiles, shoes, underwear, and virtually any product manufactured. The average American, in fact, spends $193 a year on sports apparel.[6] Eye-catching statistics like this influence both manufacturers and marketers. Not only will companies like Starter and Champion produce and distribute shirts, hats, and sweats with prominently displayed team logos, but companies such as McDonald's use licensed merchandise as a consumer inducement, i.e., the 1992 U.S.A. Dream Team Basketball cap promotion, where McDonald's customers could buy a hat with their Big Mac® and french fries.

The springboard for all sports promotions is the competition. Sporting events predictably gather audiences in person and over the airwaves. Broadcasters know that over 130 million people will watch the Super Bowl, thirty billion (yes, billion) total viewers will watch the fifty-two World Cup matches, and Notre Dame will sell every seat (59,075 capacity) at each of its home football games. With so much interest focused on competition, shrewd sponsors pay to identify and interrupt the action to promote their products and services.

The broadcast industry allows sports entertainment to be enjoyed ("consumed") by worldwide audiences. The sports advertising market has taken advantage of the expanded audience access to grow from spot commercial segments and show entitlement to integrated program *features* that increase sponsor involvement. Features like logo placement in the studio—the Prudential Halftime report, or on the field of play—the FedEx Orange Bowl, has enhanced the value of corporate sports sponsorships. The 1995 FedEx Orange Bowl logo, for example, was visible for thirty-one minutes during the broadcast. One journal, *Sponsors Report,* estimated the value of Federal Express's publicity at $15.86 million for the game.[7]

The important thing to note is that television/radio interests currently sell all elements of their broadcast, the show's name, statistical recap, replays, and interruptions such as Fox's McDonald's Game Break. The Fox network could simply cut to the studio, but it makes more sense to sell the feature to one of its largest sponsors.

Network logos appear in the corner of the television screen. Arena names (Arco Arena) are displayed on the floors of their respective venue. Sponsors, such as Levi's Dockers®, sponsor shows (the NFL on Fox) that integrate brand names and images into the programming. Fox's NFL Halftime and pregame shows are highlight, hype, and analysis segments featuring Howie Long, James Brown, Terry Bradshaw, Jimmy Johnson, and Levi's Dockers®. The show previews and reviews all of the pertinent gridiron action, and the sponsor, Levi's Dockers®, receives full mention during the segments, logo placement during specific studio segments, introductory and exit mention, as well as a commercial segment during the broadcasts. In effect, Levi's Dockers® is as much a member of Fox's football team as coach Johnson. The fixed position advertising spots, entitlement privileges, product category exclusivity, and billboard drop-ins are all negotiated elements between Fox and Levi Strauss before the first ball is mounted and kicked each year. Both the broadcaster and clothing manufacturer share the objective to maximize audience exposure through the excitement of professional football. Most importantly, Fox and Levi's are willing to invest millions for the opportunity.

Thousands of relationships like the Fox-Levi's NFL connection (the counterpart is NBC-Domino's Pizza) exist between sponsors and promoters. These contractual relationships all aim to enhance the visibility of the event and its sponsoring products and services. The efforts to capitalize on the relationship result in the many product promotions at consumer venues. Free collector drinking glasses at gas stations, cereal box poster offers, collector cups at fast food restaurants, and other sports-related inducements leverage the popularity of a team or personality to influence consumer behavior. Virtually every product category has a sports tie-in/identification with consumers and events. The 1996 Atlanta Summer Olympics had eighteen major sponsors signed up two to four years in advance. Familiar names like Coca-Cola, Anheuser-Busch, McDonald's, AT&T, VISA, IBM, Kodak, Xerox, and ten others jointly paid over $500 million to identify with the Olympic Games at the event site, during television broadcasts, and through retail opportunities like ticket application distribution, contests, and logo reproduction on commemorative packaging.

But the Olympic Games are not the only events characterized by heavy sponsor involvement in promotional applications. Budweiser's famous "Bud Bowl" is both a part of every Super Bowl commercial broadcast, and a heavily supported retail promotion in supermarkets around the country. Castrol Oil features NFL merchandise redemption opportunities (i.e., buy a case of motor oil and get an NFL logo hat of your favorite team for free) on its products cases. ESPN offered trips (1994) to the Major League All-Star game and to the NFL Pro Bowl through sponsorships sold to Suave and Radio Shack respectively. By sharing the excitement of sports entertainment with a consumer product, ESPN understands the essential element to sports marketing—consumer identification. Every promotion attempts to achieve positive identification between sponsor and event. That delicate, yet solid, relationship drives the multibillion-dollar sponsorship machine.

Furthermore, the rush to develop other revenue opportunities related to sports entertainment has ignited an interest in constructing sports arenas and other facilities. New facilities such as the America West Arena (Phoenix), the Delta Center (Salt Lake City), Camden Yards (Baltimore), and Comiskey Park (Chicago) mean swank, exclusive luxury boxes and enhanced concession and retail opportunities, not necessarily more bathrooms or improved sight lines (unobstructed views). Chicago Stadium, hallowed ground for any sports fan, was razed and replaced (by the United Center) to accommodate the owners' needs to maximize sponsorship sales potential, not to enhance the fans' arena experience. The Toronto Raptors had never played a basketball game, or even had a player under contract, but they secured an arena entitlement sponsorship from Air Canada, (a twenty-year deal for $20 million). In this case, the sponsor arrived at the stadium before the team and fans.

Who Are the Fans and Why Are They Important?

Fans are the basis for the financial growth of sports. They participate in many forms: buying tickets, watching broadcasts, listening to the radio, reading newspapers, magazines, and journals; or simply collecting cards and memorabilia. As a group they annually spend $6 billion to attend the events and, as a household, they spend 178 hours watching them on television at home. This activity means that fans are a neat, captive package for advertisers to reach. Super Bowl XXVIII (1994) had over 133 million viewers and thirty-second commercial spots were selling for $900,000 each.[8] One year later, ABC set the rate at a cool $1 million per thirty seconds. To many companies, that is a reasonable fee to communicate with more than one half of the country. The incredible fees that promoters, leagues, and broadcasters earn all goes back into the same sports cycle to create more events, attract more athletes, and upgrade facilities to keep the fans and sponsors content with their investment. The money cycle enhances the assets of sports franchises, which is estimated for the four major leagues (NBA, NFL, NHL, and

Major League Baseball) by *Financial World* magazine to be over $11 billion. Furthermore, the sponsorship and ancillary markets grow as the patronage of products associated with sports and sports personalities increases. For example, baseball card licensing fees bring an extra $80,000 to $100,000 for each player alone.[9]

Critical to the sports industry, the public's enthusiasm is never lost in the minds of shrewd marketing managers around the world. Sensing the loyalty and heightened interest in sports entertainment, companies attach their products to events in the hopes of cultivating the same infectious loyalty for their products and services. The variety of sports offers companies a wide range of promotional opportunities to reach diverse demographic targets. Companies receive proposals daily to sponsor events like basketball, football, racing, soccer, track, swimming, golf, tennis, sailing, hockey, cycling, boxing, high school, and college sports. The fundamental premise is that sports attracts a captive, enthusiastic audience. Depending upon the size and access to the audience, i.e., radio, television, arena mention/placement, and ad circulation, the cost of doing business can vary dramatically. It may only cost a few hundred dollars to sponsor a little league team, but it can cost several hundred thousand to buy advertising for a professional team, and up to $40 million to secure official worldwide Olympic sponsor rights.

The rising financial stakes, however, can also have negative economic consequences. The ESPN network recently (1992) chose to pay Major League Baseball $13 million to buy out the last two years of its broadcast contract.[10] The original agreement had a two-year option at $125 million per year. ESPN claimed that it lost almost $200 million on its original four-year deal with Major League Baseball and elected to pay the $13 million exit penalty rather than risk further financial hemorrhaging. Unfortunately, sports is like politics: not everyone participates in the windfall, and there are both winners and losers. In this case, the baseball estimates were simply inaccurate.

The key issue was not *who* will broadcast the baseball games, but at *what price.* How did Major League Baseball absorb the lost revenue? Without that revenue, were some, or all, clubs adversely affected?* Lastly, has the extra cost been passed on to the consumer, as in so many financial models? The answers are not easily found. It is certain

*ESPN renegotiated and contracted to broadcast baseball games.

that the owners do not want the risk and uncertainty of declining broadcast revenues, and it is precisely this uncertainty that has led to their insistence on some type of salary cap, which ties payroll expenses to overall revenues. The owners can slash costs, which means a lowered payroll and administration, or attempt to raise revenues, which means sponsorships and ticket prices. Well, if the television market is flat, it is likely that other sponsorship opportunities are not in high demand. There is a proportional elasticity between broadcast and event sponsors, and the owners can testify to that reality. Passing the cost to fans usually means ticket price increases, always a difficult sell, unless they are for a championship team. The relationship between sports industry management and the mechanisms that they use to earn money from the corporate world, i.e., radio, television, and event sponsorships, drives the rising cost of sports entertainment.

The Industry's Players

Sports marketing participants can be categorized in five separate ways.

1. *Buyers of sports marketing opportunities:* This includes broadcast interests, retail licensing rights, licensed manufacturers, event promoters, and all sponsorships.

2. *Sellers of the above interests and events (suppliers):* Networks, leagues, team representatives, event organizations such as the Atlanta Committee for the Olympic Games (ACOG), licensors, and promoting organizations (such as International Management Group [IMG]) all sell the excitement and opportunity of sports entertainment. Skating exhibitions, baseball card shows, and consumer product companies like Nike and Reebok use performers' personalities to attract audiences.

3. *Operations employees:* A wide array of publicists and intermediaries cooperate to ensure that an event occurs. Porta-potties, remote concession stands, and grand stands for spectators take a lot of manpower to place, monitor, serve, and put away. Golf courses are not roped, staked, and plastered with billboards by ghosts or other-worldly creatures.

4. *Athletes:* The men and women whose exploits thrill diverse groups around the world market the product of sports entertainment

each time they compete. Their actions keep billions of dollars churning to perpetuate the industry cycle.

5. *Large conglomerates like Disney and Blockbuster Entertainment:* This is an emerging group that will quickly have an impact on the leagues. Sports authorities clearly depend upon corporate subsidy through sponsorship. By encouraging actual ownership, the leagues virtually guarantee permanent subsidy. These groups bring much more than money. They bring significant savvy, promotional expertise, channel alliances (i.e., television stations and media contacts, sales forces and retail access), and a desire to succeed in family entertainment.

SELLERS (PROMOTERS)

Sellers (promoters) package and price the broad appeal of athletic competition for sponsorships that take effect both on and off the field of competition. Ticket sales, broadcast rights, event entitlement (i.e., MCI Heritage Classic) and endorsement sales efforts transfer the perception of excitement and purity in sports, all for the purpose of profit.

BUYERS (SPONSORS)

Buyers (sponsors) negotiate on behalf of their companies to build sales programs that spark enthusiasm in the retailers, draw customers off the streets *and* excite these companies' employees to execute these campaigns. Their financial commitments to leagues, events, athlete endorsers, broadcasters, and their industry trade establishes a market price for all facets of sports entertainment. CBS bought the 1998 Winter Olympic broadcast rights for $375 million because they feel that they can sell advertising and programming that will generate an amount greater than that. Quaker Oats, Nike, McDonald's, and Hanes pay Michael Jordan a total of $30 million annually based upon the perception of a return on that investment. Corporate promotional managers receive a plethora of proposals for their budgets. Until the emphasis of advertising and promotional concepts changes, the corporate sponsorship buyers will continue to influence sports both on and off the field. The Fox network, for example, petitioned the NFL for a prime time airing of the 1995 NFC Championship Game, anticipating a Cowboy-49er contest. Their prior game (November 13, 1994) drew a record sports audience for the network, and they believed that a prime time start in all markets would eclipse the regular season audience, and it did.

Furthermore, sponsor influence affects regions. When St. Louis was left without a football team in 1987, the league's biggest sponsor, Anheuser-Busch, was left without a home team. The Cardinals left for a better stadium in Arizona, but Anheuser-Busch and its family of products quietly lobbied for another team. St. Louis was passed over in the first expansion rounds as Charlotte and Jacksonville won the rights to become franchises, but the league did not discourage a new football facility being constructed in the early 1990s. By 1995, the Los Angeles Rams announced their intentions to move, and although Anheuser-Busch stayed publicly quiet on the subject, their influence had to be a significant factor in the process.

As sports entertainment's reliance upon sponsorship increases, the competition for sponsor participation develops different dimensions. Selling a sports promotion in Los Angeles, for example, means that the event competes with the Lakers, Clippers, Angels, Dodgers, Kings, Mighty Ducks, USC, UCLA, and individual events like the PGA's Nissan LA Open. It is definitely a buyer's market for sponsors. Corporate America enjoys a favorable position to choose the teams and events with which it wishes to identify. Companies gradually achieve more negotiating leverage as sports sponsorship evolves into integrated media and retail marketing activities. A company like Anheuser-Busch, through experience, knows exactly what to seek from its events and negotiates based upon that information.

Small market, single team towns like Portland and Sacramento, which have only one professional team to root for, the Trailblazers and the Kings respectively, have other sponsor-promoter dynamics that affect their relationship. Franchises like these retain certain benefits from being the only "team/show" in town, but they compete in smaller media and retail markets, which have inherently smaller advertising budgets—meaning a smaller gross revenue opportunity. Teams that fall into this category, therefore, cannot afford arrogance or oversight in their negotiations and relationships with potential sponsors.

The Selling of Sports

The objective of sports marketing is simple: *sales*. The excitement of competition is sold on floors, fields, fairways, and airwaves all over the world. The sales cycle between fans, events, and their sponsors is never precise, but it is consistent. Event promoters and sponsors attempt to maximize their financial potential through the attentive, loyal sports fans who gravitate toward the unexpected of the sports world.

The NBA is a great example of growth through successful promotion and sponsorship. Its phenomenal progress is supported by the numbers. League revenues have increased from $140 million in 1983 to $1.1 billion in 1993.[11] The NBA's broadcast agreement with NBC and Ted Turner's TNT network reflects the progressive and cooperative spirit that has guided growth and prosperity. The two sides will share advertising revenues earned over certain thresholds, $1.06 billion with NBC and $350 million with TNT.[12] By having equal interests in promoting and selling the popularity of basketball, the NBA will be responsibly promoted for everyone's interests, not only one party. The financial stakes really dictate a shared risk philosophy that is becoming popular with new agreements between events and sponsors.

Competing in the marketplace also means undermining sponsorships, a tactic known as *ambush marketing,* i.e., getting Olympic game identification without paying the governing body of the Olympics for the privilege. A classic case happened during the 1994 Winter Olympics with VISA and American Express. VISA's famous tag line with its Olympic advertising states; "and if you're going to the Olympics, you better take your VISA, because the Olympics don't accept American Express." American Express countered this effective campaign by buying network advertising during the games showing that it has had an enduring presence in Norway for many years.

The American Express campaign implied that a visa (travel permit) was not necessary in Lillehammer. American Express certainly felt that the campaign was clever. VISA, however, felt otherwise. It had spent $40 million to be a category exclusive sponsor, and it did not want a competitor to dilute the impact of its investment. The International Olympic Committee (IOC), the governing body of the games, lambasted American Express for its attempts to undermine a chief sponsor. CBS, meanwhile, had sold the commercial time to American Express because the network had to move its advertising inventory. In this case, conflicting interests allowed the situation to develop, and the IOC's remedy is to protect future sponsors through broadcast exclusivity as part of the sponsorship. The Atlanta Games Committee, host for the 1996 Summer Games, even has a director of sponsor protection, a signal of the IOC's sentiments toward ambush marketing.

The Atlanta organization has already been busy foiling an effort by Sony to access the Olympics in spite of worldwide sponsor Panasonic. Sony offered to donate one of its famous Jumbotron® stadium replay screens to the Atlanta Braves for placement in Fulton County Stadium. Sony wanted the screen to linger through the Olympic Games as well, but Panasonic recognized Sony's shrewd maneuver and had the installation of a video board written into its own sponsorship package, effectively taking Sony out of the picture. Sony's calculated attempt failed, but it shows that ambush marketing is an external nature of the contemporary sports marketing industry.

Old-fashioned luck is another external feature in sports marketing. In 1992 Adidas and Nike had advertising budgets of $23 million and $150 million, respectively.[13] Yet, at the Final Four* that year, each company had two teams wearing their shoes in that elite group. Adidas sponsored Duke and Indiana, and Nike shoes were worn by Michigan and Cincinnati. Due to the pairings, each company was guaranteed to be present for the championship game, where seventy million fans watched.[14] Commercial advertising rates were $300,000 per thirty seconds, but Nike and Adidas were there, in part, for free, having paid the schools a fee prior to the season. Adidas only sponsored three of the sixty-four teams that entered the sixty-four team tournament, and Nike endorsed twenty-nine, but both had two of the four finalists. Adidas was thrilled, to say the least, and Nike had hedged its significant bet and had to be pleased as well. As a footnote, the next year, Nike paid Duke and Coach "K" millions to wear its shoes—the price of success for all of the parties.

But how effective was Adidas's sponsorship of Duke and Indiana University in 1992? With all of the promotional clutter of the tournament, could Adidas define any degree of success through its involvement with the two universities? Given the popularity of the schools, and

---

*NCAA Final Four is college basketball championships for men and women. It is one of the two top-rated televised sports events (the other event is the Super Bowl).

their place within the sport of college basketball, Adidas had the opportunity to publicize its association and did so in *USA Today* and other publications. Whether or not it penetrated the saturation of other advertising is another issue. Adidas could not quantify actual sales tied to the Final Four, but its exposure in one of sports' truly glamorous events made their investment a good one.

The sports entertainment industry, therefore, seeks ways to make events meet sponsor goals so that the event has a realistic future. Event promoters need to give sponsors the vehicles to meet their promotional criteria: e.g., the generation of impressions, ad recall, retail licensing opportunities, and increased sales based upon retailer participation. Many companies want to quantify the results of their sponsorship and seek to evaluate the sponsorship from a cost/benefit standpoint. Many former sponsors and analysts feel that the value of sports advertising has been diluted due to the development of sports programming and sponsorship opportunities (arena football, college football, foreign football, the NFL, etc.). The industry continually needs to prove its merit and quantify its impact.

In many ways the sales job never ends. Easy profits are not a foregone conclusion, for promoters or sponsors. Coca-Cola does not buy an NBA license and immediately sell more twelve packs. It needs to invest more money into a campaign and develop it in many markets in order to see a return on its investment. All involved parties, from athletes to owners to administrators to marketing managers, know that the financial results are truly more important than the games' results. The reality is that the genuine nature of sports competition has eroded at the professional, most collegiate, and even the high school levels. For example, Nike's high school basketball camps not only offer competitive instruction, but advanced recruiting opportunities for college coaches. The conflict is that the real motivation might be for the perpetuation of the star system, not the advancement of the student athlete.

The marketing and financial constraints of professional franchise ownership has created a new breed of management. Disney owns and operates the Anaheim Mighty Ducks in addition to being a minority owner of the California Angels. Blockbuster Entertainment's chairman, Wayne Huizenga, owns virtually every Miami team (the Dolphins [NFL], the Marlins [baseball], and the Panthers [NHL]). This gives Blockbuster direct access to the local professional sports marketplace.

It can approach movie studios such as Warner Brothers and offer game-day promotions to premiere the studios new releases in conjunction with Marlins, Dolphins, and Panther games. Disney, likewise has an abundance of cross-merchandising possibilities through their retail interests, theme parks, television stations, movie studio, video game division, and recording companies. Mighty Ducks paraphernalia can easily be sold at all retail venues, and all characters from Mickey to Goofy can be licensed on appropriate sportswear.

Disney's move into the sports world makes sense. No other company arguably competes more successfully for the international family entertainment dollar.* Buying into professional hockey is cheaper and less costly in terms of negative publicity if merchandising campaigns fail. Furthermore, by cutting its sports teeth with the Ducks, it can move into other professional sports with value-tested programs in hand. Disney's example provides a window to the near future of the expanding demands in sports franchise ownership.

The trend indicates that penurious misers like Charlie Finley† no longer have the sufficient resources to operate professional franchises. Corporate owners bring efficiencies, relationships, and resources to maximize franchise revenues. Paramount, for example, had owned the New York Knicks, the Rangers, the Madison Square Garden facility, and the broadcast arm (the Madison Square Garden Network) that carried the cable broadcasts of these teams. Paramount took advantage of scale (sold sponsorship of three different teams or properties to one sponsor as opposed to three separate sales pitches). The package of the Garden, the Madison Square Garden Network, the Rangers, and the Knicks eventually was sold for $1.075 billion to ITT Corporation and Cablevision Systems, Inc.

Another sports monopoly belongs to cable mogul Ted Turner. Turner owns the Braves (baseball) and the Hawks (basketball). More importantly, he owns significant cable networks, TBS and TNT (among others), which broadcast baseball, basketball, and football. Turner also promotes (and subsidizes) the Goodwill Games, an Olympic style international competition. It is no wonder that there is a Turner Sports divi-

---

*Disneyworld is the most visited attraction in the world at twenty-five million customers per year. Disneyland is second at thirteen million. San Francisco's Pier 39 is third at eleven million.

†Former baseball owner of the Athletics who sold players when their value peaked. Commissioner Bowie Kuhn had to rescind some of these trades, terming them "detrimental to the game."

sion that supervises the integration of the individual sports teams and events with the broadcasting interests. To Ted Turner's credit, he does not try to manage it all under one sports umbrella. Instead, he gives each entity its necessary autonomy, but he can bring in relevant and critical expertise from other divisions for valuable promotional and financial advice. The resources that a large organization has in terms of sales staffs, merchandisers, and marketing support allows a team to maximize its financial potential. Large entertainment conglomerates bring operating efficiency and capital to teams. There are constraints, however. As publicly held companies, they have shareholders to answer to, and, therefore, need to turn a profit. This reality will make sports franchise earnings and finances more accountable to the public.

Another extension of scale advantages in sports marketing are the "properties" divisions of the major sports. These divisions manage and police the extensive licensing and marketing of their parent leagues' images. Video and image reproduction on products and in advertising campaigns is a multibillion-dollar industry in itself, and the licensing of manufactured goods totals in the tens of billions. Going one step further, and to prove that academics acknowledge the sports business, the 681 colleges and universities that play football at the intercollegiate level have formed an organization called College Football USA. It is a joint venture between the athletic directors and coaches' association intended to develop college football as a brand entity. College Football USA will sell licensing, sponsorship, publishing, and broadcast production opportunities for its members and business clients. College Football USA is part representation, part trade group. It will probably be very successful as the close-knit world of college sports runs its business through the organization. (See Figure 1 at the end of the chapter for a sports marketing Flow Chart.)

Sponsorship Packages for Sale

Teams and rights holders submit proposals to corporate buyers to elicit their interest and money. (See Table 1 for sample sponsorship fees.) Packages for golf tournaments, baseball games, and car racing teams arrive daily on corporate decision makers' desks.

• Fireworks Night at the Los Angeles Dodgers' April 12 game was priced at $40,000 for the official fireworks designation, four premium seats, and fifty others. The Dodgers included forty radio spots, five television commercials, and give retail logo usage rights to the sponsor.

• The 1995 SCCA Trans-Am Championship will cost a sponsor $185,000, for signage; television (Prime Network), tickets, and hospitality. Retail privileges are included.

• To entertain clients in an exclusive luxury box (built right on-site for the tournament) at the Kemper Open (Potomac, MD), all one needs is $12,500. The box will seat twenty for all four tournament days, in addition to a full-page black-and-white program advertisement, and thirty tickets per day.

• The Philadelphia Phillies sell a Sunday giveaway for $65,000. The sponsoring company's logo will be printed on 20,000 items (hats, shirts, etc.) The team will also provide a pre-game brunch for fifty guests, and the owner's Super Box for game viewing. The Phillies will also give the sponsor 50,000 game schedules with the sponsor's logo, two Phanatic (mascot) appearances, some media time, and a kids clinic for 100 kids on the field before the game.

Table 1
Sample Sponsorship Fees[15]

Company	Amount	Consideration
Anheuser-Busch (Ice Draft®)	$750,000	Official Beer NHL (hockey)
Ameritech	$250,000	WTA Title sponsor Chicago event (women's tennis)
Fiat	$8,300,000	1995–1997 Tour de France (bicycle race)
Motorola	$2,000,000	Title sponsor cycling team
Infiniti® (Nissan Motor Co.)	$250,000	Presenting sponsor ATP (LA event) (tennis)
Group Health Plan	$250,000	Title sponsor LPGA (St. Louis event) (ladies golf)
Coca-Cola	$1,000,000	Davis Cup 1996–1998 (international tennis)

Historical Images and Impacts

Some famous images include

- Mean Joe Greene chugging a Coke® given to him by a young fan
- Michael Jordan and Larry Bird playing "H-O-R-S-E"* for a Big Mac® and french fries
- Bo Jackson rehabilitating his hip with Nike Cross-Trainers®
- Joe Namath wearing panty hose
- Dan and Dave's truncated showdown in Barcelona to determine the world's greatest decathlon competitor
- Joe Montana playing pick-up basketball with Hakeem Olajuwon and Karl Malone
- Joe DiMaggio, a national sports legend who hit 361 career home runs (with only 369 career strikeouts), is best known as "Mr. Coffee" to many.

Miller Lite® launched an entire industry (low-calorie beer) with its humorous ads featuring retired athletes wanting a less filling beer that still tasted great. Jack "Hacksaw" Reynolds, "Marvelous" Marv Throneberry, Dwight Clark, Grits Gresham, Bob Uecker, John Madden, Carlos Palomino, and many others appeared in memorable ads over a decade as Miller Lite® became one of the top-selling beers in America. The ads played upon the reputation the athletes created during their careers and popularized a low-calorie beer for sports fans.

The entire multibillion-dollar athletic shoe industry is a study in the effects of sports advertising. Slogans like "Just Do It" and "Life Is Short. Play Hard" are a part of society's lexicon. Michael Jordan and Bo Jackson are as responsible for Nike's prominent cultural status as its financial growth. These athletes gave Nike the platform for creating personalized shoes and new categories of products. In the early 1980s Converse's Superstar® shoe was worn by Julius Erving, the NBA's most exciting player. Converse decided to emphasize the shoe, not the player, in its related promotions. On the other hand, Nike decided to create a line of products based on the athlete. The Air Jordan® is simply the

---

*A playground favorite where shots are created and attempted by the competitors. When one shot is executed by one player, and not the following one, the second player (who missed the shot) receives a letter. When he spells H-O-R-S-E, he is disqualified.

most popular shoe of all time, and the cross-trainer (inspired by Bo Jackson) is the most successful new shoe category in the industry. The visionaries at Nike recognized the equity in the athletes and capitalized on the opportunity.

Nike's main competitor, Reebok, is not far behind in contributions to the sports marketing industry. The technological contribution of the pump system has brought more than simple gadgetry to the field of performance and technology in athletic footwear. The campaign of "Dan and Dave" cost Reebok more than $20 million in financial commitments for advertising, agency fees, and advanced promotional hype leading into the games. Reebok kept telling the public that the two best decathlon participants, traditionally dubbed "The World's Greatest Athletes," would meet in Barcelona and settle the issue at the Olympics. That was before Dan O'Brien shocked the world by not making the Olympic team. The improbability of this great athlete failing to qualify for the U.S. Olympic team (he got zero points in the pole vault event at the qualifying meet) was only surpassed by the amount of publicity that Reebok received for its involvement in the lame-duck promotion. The promotion was actually anything but a failure. Reebok's name, and the campaign, received international coverage for the unexpected twist of fate. Reebok wanted to create an event, Dan versus Dave, within the larger event of the Olympics. By capitalizing on its endorsement of America's top two decathlon participants, the shoe manufacturer wanted to bring corporate America to the compelling drama of two friends and competitors. The concept was extremely well conceived. For the dénouement to be delayed by one of the athlete's failures was never anticipated.

Most sports promotions are more straightforward as sales tools. Gillette, for example, introduced its Sensor® razor in 1990 and planned to use Super Bowl XXIV as its introductory media vehicle. The target demographic was the male audience, and Gillette spent $3 million on the Super Bowl commercial purchases, and millions more on print support.[16] By focusing on America's premier event, and supporting the campaign in print, Gillette sold out its Sensor® inventory through the February and March following the broadcast. The feedback also encouraged Gillette to increase their 1991 shaving budget by 25 percent.

Evolution

Before the integrated, multimedia promotional age of Gillette's Sensor® and other contemporary products, sports advertising was more simplistic and limited. Stadium advertising was done by the facility managers and their outfield walls were covered with sponsor messages. Today, billboards are a significant part of facilities, not for the audience in the stands, but for the television audience to see at home. The most popular camera angle is from center field to home plate. Therefore, the most expensive billboard for baseball is directly behind home plate—where it will get the most camera attention. The focus from a sponsor's point of view includes both the fans in the stands and the ones at home. Furthermore, as the sports industry has grown into established identities, the teams, athletes, and sponsors have standardized the use of sports in both media and retail promotions.

Athlete endorsements were not equity deals like Shaquille O'Neal's Reebok agreement, but Ted Williams had his name on a root beer, and Joe DiMaggio even pitched Camel® cigarettes. The great DiMaggio's defining accomplishment of the fifty-six-game hitting streak had one little known casualty. He was to receive a $10,000 endorsement from Heinz 57® if he could have made it to just one more game. The simple concepts of advertising vehicles were in place before mass merchandising, even though they were not as prevalent as today.

Teams themselves were more barnstormers than league franchises. With population concentrated in the Northeast, and travel done exclusively by rail, professional athletic events were confined primarily to this region. The media also had a limited range, and that contributed to the restricted appeal and support of sporting events. Professional sports did not have an established identity. College sports garnered the attention and crowds. The campuses had traditions and established fan bases and rivals. Most importantly, universities had funding sources (government and alumni) for stadium construction, the place where the fans created their sports addiction. Professional sports could not as easily turn to the public for a subsidy. The original Yankee Stadium was called the "House that Ruth Built" because Babe Ruth drew the crowds that generated the capital to build the historic facility. In the early days of sports, before guaranteed broadcasting rights, concession contracts, and lucrative advertising packages, owners were noted for their frugality, and for legitimate reasons. The lack of a predictable, consistent cash flow put a lot of pressure on investment decisions.

Also, there was not much precedent for municipalities to work with leagues and owners to construct and maintain facilities. Today, of course, cities prostitute themselves to attract professional franchises, but that was not always the case. The Great Depression, and the lack of organization in every sport (except baseball), diminished the priority of sports in the minds of the public and corporate America. The psychological impact of sports never lost its influence, but the expansion of teams and fans slowed. Despite the obvious difficulties, the persistence of promoters caught the curiosity of the fans. Successful barnstorming developed the fan base and laid the groundwork for the extension of professional sports into mainstream American life.

The early twentieth-century American sports figure Red Grange provides excellent reference to the glory of the barnstorming era. (See Table 2). He was rewarded with several thousands of dollars when he left the University of Illinois to help George Halas, coach, owner, and promoter of the Chicago Bears, bring professional football to the masses. His legend and nickname, the "Galloping Ghost," were created on the college gridiron, and Grange's agent, C. C. Pyle knew that the "Galloping Ghost" had that inscrutable element that packed the house and charmed the press. Pyle convinced Halas to use Grange's appeal on a barnstorming tour across the country. Pyle reasoned that Grange's talents would generate fan interest and money. In a carefully choreographed exhibition series, Halas showcased the multitalented Grange against semipro and all-star teams.

Table 2
Red Grange's Impact on Tour[17]

	Site	Attendance
Game #1	St. Louis	8,000
Game #2	Philadelphia	35,000
Game #3	New York City	73,000
Last Game	Los Angeles	75,000

Grange, Halas, and Pyle made hundred of thousands of dollars together and spread the credibility of professional football. Grange's appeal was such that he even made a movie when he was in Los Angeles. His creative play paved the way for future teams, leagues, and rivalries. The "Galloping Ghost" proved that one charismatic individual can make a difference to a legion of devotees. In the 1920s professional football lacked the marquee status it has today, but the roots of modern football are in the efforts of Halas, Grange, and the Bears.

Barnstorming was more of a party-by-rail than a multimedia festival like the Dream Team's* 1992 Barcelona debut. The players of the past did not have the world's attention, nor did they enjoy first-class accommodations as their sports' appeal was not established. The compensation for the participants were lower, and the stakes were significantly higher. Without the plethora of revenue sources such as broadcast contracts, licensing, and sponsorships, the athletes and promoters of the early twentieth century made our present generation of millionaires and media stars possible.

Today's sports machine is driven by earning potential more than competitive outcomes. The drama and thrills of competition are given elements of the sports entertainment equation. The maximization of profits is the primary objective. The IOC, for example, decided to stagger the Winter and Summer Olympic Games beginning in 1994 so that the two events would not compete for advertising dollars. The IOC knew that the format change allowed the two events to achieve their highest profits, the goal of virtually every industry's management decision. Prior to the alternating format, the Olympics encountered resistance in selling two annual sponsorships at $40 million each. Add the necessary media and print support, and a company could spend over $100 million on the Olympic Games in one year. By staggering the games, the Olympics remained in the news and the sponsor clutter between the winter and summer events ended.

The "old days" of professional sports had higher stakes because revenues were strictly a function of event attendance. Leagues and teams often survived from year to year. The St. Louis Browns, Kansas City Monarchs, and Fort Wayne Pistons did not receive a fixed percentage

---

*The most talented compilation of professional athletes ever to assemble for Olympic-team competition. They easily won the Gold Medal and all members of the team became international stars. The team consisted of Michael Jordan, Patrick Ewing, Chris Mullin, Karl Malone, John Stockton, Magic Johnson, David Robinson, Clyde Drexler, Scottie Pippin, Charles Barkley, Christian Laettner, and Larry Bird.

of licensed merchandising income, network television contracts, stadium sponsors, and luxury box tenants. Teams were sold in order to leave one unprofitable city in the hopes of finding one where fan interest thrived. Whatever happened to the Rochester (New York) Royals? They eventually became the Sacramento Kings, via stops in Cincinnati, and Kansas City-Omaha. Financial stability and audience popularity corresponded with the rise of the television set as the primary entertainment medium. Preceded by the radio, television enhanced the excitement and brought the unpredictability of sports into the fans' living rooms. Millions watched the entertainment in their social comfort zone and familiarized themselves with the personalities and exploits of their athletic heroes.

The broadcasting industry created a perpetuating cycle of advertising commitments that, in effect, provides an annuity for professional sports. Sports programming delivers a reliable audience, and broadcasters are paying billions in rights fees for the opportunities it provides. The spiraling rights fees now total more than $1 billion annually for the four major leagues, NBA, NFL, NHL, and Major League Baseball. The networks, in turn, are charging more and more for the commercial privileges, up to $500,000 for a thirty-second segment for the NFC Championship game.

Football exemplifies the made-for-television bonanza of sports entertainment. In 1991, the NFL generated $1.4 billion in revenues, earning twice as much from broadcast revenues as ticket sales.[18] Eight hundred fifty million dollars came from radio and television, $783 million from network television contracts alone.[19] On the other hand, ticket sales added up to $402 million, or approximately 30 percent of league revenue. Figures like that explain the power that networks have over issues like scheduling (which teams play each other and when) and game times. Monday Night Football, bye weeks (when each team takes a week off, which extends the season an extra week, giving the broadcasters one more week to sell ads), extended seasons, and delayed starting times are changes the league has made in order to give television interests the best chance to expand the audience for and sponsor revenues from football.

It all goes back to the fans. Depending on the event, millions if not billions tune in and/or show up for the games. Advertisers and merchandisers keep investing money into sports entertainment because they receive a satisfactory return on their investment. But that may change as the current image problems of Major League Baseball demonstrate how the event-sponsor-fan relationship can be threatened. Franchise values will diminish as merchandise sales, broadcast contracts, and ticket revenues decline in response to the unresolved labor disputes. There is no shortage of sports entertainment, but there is a shortage of smooth event operations and positive public image in professional sports. If the fans' loyalty wanes, the money spiral will reverse.

In 1990, CBS paid a whopping $1.06 billion to Major League Baseball for four years of broadcast rights.[20] With the newfound revenue, owners went on spending sprees and drove up their payroll costs. CBS, however, encountered a flat advertising market, and poor World Series matchups (either too short: Oakland versus Cincinnati in a four-game Reds sweep in 1990), or wrong markets (Toronto versus Atlanta in 1992). CBS subsequently lost millions on the deal. When the broadcast agreement expired, the owners' earned income fell. The new broadcast arrangement became a shared risk venture between ABC, NBC, and baseball. It projected first-year revenues at approximately $140 million, or more than $100 million less than they earned with the CBS deal. Unfortunately for ownership, the salary scale did not automatically adjust for revenue declines. This is the basis for the baseball owners' salary cap demands. They want operating expenses, of which player salaries are the main component, to be directly tied to revenue. The players disagree with the notion that earning capacity has to be restricted. As a result, the fans are unfortunately learning more about arbitration and negotiation processes than baseball strategy and shared excitement.

The uncertainty of revenue sources does threaten the stability of labor-management agreements. Even the NFL experienced significant uncertainty during its last television contract negotiations. In the early 1990s, the main broadcasting networks, ABC, CBS, and NBC, claimed substantial losses on their broadcasts.

The advertising climate was indeed a bad one, and NFL owners knew it. Art Modell, the influential Cleveland Browns owner, led the leagues' broadcast committee and even recommended that the league restructure its agreements to accommodate network losses. He wanted to extend the current agreements at a fixed rate, which would give the league financial security, but at a reduced fee. The owners didn't take Modell's advice and decided to take their chances that the advertising market would rebound.

Waiting turned out to be a good idea for the NFL, because another network, Fox, decided to enter the sports mainstream. The presence of a wealthy, curious competitor usually drives up the bidding price, and that is exactly what happened. The upstart network paid an almost obscene $1.58 billion to the league for four years of broadcast rights, almost $400 million more than CBS offered.[21] In 1992, the networks looked as if they had finally turned the momentum around on spiraling rights fees, but that changed in a hurry. Fox's bid had two essential elements. The network wanted to enter the world of professional sports programming and, more importantly, use the reliable franchise of football to solidify its network affiliates and other programming interests. CBS brilliantly used its NFL programming to develop core audiences for programs like "60 Minutes" and "Murder, She Wrote." Fox knows that they will not sell advertising in excess of their rights fee, but they are banking that they will develop other programming opportunities and station affiliations that will help them penetrate the mature, yet profitable, American market. Hence, the premium paid for the NFL can be justified. Furthermore, Fox bought the National Football Conference (NFC) rights, featuring high-profile teams in key markets such as Chicago, Dallas, New York, Philadelphia, and San Francisco. Time will provide objective evidence for analysis, but from the very beginning, the logic of the precocious network's gamble must be acknowledged.

Television and its effects on sports will be discussed in greater detail in chapter 7, but as in virtually all sports marketing issues, it is tied into the past, present, and future success of all sports entities. As broadcasting matured, it brought a heightened corporate presence to both sporting events and brand marketing. The billions invested into broadcasting can be traced to larger audiences, new markets, and sponsor involvement. Furthermore, broadcasters have convinced corporate advertisers and marketers to promote sports as they promote their products and services.

An Olympic Balance Sheet Shows Sports' Financial Context

Perhaps the world's greatest sporting event, the Olympics creates athletic heroes, huge television audiences (the Games are watched by 64 percent of American families), and millions of dollars in sponsorships.[23] A look at the balance sheet for the 1996 Summer Olympics, as prepared by the Atlanta Games Committee (this statement was prepared in 1994), reveals the financial dimensions of staging the Olympic Games.

Projected Revenue		Projected Expenditures	
Broadcast rights	$555.5	Construction	$516.6
Domestic sponsors	513.4	Operations	405.4
Ticket sales	261.2	Executive/Administrative	182.9
International sponsors	114.4	Sports and international organizations	147.6
Merchandising	28.7	Operating contingency	60.0
Other	107.5	Other	161.9
Total	$1,580.7		$1,580.7

According to the Atlanta Committee for the Olympic Games (ACOG), the opening ceremonies' costs alone will eclipse the $24 million mark. The ticket sales and distribution network will manage a total of eleven million tickets, ranging in price from opening ceremonies at $600 each to an average event price of $39.72. Initial sales estimates suggest that ACOG can sell 62 percent of the eleven million tickets ($261 million). And it is safe to assume that sales representatives will be requesting that customers use their VISA® cards for all ticket purchases.

The Games attract more than money, though. Thirteen thousand volunteer groups totaling 484,000 people volunteered over two years prior to the Games. And ACOG expects the Games to bring $500 million in capital improvements to the city, a nice legacy.

Fig. 1.
Sports Marketing Flow Chart

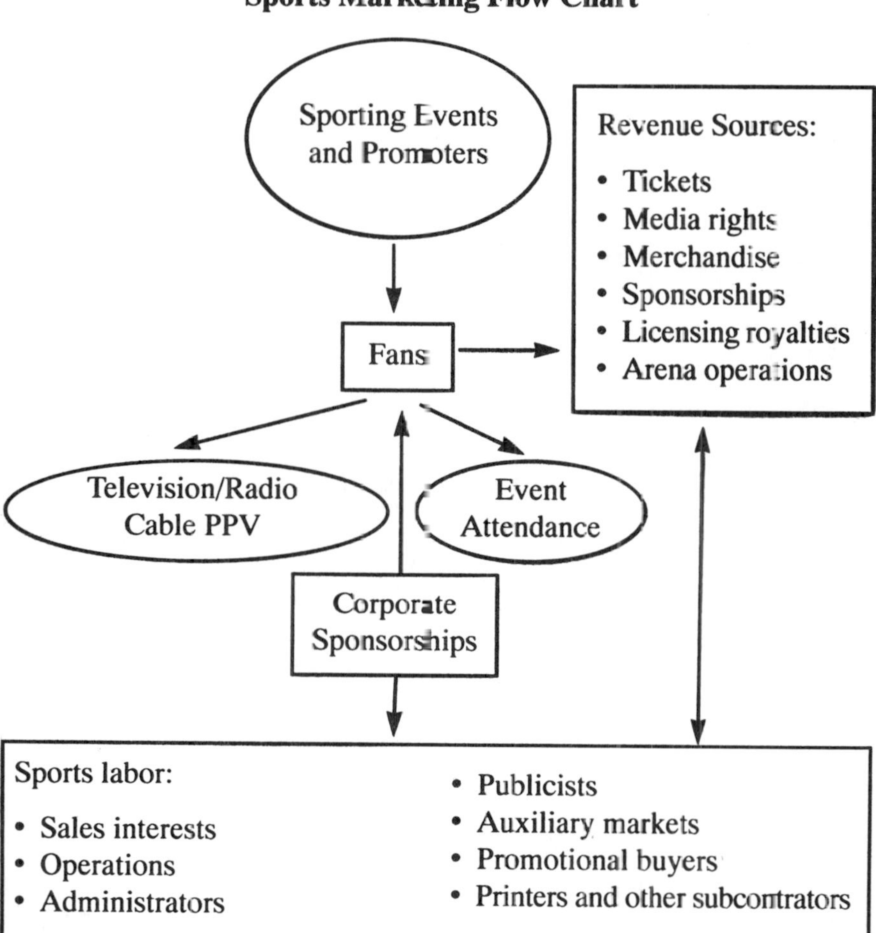

Sports marketing is not to be confused with board room deals and fast-paced excitement. Certainly, that is part of the business, but the vast support network of publicists, administrators, sales support staff, media, and concessionaires know that their jobs are more about subordination and execution than competitive participation. Fans pay top dollar to watch Patrick Ewing play basketball, not for a statistician to record his exploits. The competition ultimately relies on the producers and their minions to deliver the high standards of entertainment that the sports world expects. Each game or event is a highly orchestrated production dependent upon an invisible cast of characters doing their jobs so that fans can enjoy the competition and be exposed to the sponsor messages.

2

The Event Triangle

An Event and Its Participants

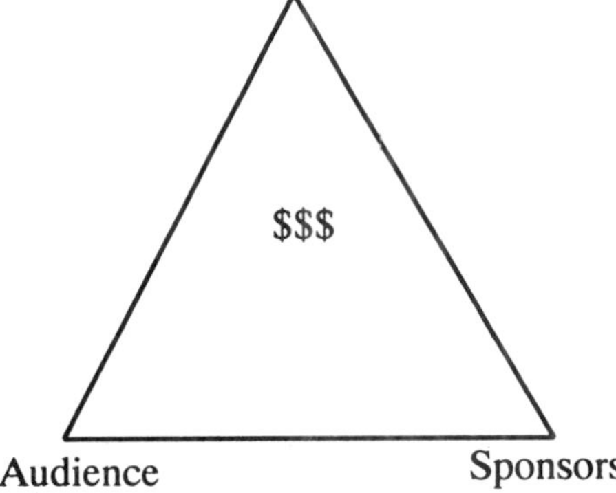

> I don't understand what is going on. But if it gets down to the nitty gritty, where X amount of money is available, I think the players deserve it and not the promoter. But I think the whole thing is totally out of control. . . . The players are so insulated, so selfish. They don't give anything back. They think they are doing a great thing by standing around signing autographs for a couple of hours and then walking away.
>
> —John McEnroe[1]

Tennis star John McEnroe has certainly experienced the pressures and pleasures of international sports fame. The glory of Wimbledon championships, celebrated comebacks, and animated competition have created lucrative opportunities for him. As a commentator for NBC and the USA Network and a product spokesman for Dunlop and Nike, McEnroe also generates tremendous fan response in exhibitions around the world. While McEnroe likely realizes that his profession has evolved through the cooperative work of players, promoters, and sponsors, he laments that today's beneficiaries, the present generation of tennis stars, may not appreciate that fact.

Perhaps McEnroe could tell contemporary athletes that Billie Jean King's prize for her first Wimbledon Singles Title in 1966 was a £50 clothing gift certificate.[2] Furthermore, it took Billie Jean another five years before she won $100,000 in prize money. McEnroe could close his sports business appreciation seminar with this fact: the 1994 Women's Tennis Association had $35,000,000[3] in prize money, which is millions less than the men's tour.*

This prize money did not materialize out of thin air. The financial rewards in tennis, and other sports, can be attributed to the entertaining talents of the *athletes* and the corresponding demands of worldwide *audiences* and *sponsors.* This financial growth only came through the three groups working together to maximize the sports' exposure, they all contributed equally.

Also, events generate significant revenue. Super Bowl XXVIII, the January 1994 extravaganza featuring the Buffalo Bills and Dallas Cowboys, generated $4.25 billion in marketing and sponsorship costs[4] and the 1994 Soccer World Cup accounted for $4 billion in spending during the summer of 1994.[5] The Event Triangle model is a simplistic description for the financial interdependency between sporting events, their consumer audiences, and commercial interests, i.e., sponsors, broadcasters, and licensors.

The Event

Events are either sanctioned activities as part of a league, i.e., baseball's New York Yankees versus the Boston Red Sox, or one-time promotions such as the Chicago Marathon, the Iditarod (Alaskan dog sled race), or

*As heard on the Wimbledon broadcast, in 1968, Wimbledon champion Rod Laver earned $3,200; in 1980, Bjorn Borg earned $32,000; and in 1994, Pete Sampras earned $584,000.

Shell's Wonderful World of Golf. Events such as golf's Skins Game, the Superstars Competition, and the Quarterback Challenge are especially created for television to be broadcast and sold to sponsors during times when there is a scarcity of valuable sports programming. Both sanctioned and contrived events using firmly entrenched athletes like Arnold Palmer, Dan Marino, and their peers, successfully attract audiences and sponsors.

League events that benefit from administrative support, planning, and marketing indicate the financial link between sporting events, their fans, and their sponsors. In 1980, Major League Baseball's gross revenues were $500 million.[6] Fourteen years later, it quadrupled to almost $2 billion. The 400 percent growth is due to the explosion of broadcast, licensing, and stadium revenues. Baseball marketed key personalities like Ken Griffey, Jr., Roger Clemens, Jose Canseco, Nolan Ryan, and others into the fabric of its consumer product identifications. By bringing more fans to the game, baseball sold itself to corporate marketing interests and increased its value. The labor problems are not attributed to the popularity and financial growth, but the disparity in participation. Major League Baseball knows that the 1993 New York Yankees generated over $106 million in revenues and the Montreal Expos barely $46 million, but they do not know how to bridge that income gap.

As the revenues grow in sports, athlete compensation increases. As athletes earn more money, the iron fisted management of the past has given way to revenue sharing, i.e., teams dividing total revenues earned (i.e., radio, television, etc.). Basketball star Glenn Robinson, after being drafted first overall by the Milwaukee Bucks, hinted that he wanted a contract for a staggering $100 million. Robinson eventually settled for $68 million, but without ever having played a game.[7] Glenn Robinson's contract is certainly a byproduct of the growth in sports popularity, as Table 1, which lists the progression of NFL salaries, shows.

Table 1.
NFL Salary Changes from 1933–1993

Year	Average Salary[8]
1933	$ 8,000
1946	$ 12,000
1963	$ 20,000
1974	$ 33,000
1980	$ 79,000
1983	$133,800
1987	$203,300
1990	$351,800
1993	$600,000

"Pudge" Heffelfinger of Dayton signed the first NFL contract, which was worth $500 back in 1892,[9] and over 15,000 have signed since then. Dallas Cowboy Troy Aikman, one of football's biggest stars, became one of the financial beneficiaries of professional football's commercial growth more than 100 years later, and earned a contract worth $50 million. The dramatic increase reflects the infusion of revenue through the events' broadcast rights fees, ticket sales, and licensing interests, such as cards, hats, shirts, etc., all consumed by the millions of American football fans.

The Audience

The audience is both the physical attendance at the event site and the electronic presence via radio and television. Only 68,000 fans sat in Candlestick Park for the NFC Championship Game between the San Francisco 49ers and the Dallas Cowboys, but over 85 million people tuned in through the airwaves. The game's audience is also represented through print media outlets such as newspapers, magazines, and journals. Many of the same fans who watched the Championship Game read about it the next day and week in their local papers and in *Sports Illustrated, The Sporting News* and *USA Today.* All forms of media use the description and commentary of sporting events to attract audiences and sponsors.

When the Fox network sells advertising time, it does so by mentioning the anticipated audience size. Likewise, when *Sports Illustrated* sells an ad space, the price is determined by circulation size and page position. Both Fox and *Sports Illustrated* also define the demographics of their viewers and readers, a matter of great importance. The audience, in reality, entertains several sales pitches. First, the event is sold to them through physical or electronic attendance. Once fans are in some form of attendance, the sponsors, the pivotal Event Triangle member, bombard them with commercial images and messages.

The Sponsors

According to *Beverage World,* the beverage industry's main trade journal, Coca-Cola products are sold in 195 countries. The soft drink giant supports sixty-seven sports programs on a regional, national, and worldwide level. The billions invested by Coca-Cola and other companies in sports finances player development and payrolls, arena and stadium upgrades, and the publicity machine that attracts sports fans throughout the world. Sponsorships that Coca-Cola and other companies purchase give them access to a variety of promotional packages including all forms of media advertising (print and broadcast), licensing rights, and stadium promotions featuring giveaways, sampling, signage, billboards, VIP receptions, and merchandise sales opportunities, a significant part of a sponsorship.

For the purpose of commercial industry context, advertising and promotions expenses in the United States total $400 billion per year, which amounts to $1,600 per person.[10] Two hundred billion dollars is spent strictly on promotions, including items like those giveaway pens and calendars from the neighborhood filling station to the sophisticated multilevel promotions like Gatorade®'s "Be Like Mike" campaign. Individual brands like Frito Lay's Dorito's® Tortilla Chips (annual sales of $1.3 billion) have $50 million budgets for media and marketing investments.[11]

The prices to communicate with the sports world's audience continue to increase. Companies spent $3.2 billion in 1992 on event sponsorships, and almost $5 billion three years later.[12] As long as events effectively achieve strategic marketing objectives, corporations will cultivate and develop sports promotions. It is essential to understand that the sponsor-event relationship depends upon corporate commitment of much more than money. Successful event marketing occurs when the sponsors take ownership of their participation and involve their employees, channel marketing chain, and consumers. When companies commit labor resources to a sporting event, they substantiate the notion that a significant audience will respond to their marketing message through a sports medium.

Why advertising and promotions? In the last eleven years (1983–1994) Quaker Oats' Gatorade® sports beverage grew the market for its beverage category from less than $100 million to $1.2 billion. Gatorade®, despite competitive efforts from both Coca-Cola and PepsiCo, holds 87 percent of the market share.[13] For companies like Frito Lay, Quaker Oats, and Coca-Cola, the advertising and promotional budget (sponsorship source) is the weapon that maintains and increases valuable market share, the ultimate promotional goal.

Why Do Companies Use Events?

Exxon, the world's largest petroleum company, purchased a NASCAR sponsorship to position Superflo® motor oil as a premium retail product. Exxon wanted NASCAR, a thirty-one-event race series during the spring and summer, to help its retail sales team develop integrated promotions between the rotating car races and its regional sales efforts. Exxon did not write NASCAR a check and forget about its marketing needs. It invested in the promotion in order to enhance existing relationships and to develop new ones.[14]

Exxon buys more than the name of NASCAR and its competitors', names like Petty, Earnhardt, Waltrip, Wallace, and Irvan. As a sponsor, Exxon buys the storied tradition of stock car racing in addition to tickets, event access, billboards, and licensed merchandising rights. By paying for the right to be included in the events, Exxon has the opportunity to link the racing events, consumers, and key industry personnel. Over six million people attend NASCAR races, and 178 million more watch them on television.[15] Furthermore, the total U.S. car racing audience is twelve million people in physical attendance and 400 million over the airwaves, a significant secondary market for NASCAR sponsors like Exxon.

The obvious connection between auto racing, motor oil, and the audience also pertains to other products and the same audience in the contemporary event marketing industry. Procter & Gamble, Miller Brewing Company, and Winston® cigarettes effectively use NASCAR to promote and sell their products. Country Time Lemonade® introduced a series of collector tins featuring six prominent NASCAR drivers. The tins containing the product were introduced in January 1992, before the Daytona 500, NASCAR's most popular race. Sales in the immediate Daytona Beach area increased by 68 percent, and the impact of the promotion was felt as far away as Columbus, Ohio.[16] Overall, Country Time Lemonade® experienced a double-digit sales increase during the first quarter of 1992.

Measured results, as the ones in the above example, justify both the participation and effort in a managed sports promotion. For both the sponsor and the promoter, it validates the premium placed on the event and reinforces the intangible elements that draw audiences to sports entertainment. Furthermore, sponsorships are costs that are inevitably passed to the consumer through the involved labor and promotional expenses. But success like Country Time®'s breeds confidence in the product. Ford Motor Company is another NASCAR sponsor that has enjoyed effective results from its event identification. After their Thunderbird® won thirteen straight 1992 Winston Cup (NASCAR) races, Thunderbird® sales went up nearly 20 percent in the Southeast, NASCAR's primary event region.[17] Ford cannot attribute 100 percent of its sales increase to its NASCAR sponsorship, but no one would dare deny that it is a significant factor. In most marketing schemes, including sports marketing strategies, it is difficult to directly correlate a promotion with subsequent sales success. However, there is no doubt among sports advertisers that associating with a winner is a great idea. The opportunity to bring the excitement, enthusiasm, and success of sports identities to a product perpetuates the sports sponsorship cycle.

SPONSOR STATISTICS

Table 2 shows the top paying event sponsors in 1992.

Table 2.
Top Paying Event Sponsors in 1992[18]

Philip Morris Companies: Philip Morris (Marlboro), Miller Brewing Company, Kraft etc.	$90–95 million
Anheuser-Busch	$85–90 million
R.J. Reynolds, Nabisco, Coca-Cola, General Motors, and Eastman Kodak	$35-40 million
PepsiCo.: Pepsi, Doritos, Pizza Hut, and KFC	$25–30 million
Mars, AT&T, Quaker Oats, Chrysler, and McDonald's	$20–25 million

Financial Interdependence

As stated, the Event Triangle depicts the relationship between events, sponsors, and the audience. It explains the interdependency and financial scale of sports entertainment. Three principles flow together seamlessly in the Event Triangle model:

1. Events need sponsors for financial subsidy and publicity.
2. Sponsors need events for promotional exposure and opportunity.
3. Athletes/performers seek compensation for their time and talents.

With respect to the first rule, all events need seed money. Whether it is the Boston Marathon or the "NBA Game of the Week," each event needs money to finance the administrative and production costs. Some small-scale events, such as local road races and charity activities, do not benefit from sponsorships and still manage to persist. No promoter or handler, however, would say that sponsorship would not be considered.

Events seek identifying sponsors to subsidize their costs, such as facility rental, maintenance, administrative and athlete labor contracts, and the concession expenses. Promoters need to cover the advance promotional and athletes' fees. Boxers, ice skaters, football players, runners, and jockeys all require remuneration for their time. The costs have to be paid. Soccer, tennis, and auto racing are the livelihoods of their participants and players. Even autographs have a price. Wilt Chamberlain, Mike Schmidt, and the entire Griffey family are available for a price, and the public will pay for them. Promoters and sponsors, therefore, will invest money in them and their disciplines to make money for their companies.

Sponsors need events as badly as events need sponsors. Both large and small companies need to reinforce their message with target consumer groups. One of the fundamental needs for any business is to promote itself. AT&T, Nabisco, and Coca-Cola need all of those print ads, billboards, commercials, and retail promotions to maintain their market share and product distribution channels. No successful company can be lackadaisical in its efforts to communicate with its public in order to maintain and increase its product's share of the market. From a sponsor's standpoint, it needs to get the correct event to develop the best market program for its target consumer. Goodyear Tire Company may not want to sponsor the Iron Man Triathlon in Hawaii, but it certainly wants to be involved in some part of NASCAR; not only for consumer purposes, such as product-testing data, but for direct sales opportunities (i.e., sales to the actual racing teams). Goodyear generates revenue from the annual sale of 200,000 tires to NASCAR racing teams. Furthermore, Goodyear gets feedback from professional drivers and mechanics on product development issues, valuable information. Where else could Goodyear get more applicable information for consumer product issues than from professional drivers?

Goodyear sponsors professional racing for the direct sales opportunities, event product inclusion (tires on the actual car), and media image generation (capturing those tires by television cameras). Racing fans buy related products when they are away from the racetrack. Concerning the auto parts market alone, fifteen million high performance tires are sold annually. Goodyear has 22 percent of that market, or 3.3 million tires sold. Their Eagle Aquatred® design, in fact, is a derivative of their Formula One® race tire. This technology transfer is one of the best external features of their race sponsorships, and demonstrates that event marketing results in both exposure and sales. This Goodyear example is analogous to the Air Jordan® phenomenon. Fans witnessed Jordan's greatness on the court, and bought his shoe as a tribute to his game, his charisma, and his performance. The fact that the Air Jordan® is a superior quality shoe, designed with Michael Jordan's input, also helps considerably. Both Nike and Goodyear use their sponsorships to gauge consumer and product feedback that can be applied to future marketing issues—perhaps the most valuable information dividend any sponsorship can provide.

EVENT REVENUE SOURCES

The U.S. Open, one of golf's four major tournaments (along with the Masters, British Open, and the PGA), is also one of its most lucrative. Backed by a three-year $40 million television rights fee from NBC, the USGA (the event's governing body), expects to gross approximately $35 million at Shinnecock Hills, the 1995 tournament site.[19]

Revenue Sources

Television (domestic)	$13,000,000
TV (foreign and cable)	$ 6,000,000
Merchandising	$ 5,000,000
Tickets	$ 4,500,000
Corp. Hospitality	$ 3,750,000
Food Concessions	$ 1,300,000
Entry Fees	$ 600,000
Program Ads	$ 350,000
Total:	$34,500,000

The USGA has been criticized by players for the difficult way it set up its golf courses (high rough and fast greens), but no one can question its ability to maximize revenue sources.

The USGA's mission is not solely about generating profits through high-profile events. The association develops the game by investing its resources into amateur events and by funding programs that enhance access to the game for minorities and youths.

Sales Vehicles

As in the NASCAR-Country Time Lemonade® Collector's tin retail licensing case, events can be wonderful sales catalysts for sponsors as well as the promoters and participants. As the world knows, athletes get paid for their services and are often able to enhance their images in the process. Some athletes such as Babe Ruth, Joe Louis, Joe Namath, Willie Mays, Michael Jordan, Wayne Gretzky, and Joe Montana become icons. The publicity these professionals receive can translate into wealth and prestige, although not every athlete who wears a uniform enjoys the same privileges. However, all of them enjoy the association of star appeal. And promoters benefit, too. They sell everything associated with events, from tickets to concession rights and all media rights. They enjoy the opportunity to shape the image of the action and create heightened publicity for the event and its participants in the process.

The most important sales concept associated with events is *sponsorship.* Through sponsorships, companies integrate their products and services with sports entertainment. Sponsorship can manifest itself in many ways. One popular form is *entitlement,* such as the MCI Heritage Classic, the FedEx Orange Bowl, and the Equitable Old-Timers game. Entitlement privileges cost companies millions of dollars because they generate significant media traffic. (See Table 3.) If entitlement fees are too high, companies often sponsor a portion of an event, for example, "Domino's Pizza Halftime Report." Domino's could probably make a bid to sponsor the entire day of football programming, but that would not be a cost effective way to advertise. The impressions generated through the halftime show and related advertising gives the pizza delivery company ample exposure to the viewing audience.

Table 3.
Entitlement Beneficiaries[20]

Bowl and Sponsor	Date	Network	Team Payouts
Las Vegas Bowl	12/15	ESPN	$ 200,000
Jeep Eagle® Aloha Bowl	12/25	ABC	$ 750,000
Poulan Weedeater® Independence Bowl	12/28	ESPN	$ 750,000
Builders Square Alamo Bowl	12/31	ESPN	$ 750,000
Carquest® Bowl	1/2	CBS	$1,000,000
CompUSA Florida Citrus Bowl	1/2	ABC	$2,500,000
USF&G Sugar Bowl	1/2	ABC	$4,450,000
FedEx Orange Bowl	1/1	NBC	$4,500,000
Rose Bowl	1/2	ABC	$6,500,000

The payouts are what each team earns, not the sponsorship price. The payouts, however, reflect the bowl revenues. And revenues are a function of broadcast rights fees, sponsorship contracts, and ticket sales.

Ironically, for the 1995 Rose Bowl, there was no title sponsor, yet the highest team payout. The Rose Bowl, however, had the highest attendance figure (102,247 frenzied fans). By not selling entitlement rights, the Rose Bowl definitely forsakes income opportunity that other bowls earn to invest in upgrading their product. The Fiesta Bowl will pay $12 million each to its participants, because of its lucrative television deal (CBS) and sponsorship agreement (IBM OS/2®).[21]

Product exclusivity is another popular sponsorship premium. Pennzoil paid a reported $1 million in order to be the official motor oil of the 1994 Brickyard 400, the first NASCAR race at the Indianapolis Motor Speedway. Coca-Cola paid $47 million for its worldwide sponsorship privileges and rights to the 1996 Summer Olympics, primarily to be the official soft drink of the games.

Event sponsorships are flexible in what they can provide participating companies. As mentioned, sponsors can pursue the media options that are available through the event. They can buy arena signage opportunities on the scoreboard, floor boards, and rafters. Companies can also conduct promotions during the athletic events. One famous stadium promotion involved a young man (Don Calhoun) from Illinois who stepped out on to the court during a 1993 Chicago Bulls-Miami Heat game and sank a three-quarter court shot that earned him $1,000,000. He had the opportunity because the sponsors, Coca-Cola and Lettuce Entertain You restaurants, deemed that the promotion had commercial benefits and paid for the rights to conduct this promotion at twenty Bulls games. When Mr. Calhoun made his shot, he brought significant publicity to the Bulls, Coca-Cola, Lettuce Entertain You restaurants, and the promotion. The replay footage made it on CNN, "Good Morning America," NBC's "Today" show, and the MacNeil-Lehrer Report on PBS. National Public Radio even requested the audiotape of the fan reaction, it was that spontaneous. The lesson from the "million dollar shot" is that promotions also generate publicity in addition to sales activity.

The Triangle at Work

The Event Triangle explains three basic things about event marketing:

1. Events showcase and sell the personalities and competitive talents of the athletes.

2. Events demonstrate the promoting organizations' marketing skills.

3. Events promote and sell the products and services of its sponsors.

Conveniently, the three Event Triangle members promote interdependence and financial success for each other. The simple act of the audience seeking event entertainment sets into motion the sponsor subsidy mechanism, which further promotes the event and the product's dependence upon it throughout its sales channels. There are three related, but different paths that link sponsors and the event to an audience.

1. Sponsors pursue their target consumer/audience through an event and its participants. (See Figure 1.) Games attract an audience, and there are two basic ways to exploit the opportunity: in person and through a broadcast. Fans can walk out of the room during a commercial or switch the channel, but if they watch a hockey game, they cannot miss the corporate banners on the sideboards. More than likely, some broadcast commercials do make it through to the viewer/listener. Taking advantage of media opportunities is the most expensive form of sponsor-audience communication, and the fees vary (see chapter 7). Nike pays Andre Agassi, Curtis Strange, and Jim Courier millions to wear the famous swoosh logo because they are fabulous competitors who, in effect, are moving billboards as they play. The Nike logo also has shown up on the famous Penn State uniform, the classic college football team with an extremely talented program.

Consumer incentive programs, such as Anheuser-Busch's famous Bud Bowl, are sponsor driven events that leverage product sales with sports entertainment. Starting in 1989, Anheuser-Busch created and perfected a media and retail promotion in conjunction with the Super Bowl. As a marquee sponsor, Anheuser-Busch has the influence with the league and distributors to execute one of the biggest promotions in America. The Bud Bowl offers the winning consumer a $1 million dollar prize, and has displays set up at virtually every retail location available. Advertising to promote the actual event of the Bud Bowl, a fictitious game between brands like Bud Light® and Budweiser®, begins a month in advance and the cases of beer are shipped and stacked everywhere Budweiser® is sold. During the Super Bowl a series of advertisements run featuring personalities like Chris Berman, Joe Namath, and

Figure 1.
An Event and Its Participants

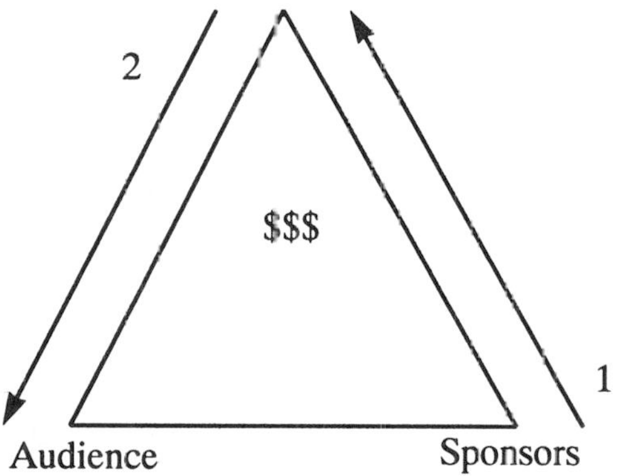

This is the direct path.

Sponsors purchase event identification opportunities from rights holders. Buying a Super Bowl spot delivers more than 130 million viewers.

Buying an Olympic license allows Kodak to place the five-ring logo on specially marked packages. More importantly, the license allows Kodak to appeal to Olympic fans.

Cadillac knows that Arnold Palmer has a loyal following. Its relationship with the most popular golfer ever bridges "Arnie's Army" as potential customers for the car manufacturer.

---

other notables, and a game between the two competing brands unfolds. Viewers need to record the score and mail in the results on forms that are available at Budweiser® displays in local stores. Anheuser-Busch does not care about the outcome. They want people to purchase Budweiser®. To accommodate fans, Anheuser-Busch even has an 800 (toll-free) number where consumers can call and get the "game" results so that the mail-in forms can be accurately completed and the consumer can qualify for the sweepstakes. It also allows the brewer to quantify the reach and popularity of the promotion, among other demographics.

By combining the biggest sports event in America with comprehensive retail and media support, Anheuser-Busch has turned a relatively poor sales month (January) into a good one. After the very first Bud Bowl, sales for that January rose 17 percent over the prior year, easily covering the cost of the promotion.[22] The strange graphics and video-game feel to the campaign is not in vain. Anheuser-Busch even considered the Bud Bowl to be a significant contributor to a record first quarter in 1991, the best promotional feedback for any marketing planner. And the most reliable evidence of its success is that Anheuser-Busch continues to fund the venture.

2. The second Event Triangle sponsor-audience identification route is sponsor participation in direct association with an event's competition: for example, the ubiquitous appearance of Gatorade® cups, coolers, and squirt bottles at every sporting event at every level of competition. (See Figure 2.) Little League, the Major Leagues, colleges, high schools, the NFL, and the NBA all use Gatorade® jugs, bottles, and cups, especially on the benches and sidelines. Gatorade® pays a significant amount of money for these identification opportunities, so when there is a time-out during a game, Gatorade®'s squirt bottle and cups carry the liquid for refreshment—even if it is only water. By being involved with the action, even if it is only for the ceremonial and celebratory coach drenching, then Gatorade® reinforces its status of being as much a part of a team as the equipment. During games, Gatorade® and other associated products (uniforms, spectacles, protective padding, and equipment extras) receive free billboard space as cameras pan the sidelines and benches.

Entitlement packages operate in a similar fashion. The FedEx Orange Bowl is an excellent example, because the logo appears at midfield and is played upon during the broadcast. The value of that is audience size multiplied by visual broadcast time. As noted in chapter 1, the value to FedEx and the Orange Bowl committee of their National Championship game between the Nebraska Cornhuskers and the Miami Hurricanes was estimated at more than $15 million. The sponsor knows that viewers (and fans at the game) cannot ignore the sponsors' collective association with the event.

Two other creative entitlement sponsorships are through high school sports programs and event facilities. Reebok bought the rights to California high school sports, the California Interscholastic Federation (Reebok CIF®). In this sponsorship, Reebok was the official sponsor of virtually every state sanctioned sports activity. Reebok gained additional access to the coaches, trainers, administrators, parents, and students throughout America's most populous state. Not only are high school sports programs vital to communities and kids, they can be fabulous marketing tools. Reebok blanketed the state with one comprehensive promotion. Of course, it was Reebok's responsibility to maximize its opportunity through the events and sales channels, but by paying for the rights to identify with the CIF, Reebok's name was attached and event access guaranteed. The Reebok CIF sobriquet and other entitlement opportunities, event facilities like the Target Center (Minneapolis), United Center (Chicago), Arco Arena (Sacramento), and the Great Western Forum (Los Angeles), generate media traffic and access, a key feature of any sponsorship.

Any sponsor who purchases the display opportunities associated with an event such as program advertisements, ticket coupons, arena promotions and billboards, mentions, and all media considerations does so to communicate and reinforce sponsor messages. By merely associating with the event, fans cannot miss sponsor messages. Michael Jordan made the sports highlight films nationwide virtually every evening. At Bulls home games, his dunks, shots, and spectacular plays frequently caught the arena's main scoreboard in the background with its prominently displayed Winston® logo. Fans at the game, at home, or in a bar cannot avoid the commercial presence of sports entertainment.

Figure 2.
An Event and Its Participants

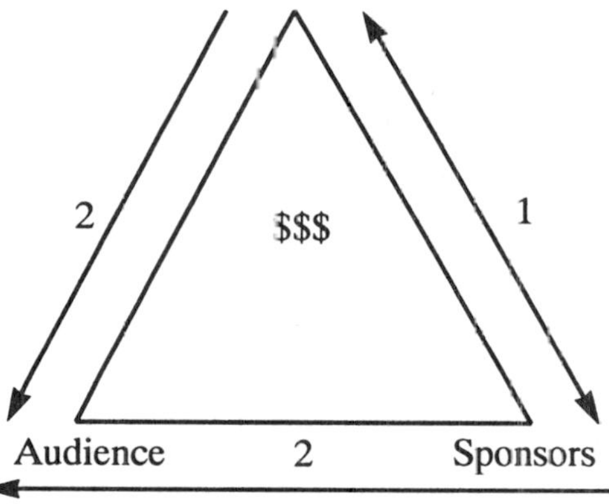

This is the participation path.

Direct association with an event, or athlete(s). Wilson footballs are a part of every NFL game. Nike shoes are a part of runner Jeff Atkinson's workouts.

Ownership, and entitlement privileges give a sponsor event-audience image access.

Property rights holders and event promoters are able to subsidize their events through sponsor participation, therefore gaining an audience. Property holders sell sponsorships based upon the identifiable audience.

3. The third route of the Event Triangle allows fans to access the event through a sponsor's product. (See Figure 3.) Pay-per-view television is the most obvious example of this method. Most championship boxing is available through this method—for example, TVKO. Currently, nineteen million homes have cable television, and as the infrastructure grows, pay-per-view becomes more profitable. For short events like boxing (broadcast time is less than an hour for one fight), pay-per-view generates better revenues. A marquee match on live network television only earns $8 million, as opposed to a conservative estimate of $20 million on pay-per-view.[23] Mega-events like Evander Holyfield versus George Foreman can gross over $50 million. College football, wrestling, and other events are pioneering this industry of consumer choice in sports entertainment.

Other consumer incentive programs represent fans purchasing consumer products to identify with their sports entertainment icons. Promotions like "Find the Nolan," or other autographed merchandise in packs of trading cards give fans a consumer opportunity to collect memorabilia, an otherwise expensive hobby. Nolan Ryan, Ken Griffey, Michael Jordan, Wayne Gretzky, Larry Bird, Mickey Mantle, Joe Montana, and Joe DiMaggio have retail autographed merchandise for sale through contractors like Upper Deck, Topps, Fleer, Scoreboard, and other manufacturers. The likelihood of meeting Nolan Ryan, Shaquille O'Neal, or other stars at the filling station is low, and the price for retail products like balls, prints, and jerseys is extremely high, from $45 to $500, depending on the athlete and the item. These card companies frequently run promotions whereby they insert a limited number of cards signed by the athlete, and consumers are given the incentive to buy packs and packs in the hopes of finding one of the lucky mementos.

Sporting events are getting priced out of many people's reach. Football and basketball tickets can cost between $30 and $100. Not too many paper routes pay that kind of money, so children subsequently are getting excluded from live sports entertainment. Many watch on television and participate through more affordable means, like merchandise purchases. These same consumers who pay less than a dollar for trading cards are the ones who are buying the Pepsi®s, Coke®s, LifeSaver®s, and chewing gum that advertisers sell through sports.

Small, affordable premiums like collector cups (available at McDonald's and 7-Eleven), trading cards, and other retail ventures, like proofs of purchase redemption programs, bridge the gap between the growing income disparity for the professional sports fan. This is something that companies can develop through their sponsorships to bring sports to fans in a cost-effective manner. Companies, through their sponsorship investments, have unintentionally driven up the prices of sports entertainment, so that companies, in some cases, are the only ones who can afford to bring sports to the fans.

Figure 3.
An Event and Its Participants

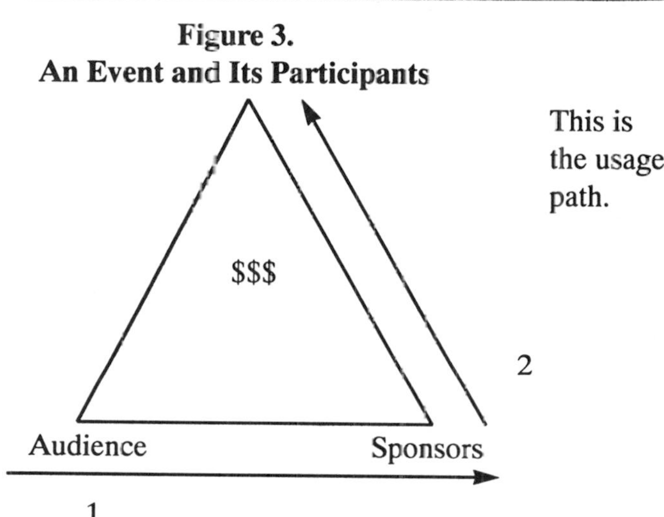

An audience will seek a sponsor product or service to enjoy an event. For example, fans need to tune into ABC for Monday Night Football.

Pay-per-view events such as boxing also demonstrate ways that fans need sponsor services to enjoy an event.

The earliest tickets for the 1996 Summer Olympics were available at Coca-Cola® retailers such as Kroger. For fans to enter the ticket lottery, they had to seek out the Coca-Cola® displays at participating retailers.

Bringing the Three Paths Together

Interactive Network (IN), a technology firm that specializes in interactive programming entertainment, used a sports promotion that reflects the three Event Triangle paths working together. The IN hand-held unit allows television audiences to play along with live sports entertainment. As each play unfolds, the IN players choose options that correspond with the actual game. For Super Bowl XXVII, IN contracted Ronnie Lott to be a celebrity player. Lott, a four-time Super Bowl participant, brought credibility and realism to the promotion.

In IN's football programming, scores tally after each play and members could compare their results to Lott's instantaneously. Interactive network did not have to promote the Super Bowl, but chose to capitalize on its widespread appeal. Bringing Lott "on-line" to the growing computer audience highlighted the spectacle of IN's involvement with subscribers, its primary revenue target. Having Lott endorse the technology validated the entertainment medium, and gave Interactive Network consumer feedback on the merit of celebrity participation. They followed up this promotion with similar ones featuring Gary Fencik and Jerry Glanville.

Event Sites and Facility Sponsorship Issues

The emerging model in effective event management accommodates several interests regarding facility use. Before television, the facility was the primary focus in sports revenues, and now as sporting event standards rise, the importance of having a revenue-friendly arena/stadium is critical to drawing fans and generating income.

FACILITY CRITERIA*

- Event audience—luxury suites and regular seating
- Merchandise sales opportunities
- Soft concessions—food and beverages

*This doesn't include logistics like parking access, public transportation, and environmental/neighborhood issues.

• Multipurpose capacity—a choice of use as a single sport stadium such as Camden Yards or a dual purpose sport arean (basketball and hockey) as in the Great Western Forum.

Facility revenue distribution is a core issue as cities and countries compete for sporting events and the prestige and revenue they bring. Atlanta has to construct over $540 million in facilities to host the 1996 Summer Olympic Games.[24] To host a Super Bowl, for example, a city needs to have a stadium providing a minimum of 70,000 seats, plus luxury suites. Super Bowl XXX, to be played in the Phoenix metropolitan area (Sun Devil Stadium), will bring an estimated $187 million to the Valley of the Sun.[25]

McDonald's, the concessionaire at Toronto's Sky Dome, annually grosses $50 million in event business at the facility.[26] Staggering figures like these underscore the importance of sports and municipalities. If a franchise/event planner cannot maximize revenue at a current site, ownership will entertain competitive bids from other cities. An ongoing case in point involves the NFL's Raiders franchise. Al Davis, the managing general partner, left a loyal fan base in Oakland, California, for the sunnier skies in Los Angeles and facility benefits that he could not get from the Oakland-Alameda County Coliseum (in 1982—the time of the move). The Los Angeles Coliseum's board offered expanded seating capacity (almost 40,000 extra seats) and guaranteed the construction of profitable luxury boxes. Unfortunately for Mr. Davis, the Los Angeles Coliseum did not deliver on its promises. The NFL discussed constructing (with prominent sponsor NationsBank) a facility near Hollywood Park, that would host other league events (Super Bowls) in the years to come. But the NFL and the Los Angeles authorities did not not react to the competitive market, and the Raiders moved back to Oakland in the Summer of 1995.

Sponsor participation in event facilities and sites is critical. Coca-Cola sponsors the NBA and individual teams like the Chicago Bulls. The soft drink bottler obviously wants Coke® and its other beverage products sold at the United Center. Leveraging sponsorships for advertising purposes only makes sense if the efforts influence sales. Having a sponsor place products at an event for the athletes and/or fans fulfills the main objective of event-product identification. Kodak's $40 million Olympic sponsorship means more than licensing the famous ringed logo on packaging, it means selling film and camera products at the event site. Companies want fans to use their products in association with events. This applies to usage issues as well. At golf tournaments, participating players receive automobiles at tournament sites to transport them from their hotel to the tournament. If it is a Senior PGA event, Cadillac provides a car for the players and tournament administrators. If it is the Buick Open, Buick donates the cars.

Facility entitlement is a popular way to leverage event access. By purchasing the promotional rights to a stadium, companies tie-in with regional and national events. Not only are professional events held regularly, but rodeos, ski and boat shows, wrestling matches, concerts, track and field competitions, and charity contests as well. The Great Western Forum in Los Angeles started the popular trend, and now it is an integral revenue stream for many facilities. The sum of these events attracts a large and diverse audience. And though measuring returns is not easy, the media traffic and exposure opportunities obviously keep the sponsors happy, because very few entitled facilities change hands.

Table 4.
Facility Financing Choices

Facility	City	Sport(s)	Financing
America West Arena	Phoenix	Basketball	Public
Arco Arena	Sacramento	Basketball	Private
Coors Field	Denver	Baseball	Private
Delta Center	Salt Lake City	Basketball	Private
General Motors Place	Vancouver	Basketball, Hockey	Both
Great Western Forum	Los Angeles	Basketball, Hockey	Private
Target Center	Minneapolis	Basketball	Private
United Center	Chicago	Basketball, Hockey	Private
USAir Arena	Washington, D.C.	Basketball, Hockey	Public

Table 4 demonstrates two main points. First, there is significant commercial value and interest in entitlement opportunities and efforts to make the sponsorship fit into marketing objectives. Second, the growing number of private facility financiers, normally a municipal or public domain, indicates that facility ownership and control generates revenues and profits. Hard and soft concessions, luxury box sales, parking, and scoreboard and billboard advertising are facility profit centers.

The two types of income are related to costs. Luxury suites are expensive to construct. Electronic scoreboards likewise cost owners a few more dollars. But the purchase and construction expenses can be payed out over the facility's life and the cash they immediately generate adds value to the franchise and the profit/loss statement. Electronic messages like scoreboard advertisements, announcements, and half-time entertainment acts do not cost the promoters extra money. They are "soft" costs, with incredibly high margins. Suite construction, and/or ticket packages do cost money in both fixed and variable cost terms, i.e., "hard" costs. Cash flow dictates a facility's economic viability, and a team's stability. By hosting several events, and generating rental fees, concession sales, and media opportunities, facilities can pay their debt service (schedule of payments to retire financial obligations) and turn a profit. On the other hand, without tenants, or when there is a scarcity of activity, the facility will quickly build up losses. This is the current plight of the Target Center in Minneapolis. Basketball's Timberwolves franchise also owns the facility, and the financial onus hangs over it as the owners try to negotiate a debt payment agreement with city officials.

Another debt service situation applies to the Florida Suncoast Dome in St. Petersburg, Florida. The largely unoccupied, publicly financed facility was built to lure a professional baseball team, and was constructed for $138 million in the early 1990s.[27] The Suncoast Dome, more recently renamed the ThunderDome, had potential tenants in both the White Sox and the San Francisco Giants, but lost to last minute "save the franchise" bids by the city of Chicago and new ownership in San Francisco. The St. Petersburg facility, though, makes the best of the situation by housing the NHL's Tampa Bay Lightning, Arena Football, and several concerts, exhibitions, trade shows, and entertainment events.

The ThunderDome encourages activity. To use the ultra-modern facility, a promoter only needs to pay the $9,000 rental fee, or 12 percent of the gross ticket sales, whichever is greater, plus expenses (security, concessions, etc.). Expenses range between $20,000 and $70,000 depending upon the event size.[28] The ThunderDome was intended to bring business to the Tampa-St. Petersburg economy, and it has, just not the stable, consistent revenues of Major League Baseball. Whether its construction pays off in the long run remains to be seen, but it demonstrates the financial and political (bond issuance/debt service for construction and maintenance) clout of sports in communities.

Table 5.
Franchises' Facility-Generated Revenues
(As estimated by *Financial World*)

Stadium	Team	1991 Revenue (millions)	1993 Revenue
Comiskey Park	Chicago White Sox	$19.3	$21.8
Dodger Stadium	Los Angeles Dodgers	$18.0	$13.1
Joe Robbie Stadium	Miami Dolphins	$18.0	$15.4
Shea Stadium	New York Mets	$16.0	$11.5
Fenway Park	Boston Red Sox	$14.3	$ 9.9
Wrigley Field	Chicago Cubs	$12.0	$13.6
SkyDome	Toronto Blue Jays	$12.0	$ 6.3
Meadowlands	New York Giants	$ 5.5	$ 3.9
Great Western Forum	Los Angeles Lakers	$ 5.0	$24.0
Texas Stadium	Dallas Cowboys	$ 4.0	$30.0

Table 5 demonstrates that stadiums are a significant revenue source. Furthermore, some teams have better lease terms with respect to revenue division, and it is this issue that drives the increased mobility of professional sports franchises. Events create profit centers predicated upon the presence of quality entertainment, and facility developers and tenants naturally have opposing views on revenue dispersal.

Star Power—The Event Magnet

The main ingredient for a successful event is the presence of a legitimate star. Billie Jean King versus Bobby Riggs 1973 battle of the sexes tennis exhibition at the Astrodome in Houston attracted 30,000 people.[29] Red Grange attracted thousands in his barnstorming exhibition. Babe Ruth became the first athlete to earn more money than the president of the United States. His famous response, "I should be, after all I had a better year than he did," was remarkably accurate. Michael Jordan's minor league career (and Bo Jackson's before him) was a boon to attendance. The magnitude of the event, and its participants, initiates the sponsor-audience revenue cycle. Names like Mays, Dempsey, DiMaggio, Louis, Aaron, Ali, Chamberlain, O'Neal, Jordan, Owens, Namath, Mantle, Palmer, and Montana burn brightly on any marquee. For decades, whenever one of these stars was present, promoters have successfully sold their events to fans.

Joe DiMaggio, when queried about his source of motivation, once stated that there might be a fan in the ballpark who had never seen him play. He knew that people flocked to stadiums just to say that they saw him perform. His pride would not allow his performance to falter, and the fans always appreciated his modesty and competitive intensity. As event entertainment expands around the world, promoters take the simple principles of event management to entertain fans while creating profitable ventures.

A good example is International Management Group's (IMG) golf event, the "Skins Game." Aired by ABC during the Thanksgiving weekend, the "Skins Game" is now a golf institution. The original competition featured Jack Nicklaus, Gary Player, Tom Watson, and the King, Arnold Palmer. The concept popularizes the old skins betting concept,* except that the figures are several thousands of dollars. The participants were not in their competitive prime, when they had dominated golf, but they were still the most beloved and respected players in the world. Their participation brought instant credibility and respect to the competition. Connected via microphones throughout the broadcast, fans were a part of the banter and discussion during the competition, bringing a sense of intimacy to the event. Most importantly, the "Skins Game" brought fans. Since that original competition, the concept has been expanded to include golfers from the Ladies PGA and Senior PGA. Names like Snead, Lopez, Rodriguez, Couples, Stewart, Trevino, and Daly have thrilled golf fans of all ages through this unique event. The "Skins Game" is now a major sports "franchise," worth millions of dollars. It could never have become this successful without the enthusiastic participation of the athletes. Their efforts attracted and retained both fans and sponsors, the key to an event's success.

One athlete who has this "star" effect throughout the world is Arnold Palmer. Perhaps more than any other international competitor, Palmer's charisma, humor, and genuine modesty have attracted legions of fans, affectionately dubbed "Arnie's Army." Arnold Palmer's popularity is so unquestioned that he is given credit for bringing this sport

---

*The skins betting concept is when a bet of a particular dollar figure per hole is made. If there is a tie, the money is carried over to the next hole. Bets are paid at the end of play.

to the masses and re-establishing the significance of the British Open in America. His trademark aggressiveness, competitiveness, and sense of humor captured the imagination of generations of fans. Palmer's calendar is chock-full of appearances and obligations to satisfy the public's demand to see him play golf.

This adoration translates into financial gains for promoters and sponsors. Palmer's presence, for example, at the 1992 Ameritech Senior Open helped draw record crowds totaling over 77,000 people for the tournament week.[30] The final round saw 30,500 fans come to the course, an increase of 9,000 fans over the prior year—when he did not play.[31] His presence and a 40 percent attendance increase are not coincidences, he has been doing it for four decades. The extra 9,000 tickets represents a lot of money for the tournament in terms of basic ticket sales, concessions, and related expenditures. If each fan represents $30, that means that the promoters grossed an extra $270,000 for just one day in 1992.

Star power is pervasive in the sports world. Pele, the world's greatest soccer player and good will ambassador, played for the New York Cosmos for three years (1975–1977). Signed for $4.5 million, Pele transformed the old world's sporting pastime into a youth crazed activity in the United States. During his tenure in New York, the number of registered soccer players in the United States grew from 100,000 to 400,000, a testimony to his appeal. By the time he played his last match as a Cosmo, the game was broadcast in thirty-eight countries and attended by international dignitaries from around the world. Declared a "national treasure" in his native Brazil, Pele has truly been an international luminary of sports. His legend is so revered, his presence even stopped a war for two days in Africa (the 1968 Nigeria-Biafra conflict).[32]

HE'S BACK!!!

Michael Jordan retired from the Chicago Bulls following their third straight NBA championship in June 1993. Arguably the most accomplished athlete in the history of team sports, Jordan's retirement left a vacuum for basketball fans, but the public followed him in his path through minor league baseball (his Birmingham team sold 190,000 more tickets in 1994 with him playing). Jordan had grown weary of the NBA grind, and after the tragic death of his father, he made his baseball career a tribute to his memory.

Baseball's prolonged strike abruptly stopped Jordan's progression to the major leagues, and he reentered the NBA towards the end of the 1994–1995 season. His return, perhaps, was the most celebrated comeback since Coca-Cola rereleased its original formula (Coca-Cola Classic®). And Jordan delivered. The Sunday afternoon game against Indianapolis (a Bull's loss) drew the largest regular-season television audience in NBA history, thirty-five million viewers.[33]

The anticipation of Jordan's return was international news. The media swarmed the Bull's practice facility. They inundated coach Phil Jackson and other Bulls players with questions. Everyone wanted to know when and if Michael Jordan would play basketball in 1995. The hype over his return stimulated interest in his career and in his sponsors. Jordan's main sponsors had wisely stayed with him in his baseball career. Nike, Gatorade® (Quaker Oats), Hanes® (Sara Lee), Wheaties® (General Mills), and McDonald's knew that he would still be the best spokesman for their products.

The attention of Jordan's possible return to the NBA helped increase the stock value in these companies over $2 billion in less than one week. Of course, the ability to sustain the increase in value is up to the companies, but Jordan's incredible impact is undeniable. Already the best compensated endorser, he might even be underpaid. How many other employees or subcontractors can influence over $2 billion of defined shareholder value?

The Root of Event Interdependence

The financial success of sporting events lies within the framework of the Event Triangle. Each participant, event, audience, and sponsor(s), has goals satisfied by the other groups. Because sports has maintained its audience, sponsors invest billions of dollars to communicate through them. Furthermore, the reliability of fans attending and tuning into sports events, has brought the expansion of proved event principles into new markets. No one in the fifties or the seventies for that matter, would have forecasted thriving hockey teams in San Jose, California, or Tampa Bay, Florida. But through unforgettable performers, and successful media promotion, hockey is in the Sun Belt and California.

Fans are responsible for the unflagging enthusiasm that supports sports entertainment. They justify the billions invested and returned from sports sponsorships. The fans, in essence, are a docile, cooperative group that faithfully support their teams and athletes. The Olympics earn the highest sponsorship fees because they sell nationalism. No one's patriotism can be questioned, and sponsors enjoy the association with predictable goodwill.

As the "global village" (the digital age of shared information) approaches, an evolving case worth following will be the eastern European market. The now emancipated East has produced fabulous athletes for decades, as they proved by their superior Olympic performances. Now, as economic opportunity awaits in the West, many compete in America and western Europe. Sarunas Marciulonis made history as he became the first Soviet born athlete to score a basket in the NBA, but now other eastern Europeans like Vlade Divac and Toni Kukoc are household names. The NHL, in fact, has more eastern European born stars than American bred ones. But the tide of athletic talent will stop as events find their commercial ground there. Contemporary sports marketing principles will go there to influence sponsorships and entertainment. One sports capitalist, Howard Baldwin, owner of the Pittsburgh Penguins, purchased a stake in the Russian National Team and integrated some NHL marketing standards to generate fan interest and revenue.

Fancy uniforms, rock music, and fan participation promotions have increased attendance by 600 percent, and helped give the players a raise.[34] And Mr. Baldwin's goals are not entirely altruistic. He now has significant licensing opportunities with obscure, mysterious graphics, exactly the formula that has worked for other franchises. He hopes that his Russian hockey fatigues will make his Russian Penguins a new rage and add to the NHL's approximate $1 billion licensing industry. Furthermore, he has a feeder system* in hockey-rich Russia that will help keep his own hockey team staffed with exciting players.

Case Analysis: Totally Super[35]

Some vital statistics of America's most popular sporting event, the Super Bowl display how sponsor investment works with an event to

*Setting up a business presence to both entertain the fans and scout talent in the area.

influence an audience. Played on the last Sunday in January, the Super Bowl benefits from the hype of an entire football season, no significant sports entertainment competitors, and inclement weather conditions in almost 80 percent of the United States. It truly is the ultimate one day television event, with over 133 million viewers (41 percent female) in demographic reach. Lastly, due to the integrated marketing capacity of sponsors, networks, and licensors, the Super Bowl accounts for $4.25 billion in marketing expenditures.[36]

Attendance: All but the first Super Bowl have been sellouts.
Super Bowl I tickets cost $6–$12.
Super Bowl XXIX tickets cost $200 each.

Television audience: Super Bowl I—77 million viewers, 22.6 percent rating.
Super Bowl XXVIII—133 million viewers, 45.5 percent rating.
Seven hundred fifty million viewers worldwide. Broadcast in 141 countries.
Ad time cost $42,500 per thirty-second spot in 1967, $900,000 in 1994 and $1 million in 1995.

Advertiser impact: Sixty-six percent people tested recall Super Bowl commercials. The average recall for a commercial airing during any given broadcast is 23 percent. ABC's ad revenues from Super Bowl XXIX was $75 million.

Host economic impact: Super Bowl XXX estimated to bring $187 million to Phoenix. Super Bowl XXVI (Minneapolis) generated $121 million. Two thousand jobs were created for the event.

Promoter's angle: The NFL sold the broadcast rights for XXVIII for $41 million. NFL Properties, the licensing arm of the league, sells approximately $200 million in merchandise for the game. For Super Bowl XXIX, Sears sponsored the Legends Bowl featuring flag football contest and player appearances at Sears stores, and an individual apparel line. "NFL experience" brings carnival atmosphere and convention of the sport and its sponsors to the host city.

Player's Share: Super Bowl XXIX winners received $42,000 each, and losers $26,000, a pay cut for most players.

Ticket distribution: NFL gets 25 percent of facility capacity, host team 10 percent, two competitor teams receive 17.5 percent. The other twenty-seven teams in league get 1.2 percent each. The rest go to season ticket holders in lotteries. So where do the scalpers get theirs?

News media: Three hundred thirty-eight credentials were issued at Super Bowl I.

Six hundred forty-six news organizations, 407 international media representatives, 136 international news organizations and a total of 2,846 journalists received credentials for Super Bowl XXIX.

Gambling action: Between $35–60 million in legal gambling. Illegal estimates are much higher.

Obscure "Super" fact: The Super Bowl is the third biggest eating day in America (behind Christmas and Thanksgiving).

The Super Bowl is not just about the actual game, it has evolved into a cyclical business event, as shown by the $4.25 billion of marketing activity. Activities like season-long promotions giving trips to consumers, i.e., Savane®. Onsite promotions like the NFL Experience brings a festival atmosphere to the host city, and, of course, involve sponsors. Super Bowl XXIX's NFL Experience was sponsored by Coca-Cola and American Express®. At the "Experience," fans could go to the super sized Foot Locker, or run in the UPS forty-yard dash, or take a photo in the Fuji end zone.

Game advertisers also receive "added-value," doubling their exposure. Business sections of international newspapers discuss, analyze, rate, and report the commercials run during the game. *USA Today,* for example, analyzes each ad, and devotes cover-story space to the commercials of the broadcast. Advertisers often get maligned for paying the exorbitant fees for advertising, but secretly laugh, for they know that the related publicity often doubles the exposure.

So Who Actually Attends the Game?

An NFL survey shows:

35 percent attend on a corporate expense account.
33 percent earn more than $100,000 annually.
27 percent own their own company.
25 percent are corporate officers.
22 percent sit on a board of directors.

3

Big League Sports

The World Golf Tour is the reward for the best players in the world. . . . It is set up for the best to compete against the best.

—Greg Norman, November 17, 1994

With proposed financing of $25 million from Fox Sports' programming war chest, Greg Norman consulted with the directors of the World Golf Tour on the feasibility of their business plan. The World Tour would guarantee event purses of $3 million per eight international competitions. Winners would receive $600,000 each (last place finishers earn $30,000). Furthermore, a $1 million bonus would go to the player with the highest point total at the year's end. The objective was to gather the thirty top golfers in the world, add ten more from the event site (the country) and have the forty best golfers compete in a championship setting.

Beamed throughout the world by Fox's extensive broadcasting network, the new World Golf Tour would give the international game of golf further definition. In retrospect, the World Tour was off to a fabulous start. It had:

- A charismatic, enthusiastic supporter: Greg Norman
- A broadcast partner: Fox
- A seemingly bullet-proof business plan: the best competitive golfers in golf's best international settings (Scotland, Spain, USA, Japan, and Canada)

The World Tour's task was to broker the deal to the international golfers and their governing bodies, the PGA and the European PGA. The players were enthusiastic about the opportunity and the concept, but they were reticent about diminishing the PGA's entertainment machine. "It's a good idea," said golfer Fred Couples the day following the announcement, "but only if the PGA is included."

Couples' statement proved prophetic, as the World Tour did not receive overwhelming player support. With eight events occurring in five countries, the United States, Canada, Spain, Japan, and Scotland, players knew that this new Tour would take name attractions out of other tournaments' fields, and that would displease loyal, longstanding sponsors. If a World Golf tour event coincided with the Buick Classic, and Fred Couples, Davis Love III, Greg Norman, Nick Price, Ben Crenshaw, and the other top draws are in Spain to play for $600,000, then the promotional package sold by the PGA to Buick is diminished.

If the PGA gives a rebate to the sponsor, they lose money and prestige. If the golfing audiences watch the world event on Fox rather than the Buick Classic on CBS, then the sponsors lose return on their investment. Thus, someone would lose on this new deal, but not necessarily the forty competitors. The World Tour's original business plan wanted players to commit to all eight events, and for that commitment, they would receive an expense stipend ($50,000 each). Ultimately, the World Tour was too much, too soon. The security and sanctity of the PGA tournament schedule and membership remained intact, as did its healthy $82 million worth of sponsorships.[1]

In the near future, the PGA must be leery of promotional competitors. Golf stars should not have to endure less opportunity. That would be monopolistic bias and restraint of trade resulting in a skewed form of wage discrimination. In fact, the Federal Trade Commission (FTC) is investigating the PGA Tour exactly for those reasons. Golfers are independent contractors, and if there is no legal structure, professional golf would be nothing more than disorganized exhibitions. However, in the new age of "Big League Sports," athletic competition is going to the highest combination of broadcast and sponsor bidders. No one connected to golf wants to see it become a promoter-driven entity like boxing, but that could be a part of its future.

Golf (like boxing) is an international sport that has no real borders for its best competitors. Arnold Palmer, Jack Nicklaus, and Gary Player set the precedent for international travel in the sixties (to maintain the analogy, Muhammad Ali had celebrated bouts in the Philippines and Africa during the seventies). Today's stars certainly have made international play an important part of their schedules. Nick Price, the acknowledged best player in the world after record-setting years in 1993 and 1994, planned to play in Dubai (United Arab Emirates), Manila (Philippines), and Johannesburg (South Africa) in addition to America in the first six weeks of his 1995 golf season. Television brings the charisma and greatness of golfers like Olazabal, Price, Ozaki, Norman, and Couples to the masses. And the masses want to see them in person, as well as on screen.

Some of the sports' organizational structures, (Major League Baseball, the NFL, the NHL, the PGA, etc.), are losing ground to the athletes and corporate interests that financially support one another. As the Event Triangle demonstrates, events attract audiences, and those audiences are a desirable commodity driving up the price for the athletes and sponsors. The World Tour is not a revelation. It is a potential revolution. The best players are given the chance to seize an opportunity. They can create an international audience that can be captured by global networks, and earn millions in the process.

Sports' governing bodies—e.g., NFL, NHL, WBC, and the PGA—have so much power that competitors are compelled to enter the industry and participate in the financial windfall. The problem in all of the major sports leagues is that there is not enough room for the splintering (dilution) of leagues and teams. In professional golf, the current setup mandates a tour commitment. The PGA requires its members to play in a minimum of fifteen events in order for the players to maintain exempt status (players qualify for exempt status through money earnings and tournament competition results—the top 125 money winners immediately qualify for next years' events). Without making this commitment, players cannot play in more than eight PGA tournaments, even if the sponsor pleads for an exemption. Thus, esteemed foreigners, such as Sandy Lyle, Ian Woosnam, Jose-Maria Olazabal, Bernhard Langer, Jumbo Ozaki, Ian Baker-Finch, Colin Montgomerie, and Seve Ballesteros only play in the U.S. Open, the Masters, and selected other events because of the travel burden.

Spain's Jose Maria-Olazabal, one of the world's best players (1992 Masters Champion) has frequently lamented the strict PGA policies.

When he heard of the World Tour concept, he sent a letter (November 15, 1994) to Greg Norman. The World Tour reprinted it and distributed it to the press at the inaugural conference:

> Dear Greg,
> I'm most excited about the World [Golf] Tour project you submitted to me last week. The idea and philosophy of a great project has got to me. It is the kind of step forward I've been dreaming of for the last years. . . . With . . . the best players competing in more tournaments around the world. Please feel free to use my name as a strong supporter of the idea. I am writing to get full details of the development of that project to commit to the World [Golf] Tour.
>
> Sincerely,
> Jose Maria Olazabal

This endorsement was the public statement that the fledgling World Golf Tour needed in order to build player consensus. Olazabal felt restricted by the protectionist policies of the PGA. No one doubts the PGA has developed golf entertainment for golf fans, sponsors, and broadcasters, but at what price to the competitors? The ultimate answer to the World Tour was that the players did not support it—this time. The World Tour did not have its origins in the PGA, and hence, will probably never receive cooperation from the governing body.

Organized, sanctioned play by the worlds' greatest athletes, whether they are golfers or basketball players, is a certainty. Only the financing and revenue distribution needs to be determined. Unlike the PGA, the NBA anticipated the growth of international basketball. Not only did several American players (Bob McAdoo, Brian Shaw, and Danny Ferry) enjoy careers overseas, but foreign leagues were gaining financial strength to lure more athletes.

USA Basketball was formed to govern the United States' amateur tournament entries, and the NBA lent their experience and management to the process. The 1992 Dream Team was the answer to the United States' international competitive presence. Stars like Larry Bird, Michael Jordan, Magic Johnson, Karl Malone, Chris Mullin, Charles Barkley, Clyde Drexler, John Stockton, David Robinson, and Patrick Ewing gave instant credibility to USA Basketball, and entrenched the NBA as the organizer and profiteer from the venture. By the time the league needed to form the second Dream Team (Dream Team II) for the

World Championship of Basketball, the NBA had sponsorships, licensing, and television issues in place. Dream Team II represented the United States in Toronto and will form its third team for the Atlanta Summer Games in 1996.

Organizational Overview

Sports activities have created a platform for owners, players, and sponsor participants to profit from the public. Leagues and teams package athletes in showcase surroundings to sell to an audience. The athletes directly associated with the competition and publicity of the event(s) express their talents and personalities through their performance. In revealing their competitive spirit and showcasing their abilities, the athletes and franchises create a loyal bond with their fans and the entire community of sports enthusiasts.

The relationship between the vehicle (management), and the fuel (athletes/participants) has gone from complete and abject exploitation (baseball under the reserve clause system when the club reserved the rights to a players contract, restricting *any* movement) to a system of debated compromise (major league sports as we know them today). Owners initially had the leverage, but are slowly dividing the wealth with labor.

Big league sports are now defined by money, not the level of competition. High school programs even seek and sell sponsorships because they actually have commercial value. This is not a condemnation of the prevailing circumstances, merely an objective analysis. A "big league sport" is defined by its revenue potential. Given that broad latitude, the following sports can be classified in the categories listed in Table 1.

Table 1.
Classification of Big League Sports Based on Revenue Potential

U.S.A.	International	Large-Scale Events
Football	Soccer	Olympics
Basketball	Track and Field	World Cup
Baseball	Auto Racing	Goodwill Games
Hockey	Horse Racing	America's Cup
Tennis	Tennis	World Championships of Track and Field
Golf	Golf	
Auto Racing	Boxing	
Horse Racing	Skating	
College Basketball	Gymnastics	
College Football		
Boxing		
Skating		
Wrestling		

THE FINANCIAL SYNDROME OF SPORTING EVENTS

The syndrome simply creates financial feedbags for the administrative and sales interests of the sports industry. Once the financial viability of an activity is proved, then the resources to uphold, enhance, and nurture it come together, i.e., media support, properties divisions, marketing arms, charitable concerns, and other related activities. It also brings progressive attempts at further development. Wimbledon, the most prestigious event in all of tennis combined its merchandise, television rights, sponsorships, and ticket sales to earn a record $25.6 million in 1993, and it increased that by 71 percent in 1994 to $43.7 million.[2] Excellent management, international appeal and the biggest names in both men's and women's tennis equally contribute to the financial success of the event.

The Promoter's Equation can be written as follows:

Top Celebrities + Legitimate Competition = Fan interest = Sponsor dollars and television exposure.

Team sports, supported by league structures, generate excitement, publicity, and money around the world. *Financial World* magazine has made estimates of America's major sports' franchises and their 1993 net worth.

Table 2.
1993 Estimated Value of America's Major Sports Franchises

Sport	Average Franchise Value	Minimum Salary
Football (NFL)	$153 million	$108,000
Major League Baseball	$107 million (prestrike)	$109,000
Basketball (NBA)	$99 million	$150,000
Hockey (NHL)	$61 million	$100,000

The total value of 107 franchises analyzed came to $11.4 billion, on revenues of $5.1 billion. Even as operating expenses (primarily salaries) increase, franchise value increases. Football's Philadelphia Eagles, purchased for $65 million in 1985, sold for S185 million in early 1994, and the New England Patriots, purchased for $106 million in 1992, sold for $160 million in 1994. Perhaps the greatest argument for the power of ownership is exemplified through the sale of the Tampa Bay Buccaneers. One of the most woeful football franchises, the Buccaneers were sold for $192 million in early 1995. The value for the Buccaneers and other teams have skyrocketed for many reasons: *prestige, power,* and *profitability.*

The *prestige* explanation is simple and straightforward. There are only 107 major league franchise owners in America. The position of team owner has many perks besides money—most particularly media exposure. How many times had Jerry Jones appeared on national television before he bought the Dallas Cowboys? After one Super Bowl victory, he was featured in a nationally broadcasted Apex apparel advertisement with some of his employees, including former coach Jimmy Johnson. Furthermore, the fraternity of professional sports is an elite one with access to other entertainment outlets and other personalities. Simply put, franchise ownership is an impressive addition to any resume, or annual report, as in the case of Disney (which owns the NHL's Mighty Ducks).

Back to Jerry Jones. There is more to his ownership than simply publicity. Led by stars such as Troy Aikman, Emmitt Smith, Jay Novacek, and Michael Irvin, Jones's Cowboys are one of sport's most popular teams. He paid $140 million ($65 million for the franchise and $75 million for the stadium) in 1989, and the value for both has almost doubled. Most importantly, his Cowboys have turned $60 million in profits the past three years because the Cowboys market the product on the field and off. The Cowboys merchandise virtually all of their promotional entities: they sell tickets, media rights, luxury suites, and team sponsorships. Their famed Dallas Cowboy Cheerleaders division even earns $250,000 a year. The team's newsletter is printed both in English and in Spanish, and the radio broadcasts are in both languages as well. Jones is so confident about the Cowboys' drawing power that he wants to spend (financing through the Cowboys and the city of Irving) approximately $200 million to expand Texas Stadium to accommodate 40,000 more seats—and more revenue.[3] This type of hands-on management has enabled the Cowboys and Jones to think "big"—just like the state of Texas.

The *power* of franchise ownership is relatively simple as well. First, ownership means political clout. Team owners bring millions of dollars in business activity to municipalities, industries, and federal tax collectors. Sports franchises and related businesses (licensed goods, trading cards, etc.) employ people. Professional sports entertainment production and distribution needs athletes, administrators, and operations executioners. Wayne Huizenga bought the Florida Panthers (NHL, $50 million), Florida Marlins (MLB, $95 million), and he purchased controlling interest in the Miami Dolphins (NFL, $138 million).[4] Huizenga also owns Joe Robbie Stadium. He is an important civic leader whose decisions influence Miami's business community.

Professional teams bring positive external factors to a city that define elements of the community, i.e., the enthusiasm and heightened emotion. The Pittsburgh Steelers of the early 1970s were dubbed "The Steel Curtain" for their stingy defense and blue-collar approach to the game, but those teams had a star wide receiver named Lynn Swann who took ballet lessons and exhibited a graceful style that made him one of the league's all-time great players. Similarly, some of the great San Francisco 49ers teams of the eighties were referred to as a finesse team, because of the personality of their sophisticated coach, Bill Walsh. Yet nothing could have been farther from the truth, as those 49er teams had top defenses featuring tough personalities like Jack "Hacksaw" Reynolds, Ronnie Lott, Fred Dean, Michael Carter, and Mike Walter. The reality in the late twentieth century is that much of the news tends toward the negative, and a winning team helps the morale of a community. Mayors and governors frequently place friendly wagers with their counterparts when a big game grabs the headlines. The wagers usually consist of local Epicurean delights, such as fish from Florida and ribs from Chicago, but they always make the headlines.

The point is not the actual sociology of sports, but the fact that sports do have a sociological impact. The Colts' departure from Baltimore, and their associated history/identification with the city, created a withdrawal of the city's identity.* Any Brooklynite would say that the town has not been the same since the Dodgers left. But the teams did leave, and it has always been for the same reason: owners look to make (more) *MONEY.*

Franchise relocation is a sticky issue. Movement indicates the instability of the league, and the selfishness of an owner. Therefore, leagues frown upon relocation, but the owners have won the right in court (*Raiders* v. *NFL,* 1982), which means their value is enhanced because competitive cities continually and persistently attempt to lure teams. Thus ownership is about being in the news and making the news. Most importantly, it is about generating revenues and profits. The money comes from all the usual sources: stadiums and arenas, radio and television, merchandise, and integrated sponsorships. Total 1993 franchise revenues were $5.1 billion, and operating income almost $375 million.[5] With cash sources coming in so many forms, and with operating expenses being primarily player salaries ($2.85 billion in 1993), ownership of professional franchises is a simplistic equation.

But in sports, where winning is everything, it has a definite price—salaries. Rickey Jackson, one of the best linebackers in NFL history (among the league's all-time sack leaders, six-time Pro Bowl participant) signed with the San Francisco 49ers for the league minimum of $162,000 in 1994, after a storied thirteen-year career with the Saints. Jackson felt the 49ers could make it to the Super Bowl with his help, and he was willing to take a huge pay cut to prove it. He wanted a reward for his efforts, though, and he had a bonus clause written into his contract giving him $838,000 if the 49ers made it to Super Bowl XXIX. Jackson's more celebrated teammate Deion Sanders had $750,000 in bonuses for making it through the championship game to the same Super Bowl. The 49ers did not mind giving the performance bonuses, because they rewarded results, not statements.[6]

---

*To see how important this departure was, one should see the movie *Diner.*

Incentive structures, however, are not unique to linebackers and cornerbacks. The defending World Cup champions (1990's champion), Germany, saved $1.27 million by not repeating as champions in 1994. The players were to be rewarded with $80,000 bonuses if they repeated as World Cup champions. By only reaching the Quarterfinals, the players received $22,000 each.[7] Of course, the German Soccer Federation would have enjoyed paying the extra money, if only to keep the national press from second guessing the coach and players.

Big League Motives

The ripple effect of the 1994 World Cup was not in the bonuses paid to the players, nor in the amount of Budweiser® sold at the promotion. It was about selling soccer to the host country. Though not the primary objective, the world's most popular sport wanted to make it as a "Big League Sport" in America. The World Cup was well attended, reported, and commercialized in the United States, and the organizers wanted to capitalize on the favorable U.S. reception.

Soccer had never enjoyed sustained success in the United States. Television and gate receipts never subsidized leagues, such as the North American Soccer League (NASL), for long periods of time. But the 1994 World Cup gave soccer another chance in the United States, as the organizing committee devised a business plan that it believed would make professional soccer finally succeed in the United States.

BIG LEAGUE BUSINESS PLAN FOR: *MAJOR LEAGUE SOCCER (MLS)*

The league will own all players and franchises.

A central management authority will control salary expenditures—parity.

Financed partly by World Cup Organizing Committee.

Team operators will have to pay a minimum of $5 million. The league goal is to raise $50–$100 million for league startup costs. Operators invest in the MLS, but run a franchise, hire the front office and coaches, manage player personnel, and run local marketing programs.

League Set up

By late 1994, The MLS had:

A league logo.
An official game ball.
Commissioner Alan Rothenburg (1994 World Cup Executive Director).
Television partners—ABC and ESPN.
Ten teams: New York (Long Island); New Jersey Meadowlands; Boston; Kansas City; Los Angeles, San Jose; Columbus; Orlando; Washington, D.C.; and Chicago.

Sponsor Packages:

Nike agreed to pay $150,000 to its five sponsored teams.
Nike will spend $100,000 each in marketing support (uniforms and footwear).

The league was scheduled to start in the spring of 1995, but the kickoff got put back a year as financing, investors, and other issues went unresolved. Flush with success as the World Cup's organizer ($40 million profit), MLS hopes to capitalize where others (six leagues) have failed. By centralizing and standardizing operating expenses, the league forecasts financial stability for all teams.[8]

Approaching the league concept with this conservative emphasis puts the focus on league longevity, *not* independent franchise success. Organizers feel a united beginning and loyal television backing will result in long-range growth that finally transfers the enthusiasm to *play* soccer into an interest in *watching* soccer. Many detractors claim that by not starting the league immediately following the success of the World Cup, the ground swell of enthusiasm would be lost. But owners were not discouraged or dismayed by the nay sayers, placing their faith in their conservative business plan. Colloquially stated, Major League Soccer is in no hurry to make headlines for hastiness.

The concepts of power, prestige, and money pertain to college sports as well. The merging of conferences and alliances is done for its fiscal implications, not geographic or academic. The most obvious case involves Penn State's Nittany Lions. Long a college football powerhouse, Penn State has a loyal national following buoyed by a great tradition and respected head coach, Joe Paterno. Not satisfied with merely selling out Beaver Stadium and picking on Eastern schools, Penn State joined the big 10 for football. The reward was threefold:

- More television coverage
- Better, consistent, guaranteed exposure
- More money

Penn State went to the Rose Bowl after the 1994 season, its first in the new and improved conference setup. The only problem was that the Rose Bowl ("The Granddaddy of Them All") precluded a true national championship matchup. The Rose Bowl features the Pac-10 champion versus the Big 10 conference champion. If either conference's representative has the number one ranking it can participate in determining the national champion, but if the game features the number two team, as the 1995 Rose Bowl did (Penn State [number two]) versus Oregon [number eight]), then Penn State had virtually no chance of winning the coveted title if the top-ranked team won its Bowl game. So Penn State's security blanket worked against them in 1994. The Nebraska Cornhuskers, the number one team, played Miami, the number three team, in the Orange Bowl. Of course, everyone wanted Nebraska vs. Penn State, but as the winning member of the Big 10, the Rose Bowl was the Nittany Lions' only option. Nebraska beat Miami in a thriller to eliminate any possibility for Penn State's championship hopes, a byproduct of its conference commitment.

The Underpinnings of Big League Fanaticism

Basketball's Washington Bullets traded for superstar Chris Webber in November of 1994, signed his college buddy, first round draft pick Juwan Howard, on virtually the same day, and sold 1,200 season ticket plans in less than forty-eight hours. Less than three months later (and 3,000 miles west), over 300,000 fans jammed the streets of downtown San Francisco to welcome the 49ers after their fifth Super Bowl victory in January 1995.

You don't always have to be a winner to be loved, either. Basketball fans in North Carolina are willing to put their money where their hearts are for the Hornets. Rights to eight season tickets for the Charlotte Hornets were auctioned for $160,000. And that is only for the rights, the tickets still needed to be purchased.[9] Fan hysteria and pure pandemonium rules when the right combination of charisma and potential steps in the ring (Muhammad Ali), on the court (Bird versus Magic), or on the diamond (Roger Clemens). These individuals have an outlet for their specialized abilities. But unlike a cost accountant (another highly paid specialist), athletes command interest and attention from the general public.

Most importantly, athletes have a structure, and/or platform to display their talents. Teams, leagues, and networks have evolved to package and present the athletes in all of their glory. Yes, Michael Jordan paid the price to dominate and excel in professional basketball. He combined his enormous talent with discipline and hard work to use the outlet of the NBA and the Chicago Bulls to charm the world with his charisma and abilities. The Olympics, the World Series, the Super Bowl, and even the Superstars event are all platforms that showcase the athletes. The degree of audience reach and attention define the influence and potential of the platform.

But fanaticism and its corresponding attendance/viewership is usually based on winning, and competitive opportunity. Hence, the NFL's stated embrace of "parity" intends to keep all thirty franchises legitimately in the hunt for postseason glory all sixteen weeks of the regular season. By maintaining relative competitiveness with the opponents, the predominant thinking is that the fan base will stay interested. If not, the fans will stay away. For example, the 1994 Houston Oilers went into the fourteenth week of the season with a 1 and 12 record. Only 31,453 fans decided to attend their December 11 contest against the Seattle Seahawks (a 16-14 loss). Attendance figures also showed that there were 14,358 no-shows. The prior weekend, amid swirls of franchise relocation rumors, the Los Angeles Rams played what was one of their last games in Los Angeles before only 34,960 fans, one of the lowest attendance figures in their tenancy at the "Big A" stadium in Anaheim.

Fans have proved that they will support both winning and losing franchises, and the owners like to see evidence of that through ticket sales. When an expansion franchise opportunity, or relocation opportunity, arises, the first thing the tentative ownership committee does is sell tickets to prospective fans. By selling tickets the city shows the revenues a team can expect by playing/moving to that region. Depending on the sport, owners equally share some national broadcast revenues, and local broadcast revenues (in the individual teams' areas) are determined by market size, i.e., New York City is greater than Cleveland, Ohio. Therefore, ticket sales are normally the teams' primary source of revenue. Hence, when team ownership wants an indication of revenues, this means ticket sales.

No recent case exemplifies this better than the 1994 Rams, who were courted by the city of St. Louis. Oddly, the eighteenth largest U.S. market proved that it was more attractive than the second largest consumer market.[10] To warrant a move, the Rams wanted a guarantee of 55,000 tickets sold for the 70,000 seat domed facility being constructed.[11] The ticket sale guarantee is, in effect, nothing more than the financing of guaranteed profits. At an average price of $29.13 (1994 average Los Angeles Rams ticket price)[12] for the ten annual home games (eight regular season, plus two exhibitions), Ram management would earn a minimum gross ticket sales revenue of $16,021,500, which is almost $2.5 million above the 1993 league average of gate revenue ($13.7 million), as reported in *Financial World* magazine.

Furthermore, the St. Louis Rams pulled a page from the Carolina Panthers' play-book and had an ambitious seat licensing program, whereby individuals purchased lifetime, permanent rights to a seat, or seats, for a fee (from $250–$4,500 each), depending upon location. The fans then have to purchase the annual tickets for those seats at the $25–$45 ticket price, depending upon the seat location. The Rams intend to raise $60–$70 million with this program. (The Carolina Panthers, according to Raiders owner Al Davis, raised $150 million in seat licensing revenue.) If, however, the franchise had not sold 40,000 permanent seats by a drop-dead date (March 10, 1995), the Rams could have called off the deal.[13] Prenuptial agreements obviously apply to professional sports marriages as well.

Ram ownership wanted to move in spite of the fact that the NFL's Cardinals left St. Louis (1987 relocation to Phoenix) and that Los Angeles is the United States' second largest media market. Commissioner Paul Tagliabue also had concerns, because the best scenario for the Rams is not necessarily the best one for the NFL. Unfortunately for Tagliabue, the Raiders lawsuit against the league over their 1982 move dilutes his influence and power over such issues. Currently, the NFL needs twenty-one owners to approve a move, but legally cannot enforce it. He stated on the radio (in regard to the Rams-St. Louis situation):

> Obviously when you're talking about one of the two largest population areas in the country, you really need an in-depth review to see what the implications are. . . . That's what we're preparing to do if we receive a proposal from the Rams or Raiders. We will focus on our policy guidelines on team location.

But the reality of the Rams' Anaheim situation is not the most favorable from an ownership standpoint. Since leaving the dilapidated (in the Rams' opinion) Los Angeles Coliseum in 1980, the Rams drew an average of 62,550 fans per game in their inaugural year in Anaheim. Ten years later, when the team went all the way to the NFC Championship game, the club averaged 59,919 fans per home game.[14] By 1994, attendance sunk to an average of 42,312 and the St. Louis offer estimated 1995 profits in the Show-Me-State at $20.8 million. Compared to their reported loss of $6 million for 1994, ownership believes that the sunshine of southern California can be traded for a $26 million revenue swing.

The key factor, though, is not just 1995, it is the time beyond that. The NFL does not want to promote a barnstorming approach to ownership. Regional stability is integral to maintaining a fan base and national market share. The obvious temptation for the short-term solution, i.e., moving, had to be weighed against the long-term implications of staying in Southern California. Clearly, the Rams think that with a guaranteed broadcast revenue stream that evenly divides national rights fees, they will make more independently in St. Louis from their stadium, ticket, and broadcast revenues than in Los Angeles. In St. Louis, the Rams chose from three different sites for a $15 million practice facility, which will compare dramatically to the converted high school they used in Anaheim. Furthermore, the city of St. Louis will additionally pay $15 million in relocation fees, retire $30 million of debt to the city of Anaheim and provide a $260 million state-of-the-art domed stadium for the Rams to call home. Lastly, the thirty-year lease payment is set at the bargain price of $250,000 per annum.[15] Not a bad deal if you are a Rams management executive.

The competitive interests for the Rams have different objectives: St. Louis versus Los Angeles and the NFL's league interests versus Georgia Frontiere, the Rams owner.

The best decision for one city will hurt the other, and the best decision for the league may or may not benefit the franchise owner. But in early 1995, the Rams (despite many objections) moved east to St. Louis. Ironically, the Rams were the first professional sports team to move westward (from Cleveland in 1946), but after forty-nine years in southern California, they returned to their midwestern roots amid great fanfare. How long will the honeymoon last between the team and their new city?

Labor

In the sports world, October 1994, will be remembered as the first October in ninety years without a World Series. Attorneys and mediators such as Donald Fehr, Richard Ravitch, and William Usery became household names as the public acrimony between labor and management overshadowed the game of baseball. The ongoing distrust between the purveyors of the national pastime led to this inevitable development. At one time, the frugality of Major League Baseball owners was legendary. It is even mentioned as the root of the 1919 Black Sox scandal (the White Sox were proved to have thrown the World Series). Some critical timeline highlights illuminate the status of baseball's labor-management relationship:

- 1947: the minimum major league salary was $5,000[16]
- 1968: it doubled to $10,000
- 1975: the players won the right to free agency (the rights to sell services to any team after a certain number of years in the league provided the player's contract has expired)
- 1994: longest work stoppage in the game's history, ostensibly due to disagreements over a proposed salary cap.

By the time the players walked away from the game in August of 1994, they had eight separate work stoppages in the last twenty-four years. They also had an average salary over $1 million. The players resolutely stood behind their leadership in opposition to management and gained ground in arbitration, full benefits, and a pension plan. They weren't about to back down in 1994.

Management, on the other hand, had a far different outlook. Bud Selig, the acting commissioner of baseball, claimed that Major League Baseball was a break-even operation since 1978, losing money in the years between 1975–1985, and earning money from 1986–1993.[17] In 1975, baseball's revenues were $162.5 million. By 1993, they had climbed to $1.879 billion. In the eight fiscal years from 1986–1993, operating profits were almost $763 million, excluding expansion fees. But on the bleaker side, owners paid out $280 million in collusion damages to players, and absorbed over $300 million in losses in the early 1980s. With all of the financial gains and losses for both owners and players, it is no surprise that both sides distrust the other's financial analysis. Furthermore, the cause of the revenue increase is another subjective debate. The players, naturally, claim that their appeal has led to the heightened interest and revenue whereas the owners believe that their management and marketing has enabled the game to grow. How could a working agreement sensibly evolve given the inability to agree on anything? That is where the lawyers come in.

The players went out on strike formally after the Oakland A's-Seattle Mariners game on August 12, 1994. The two sides publicly stated that they wanted a swift solution so that the postseason could be saved. The sides met often, but with no tangible results. The task to negotiate a settlement in the disagreements between the operative elements in baseball, i.e., the players and the owners, had passed the president's desk in late 1994, and President Clinton appointed a proven winner, Bill Usery, to break the stalemate. Usery was paid $120,000 per month to negotiate an agreement that would divide almost $2 billion in annual revenues between 700 people (baseball owners and players).[18] The owners, incapable of solving the revenue disparity between large and small market teams, determined that the solution was to impose a salary cap that defined player salaries to be 56 percent of annually defined revenues ($1 billion). The players balked at the suggestion, implying that any wage control was not in anyone's best interest.

Baseball's 1994 off season was a series of legal updates, proposals, and counter proposals. One side would submit a proposal, and the other side would crunch the numbers based upon the complicated taxations, licensing, and allocations and then declare the proposal untenable. The issues always came to the payroll tax concept. Donald Fehr, a union negotiator, consistently interpreted the tax and other measures as a salary cap. The owners continually threatened to impose an across-the-board salary cap if an agreement on a new labor contract could not be met. The players maintained that, as an integral part of the game, they wanted some say in the decision-making powers of the game, i.e., naming a commissioner, community development issues, broadcasting agreements, and international play. The union also wanted to contribute to an industry growth fund for promotional and community applications. Each side antagonized the other's position until the efforts of mediator Usery and the will of the players and owners ultimately ended in an imposed salary cap on December 23, 1994—Merry Christmas.

But that was not the end. The players said that they would not play under those circumstances. Owners prepared replacement rosters and adjusted ticket plans. Fans and sponsors passed judgment on baseball's inability to resolve its disputes. The future of the game, with or without its real players, was very much in doubt. President Clinton formally involved himself and imposed a target settlement date of February 6, 1995. A few days after President Clinton made his concerns public, the owners backed off the salary cap, and threw it out of their agreement.

By doing away with the imposed cap, the owners appeased the National Labor Relations Board, the Federal Trade Commission, Congress, and the Players Association. Their steadfast position quickly eroded in the face of federal intervention. The owners charted a course that would (in their opinion) allow the 1995 season to begin anew. The players, happy to see the owners back down from their dogmatic position, were not too quick to yield in their own resolve. Therefore, just one week before the pitchers and catchers were due to report for spring training, there still was no settlement. Replacement players and unknowns straggled into the training camps, each side more determined not to back down from its position.

RESOLUTION!?

On March 31, 1995, U.S. District Judge Sonia Sotomayor became an unlikely power broker in the longest work stoppage in Major League Baseball history. She presided over the players' motion (on behalf of the National Labor Relations Board) for an injunction on the owners' labor contract. Judge Sotomayor upheld the players' claim that the owners imposed unfair labor practices and restored the terms and conditions of the last existing agreement. That agreement, as all baseball fans know, led to the strike, which started August 12, 1994.

By imposing the terms of the expired agreement, Judge Sotomayor did not resolve the strike, but allowed both sides to begin play under the rules of the old agreement and negotiate for a future binding contract.

By the time that everyone was back in camp, the strike had strained many relationships. Obviously the owners and the players (and their respective attorneys) had antagonized one another. The late start in the season (it would have eighteen fewer games) made sponsorships (both regional and national) difficult to sell. The critical time to sell sponsorships is approximately six months prior to the season, and six months prior to the beginning of the 1995 season, the future of baseball was very much in doubt. Teams did not really know what they were selling. Broadcasters had little idea how to market baseball in 1995. Radio station WABC sued the Yankees for $10 million, claiming that replacement baseball was a "sham," and that they would lose millions airing games that did not feature Major League players.[19]

But the most strained relationship, without a doubt, was between the game and the fans. For the fans, unfortunately, the players and the owners control the game. When the relationship breaks down, the fans suffer. And the fans were angry. Owners anticipated the backlash and drastically reduced ticket prices. The New York Mets sold 122,555 seats to their first three home games. Not bad, but 95,951 of those tickets sold for only $1, which was more than a $400,000 loss in revenue. All around the league, in Atlanta, Milwaukee, and San Francisco, attendance suffered.

Some teams had special promotions where children received free admission when accompanied by an adult. The Houston Astros even had two games where each seat in the Astrodome was absolutely free. If you were an Astro season ticket holder, your refund for that seat was in the mail. The teams definitely tried to make it up to the fans. Players lingered to sign autographs and mingle with the fans. The enthusiasm of baseball's providers (players and owners) was high, but they still did not have a formal agreement. Perhaps that was what the public needed to see.

Fabulous players like Cal Ripken, Jr., Mo Vaughn, Mark McGwire, Juan Gonzalez, and Mike Piazza will still attract millions of fans. But, a final analysis of the 1994 baseball strike will have to wait several years.

Many fans might not trust baseball until the game's controlling parties indicate that they are committed to a future characterized by trust. And, by the time the fallout from baseball's 1994 work stoppage is ultimately defined, the only thing that any observer would agree with is that the national pastime's most prominent participants might have been the lawyers.

Different Sport, Same Problems

The NHL had its own 1994 version of labor problems. A predominantly Canadian and Northeast American game, hockey won over the whole North American continent by the early 1990s. But with the successful expansion came the inevitable disagreements over compensation, salary caps, and revenue distribution. The labor rift evolved into an eventual cancellation of all 1994 games, and the settlement came down to the wire in early 1995. The two sides eventually agreed to play, but the resolution was not entirely amicable.

Overshadowed by the baseball strike, the NHL's work stoppage was damaging to hockey and the contemporary sports entertainment business. Amazingly enough, the labor disputes in baseball and hockey curtailed the number of professional sports contests by more than one thousand games between 1993 and 1994. In 1993, there were 4,889 games played in the four major leagues. In 1994, that number fell to 3,730, representing millions of dollars of lost revenue opportunity for athletes, owners, sponsors, and facility operators.

Furthermore, consumers accustomed to attending sports contests now had to find other entertainment alternatives, and no event manager wants to lose fans to their competitors. The goodwill between the franchises, players, and fans cannot be underestimated. Fans fall in love with the images, sights, and clothing of athletes and teams. In a cynical management point of view, the actual athletes are more or less as interchangeable as the uniforms and equipment. On the other hand, certain key personnel, i.e., Jordan, Ripken, Mattingly, and Ewing can transcend the game; and their teams do promote them.

The cynical view states that it is the uniform, the city, the facilities, the *constants* of a franchise with which owners hope fans gravitate toward in order to establish the loyal bond that eventually sells tickets, cable subscriptions, merchandise, and sponsorships. To jeopardize that profitable relationship with a labor dispute diminishes the threads that support the profit cycle between professional sports franchises and their fans. And the ripple effect can be gauged through sponsor involvement, or lack thereof.

The reality is that the players are the stars. Fans have always gravitated toward athletes such as Jesse Owens, Mickey Mantle, Steffi Graf, Cecil Fielder, and their peers. People do not pay money to see sports owners or league governors negotiate and promote the sports. Everyone wants to see the athletes. It is management's job to be efficient and faceless. Their job is to package and price the entertainment, and its supplementary elements, so that fans can purchase access. And it is in the pricing of sports entertainment that management becomes visible, because the price reflects the *cost* of producing sports entertainment, and that means *labor.*

But What Is a Player to Do?

This situation of imperfect competition, pervades all major sports and is the root of rival leagues, i.e., the WFL, the USFL, the ABA, the WHL, etc. The concept is always to lure the stars from the established league by offering more money and to try to build loyalty and a franchise around the short-term attraction of big stars and novelty. This concept worked fabulously with the American Football League in its battle for equality with the established NFL. When Joe Namath became the darling of professional sports, the NFL opened up to the American Football League (AFL). Likewise, Julius Erving was the Michael Jordan of the 1970s, but for the New York Nets, an American Basketball Association (ABA) franchise. The ABA had no national television exposure, so his acrobatics spread via word of mouth and his legend and true greatness eventually led to the assimilation of several ABA franchises into the NBA (Nets, Spurs, Pacers, and Nuggets). But political issues in sports distract fans' attention.

Placing attention on a conceptual, abstract, philosophical debate that athletes are not necessarily prepared to discuss. It is similar to asking athletes about their political leanings in a primary. By having the athletes focus on the business side of a sport, the competition/entertainment is bound to suffer. Players embroiled in labor disputes are seen out of their competitive arena. Probably not a place where they want to be. The athletes do not want to diminish their bond with the public as performers. A prolonged and aggravated round of difficult negotiations puts athletes in uncharted territory with their fans. Sports are simple to analyze: a winner and a loser, highly skilled performances, cheers and boos. When the politics of sports overshadows the competition, everyone is in danger of the emphasis shifting from the drama of competition to the jousting of attorneys—an unenviable fate for everyone.

Without the established structure of a competitive league, athletes compete in other venues. Wayne Gretzky, "The Great One," took a team of hockey All Stars and toured Europe in the winter of 1994. Fed up with the politics of waiting, Gretzky went on an old-fashioned barnstorming tour to get out on the ice, and pay homage to the international roots of ice hockey. Unfortunately, not too many athletes enjoy the popularity or widespread acceptance of Wayne Gretzky, and not too many superstars would take the initiative that he did. The world of sports needs more Wayne Gretzky's. His example is one of a true competitor. As an athlete, he needs to test his skill in competition. It is a shame that petty reasons prohibited him and his peers from competing on the accepted basis of the NHL in 1994.

But the real issue in sports work stoppages for competitors is lost wages. Baseball players such as Barry Bonds, Frank Thomas, Ken Griffey, Jr., Kirby Puckett, Bobby Bonilla, Roger Clemens, and others lost over $30,000 per day. How the players cope with the lost wages and strained emotional loyalties will determine the future of their union.

ALIENATION: SPOILING THE BUYER-SELLER RELATIONSHIP

Alienation is a new element to big league sports as players and owners antagonize one another to the detriment of the institutions that have benefited both parties. Labor-management problems demonstrate the lack of regard for the sport, the fans, and the sponsors who subsidize their teams, the leagues, and the events. In response, political action groups are formed, mediators deployed and talk show hosts enraged. Yet, the business of sports goes on. During the baseball strike, the Oakland Athletics (A's) gave away autographed baseballs from Tony La Russa, their manager. They also reduced prices 78 percent for "replacement" baseball. Their cross-town rival, the San Francisco Giants, anticipating their fans' burnout, offered a unique solution. Direct calls from top management and broadcast personnel were made to season ticket holders. The goal was to show the Giants humility about the strike and concern for fans. Calls were placed to the top 2,800 season ticket holders, and all verbal abuse from frustrated fans was tolerated.[20] *The Telephone Dream Team* included:

Peter Magowan:	Team Owner
Bob Quinn:	General Manager
Dusty Baker;	Team Manager
Hank Greenwald:	Announcer
Ted Robinson:	Announcer
Mike Krukow:	Announcer
Duane Kuiper:	Announcer

The goal of the celebrity telemarketers was to reassure fans of the Giants' commitment to fielding a competitive squad, and that their fans' voices were heard. The Giants' efforts echoed those of other owners. The Kansas City Royals gave away pieces of their field. The Detroit Tigers gave away theater tickets. The Milwaukee Brewers promised that prices would decrease if baseball in 1995 featured replacement players. The Toronto Blue Jays were not even trying to sell off season ticket plans. They had a different problem. Local laws in Ontario (the governing Canadian province), prohibit the use of replacement workers during any strike, which includes a baseball strike. To comply with the laws, the Blue Jays made contingency plans whereby they would temporarily relocate to Dunedin, Florida, and play at Dunedin Stadium (capacity 6,218) during their spring training home. Fittingly, the Blue Jays, if they had been forced to play exhibition baseball, would have played in an exhibition venue (ironically, their first stadium in Toronto was called, "Exhibition Stadium").

All of this shows that even as the owners remained united (apparently) on one front (the salary cap), they *still* had different ideas about how to market their teams. Traditional avenues of emphasizing stars like Cal Ripken, Jr., Don Mattingly, and Mark McGwire were forsaken for other methods. Owners used to rely on the product to sell itself. Now that the product (the game) has changed and is being questioned: the owners had to repackage and promote it to the once loyal and docile fan base.

Critical to issues regarding labor unrest in big league sports are the feelings of the sponsors. What are the sponsors supposed to do in the wake of the strike? Do they give up on the years of promotional investment in baseball? Do they ask for a reduction in sponsorship fees to continue their relationship with baseball in any of its forms, i.e., real versus replacement players? Or, do they risk crossing a picket line through their sponsorship and potentially alienate their employees and consumers. Would the unionized employees of Miller Brewing Company attend a game by replacement players who are essentially strike breakers? Would these same employees watch games and respond favorably to the advertising and promotional efforts?*

Lastly, would the thousands of companies who advertise through baseball's mediums be taking sides through their sponsorship? The reality is that companies will decide on the basis of baseball's value. If the image and reputation of the game is so tainted that its value is diminished or questioned, sponsors will stay away from the league and its players until they demonstrate that they can work together. Without cooperation between labor and management, how can Coca-Cola, Anheuser-Busch, General Motors, and the other sponsors have any confidence in their investment?

Franchise Winners

Franchises with tremendous traditions, such as baseball's Yankees, football's Cowboys and 49ers, and basketball's Celtics, are easy to analyze. For every team that has achieved success, there are others that have not. Analyzing the Los Angeles Clippers basketball team can be painful from a fan's perspective, but profitable from an accountant's.

To look at the Clippers' past twenty-five years, for example, they compiled a record of barely 700 wins and more than 1,200 losses. In addition to that, they have had sixteen coaches, four owners, and fourteen public relations directors.[21] They had only won one playoff series in that time, and their teams featured just seven All Stars. Yet their franchise was valued at more than $80 million. Why? Because the team

*In Boston, unions representing beer delivery and telephone repair line personnel came out after the president's intervention in early February and said that they would not cross a picket line at Fenway Park.

generates significant revenue streams: $16 million in media revenues and $11 million in ticket sales for the 1992–1993 season.

Obviously, the Clippers do some things correctly. They had followed the success of the NBA in their own market *off* the court, if not on it. The NBA had revenues of $140 million in 1983, and $1.1 billion in 1992.[22] In many ways, the Clippers rode the wave of popularity, and in spite of competitive difficulties, managed to achieve a degree of business success. In spite of the presence of the cross-town Lakers, the plucky, scrappy Clippers have overcome some obstacles to make money.

Franchise Movement

Franchises move to make money. The Brooklyn Dodgers and the New York Giants left their loyal New York City boroughs in the 1950s for the greener pastures of California. Al Davis's Raiders were already in California, but he moved them from Oakland to Los Angeles and back to Oakland for a facility that promised an upgrade in revenue vehicles, such as luxury boxes. The Chicago White Sox almost moved to Florida (Tampa-St. Petersburg), but got a new stadium in their hometown. The San Francisco Giants were the next team lured to Florida's sun coast. In fact, an ownership group from the Tampa-St. Petersburg area had a signed agreement of sale from Bob Lurie (Giants' owner) in 1992, but the sale was not approved by Major League Baseball.

In the meantime, a local San Francisco ownership group stepped forward to buy the Giants. The new deal with San Francisco included one key element: an improved deal on Candlestick Park, the Giants' ballpark. The situation of the White Sox, the Giants, and their Florida suitor indicates the critical issue of a facility lease. It used to be that teams went where the fans were located. Now that is only half of the issue.

Tracing One Team's Mobility

The Rochester Royals (NBA) began in 1948.
They moved westward and became the Cincinnati Royals in 1958.
The franchise changed their name to the "Kings" and moved to Kansas City and Omaha in 1972.

In 1975 the Omaha part of the franchise was dropped.
In 1985 the Kings continued westward to Sacramento, their current home.

Sponsor Odyssey

The franchise movement concept is applicable to sponsor associations. The most critical aspect of event management is to secure sufficient revenues to run the event. In today's terms, that means sponsorship. In the "old days" (pre-1980) of events, promoters emphasized ticket promotions. Money was primarily made at the ticket booth, not the television ratings report. Oftentimes, golf tournaments added appeal by identifying with a celebrity, as popularized by Bing Crosby and his famous Carmel "Clambake," or Andy Williams's San Diego Open. Both tournaments remain in existence (same sites, but different title sponsors). An event's name can show the changing complexion of major sports promotions, as shown in Table 3.

Table 3.
Tracing an Event's Title

Year(s)	Event Name
1945–1960	Tucson Open
1961	Home of the Sun Invitational
1962–1972	Tucson Open
1973–1975	Dean Martin Tucson Open
1976	NBC Tucson Open
1977–1983	Joe Garagiola Tucson Open
1984–1986	Seiko-Tucson Match Play Championships
1987	Seiko-Tucson Open
1988–1990	Northern Telecom Tucson Open
1991–present	Northern Telecom Open

No offense to Joe Garagiola (a former baseball player and well-known announcer), but he would seem to be an unlikely inspiration for a PGA Tour event. But his name was printed on all of the press releases, ticket stubs, and programs. Furthermore, all of the newspaper articles and media coverage cited the Garagiola name. Ultimately, the PGA learned that it could earn more money from companies like Seiko and

Northern Telecom by replacing Joe Garagiola's name with theirs—and it was right!

Generating Big Revenues

There are four main ways that sports rights holders and promoters earn money and craft sponsorship packages:

1. Gate receipts: the fans in the bleachers or the stands.
2. Broadcast sales: radio, television, cable, pay per view.
3. Licensing: merchandise product sales featuring sports property likenesses.
4. Facility revenues: luxury box, concessions, parking, venue advertising (signage).

GATE RECEIPTS

"The Gate" is the historical profit/loss determinant. The University of Michigan plays in a stadium holding over 106,000 people. If the average price of a ticket is $20, each sold-out game grosses the Wolverines $2,120,000. Notre Dame Stadium holds 59,075 fans and its average ticket price is $28.00, meaning gross sales of $1,654,100 for each home game. Revenues are easily predicted if attendance is a constant. For the Minnesota Twins baseball team the average 1994 gate was $257,447; for the Yankees, $430,000.[23]

Originally, sports marketing emphasized increasing ticket sales. As the broadcast industry matured, the attendance issue expanded to those who could *potentially* watch and/or listen. But the basic goal of every event promoter is to sell tickets. Even if the event is to be televised, they want the seats full, and the arena loud. An enthusiastic atmosphere is an essential ingredient in the sports entertainment experience. If athletes competed in silence, the emotion of their effort would certainly not be as evident as with a cheering audience. To promoters, cheering fans mean churning turnstiles, and money in the bank.

Most promotions like "Bat Day," or "Cap Day," were originally conceived to draw fans to the park. The NBA, the recognized league marketing guru, used to schedule doubleheaders (sometimes featuring teams like the Harlem Globetrotters) in order to draw fans as late as the 1960s. Maverick owners in all sports would stop at nothing to establish a fan base. Bill Veeck (of the St. Louis Browns and Chicago White Sox) developed sideshows like exploding scoreboards and other gimmicks to entice fans to the games. Veeck even signed midget Eddie Gaedel to play in one memorable game. Gaedel's single major league at-bat was a four-pitch walk, but baseball fans still talk about it to this day. Veeck knew that the publicity alone would be worth the criticism, and it remains his legacy to professional sports promotions.

Broadcast Sales

Perhaps the most important thing to any event is broadcast exposure. Sports promoters accommodate the media because they generate publicity. In buying the rights to radio and television coverage, broadcasters assume the obligation to sell the event to both sponsors and an audience. For promoters and team owners in the big league sports world, broadcasting means more than just publicity, it means money, as displayed in Table 4.

Table 4.
1993 Media Revenue[24]

League	1993 Media Revenue per Franchise (millions)
NFL	$41.3
Major League Baseball	$27.7
NBA	$14.9
NHL	$ 5.4

Media revenues are also the boon or bane for the small-market and large-market franchises. Large-market franchises, i.e., anything in New York City, obviously has a larger metropolitan coverage area than Milwaukee's teams. That means more revenue for the Yankees than for the Brewers, as shown in Table 5.

**Table 5.
Small versus Large Market Media Revenues:
Milwaukee versus New York**

Team	Revenues (millions)*
Basketball	
New York Knicks	$16.3
Milwaukee Bucks	$10.1
Baseball	
New York Yankees	$63.0
New York Mets	$46.1
Milwaukee Brewers	$21.5
Football	
New York Giants	$42.8
New York Jets	$41.0
Green Bay Packers	$40.5

*The NFL shares and divides all television broadcast revenue (except for preseason games), meaning the disparities are due largely to radio income.

Broadcasting means money, or the relative lack thereof, depending upon which franchise one discusses. Teams argue among themselves that the income disparity broadcast contracts (national, regional, cable, and radio) create will eventually lead some teams to an irreversible state of noncompetitiveness.

FACILITY REVENUES

Orioles Park at Camden Yards; the Ballpark in Arlington, Texas; ARCO Arena; the United Center; Coors Field; and the other facilities that are homes to modern sports entertainment are the latest sources for maximizing profit. Television revenues, luxury boxes, and hospitality issues like concessions can often spell the difference between profit and loss in the world of big league sports (see Table 6). Facility-generated revenues are the new frontier in franchise profit fulfillment.

Table 6.
Average Facility Revenues

Sport	Average Facility Revenues (millions)	Average Franchise Revenue
Major League Baseball	$9.0	$63.4
NBA	$5.2	$38.2
NFL	$4.6	$62.6
NHL	$4.2	$29.0

These totals (computed by adding figures published by *Financial World*) are misleading, for they only show the income that the average franchises earn, they do not show the income to the facility operators and owners. In the case of the Los Angeles Dodgers, who both own and operate Dodger Stadium, the revenues are $13.1 million. Football's Miami Dolphins own their stadium and its revenues are $15.4 million, by far the highest in the NFL. Likewise in the NBA, where the Los Angeles Lakers own the Great Western Forum, the facility grosses $24 million annually, almost $10 million more than the next highest team. That means that over the course of a regular season, forty-one home games, the Los Angeles Lakers earn almost $250,000 more per event than their closest competitor, the Detroit Pistons. By comparison, the cross-town Los Angeles Clippers only earned $1.9 million from their venue, the Los Angeles Sports Arena.

Facility managers, teams and/or municipalities, have great financial clout. Their venues can generate media traffic and business opportunities, two prime sponsorship items. A perfect example involves Mrs. Fields Cookies, a premium baker/retailer of cookies, brownies, and other similar sweets. Mrs. Fields opened a franchise at Giants Stadium in East Rutherford, New Jersey. Their first season in operation at the franchise site averaged approximately $15,000 per game in revenues![25]

Naturally, the Meadowlands could have opened its own baked goods outlet, but it is not the same as Mrs. Fields. Mrs. Fields has a reputation that has cost millions in promotional investment. Furthermore, its established reputation upgrades the efforts of the facility to meet the public's heightened expectations for both high quality entertainment and conveniences. To further accommodate all retail opportunities, and to facilitate impulse purchases, facilities are installing automated teller machines (ATMs) and accepting credit cards at their venues and concession areas.

SMALL BUDGETS IN BIG LEAGUE PROMOTIONS

Coca-Cola, Exxon, Anheuser-Busch, General Motors, IBM, and the financial heavyweights that can afford creativity and experimentation in the promotional field are indeed easy to profile. Advertising and integrated promotions create case studies that all marketing interests can analyze. But what about the smaller companies? What do the start-ups, and/or niche manufacturers who want to access the mass market do? How do they overcome the obvious financial barriers of entry?

Some companies take the "Venus Flytrap" approach: situate themselves so that if opportunity befalls them, they can snatch the benefit. Odyssey Sports, Inc., manufactures a putter, and company executives wanted to get it into the hands of the best golfers in the world. Rather than formally approach tour players with endorsement contracts in their hands, they handed out free putters to the players. Some tried it and liked it. Tom Wargo and Jim Albus, two top Senior PGA Tour players, had significant success with the Odyssey® putter. Albus even became the top money winner on the 1994 Senior Tour.

The Odyssey® was a success. Sales quadrupled to $3.5 million.[26] The firm then established a tournament bonus pool for the top ten finishers using the Odyssey®. The bonus division is a standard promotional practice in golf whereby players using the selected merchandise divide bonus money based upon tournament performance. This gives the company flexibility in terms of promotional expenditure. In this case, Odyssey® is not relying upon one player, it is spreading its risk and encouraging widespread use of their product. The downside is that Odyssey cannot forge and reinforce the identification with a personality, i.e., Lee Trevino and his comprehensive Top Flite® agreement.

WHEN BIG LEAGUE SPORTS CAN REALLY PAY OFF

The San Francisco Giants hosted the first baseball game focused on raising awareness and money in the fight against AIDS. The Giants donated a portion of game proceeds to the cause ($1 per ticket), and time before the game to invoke the significance of the disease and the need to fight it. Giants' owner Peter Magowan spoke to the crowd before the game. Manager Dusty Baker also shared his personal, stirring feelings. Team members Royce Clayton and Rod Beck joined actor

Danny Glover and singer Bobby McFerrin in reading names of AIDS victims in a well-conceived and moving presentation.

The game showed that professional franchises can promote a cause rather than a product. Players wore prominently displayed AIDS ribbons on their uniforms during the game and devoted extensive pregame publicity in the news media to maximize their efforts. In addition to their own staff, the team involved ticket vendors Ticketmaster and BASS to contribute to the cause. Event specific merchandise sales also added to the charity coffers. The final total for the game and related events topped $100,000.[27] So despite some instances of negativity, professional sports can galvanize the public to support worthy causes.*

A Benchmark Event and Legacy: The 1992 Dream Team

USA Basketball, the international arm of the NBA, took charge as the governing body of the United States' international competitive efforts. By administering the team selection and merchandising, the NBA retained control over the packaging and marketing of this historic venture. Many observers would say that selecting the coaches and players was the most difficult task associated with the competitive gathering, but it might have been maximizing the enormous potential of a team consisting of Larry Bird, Magic Johnson, Michael Jordan, Scottie Pippen, Chris Mullin, Karl Malone, John Stockton, Clyde Drexler, Charles Barkley, Patrick Ewing, David Robinson, and Christian Laettner, some of the greatest names in the history of basketball. USA Basketball wasted no time in assembling sponsors:

- AT&T
- Champion
- Chock Full O' Nuts Coffee
- Converse
- IBM
- ITT Sheraton
- Kraft USA
- McDonald's
- Philips Lighting
- Quaker Oats (Gatorade®)
- Schick
- Skybox
- VISA USA

*The Cover's backdrop features a photo from that event at Candlestick Park.

USA Basketball also made no oversight in offering sponsors maximum leverage, coverage, and identification with this historic team.

- Licensing, merchandising options, logo usage in packaging and advertising.
- Television rights to the "Tournament of the America's," the competition preceding the Olympics, including rotating court signs.
- Exclusive television inventory to four Olympic broadcasts, two each on NBC and TNT.
- Ad purchase options in *USA Today* featured section (1.6 million subscribers).

But it is not so simple when you merchandise world-renowned superstars. Each player had a shoe contract, only two (Bird and Johnson) with Converse, the official shoe of USA Basketball. Converse, thus, used only its spokesmen, and not the whole team in related advertising. McDonald's did a commemorative cup and trading card promotion. They also sold a logo hat at restaurants featuring the USA Basketball association. Reebok, as the medals sponsor, became embroiled in a controversy when it became apparent that Michael Jordan, Charles Barkley, David Robinson, John Stockton, Chris Mullin, and other Nike spokesmen would have to wear a Reebok outer garment. These loyal Nike pitchmen obviously did not want to wear the jacket, but compromised by folding over the portion that showed the Reebok name.

The dimensions of the original Dream Team were more fabled than France's "Maginot Line." The hype and excitement that preceded the team's every announcement and action was extraordinary. And the team delivered. Not only by winning the Gold Medal, but by living up to the unreal expectations of the public through the appeal of their play.

Dream Team II—The Marketing Continues

Estimates for the "Dream Team" have approached $100 million in sponsorship and licensed activity. Their widespread appeal, and marketing support unparalleled, the Dream Team concept is an enormous success. The response, however, is both a boon and a bane for USA Basketball. In a positive light, the franchise of the "Dream Team" registers high on the sponsorship scale. Furthermore, programs can be seamlessly run through the experienced NBA.

So what's the problem? Simply put, it is living up to the standards of the first team. Can any future team capture the imagination and attention of the world quite like the original Dream Team? That answer is both yes and no. The original Dream Team was a novelty. Fans knew that the outcome was predetermined. Viewers did not watch to see the Angola National Team compete. They wanted to see the superstars mesh. To see if they could play well together, subordinate their individual wills on behalf of the team. By seeing that occur, the marquee value of the players skyrocketed.

Thus, when Dream Team II assembled, they had huge expectations, both on and off the court. The team had great stars such as Alonzo Mourning, Shaquille O'Neal, and Kevin Johnson. McDonald's, Coca-Cola, and Kraft stepped up to sponsor the team, and they thumped the competition at the World Championships in Toronto. Of course, the novelty of a superstar team competing was lost, but Dream Team II proved that basketball has a definite international audience, and the at the NBA has the best talent—both on the court and in the marketing departments.

Dream Team III will form and compete in Atlanta for the 1996 Olympic Games. Head coach Lenny Wilkens has been chosen, but no players. There are rumors that Magic Johnson and other original Dream Team players want to compete at Atlanta. Stay tuned.

4

Turning Sporting Events into Sponsorships and Sponsorships into Promotions

> Sponsorships allow us to get close to our customers. Together, we strengthen relationships—which ultimately means product sales.
>
> —Art Morley, Nabisco, Inc.

Companies purchase various *sponsorship rights,* e.g., radio/television broadcast rights, stadium billboard placements, product logo on the event tickets, etc., to turn sporting events into important promotional campaigns for their products and services. Simply put, *sponsorship is the promotional mechanism by which sports entertainment penetrates consumer markets to create identifiable publicity and profits for corporate buyers/participants.* Therefore, the most important task facing an event's corporate sponsor is deciding how to best use the sponsorship. Six popular ways in which companies implement sponsorships:

1. Retail Promotions.
2. Media Traffic, brand imaging through electronic and print media.
3. Arena/On-Site Event Promotion.
4. Internal Sales/Marketing Tool.
5. Product Introduction.
6. Rights Acquisition to Generate Alternative Profits, i.e., licensing.

Retail Promotions

The NBA, and its chief broadcast partner, NBC, wanted to enhance revenue for the 1993 playoff broadcasts. They approached the Miller Brewing Company and created a promotional package to attract Miller's interest and financial commitment. Thirty million dollars later, NBC, Miller Brewing Company, and the NBA agreed to an advertising campaign involving the NBA postseason playoffs. The main elements of the promotion would be integrated into a combined broadcast and retail effort to highlight the Genuine Draft® brand's relationship with the NBA. The main elements of the package included:

- Point of sale sweepstakes at retail supermarket locations.
- Television commercial broadcasts.
- Twenty-eight-page color guide to the Finals, including NBC's coverage, placed in twelve packs of beer.
- The now former New York Knicks coach Pat Riley to be involved in relevant parts of promotion, e.g., his thoughts on the NBA Finals in the brochure and his likeness at display point of sale.

Miller estimated that they would move ten million copies of the color guide, or ten million twelve packs of beer through the promotion.[1] This promotion is akin to the Bud Bowl in many ways, especially in sales success. Different sports, same retail/broadcast formula and same championship theme equals product sales for the two beer giants.

Procordia Food Norway bought a sponsorship for the 1994 Lillehammer Winter Games, and put the Olympic logo on their sardine cans sold in local supermarkets. Its Norwegian domestic sales immediately tripled. Sardines weren't the only products moving briskly, because the Lillehammer Organizing Committee (LOC) sold similar licensing agreements to other companies that resulted in over $15 million dollars in profits to the LOC by the start of the games (February 1994).[2] The Lillehammer Organizing Committee's profits were based on a 10 percent sales royalty on the sale of officially licensed goods, i.e., ones which featured the Olympic five-ringed logo. The agreement, therefore, identifies $150 million in related licensed sales in the host country alone!

ABOUT THAT BIG MAC® AND FRENCH FRIES

McDonald's is the world's largest restaurant chain in terms of both size and service. Like many companies, it uses sports promotions to expand its broad consumer base. The following two examples show how McDonald's integrates sports properties with its restaurants and consumers.

1. McDonald's spends approximately $50 million annually as an NBA sponsor. A sponsorship of this magnitude translates into leverage in promotional creation and application. With the Dream Team II, a team comprised of hand-picked NBA stars for international competition in 1994, McDonald's put the likeness of each player on a super-sized french fries box and extra large drink cup. Film footage of the players and studio-produced commercials featuring the athletes was used. Customers were even offered the opportunity to purchase additional cups at fifty cents a piece on their place mats.

The order form was a way for customers to take more away from the restaurant than memories, and a chance to earn revenue off of officially licensed products. Of course, the only beverages poured into these cups were Coca-Cola products, which created a conflict for mega-superstar Shaquille O'Neal and his primary endorser, PepsiCo. The two sides, however, worked out the differences so that McDonald's could put his likeness on a cup, and pour Coca-Cola® in it. The important element is that McDonald's placed its sports identity directly on its products, the french fries, and drinks, both to sell products to customers, and to reinforce the promotional connection.

2. McDonald's made a $40 million four-year advertising purchase of the Fox Networks' NFL broadcasts.[3] The promotional hook for 1994 was the Super-ticket watch and win game. The hamburger giant awarded 200 trips for two to Super Bowl XXIX in Miami when consumers purchased super-sized extra-value meals. As in the case of the Dream Team II promotion, contest tickets were attached to the french fries package (talk about tying-in to the brand!), and thirty million total cards held possible winning numbers.

Fifty winners were announced for four weeks during Fox's pregame shows, and McDonald's supported this promotion with in-store signage and radio advertisements. Hershey, Sears, Prodigy, and Ocean Spray were all secondary sponsors to this Fox Network promotion. These advertisers received access to Fox's commercial inventory, as well as entry into McDonald's point-of-purchase materials at the thousands of participating restaurants.

Media Awareness and "Traffic"

Mentions, frequency, impressions, cost-per-viewer, and all of the related terminology applies to the important concept of media efficiency, i.e., the cost of reaching a viewing/listening audience of a particular demographic. Originally the principal element of traditional sponsorships, media efficiency needs such as reach, impressions, and total audience are still important factors in the profitable continuation of sports sponsorships.

All broadcasting and print efforts can be categorized as generating media traffic. A common method to generate the most effective media exposure is through event *entitlement.* It is a premium promotional tool that generates a significant amount of impressions. Sponsors have devised creative entitlement plans to enhance this concept, resulting in events, arenas, and programming featuring a corporate cognomen. The primary difference between the Poulan/Weedeater® Bowl, USAir Arena, and Shell's Wonderful World of Golf are the vehicles that carry the names. Broadcasters mention the event's title and location, so if they buy the name rights to an event, they will produce media traffic.

The most important use of commercial air space is *audience reach,* or the number of viewers watching/listening to an event's broadcast. Some events, such as the Olympics and the World Cup, capture a significant portion of the world's attention and thus provide consumer product companies with a tremendous opportunity. The 1994 World Cup was seen by a total of thirty-two *billion* viewers over the course of four weeks and 100 hours of soccer broadcasts. The 1992 Summer Olympics, by contrast, captured sixteen billion viewers in 200 hours of televised competition. Given the potential market, the 1994 World Cup offered a rare promotional opportunity to several multi-national companies:

- Known popularity of soccer in Europe, Latin America, and Asia.
- New market development in North America.

The important Latin American demographic was delivered by the Spanish language station Univision. Univision sold $24 million of advertising time during the four-week event, as advertisers responded to the opportunity to promote their products in Latin America. Univision clients include:[4]

$3 million advertisers: Anheuser Busch, AT&T, Coke, General Motors, Honda, and McDonald's.
$2 million advertisers: Reebok.
$1 million advertisers: Levi Strauss, MasterCard®, Pennzoil, and Snickers (M&M Mars®).

Univision sold $11 million of advertising time for the World Cup in 1990, but more than doubled sales for the same 1994 event. It delivered an audience that was 33 percent larger than anticipated and trounced its competitor, Telemundo, by capturing a 72 percent audience household share. The effectiveness of television advertising is not coincidental. Sponsoring companies know that consumer behavior is enhanced by advertising support, and a necessary pursuit.

Sara Lee, specifically its Champion® sportswear division, is a licensee of the 1996 Summer Olympic Games in Atlanta. To capitalize on its investment in the host city, the textile company invested $1 million dollars to create and erect three of Atlanta's largest billboards.[5] Sara Lee built the visual impressions vehicle outside Fulton County Stadium, home of baseballs' Braves and the future Olympic site. The billboards display the manufacturer's merchandise to the almost six million fans expected to attend Braves games in the two and a half years prior to the Olympics. (The baseball strike of 1994 obviously lowered that figure.) Sara Lee knew that aggregate merchandise sales for the 1996 Games already totaled more than $75 million before the billboards went up, and decided that the billboards would be a proactive effort to maximize its involvement on-site in Atlanta.

Media traffic such as radio and television commercial segments, is the root of all electronic advertising. Radio commercial spots in minor league baseball (a thirty-second spot can sell for as low as $50) and the Super Bowl (a thirty-second television spot sells for $1,000,000) offer participating sponsors an audience through a sports entertainment vehicle.

By the same token, stadium entitlement wedges corporate mentions into the every day news. As chapter 2 detailed, companies use event facilities as the advertising medium, and a dozen facilities bear corporate identities, for example, Arco Arena. Miller Lite® wanted to join the elite facility sponsorship group and offered $1 million to be the title sponsor to San Antonio's minor league baseball facility.[6] The city council, however, rejected the beer company's proposal because they did not want an affiliation with an alcoholic beverage. Of course, Coors Field and Busch Stadium are examples where other municipalities do not have the same concerns.

Clarity and *exclusivity* are important elements in media traffic. John Hancock became the entitled sponsor of the Sun Bowl, and paid the organizers an extra $150,000 to drop the three letter word Sun, because people were still referring to the football game as the Sun Bowl, and not the John Hancock Bowl, thus confusing the sponsor's message.[7] Similarly, when Great Western Bank purchased the rights to name the Great Western Forum, it dropped the old moniker, the "Fabulous Forum."

Stadium and On-Site Event Promotions

Companies have been giving away tote bags, caps, T-shirts, posters, mugs, key chains, and food items at sporting events for years. By spending money to be associated with the audience at a sporting event, companies buy the enthusiasm of the fans of that particular event, the access to the crowds, and all of the associated media efficiency benefits such as broadcast announcements, printed mentions in newspapers, printed mentions on schedules, etc.

Companies normally receive extra tickets to the games where an event is staged that allows the companies to capitalize upon entertainment privileges. The stadium event is the oldest form of sponsorship, but that does not mean that it has not developed with the times. Companies look to tie-in with the audience, retailers, and other key relationships. For example, Nabisco and its brands, e.g., Planters Peanuts®, SnackWells® cookies and crackers, Care*Free® gum, and LifeSavers® used their sponsorship with the Oakland A's to create a unique game promotion with Target stores, a major retailer. Capitalizing on the phenomenon of collectibles, Nabisco reproduced the players', coaches', and the team's likenesses on cardboard cutouts called Collector Kaps®. On the front side were four-color reproductions of the players, including autograph reproductions, and on the back were the logos of the products. By placing Target's logo on the front of the cardboard piece, Nabisco identified with the retailer and with the A's.

Four separate sets of six images were produced and scheduled to be given out over the course of the season, reinforcing the connection of Nabisco and Target with the A's. The A's promoted the event in their normal press releases, radio mentions, and print advertisements. Additionally, the team provided a reception, game tickets, and a scoreboard announcement on the scheduled promotion date. The "Kap" itself could be used as a coupon, or incentive, to draw consumers/fans back to the retailer and the associated brands, i.e., go back to Target and collect a free A's poster, other Collector Kap®, etc. Or, fans could keep the item as a souvenir.

Many promotions originate through the *cooperative advertising* funds that manufacturers and retailers (Nabisco and Target) accumulate. "Co-op money" is a percentage of the total cost of product purchases by the retailer, for example, 100,000 cases of *xyz* product at $15.00 equals $1,500,000. If the co-op rate is 1.5 percent, then co-op funds are $22,500. This Collector Kap® venture was a way to use those promotional dollars. The money is mutually distributed to joint advertising/promotional ventures conceived and developed by the involved manufacturer and distributor.

SOME CONCLUSIONS FOR THE PARTICIPANTS

- Target used Nabisco to associate with the A's, i.e., Nabisco paid for the Kap® event.
- Nabisco implemented their A's sponsorship with Target to sell more product.
- The A's provided necessary promotional inventory (photos and tickets) to execute the promotion.
- All three participants received feedback on a promotion that can be used or changed to meet future promotional needs. The A's can use this promotion with other sponsors, and Nabisco and Target can use this same program with other teams and event vehicles, such as basketball, hockey, or football.

The NFL plans to bring the virtual reality of the total football dream to fans who love the live action of the gridiron, but have become attached to their updated highlight shows. Fans will see in-stadium highlight shows with video footage supplied by both NBC and Fox. Video clips will be played between quarters and at halftime to the stadium crowds. Of course, the main issue to be determined is who has the sponsorship rights: the networks, league, or individual teams. That issue will be worked out as the league further expands its pervasive, endless tie-ins to entertainment-driven sponsorships.

Internal Marketing Tool

Sponsorships also encourage corporations to leverage them in three productive manners within their own companies.

1. Maintain old business clients.
2. Attract new business opportunities.
3. Develop in-house enthusiasm and camaraderie.

John Hancock Insurance Company purchased an Olympic sponsorship that covered the 1994 Games in Lillehammer, and the 1996 Games in Atlanta for approximately $24 million dollars. They conducted a sales promotion awarding top producers trips to the Winter Games. Hancock saw revenues related to the sales contest increase by $50 million.[8] Furthermore, two of every three company employees participated in some type of Olympic promotion, and 95 percent of the employees attended some form of corporate Olympic event. These rewarding results are attributed to the creative and successful use of a high-profile sponsorship.

But the Olympic spirit did not stop there. Hancock employees increased corporate merchandise purchases of sweatshirts, duffel bags, etc., by almost 450 percent after the Olympic rings adorned the products. The response to the incentives and client opportunities shows that Hancocks' employees took a degree of ownership in the corporate sponsorship and enthusiastically participated. Clearly, the Olympic sponsorship worked for Hancock, and demonstrates that sponsorship is about selling to your own employees as well as to your customers.

Smithkline Beecham ran a sales contest where top performers received an all-expenses paid vacation to the 1992 Olympics in

Barcelona. The pharmaceutical company had entered into an advertising agreement with NBC, which combined advertising time with event accommodations, tickets, and off-site entertainment. Sales representatives had to build retail displays and increase sales volume at retail locations. The top performing sales representatives received an all-expenses paid vacation to Barcelona and ticket privileges for any desired event. The results were positive:

- Motivated the sales force.
- Sold more product at retail.
- Top sales people saw the original "Dream Team," Matt Biondi, Carl Lewis, and other Olympic greats.

Amax, an aluminum producer, has sponsored Tony Bettenhausen in the Indianapolis 500, racing's greatest event, for several years. Amax uses Bettenhausen exclusively for internal purposes. He serves as a motivational speaker and as a merchandise commodity. Amax even has a product catalog featuring autographed items by Bettenhausen available to employees.

Product Introduction

Sports are an excellent vehicle for new product introductions. Most sports deliver a quantifiable demographic. For example, major clothing manufacturer Farah is fighting Levi's Dockers® and Hagar® in the men's casual clothing category. To introduce their Savane® product line, which includes khakis and shirts, as a superior wrinkle-free textile product, they assessed their target market: adult males with a medium to high income.

Farah bought a $4 million ESPN-NFL advertising package in 1994 to reach its audience.[9] It wanted to differentiate this promotion from a straight buy of advertising time and incorporated the "Football Legend Sweepstakes" into its promotional relationship for the 1994 season. The Football Legend sweepstakes was an interactive fan/consumer-advertiser/sponsor promotion that consisted of the following basic items:

- Savane® is the presenting game sponsor, i.e., "Brought to you by Savane®."

• Savane® received billboard exposure during the game. For example, the logo/name on game statistics and, score updates.

• Sweepstakes winners receive tickets to four regular-season games and the Super Bowl.

• During telecasts, ESPN's cameras zoomed in on contest winners, giving the promotion some value-added exposure.

• Commercial advertising time, for example, thirty-second fixed-position spots.

• Billboard mentions for the Football Legend Sweepstakes during other broadcasting times, such as during "SportsCenter."

Not only does promotion tie-in a new product, such as Savane®, with a popular sales vehicle, i.e., the NFL, it integrates the four fundamental tools that companies negotiate for in a contemporary sports promotion. These are:

Media Time: Billboards, broadcast mentions and commercials.
Merchandise: Game tickets—regular season and Super Bowl.
Licensing/Entitlement: Rights to identify with NFL on ESPN, "Brought to you by Savane®," etc.
Event Access/Exposure and "Added Value": By buying into the NFL's regular season, Savane® can tie-in with the Super Bowl, even though ESPN is not the broadcaster.

Over 70,000 people entered the contest, and the winner was featured in lengthy spots during ESPN programming. The added-value elements of Savane® and ESPN increase as the promotion gains recognition. Effectively, the franchise of a promotion is validated. Much like the "Bud Bowl," Savane®'s 1994 ESPN consumer contest is a developing *advertising* franchise for both the network and the sponsor.

Alternative Profit Source

NBC, as the 1992 Summer Olympics broadcast network, gambled that the Olympics were a potential pay-per-view revenue opportunity. In fact, when NBC bid $401 million to the broadcast network, it factored in revenue from this pay-per-view venture to help recoup its investment. The result was the fabled "Triplecast." It offered subscribers exclusive and complete coverage of the entire Olympics. No event programming would be spared! If NBC could get a camera crew to the event, it would be broadcast to the Triplecast customers. NBC's promotional partner, Cablevision Systems Corporation, joined the venture to expand the boundaries of cable programming and earn profits. Both parties knew that pay-per-view was extremely successful in single-event formats, primarily boxing super matches, and they hoped for a similar customer response in this international television extravaganza.

The sales premise was that sports fans would spend over $100 to get the latest and greatest of the world's best athletes. Heavily promoted, the Triplecast bombed. NBC lost between $60 and $70 million on the project, and Cablevision lost $50 million. The conflict between the network and cable broadcast interests were too great to overcome to package and sell the Triplecast. NBC had a primary obligation to show the best events to the general public. They could not withhold selected premier events for their cable venture. Additionally, not enough homes were properly wired to purchase the expensive service, and perhaps most importantly, the Summer is not the best time for Americans to sit at home for two consecutive weeks and justify a sports entertainment purchase. NBC was hoping for one million subscribers but, despite heavy promotional support, only 250,000 homes purchased the service.

Perhaps the largest alternative profit source in sports is in licensed merchandise sales (covered extensively in chapter 8). Hats, shirts, mugs, bean bag chairs, pennants, cards, balls, anything that can carry a logo is sold to the tune of billions of dollars. The NBA and NFL sell $3 billion in goods annually, the NHL sells approximately $1 billion. The San Jose Sharks logo is sold on $100 million worth of items alone.[10] The excitement of sports is transferred to clothes, pins, hats, golf bags, videos, and other items. The enthusiastic consumer response shows that sports products are big business and that sports identification helps that business.

Sponsors do not directly participate in the sale of all licensed merchandise, but find creative ways to participate in the licensing frenzy. Coca-Cola has a thirty-two page catalogue featuring items emblazoned with the images and logos of some of the soft drink licensors, such as the NBA, NFL, and the Olympics, and the soft drink's logo. These identifications help to promote and sell Coca-Cola's beverages and textile merchandise. Many companies, however, do not invest in logos merely to sell specifically manufactured merchandise items. They put team logos on items to be used in promotional giveaways like posters, schedules, hats, and pins. By placing an identifying logo on a product, the profits are not through directly licensed merchandise sales, as in the case of a manufactured logo Cowboys hat by Starter®. Rather, sales come indirectly through promotionally driven consumer products, as in the case when a brand (Kodak film) features an Olympic logo placed on the package. The popularity of licensing has shown that consumers buy merchandise specifically *for* the logo (Starter® Cowboys hat), and because of the logo (Kodak Olympic film).

Bausch & Lomb, manufacturer of Ray Ban® sunglasses, was the official eyewear sponsor of the 1994 Winter Olympics. Bausch & Lomb designed a special edition Lillehammer 1994 Ray Ban® to honor its association. They made the product available at retail ($85), and gave away a pair to each athlete, hoping to get some free television exposure. Ray Ban® borrows an old sports marketing standard of shrewdly distributing free product to high profile athletes in the hopes of creating consumer mayhem. In the mid-1970s, O. J. Simpson was given a strand of "puca" shells at the Pro Bowl in Hawaii. He put them around his neck, and made a rich man out of the lucky entrepreneur, as the necklace became extremely popular for a short period of time.

Creating Sponsorships— The Profitable Event Turnkey

Once purchased, sponsorship rights evolve through all forms of media and retail points-of-sale. As shown, they demonstrate an event's potential to influence new and existing consumer markets. Before sponsorships become promotions, they are packaged, priced, and sold by the promoters, or *sellers,* of the sports property.

The process by which event attributes are classified and defined for their marketability is known as *inventory.* Inventory is simply the defined commercial properties of a sporting event that are parceled and presented to corporate marketing representatives. Inventory categories include:

Broadcast Rights: Live or a rebroadcast.
On-Site Event Promotions: Giveaways, signage, and mentions.

Media Interests: Ad Time, print and electronic exposure. Also, magazines, cable television, network television, radio, newspapers, and outdoor billboards, including facility entitlement.
Licensing: Logo/likeness for retail and print identification for a specified time period.
Merchandise: Game tickets, event access, and hospitality, including luxury boxes and suites.

The ability to define, package, and price opportunities combining the above items is the promotional turnkey that drives the dynamic industry of sponsorship. Promoters vary sponsorship packages to include a variety of promotional elements, and sponsors usually enter agreements with the understanding that they are buying more than simple commercial mention. Sponsorship is the ultimate form of *relationship sales,* because both sides require cooperation, feedback, direction, and help from their promotional counterparts, i.e., the buyers and sellers, to accomplish their respective goals.

Winn-Dixie, the grocer, bought an NFL license and ran a promotion with its store brands in the Miami area whereby customers could buy discounted Dolphin tickets through their stores. Dubbed "the "Fun Zone," store-customers earned credits toward coveted Dolphins tickets through their purchases. Each week, Winn-Dixie had 1,400 seats that were available to customers through the innovative program.[11] Winn-Dixie bought the necessary merchandise and rights so that the inventory division allowed the grocer to conduct a consumer-oriented promotion over the course of an NFL season (four months).

Promotional sellers package their inventory to maximize revenue potential. The NFL sells the Super Bowl's broadcast privileges in excess of $40 million. During the game, the ball is in play for only fifteen minutes, yet there are over twenty-six minutes of programmed commercials. The return on investment is not defined merely by the sale of the twenty-six minutes of commercial time. The broadcast network receives much more than those simple twenty-six minutes of air inventory. The network gets the opportunity to do the following:

- Sell pregame advertising for the lead-in shows.
- Promote other programming, such as network shows.
- Sell postgame wrap up advertising for recap shows.
- License merchandise and conduct network specific promotions.

To inventory Super Bowl promotional assets, the list of income producing elements begins with the thirty-second commercial segments, but extends through many related issues that can ultimately tie-in sponsors with Super Bowl Sunday, the postseason, and the regular season as well. The NFL and its broadcast partners sell many types of promotions using the Super Bowl as a lure. For that reason, consumer product companies are already hyping Super Bowl promotions in the preseason, because the *franchise* of the Super Bowl event has great promotional influence with both fans and sponsors year-round.

The Atlanta Committee for the Olympic Games begins its inventory process by designating "official sponsorship categories":

Sponsor	Product Category
Anheuser-Busch	Beer
Xerox	Office Document Processing
Swatch®	Time Keeping
McDonald's	Fast Food
Coca-Cola	Soft Drink
UPS	Delivery Service
Panasonic	Electronics
Time, Inc.	Publishing
NationsBank Corp.	Banking
John Hancock	Life Insurance
Kodak	Film
Home Depot	Home Maintenance Retailer
Sara Lee	Apparel
Borg-Warner	Security (event)

By categorizing products and offering *exclusivity* in that category, the Olympic Committee is able to capture premium prices from their worldwide sponsors. After categories have been defined, the organizers divide promotional access, event tickets, broadcast interests, personal appearances, and print advertisement possibilities. In the case of the Olympics, companies pay from $10 to $40 million to become official sponsors of product categories and to use the Olympic logo on packaging in retail promotions. Not only do they advertise and entertain through the Olympic events, the Games' administrative efforts use sponsor products, from paper clips to copiers, during the Games and in the years between competitions. And all of those activities, such as product usage, produce revenue. Furthermore, they get to sell/integrate their products at event facilities. Concession stands will only sell Coca-Cola beverages and Kodak film during the games and at training centers. Furthermore, McDonald's will be the only fast food restaurant at the Athletes Village for the coming Summer Games in Atlanta. Restaurant personnel will wear Olympic style clothing, and the menu will feature more salad and fruit items to cater to the competitors' dietary requirements.

On-site usage is a critical advertising impressions catalyst and revenue source for participating sponsors. Sponsors obviously want the event business as well as the promotional inventory. Pacific Bell, for example, generated $1 million in business from their 1,366 Centrex® lines that it installed at Stanford Stadium for the 1994 World Cup events.[12] The telecommunications giant provided voice and data links to help broadcast the World Cup, including the July 4 contest featuring the U.S.A. and Brazil, from California to the world, and made money in the process, an effective sponsorship by-product. The millions of copies, phone calls, faxes, and deliveries are all important event elements that marketing managers want to pursue.

In many cases, sponsorship is the best way to earn the business. NationsBank Corp., a $40 million 1996 Olympic sponsor was one of the first sponsors for the Atlanta Games. Part of the sponsorship was a $300 million line of credit issued to the Atlanta Committee for the Olympic Games. A savvy move to fully integrate NationsBank with the Olympiad, its organizers, and the sports event business. Future events will need money loans and financing. By working with the Olympic organizations, NationsBank will be poised to judge and to evaluate future sponsorship opportunities as well as pursue new business ventures, a key banking objective.

In the case of any sports entertainment property, sponsorship also means privileged *event access.* In the Olympic example, corporate sponsors have priority to attend competitive events, establish corporate tent areas (to base entertainment activities), and access all other social gatherings focused on the spectacle of the Olympic Games. By spending the money to identify with the Games' fans, companies tie-in to the nationalism and international spectacle of the actual competition. It also gives the same companies an excellent opportunity to enhance their own international business relationships and discuss key issues like distribution, promotion, and any possible way to create a comparative advantage over their competitor. Kodak, Coca-Cola, and the select others will be discussing all of these strategies with key purchasing clients (representing billions of dollars of business) at the Sponsor Villages of the Olympic Games, something that Pepsi, BASF, and Fuji will not be doing. Sponsorship provides *leverage* in the key manufacturer-distributor relationship, one of the most important aspects of corporate sponsorship.

Who Controls the Promotional Inventory?

Promoters, and/or rights holders to sports properties, package, price, and sell a variety of sports marketing opportunities. Corporate marketing representatives are presented with promotional access and merchandise, such as inventory, and vehicles by the following sales agents:

- Teams, leagues and individual franchises.
- Broadcast media; radio and television rights-holders.
- Print media, newspapers and magazines that feature/sell sports.
- Player agents/representatives.

A common contemporary method is to offer a comprehensive menu of sponsorship entities on a regional scale. For example, the New York Knicks, Sacramento Kings, and Portland Trailblazers own the rights to all of their teams' promotional inventory: arena signage, floor promotions, radio and cable television broadcasts, and all of the advertising space in the game program. Obviously, the league office negotiates national broadcast and licensing agreements, but these teams offer one-stop promotional shopping in their regional markets.

Therefore, to sponsor one of these teams, a company needs only to dial that team's home office. There are no multiple pursuits of one sponsor by five separate interests representing the same promotional commodity. This brings efficiency to the sponsor-promoter relationship and allows the team controlling all of the promotional inventory to package and price their sponsorships accordingly. To buy an arena sign might be $10,000 for one season, but if an interested company wants to buy a $250,000 fixed-position advertising package on their cable broadcasts, that sign might be included. Of course, the sponsors paying the larger dollars get the right of first refusal on most promotional items, so if you only want a rotating courtside sign, your company will have to wait until the team has heard from other companies that are entertaining larger investment.

Conversely, the San Francisco Giants are sold by KNBR radio for regional radio advertisement opportunities—SportsChannel for cable broadcasts, and KTVU television for regional network broadcast sales. Stadium billboards and luxury boxes are sold by the Giants and the city operators of Candlestick Park. The benefit of this diversified approach is that each sales group can specialize their attention to fit the needs of sponsor clients.

The downside of this model is the cost of overhead. Several administrative agencies are handling separate inventories of the same property, thus creating higher administrative and management costs.

Events Create Sponsorship Opportunity

The following examples demonstrate ways that sporting events can be used to create and package commercial opportunities for sponsors.

The New York Downtown Athletic Club annually awards the Heisman Trophy, college football's Most Valuable Player award. ESPN paid the New York Downtown Athletic Club $1.2 million for the broadcast rights for the trophy presentation ceremony.[13] ESPN had an hour-long annual special and sold affiliation sponsorships. Wendy's was the primary sponsor and took the Heisman name, image, and history and created "Heisman Moment" commercial segments, which featured past winners and related lore. The advertisements were placed in their college football advertising spots during NBC's exclusive Notre Dame 1994 telecasts. Furthermore, *USA Today* had "Heisman Watch" updates in the sports section where the progress of America's best male and female high school athletes who vie for the "Wendy's High School Heisman Award" was chronicled. There were twelve 1994 finalists, with the winner being named and honored December 10 by the Downtown Athletic Club in New York.

In addition to using the association with broadcast advertising, Wendy's regionalized the promotion by creating the "High School Heisman," an award that honors high school students excelling in academics and athletics. In this case, ESPN took a prestigious event, gave it a numeric value and segmented it to the market. By dividing its promotional entities and rights, they encouraged sponsors such as Wendy's, to participate in promotional creation and distribution, i.e., broadcast commercial placement, retail presence, and regional emphasis.

Similarly, the burgeoning electronic billboard market in baseball broadcasts is a recent example of clubs creating a new promotional opportunity to increase revenues. By placing a rotating billboard behind home plate on the backstop, advertising sales agents maximize their opportunity to sell billboard exposure during telecasts. The Seattle Mariners, Milwaukee Brewers, and Detroit Tigers installed this feature in 1993 and earned approximately $1.5 million each.[14] Not everyone, however, is pleased with this development. The cable operators and other broadcast interests claim that this opportunity gives away cheap advertising, for example, $1,800 for a six-minute half inning segment versus $5,000 for a thirty-second commercial spot. This promotional inventory category, therefore, created a negative external feature between sales interests in the equality of revenue vehicles. CBS and ESPN banned their use in national broadcasts in 1993. Baseball's national broadcast partners for 1994, NBC and ABC, allowed the billboards, but they earned a percentage of the income, a seemingly equitable compromise.

Prime Ticket, a western United States cable broadcaster, recognizes that the Latino population living in their broadcast areas, eight million and growing, is an important target market for advertisers. Prime Ticket knows, for example, that Coca-Cola spent $20 million to participate in the global Spanish language broadcasts of the 1994 World Cup. Furthermore, advertising heavyweights like Reebok, Anheuser-Busch, and McDonald's are budgeting for similar advertising expenditures. Prime Ticket decided to meet the growing demand (from both consumers and advertisers) for Spanish language programming and created "The Prime Ticket La Codena Deportiva." It is the all Spanish sports network, and the best vehicle for consumer product companies to reach the Latin audience in the western United States.

Promotional suppliers have the ability to package sponsorships to meet market specific needs, and college football (controlled by the NCAA) is a popular vehicle that shrewdly divides itself to generate promotional business. The NCAA and Hardee's Restaurants, for example, came to a mutually beneficial agreement. The restaurant chain does business in twenty-five states, and they purchased the exclusive fast food marketing rights to the four appropriate college football conferences: the Southeast, the Atlantic Coast, the Big 10, and the Big 8 conferences. By paying an estimated $1 million for these rights, Hardee's only buys advertising in the areas where their restaurants are located. The NCAA packaged the needs of the client and sold the sponsorship.

Sponsors are also trying to solve college football's biggest marketing drawback: the inability to determine a *definitive* national champion through competition. Currently, sports writers vote for the most deserving team in a poll after the New Year's games. The current system is vague, and divides the viewers and fans. This division impinges on the revenue opportunities to game hosts, teams, the NCAA and college football broadcasters. Nike, Disney, Federal Express, IBM, and other blue-chip sponsors who support college football have made financial offers (ranging between $18 to $27 million) to settle the issue, but for now, fans and sponsors will have to accept a coalition of the following games to determine the season's best college football team. The coalition officially begins its efforts to determine a National Champion following the 1995 college football season. Its likely success will probably lead to an NCAA inspired (and controlled) championship game sometime around the year 2000. The Bowl Coalition games include the:

- IBM OS/2® Fiesta Bowl
- FedEx Orange Bowl
- USF&G Sugar Bowl

Their proposal would bring a definitive champion to college football, and end the cannibalization of profits and ratings that exists in the current Bowl format. In this case, sponsor input will change the tradition of college football, because its marketing potential has created a premium advertising opportunity for interested corporate sponsors. The ultimate price of college football's national championship will be determined by market forces, not any one governing body or Bowl committee. The Bowl Coalition is not a national championship playoff. It is the efforts of these three Bowls to form a cartel of sorts to best position one of the games to be the deciding game for the national championship. The coalition should be successful, as long as the top two teams in the country are not members of the Pac-10 or Big-10, for those conference champions are bound for the Rose Bowl.*

Virtually every element of a sporting event has a potential sponsorship angle, and each event explores new methods to capture advertising revenue. New York state recognized that horse racing presented enhanced commercial opportunity through corporate logo placement on the jockeys' clothing, and passed legislation allowing advertising space to be sold on race clothing. Much like a race car, jockeys can sell the rights to logo placement on pants, boots, and turtlenecks. The riders cannot alter their uniforms' color scheme (they are owned by the horse owner), and must receive permission for all displayed advertisements.

Anticipating potential sponsor conflict, the advertising rules dictate that a company sponsoring the race has precedence over a displayed logo on a jockey's outfit and may forbid its appearance in the event of a sponsorship conflict. This example demonstrates the creativity of event managers and participants to seek effective methods of sports promotion. Its effectiveness will be determined by the demand for logo placement on the jockeys and more accurately by the implementation of similar rules in other states.

Site fees for golf events are also profit sources. Golf brings notoriety to places like Firestone (NEC World Series of Golf), Silverado (Transamerica), and Doral (Ryder Open). Most importantly, they bring money, through lodging, concessions, restaurants, spectators, etc., and they bring advertising to the resort and make the transaction a symbiotic one. For new developments such as the Sherwood Country Club in Los Angeles (Franklin Funds Shark Shootout), this is a tremendous opportunity to achieve notoriety and credibility in the wealthy world of destination golf and living communities. For established resorts, like Pebble Beach, it is a method to reinforce the image that it is still one of golf's greatest names.

The Comprehensive Approach

Marketing managers, the sponsorship *buyers,* increasingly desire more input and ownership over their sponsorships. The control, influence,

*The 1994 Penn State team was undefeated and could not meet Nebraska because they had a Rose Bowl commitment to play with the Oregon Ducks, the Pac-10 champion.

and "hands-on" management allows sponsors to respond to consumer feedback of the evolving promotion. A good example of this is in the world of professional volleyball.

Originally ignored by everyone except beachcombers, volleyball at first found a niche, then a stampede of enthusiastic corporate support. Selling healthy lifestyles, fun, and sex appeal, volleyball has become a darling of major sponsors like Budweiser, the Miller Brewing Company, Coors, Old Spice, Evian, and José Cuervo. Other product sponsors include Bausch & Lomb for their Killer Loop® sun glasses.

Tournament entitlement privileges cost between $50,000 and $100,000 and they run year round. NBC was lured in on an experimental basis in 1990 for one broadcast, and the sponsor feedback was so positive that they went from three televised events in 1991, to ten in 1993. In this example, the franchise of volleyball was mutually developed by all three elements of the Event Triangle: the audience, the sponsors, and the players.

The Association of Volleyball Professionals (AVP) governs a two-man team format. For television, they play with a one-hour time limit, and for big purses. Miller Beer® spent $2.3 million on their 1993 men's AVP tour sponsorship, and were able to integrate volleyball elements into other promotional campaigns.[15] For example, a Miller Lite® Beach Volleyball tournament took place the week of the NFL's 1993 Pro Bowl in Hawaii at the Hilton Hawaiian Villages Resort, the same hotel where the NFL's finest were staying. Being a sponsor of both sports allowed Miller to highlight its on-site identification with athletes, fans, and key business clients.

Miller's success with the AVP inspired rival Budweiser to start its own tour. Budweiser's four-man teams play on similar sand, but appear on ESPN. Coors, meanwhile, is the title sponsor of the women's tour, the WPVA, to the tune of $1 million annually. The female volleyballers appear on the Prime Network cable outlets.

Coors recognizes the opportunity for event management and regional identity, and that is evidenced by its sponsorship of the Silver Bullets, the first modern professional women's baseball team. The team barnstorms around the United States playing local all-star teams in minor league cities, and against semi-pro teams before professional games. The team has averaged over 7,000 fans per game, showing that Coors' instincts were right in pursuing this promotion.[16] This promotion brings advertising into the barnstorming realm and offers baseball, beer, and fun in one tidy package.

Event "Franchise" Development

The college basketball bonanza referred to as "March Madness" is the tournament determining the nation's best basketball team, for both men and women. Largely through television promotion, The NCAA championship tournament has grown from thirty-two to sixty-four teams and commanded a seven-year $1 billion deal with CBS. CBS was so happy with the growth in popularity of the NCAA men's basketball championship, that they tore up the existing agreement in late 1994 and paid a whopping $1.7 billion for the broadcasting rights for seven years, the highest rights fee ever paid for a sports property.

CBS recognizes that the men's basketball franchise has significant worth and annually sells out their entire commercial inventory. General Motors paid $12 million to be a partial sponsor of the 1994 tournament. Thirty-second commercial segments of the Final Four semifinals and the championship game sell for $450,000 each.[17] The popularity of the event keeps growing with the dramatics of the college basketball players. Christian Laettner's last-second game winning shot against Kentucky in the 1992 semifinals is even credited with increasing viewership of the final three games by 920,000 homes. The fees do not got to Christian Laettner and his fellow competitors, however; it is the NCAA that cashes the rights fee check.

Given that the sophisticated, upscale audience has responded so well to the men's road to the Final Four, CBS banked on the notion that a similar franchise opportunity existed in women's college basketball. With a similar tournament format, and a dedicated, albeit smaller, fan base, CBS and the NCAA wanted to give female players an equal shot at exposure, and hopefully create a profitable sales vehicle. Going into the original billion-dollar agreement, the NCAA included tournament rights for both the male and female competitions, a true package deal.

Committing to both tournaments, CBS developed the franchise and commercial viability of women's basketball on television. The strategy worked, as CBS's ratings for all college sports viewership has steadily increased. Today, the franchise of women's basketball keeps maturing and its sponsorships are worth more to both the broadcast buyers and their advertising clients. When CBS wanted to extend its agreement with the NCAA, the women's tournament spun off to ESPN, as its product viability had been proved on CBS.

By the same token that sports events are conceived and nurtured, so are firms' sponsorship. *Exclusivity* is something that companies pursue to protect their promotional interests. Promoters charge premiums for exclusivity. For example, Miller Brewing Company paid for three-quarters exclusivity in their deal with the NBC-NBA broadcasts for an estimated $150 million through 1998. Home Depot, a $40 million Olympic sponsor, vetoed Sears' bid to sponsor only the figure skating and skiing events of the 1994 Games. Home Depot cited a potential conflict between Sears' message and the consumer, and successfully protected its interests. Sponsors, too, want to protect and develop the franchise of their advertising efforts.

Franchise development is an applicable concept to virtually any organized event, even at the high-school level. The National High School Coaches Association (NHSCA) recognizes that they are a powerful body of consumers. Their athletes need equipment (along with the coaching) to compete in their disciplines, and a national competition to determine the best in athletic excellence should be supported by companies that can directly benefit from their sponsorship. The NHSCA started formal championships for five sports in 1994, and they had $300,000 worth of sponsorship agreements. The event aims to have twenty featured sport categories, and over $1 million in sponsorships by 1996.[18] The championships are currently staged at many sites, but will ultimately be held in Atlanta. The NHSCA hopes that they will all be subsidized by sponsorship.

DEMOGRAPHICS THE NHSCA IS SELLING

- Nineteen thousand schools.
- Five events in 1994, 35,000 paid attendance.
- Twenty events, 125,000 in attendance by 1996.
- ESPN television time.

Sponsorship Packages Offer the Following

- Signage at events.
- Product exclusivity.
- Sampling and coupon opportunities on-site.
- Mailing list access.
- Right of first refusal on sponsorship renewals.
- Highlight show on ESPN: golf, tennis and wrestling in a three-and-a-half-hour special; basketball and baseball in two-hour-long programs.

The NHSCA's Angle

Access, access, and more access. These coaches buy equipment, such as shoes, balls, uniforms, and the like. A manufacturer can use this event as a trade-show opportunity and multipresentation vehicle. The NHSCA is also selling some ESPN exposure and on-site access, as well as the exclusivity premium, including right of first refusal that all sponsors use to develop marketing continuity. Additionally, these schools all have vending machines that can sell sponsor products from beverages to snacks, a lucrative market. Sponsorship in activities like this result in scoreboard placements in gymnasiums, fields, etc. More importantly, they give participating sponsors and sales representatives leverage in approaching the schools. If PepsiCo sponsors this event and asks a participating school's athletic director to put a Pepsi® machine in his/her gym, the soda manufacturer is likely to have a receptive audience. PepsiCo has had great success in placing scoreboards (featuring the Pepsi® logo/image) in school gymnasiums on similar premises. By starting a relationship on "mutual benefit" terms, PepsiCo leverages its business opportunity with its bottlers, distributors, and, most importantly, with its target—the teenage audience.

Perhaps most importantly, the teen consumer market is growing. From 1986's figure of $74 billion, teen spending grew to $95 billion by 1992, with forecasts to easily eclipse the $100 billion mark in the near future.[19] Furthermore, $60 billion is spent just by high schoolers. This is a significant demographic whose needs, interests and influences constantly change. Advertising to the high school sports category is a safe way to approach a rapidly changing, mercurial group.

Mass Market Appeal

Manufacturers essentially want to sell to the mass market a product virtually everyone uses (Coke®), as opposed to a niche market (protein supplement PowerUp®). Gatorade® was once a niche item that now has mass market appeal. Fibar®, concentrated high-energy food bars, are trying to achieve a similar growth. They ideally want to be sold at both specialty stores (bike and outdoor shops), and large retail outlets such as WalMart. Companies, to increase their potential markets, will use sports to gain the largest possible audience for their product.

Pharmative, a large pharmaceutical company, manufactures Regimin®, a vitamin supplement. Pharmative wants the product to achieve mass market distribution, and get out of the specialty store niche. The Regimin® brand sported the NFL logo in 1994 to help attain that goal. The simple licensing strategy aimed at luring customer acceptance. The brand spent approximately $4 million over the course of the 1994 season on a comprehensive print and radio advertising campaign.[20] Regimin®'s target: Active males between the ages of eighteen and forty-five.

Regimin® was promoted on CBS radio broadcasts of NFL action throughout the 1994 season and postseason, including the Super Bowl. Additionally, print ads featured slogans scripted on the side of a football saying:

> Your Body is a Temple. Don't Treat it like an Outhouse.
> and
> Sweat like a Pig. Don't Eat like One.

This isn't the only NFL licensed product that hit the shelves in 1994. Team colognes were available for those who wanted to smell like a football player.

AN EVENT'S ADDED-VALUE OPPORTUNITY

Added value in sponsorships is a frequently used term. Simply put, it is the concept that other issues and events, such as publicity, around the associated entertainment vehicle, i.e., a sporting event, will increase the actual impact of a commercial association, or sponsorship. For example, Gatorade®, Hanes, Nike, and Michael Jordan's other endorsers receive a significant bonus when he led the Bulls to their third consecutive championship. The added attention and exposure to the Bulls' star heightened the public's awareness and appreciation of his charisma and talents.

Firms know that this opportunity exists, and they seek to capitalize on the potential added value of an event. Adidas, the leading shoe in international soccer, sponsored the 1994 World Cup. Tony Meola, a star goalie for the U.S. team, was their domestic spokesman. Meola was featured in television advertising for the Predator®, Adidas' $150 top of the line shoe. Adidas is the international soccer shoe leader, and viewed the World Cup as an opportunity to increase their share in the $204 million U.S. soccer shoe market.[21] By using Meola in commercial spots, Adidas targeted American viewers with a known player. Adidas did not feature Meola in other countries, but with America as the host, Adidas recognized the opportunity to maximize its exposure in the United States. They wanted to combine the hype, attention, and spectacle of America's first World Cup, and pursued that objective through its added investment in Meola's endorsement.

The World Cup also gave JVC, the electronics manufacturer, an opportunity to use its sponsorship in regional areas. It developed the "Kick It Up" series, youth tournaments in and around the World Cup sites. These tournaments gave JVC the opportunity to create multiple events, display products to entire families of soccer enthusiasts, and use its World Cup sponsorship to promote its products at a grass-roots level.

Super Bowl XXVIII featured "Big TV," a Super Bowl program. Coca-Cola produced seven of the forty-one hours of the 1994 Super Bowl's related television. A major NFL sponsor ($50 million annually), Coca-Cola's proactive approach to the 1994 Super Bowl acts as both a football marketing tool, and as a test run for the 1996 Olympics, when Coca-Cola wants to be hitting on all cylinders in their $47 million worldwide sponsorship.[22] As the host city's top sponsor, Coca-Cola wants to take a fresh, unique approach to the event.

Not only will Coca-Cola have television production capabilities, it will also create an interactive area that will feature games, merchandise and hospitality in downtown Atlanta. By exposing themselves to the television medium two years prior to the Atlanta Games, Coca-Cola can entertain thoughts of realistically selling promotional inventory to other Olympic sponsors as well. This diversification approach will help it find the best way(s) to identify the Olympic Games with its two most important audiences, consumers and industry buyers.

Summary: Three Thoughts on Sponsorship and Promotions

1. Sponsorships continue to evolve as those who sell sports promotions recognize and accommodate the marketing needs of the sponsors, the buyers of sports entertainment advertising opportunities.

2. Sponsorships provide the tools for a marketing plan. Actual promotions, in any form of media or retail application are the implementation of some, or part, of the sponsorship by the participating corporate customer or sponsor.

3. Relationship sales is, perhaps, an overused phrase. In sports, however, the ability to communicate and listen to the needs of the promotional investors will influence their enthusiasm to consider and pursue sponsorships. Never assume that you know your counterparts business better than he/she does.

Case Study: PowerBar: Persistence Pays Off

As Gatorade defines the sports beverage marketplace, PowerBar® developed a brand new category for the sports enthusiast—the energy bar. Created by a former marathon runner, Brian Maxwell, PowerBar® is a sports marketing success story. Starting literally from Maxwell's kitchen, PowerBar® is now sold in twenty-seven countries worldwide.

PowerBar®'s original marketing strategy emphasized sampling at sporting events. Today, that has grown into an association with approximately 4,000 different events, from NCAA basketball to regional charity road races. PowerBar®'s growth, though, is not fueled by major sponsorships with the NBA and the International Olympic Committee. PowerBar® expands its markets by following creative event promotions to reach the athletes, competitors, and spectators of its target audiences.

PowerBar® is also unique because it manages its own events, i.e., The PowerBar International Women's Challenge (cycling). Progressive ideas and products have always defined PowerBar®, and as its success attracts attention and competition, the company needs to maintain its promotional edge in both new and existing markets. Company employees Mike Waite, (Promoting Coordinator for Title Events), and Scott Sowry, Corporate Communications Director, contribute their thoughts on PowerBar® in the competitive sports marketing industry.

PowerBar Today

Mike: For years, people have been using PowerBar®s as a piece of sports equipment. Cyclists take them on long rides, runners eat them religiously before workouts. It is both a good and bad thing that many consumers are in the habit of using them exclusively in such capacities. Our idea is to let our existing consumers, and new ones, know that PowerBar®s apply to other situations as well. In fact, that our product is a tasty snack for any activity in addition to high exertion sporting endeavors.

The cornerstone of our past, present, and future is to be at events and put the Bars in peoples' hands, communicating what the product is and what its strengths are. We need to educate our new markets while maintaining a presence in our more mature ones. This is an awkward phase in terms of communicating this message with a wide audience and retaining our identity with the hardcore athlete.

PowerBar looks for several things in its events, not just media-generated impressions, or retail identification rights. As a very young company, we are looking to bolster the brand name and grow our market share. This is an exciting time, because our goals have to take a broader, more definitive scope, than simply to get people to try our product. In some of our more developed markets, (it's actually premature to call any of our markets developed because we only have 40 to 45 percent brand awareness), we need to reinforce our position and exploit the available room to grow.

Growing Pains from a Promotional Perspective

Scott: We are trying to be more selective with our sampling strategy. Some of our best customers probably go to events knowing that we will be there giving out PowerBar®s, so why buy one? It is important to still sample, and educate the consumer with a PowerBar®'s taste, texture, and effects. But we're at the point where it is not necessary to give away thousands of products indiscriminately.

With a new product, and virtually no budget, PowerBars originally (in the late 1980s) needed to assume the responsibility to reach out to the marketplace. Today, the objective is to grow from this highly personal "one on one" marketing relationship to a more mass-market strategy without losing the grass-roots appeal that has been successful.

Mike: It is difficult, within our demographic profile, to get smarter with our sampling and also implement programs that allow to build brand equity on a large scale. We need the grass-roots appeal, and also need to reach the mass market, and for that we are going to develop a large umbrella campaign.

PowerBar®s used to be promoted through our company's individual marketing coordinators in independent user segments, or sports groups, i.e. running, cycling, etc. The respective coordinators made all of the promotional decisions about sponsorship participation, sampling, advertising placement, and related activities. This made our overall advertising appear a bit "schizophrenic" in the sense that our rock-climbing trade advertising was one message, and our cycling message represented another image.

With so many groups contributing to PowerBar's image, there was no focused effort on a consistent message. Therefore, the company grew through individualized market attention by our staff. It worked well to get us to this point, but now we need to shift gears a little to identify the appeal of our brand in the various market segments, such as running, tennis, hiking, or endurance training. What links all of those participants will define our public image.

CONTEMPORARY EVENTS STRATEGY

Scott: PowerBar will always remain the proactive, market savvy company that founder Brian Maxwell began years ago. Brian and his wife, Jennifer, would gather up 'Bars and go to events every weekend, knowing that the best advertisement for a PowerBar®, is a PowerBar®. That's always been our philosophy, and the way to bring athletic energy food, *for* athletes, *by* athletes is to go to events, meet the consumer, and get them to try our product.

Some of our current events show how we plan to position ourselves. The "Six Flavors Six K" race in New York's Central Park fits our philosophy. Organized by the New York Road Runners Club, the event ultimately had a lot of satellite involvement by all of our departments. Modell's Sporting Goods was our retail partner, and posters were put in Modell's windows throughout New York City where people could register and learn more about the event. ESPN's show, "Running and Racing," even did a twelve-minute segment (featuring Marty Liquori) on it.

The race attracted 3,000 runners and we featured a favorite flavor T-shirt theme. (Flavors are wild berry, apple-cinnamon, chocolate, malt nut, mocha, and banana.) Lynn Jennings (1992 Olympic Bronze medalist in the 10,000 meters), a product endorser, ran in the race, and she won as the "Top Banana." We had another runner, Mike Slinskey, and he blew away the field in the men's category as well. It was the first year of the race and we were able to bring together all of our strategic groups (sales channels, marketing, corporate communications) for a successful event. The New York market is an extremely important one, and this race was a good way to approach it and involve key business partners in the area.

On a more national level, "The PowerBar Shootout" was an NCAA basketball event featuring the University of Connecticut and University of Kansas' men's and women's teams. Aired nationally on CBS, we got 4.5 hours of PowerBar basketball, in both men's and women's sports. It turned out that the men's game was the highest rated NCAA game of the regular season (both teams were ranked highly at the time) and sales spiked considerably in that region. Prior to the games, PowerBar did not enjoy full distribution and retail access in the Kansas City region, but we picked up some huge accounts in the following weeks. This shows the influence of high-profile sporting events and the execution of sponsor objectives.

Many people ask why we don't sponsor teams officially, and have high-profile athletes endorse our products, but our idea is not to write checks to people and teams. We like to give them product, as much as they like to get them, but we just can't afford to give them the money that some other companies do. We give trainers and athletes all of the bars they need—in their locker rooms—to service the professional sector without paying the tariff of sponsorship that can come with it. It always turns out that the teams and athletes want PowerBar®s for themselves, so we can gain a presence without paying the promoter a huge sponsorship fee. For example, the Iron Man Triathlon in Hawaii is an event where the competitors will eat PowerBar®s regardless of any official sponsorship designation. In many ways, we are guerrilla marketers.

Big properties that cost a lot of money do not work for our company. We want to build up the brand without paying excessive premiums simply to access publicity and athletes. We try to go directly to the athletes and consumer marketplace.

The PowerBar Challenge

Mike: The PowerBar International Women's Challenge is one of the top three cycling events in the world. It has been in place since 1983 and is an eleven-day, twelve-stage race. Ore-Ida, the potato processor, had been the sponsor. They left after 1992, and we came in at the eleventh hour in 1994. Ore-Ida had done the race primarily as a goodwill event in its home state of Idaho. The race had no media coverage, no other sponsors, and none of the "bells and whistles" that come with major sporting events. So we saw "The Challenge" as a diamond in the rough. And our long-term strategy is to develop it to its fullest potential—which we think is substantial.

Not only is the PowerBar Women's Challenge a huge opportunity, it is a big responsibility for us. From the outset, we are using this event to enhance our image, talk to a larger consumer market (the race will be televised on ESPN), and reinforce the equity in our brand name, which is a departure from our emphasis to promote our products' performance characteristics. People wonder why women's sports. We don't consider the product to be gender specific. This is not a campaign for just women, PowerBar®s are for all athletes. Hopefully, "The Challenge" will reinforce that.

"The Challenge" is also a step towards a more comprehensive approach in our overall market development. PowerBar needs to move away from strictly niche events and into ones that will retain our identity within the athletic communities that use the 'Bars and the ones that will be customers once they are exposed to the product and its attributes.

Our thinking is that the race will become a top-line event through the investment of effort and partnerships. We want to bring in other sponsors and media partners to make the race recognized as a major sporting event. Not many people watch triathlons, but everyone knows about the Iron Man, it has the identity of being the best event in its category. This event can be appreciated on equivalent terms. A big step is to bring the event to ESPN, a major coup for the race. It will be aired twice on ESPN, in an "A-block" time ("A-block" is the best programming time possible). It will also be replayed on ESPN 2, and we could not be more pleased. So slowly, and with a lot of work, the legitimacy and structure of the race gains definition.

Also, PowerBar has a manufacturing facility in Boise, so an identity is important within that community. As far as the actual race goes, our involvement has increased the prize money ($75,000), the race stages, and the competitors in the field. We will have teams from Canada, Australia, Russia, Czechoslovakia, Germany, Switzerland, the United States, and other countries. The event requires a staff of six people working full-time and 150 volunteers during the year to pull it off. Our Race Director, Jim Rabdou, is in Idaho, and he coordinates everything on site. We have also lobbied to get UCI (cycling's governing body) sanctioning, and they finally granted it.

One problem with our growth that we've had is alienation of some bike store retailers. They are upset through our associations with discount retailers, supermarkets, and warehouse shopping outlets. Bike shops were some of PowerBar®s' original outlets and greatest advocates. With "The Challenge," we are going to run programs exclusively through bike shops relevant to the race.

We are going to execute a race-related sweepstakes in participating bike stores where we will provide promotional materials and discounts on our product. PowerBar needs to sell discounted product to large organizations and warehouse stores, and enable bike shops to make money off of our products and drive store traffic. "The Challenge" addresses both groups and hopefully meets their needs.

Another retail race sponsorship is with Albertson's, a major grocery chain. We will do aisle displays, media programs, and consumer-oriented sweepstakes. We want to find partners and sponsors who want to participate in a premier sporting event. We offer on-site access, commercial time, retail opportunities, and all of the necessary components to make this event attractive for any sponsor. We approach companies in a way that highlights the strategic benefits for the prospective sponsors. If a company can get excited about "The Challenge," we want to talk about its objectives and craft a program that will meet and exceed the expectations.

As a promoter-sponsor, we have a clear vision of what we want from the event. In taking the race on, we have control, which helps the margin of error. "The Challenge" gives us a yardstick to gauge our involvement with events and partners. After all is said and done, have we influenced consumer behavior? Have we increased awareness about our product? Has the attitude changed towards PowerBar®? Can we effectively show off our product and our business style? These are questions that will determine the effect of the event.

But there are some drawbacks to the event. For one thing, it is held in a remote area. We run into people that feel Idaho is beautiful, rugged, and dramatic—but not an important consumer product market—a critical sponsorship sales criteria. Furthermore, road cycling is not the most popular form of cycling. Nine out of ten bikes sold are mountain bikes. Mountain biking is everything in today's market. That may change, but not in the foreseeable future. One thing that we did for the race is establish an Advisory Board of ten influential people in the cycling community. The board will see to it that we are in tune with pertinent developments in cycling.

Some changes may take place to make "The Challenge" an even better event. One thing that we are considering is to make the race a regional one. We might draw a one-thousand-mile radius around Boise and take the stages to Salt Lake City, Seattle, San Francisco, and Denver. The concept of involving other areas might be the hook that brings the Challenge to the next level. Lastly, as a women's event, "The Challenge" will not draw the viewing audience that a men's event will. But overall, "The Challenge" will definitely be a success for the competitors, fans, and PowerBar.

FINAL ANALYSIS

Mike: We will always evaluate the quality of our events, the amount of people that will turn out, and its fit to our user profile. But with the bigger properties that we consider, we will conduct a quantitative analysis to see if it is the wisest investment. We want to avoid clutter and confusion in our sponsorships, and make sure that it is the best investment for our resources. We will never overlook, though, that placing PowerBar®s into peoples' hands best communicates our message. A one-on-one meeting educates individuals that a PowerBar® fits into their athletic lifestyle.

Scott: With all consumers, we want to emphasize health. Our product is nutritious, low in fat, and convenient to eat at any time. On the East coast and in our twenty-seven international countries, we need to upgrade our position as a contributor to this lifestyle. Given the passion of the people behind the product, and the enthusiasm of our customers, we will achieve that goal.

5

Event Marketing to Scale

> Not only did it [World Cup] drive our business, but we believe we brought in a lot of new consumers and we had a helluva lot of fun doing it.[1]
>
> —Bill Olson, Guinness Import Co.

Companies pay for the rights to identify with the enthusiasm, fun, and spectacle of sporting events. The term *event marketing* merely ties together various elements of the entertainment: broadcast media sales, on-site event promotions, and retail merchandising rights. To further narrow the working definition of event marketing, it usually applies to tightly defined activities, or single entities, that have an obvious premium, such as the Super Bowl, the World Cup, the Final Four, the Olympics, the Skins Game, or the Boston Marathon. In all event marketing strategies, it is the perception of a premium that lures sponsors and fans alike.

Effective preparation, publicity, and positioning of an event can reap financial rewards to both opportunistic promoters and sponsors. Through an event's unique attributes, sponsors hope to bring an added-value dimension to its promotions. Sponsors look to create, often times, recreate, the excitement of sports for the consumers and, of course, added sales opportunities for their company.

According to Guinness' Bill Olson, the brewer tied-in the heritage of the product with the international tradition of soccer. For Guinness, the high descent of Irish-Americans, and the presence of an Irish team in the competition made the World Cup a fortunate opportunity for Guinness' North American marketing efforts. And after Ireland defeated Italy at Giants Stadium (East Rutherford, New Jersey) in a highly contested game, the added-value dimensions of the sponsorship materialized for the brewer, the distributors, and the consumers of Guinness® Beer. Ireland won an important game, and many celebrated in the appropriate Irish tradition—with a foamy Guinness®.

KFC (Kentucky Fried Chicken) recognized a similar opportunity with the June 1993 George Foreman-Tommy Morrison boxing match. KFC worked with Foreman, a notorious fan of food, in his discipline, boxing, and placed him in its retail franchises with a "Punch 'n Munch" campaign theme. Both KFC and the fighters get promoted in the critical advance period before any fight. KFC placed its logo on the ring mat, on two of the four ring posts and on banner space throughout the auditorium (Thomas & Mack Center). KFC's logo also was on the program cover and featured on television billboards for fight statistics. More importantly, KFC was a part of the prefight hype, which brought the enviable added-value recognition to its franchises. Normally, boxing is a risky investment for many reasons: the violence, industry stigma (the competition is not always honest), and unpredictability (fights can last only two minutes). By developing retail programs and identifiable promotional opportunities, the promoters created value based on the anticipated potential of the entertainment. In the old days of fights, whether it be Ali-Frazier, or Leonard-Hagler, corporate advertisement and promotion only coincided with the bout. On the other hand, KFC maximized the promotional capacity of the Morrison-Foreman bout.

In this, and all event cases, the actual event is the center for promotional activity, not the only means by which the company can promote its products. The Olympics, for example, is a two-week series of events that takes years of preparation from hosts, athletes, and sponsors. Matt Biondi appeared in three Olympics that spanned eight years. His training regimen never relented and he maintained his status as the world's best swimmer. Sponsors like Coca-Cola, Kodak, and VISA take similar diligent approaches to their Olympic marketing programs. Like Matt Biondi, companies that use major events know that an opportunity like the Olympics cannot be maximized with a careless or lackluster approach in regards to work effort.

Using an event to the sponsor's financial benefit is much more than the theme of this book. It is the mandate of event marketing activities and, in sports, it obligates the promoters to attract fans. Sponsors rely heavily on the promoters to execute their marketing task, which is to get fans to show up and tune in, so that the sponsors can do their task of marketing the products and services at banks, supermarkets, gas stations, and other appropriate retail outlets where they do business. (See Table 1 for trends in event spending.) Landmark events like the Olympics and the World Cup and professional leagues like the NBA and NFL dominate the event marketing landscape, but smaller sports activities also serve the same purpose of successfully bringing consumers and products together. Sponsors target events as consumer impact opportunities, through television, product sampling, client entertainment, and on-site access.

Table 1.
Event Spending Trends[2]

Year	Amount Spent*
1992	$3.20 billion
1993	$3.70 billion
1994	$4.25 billion
1995	$4.70 billion

*These figures do not include additional spending to promote the sponsorship investments, such as media buys.

Historical Reference

Athletic competition dates back to the ancient Greeks, but the Greeks were not selling licensed merchandise, broadcast rights, or even concessions at the original Olympics. The financial development of sports waited until the twentieth century, where the event's financial potential evolved through the efficient use of media to promote and profit from sports entertainment.

In retrospect, the 1938 heavyweight prize fight between Germany's Max Schmeling and America's Joe Louis was a harbinger for the future spectacle of sporting events. Broadcast to more countries and continents than any event in the history of the world, this bout captured a record radio audience in the U.S. and abroad. The fight was the second between the two combatants, and the eighth million-dollar bout in boxing's history.[3] The hype and money generated by the event was not due solely to exciting athletic competition. It was a metaphor for divergent social philosophies well beyond the control of the two pugilists.

Louis versus Schmeling was much more than two top heavyweight champions squaring off. Louis quietly led the charge to racial equality in his own society against a fighter from Adolf Hitler's despotic German Third Reich. The free world, leery of Hitler's dogma and smarting from his snub of Jesse Owens at the 1936 Summer Olympics, looked to the humble Louis to enervate Hitler's international propaganda.

Louis had lost his first bout (June 19, 1936) with Schmeling, a shocking knockout in the twelfth round, but he was determined to exact his revenge in the ring. Prefight publicity from Louis's camp reinforced his resolve to maintain his concentration in order to quickly dispatch his opponent. The German press, directed by the mendacious Dr. Joseph Goebbels, was touting athletic and genetic superiority of the German people. As the fight drew near, its international drama transcended the boundaries of simple athletic competition. The anticipation and hype built to a feverish level and radio broadcasts around the world reported Louis's first-round knockout victory. This bout had no title sponsor, no pay-per-view cable purchase option, no outlandish promoter, no multimillion-dollar purse, no Michael Buffer shouting; "let's get ready to rumble!!!," but it did have a large audience of emotional and enthusiastic fans.

As mentioned, the fight was a million-dollar event and, in the Depression era of the late 1930s, a million dollars was a nearly incomprehensible sum of money. The *New York Times*' Fred Van Ness described the financial implications of the fight fans' interest as follows:

> While there is no way of definitely determining it, this is probably the largest number of fans ever to come to the city for a fight. . . . The visitors were expected to spend about $3,000,000 in the hotels, night clubs and other places and add a tidy sum to Mayor La Guardia's sales tax. Promoter Jacobs said yesterday that nearly 50% of the reserved seats were sold on applications from out of town. These came from as far west as St. Louis and included all important cities, such as Chicago, Detroit, Cleveland and Cincinnati.

The peripatetic fight fans who flocked to New York saw a two-minute fight where the stoic champion, Joe Louis, vanquished the only loss on his record. More importantly, he stymied the irresponsible propaganda generated by the Nazi regime (it should be noted that Schmeling had distanced himself from Nazi influences and associations). This bout could arguably be the most important sports contest in the world's history. Never before, or after, have two competitors independently represented their countries (in a purely financial endeavor) where the drama of contradictory political authority was played out in the flashpoint of a boxing ring. And while this fight did have significant political and historical meaning, it also, as usual, had financial significance.

Here is a financial breakdown of the Joe Louis-Max Schmeling fight:

Gross receipts	$ 940,096.17
Radio and picture rights	75,000
Total revenue	1,015,096.17
Federal tax	89,889.51
State tax	47,093.66
Joe Louis' share (40%)	349,288.40
Max Schmeling's share (20%)	174,644.20
Paid attendance	66,227
Gross attendance	70,025
Minimum contribution to charity	$ 7,500

Fifty-three years later, boxing may not have evolved politically or socially, but it did financially. Its pay-per-view fights generated over $120 million worth of revenue during the year. Two fights featuring Mike Tyson and Razor Ruddock combined for $75 million of that revenue. Site fees, paid attendance at the turnstiles, merchandise sales, and other revenue sources (primarily pay-per-view television) totalled into the millions. The evolution of an event's financial opportunity increased the profitability for the fighters, promoters, and commercial interests, such as the broadcasters and site-holders (Caesar's Palace, etc.). The popularity of boxing has not changed, but the financial means to profit from it have matured and given promoters a revenue producing measuring stick.

As Event Revenues Increase, So Do Event Costs

The 1994 Winter Olympics cost Norwegian organizers $1 billion.[5] The Norwegians built facilities, roads, and structures to accommodate the fans, athletes, and sponsors. Event promoters, like the International Olympic Committee and Fifa (soccer's governing body), wield tremendous influence, because their events generate significant revenues, publicity, tourism, and infrastructure. Furthermore, they are a tremendous excuse to galvanize voters to approve taxation-funded capital improvements to municipalities, such as roads, structures (stadia), and transportation systems (Munich's U-bahn subway system was installed for the 1972 Summer Games). When management effectively allocates resources, it leaves a positive legacy. The Munich U-Bahn efficiently serves millions of commuters annually. The 1984 Summer Olympics in Los Angeles effectively used sponsorships and existing structures to earn a $225 million profit. Atlanta's organizers are telling anyone who will listen that they are not trying to raise cash, but between $450 million and $500 million in capital improvements to the city.[6]

The Atlanta Committee will spare no effort nor allow any oversight in their Olympic preparation. The organizing committee is supervising eleven different construction projects, including a $25 million renovation to Tennessee's Ocoee river for the kayak events. The river reconstruction involves cooperation and input from the Tennessee Valley Authority, U.S. Forest Service, as well as the respective states. Not only will the river be altered and configured for the canoeists and kayakers, but bleachers, concession areas, parking, and other spectator needs will be met.

Niche Events

Mega events like the Olympics, the World Cup, and the Super Bowl capture the attention of the world and sponsors. Smaller events like the San Francisco Examiner Bay to Breakers (foot race), Iditarod (Alaskan dog sled race), and Iron Man Triathlon (endurance competition of swimming, running, and biking) fundamentally mirror the leviathan structure of their brethren, but not the audience. Characterized by highly skilled, specialized competitors, niche events are effective advertising vehicles with much smaller audiences. Hence, minor league baseball, marathons, Arena Football, Motor-cross, and less publicized/commercialized events are commonly referred to as niche events.

The ultimate characteristic for a niche event is its cost. And cost is always relative to audience reach/access. For example, an NFL franchise can cost in excess of $190 million (1995 sale of the Tampa Bay Buccaneers), and an Arena Football franchise costs from $750,000 to $1,000,000 (1994 purchase of the San Jose SaberCats).[7] The NFL, of course, is a multibillion-dollar business, and the sixteen team Arena League is structurally similar, even if its financial impact is not.

Both leagues pursue sponsors and market their teams to attract fans. Both have administrative staff members, league offices, and broadcast interests. The difference is the fans, both in number and loyalty. Because Arena Football plays to smaller crowds without widespread television and print media coverage, they have less ability to influence consumer behavior through its corporate sponsorships. The NFL, on the other hand, will always cost more for sponsors, owners, and fans, because it is a proved mass-market vehicle for its broadcasters, licensees, and corporate partners.

Events grow in dimension and scale. Years before the Super Bowl was conceived, football players played before empty stands on dirt fields at converted baseball facilities. Wrigley Field, Yankee Stadium, and even Chicago Stadium (an indoor basketball and hockey facility) were hosts to professional football action long before Joe Robbie Stadium and the Superdome. Other sports such as NASCAR and Indy Car, the top two professional racing circuits, have experienced corresponding growth. Professional racing's unquestioned popularity with fans and sponsors demonstrates how event planners and their corporate interests can build an entertainment machine.

1994 NASCAR Title Sponsors

Goodwrench® 500	Rockingham, North Carolina
Pontiac Excitement 400	Richmond, Virginia
Purolator 500	Atlanta, Georgia
Food City 500	Bristol, Tennessee
First Union 400	North Wilkesboro, North Carolina
Hanes 500	Martinsville, Virginia

Winston Select 500	Talladega, Alabama
Save mart 300	Sonoma, California
The Winston Select	Charlotte, North Carolina
Coca-Cola 600	Charlotte, North Carolina
Budweiser 500	Dover, Delaware
UAW/GM Teamwork 500	Pocono, Pennsylvania
Miller Genuine Draft 400	Brooklyn, Michigan
Pepsi 400	Daytona Beach, Florida
Slick 50 300	Loudon, New Hampshire
Miller Genuine Draft 500	Pocono, Pennsylvania
Diehard 500	Talladega, Alabama
Bud at the Glen	Watkins Glen, New York
Goodwrench 400	Brooklyn, Michigan
Goody's 500	Bristol, Tennessee
Mt. Dew® Southern 500	Darlington, South Carolina
Miller Genuine Draft 400	Richmond, Virginia

1994 Indy Car Titled Events

Slick 50 200	Phoenix, Arizona
Miller Genuine Draft 200	West Allis, Wisconsin
ITT Automotive Detroit Grand Prix	Detroit, Michigan
Budweiser/GI Joe's 200	Portland, Oregon
Budweiser Cleveland Grand Prix	Cleveland, Ohio
Molson Indy Toronto	Toronto, Ontario
Marlboro® 500	Brooklyn, Michigan
Miller Genuine Draft 200	Lexington, Ohio
Slick 50 200	Loudon, New Hampshire
Molson Indy Vancouver	Vancouver, British Columbia
Texaco/Havoline 200	Elkhart Lake, Wisconsin

The concentration of marquee sponsors like Miller Genuine Draft®, Slick 50®, Budweiser®, and Marlboro®, indicates that these events help name brands successfully market their products. The millions invested into these events have increased the television exposure, audience reach, and consumer impact. The conventional wisdom used to be that racing was for the good ol' boys in the backwoods, but that is a misperception. Racing has grown from the small, dusty circuits of the remote parts of the country to the boardrooms of sponsors and broadcasters. The cars move at high speeds, and always carrying a sponsor's message, for a price. Depending on the affiliation, professional racing offers traditional advertising opportunities like thirty-second spots (Indy Car advertising can sell for more than $27,000). In total, corporate sponsorship and access to events and cars costs participating companies $400 million annually, an indication that racing is not a niche event.[8]

Another well known event that experienced phenomenal growth and corporate participation is the Hoop-It-Up three-on-three basketball tournament. Originally a charity event, which began in 1986, the tournament series is now played in fifty U.S. cities and twenty-four European ones. The tournament (directed by Streetball Partners, Inc.) is sponsored by the NBA, Spalding, and NBC. The international popularity of basketball and the NBA's effective international promotion of the sport result in effective applications like Hoop-It-Up. Hardcore basketball fans who play the game look forward to this three-on-three tournament. Fans cannot expect to play under the bright lights of The Great Western Forum or Madison Square Garden, but through grassroots programs like Hoop-It-Up, they validate the promotional efforts of the NBA and its marketing partners to pass on the excitement of NBA basketball.

Looking at Events to Generate Publicity and Business

Companies get in the event marketing spirit because they can integrate it into consumer activity. They want to participate in events that directly involve and target consumers and professionals without obligating them to their business objectives.

1. Safeway Stores sponsor the Arizona Fall Baseball League (a professional residence of Michael Jordan in 1994). The minor league plays from October to early December and features top players from all organizations. Safeway sells tickets in its stores and promotes the games to its customers. By promoting the sport, Safeway hopes to increase consumer activity at its retail stores. Fans have the choice to go to Safeway to buy tickets, or other items. Safeway obviously hopes to lure shoppers as a ticket outlet. In fact, Safeway and other stores participate

in popular ski ticket purchase programs that discount lift tickets. Safeway does not want to become a ticket broker, but wants people to come into the stores. Selling event tickets, for baseball or skiing, helps accomplish that objective.

2. Discover® Card is the title sponsor for a one-mile road race on New York's famous Fifth Avenue. The emphasis is to focus on users and handlers of credit cards in the restaurant industry. The promotion encourages groups of restaurant runners (chefs, waiters, and bartenders) to form relay teams in addition to the general public. Furthermore, the race has ample sidewalk distribution of Discover® Card applications and a special $150,000 "Dine Out/Cash In" sweepstakes. The event generates publicity through radio and print advertisements and word-of-mouth within the targeted industries.

3. Chemical Bank has sponsored its own "Corporate Challenge " road-race series since 1977. The first event had only 200 runners, but now the race series boasts of 120,000 participants. This event participation growth is no accident. It is a result of Chemical Bank's marketing and management. Chemical Bank pursues corporate teams to compete and the race setting provides an informal platform to conduct other prospecting activities. Chemical Bank spends $3 million annually to support the events, and the expenditure is justified through the customer contact and grass-roots success for both regional branches and customers. In this case, the event's growth is due solely to the market's reception, *not* event audience/fan attendance, or reach. The "Corporate Challenge" has carved its own niche for Chemical Bank, and its customers, through its success in strengthening the relationships of the participating banks and its business clients.

4. The New York City Marathon is one of the most successfully marketed events in all of sports. To maximize profitability and accommodate sponsor interest, the event (the Marathon itself) diversified to include satellite activities like establishing a health and fitness exposition, a corporate challenge event (similar to Chemical Bank's event), and a five-kilometer (approximately three miles) race. By adding these three other activities under the umbrella of the Marathon, the promoters could approach more sponsors and offer them separate identification with an individual event associated with the marathon.

The race itself attracts one of the world's best competitive fields for both men and women (a total of 25,000 competitors), two million spectators present at the event and sixteen million watchers on television.[9] Given those statistics, the promoters have been able to attract and involve marquee sponsors such as John Hancock, Kemper, BFI, Mercedes Benz, and *Runner's World* magazine. Most importantly, these sponsors pay in excess of $1 million in cash and services to identify with the event. The promoters do not sit back and cash checks, however. They spend hundreds of thousands of dollars on local advertising campaigns and sponsor services to give their corporate partners media and audience access through the event. Running such events galvanizes cities, because of the coordination and cooperation involved with event officials and local government. In the case of the New York City Marathon, the event brings $80 million to the Big Apple, so companies, the city, and the race representatives have incentive to make the event a success for everyone involved.

The marathon exploits all of its opportunities, it even licenses Asics, the event shoe sponsor, to develop its own line of marathon-related apparel. But the marathon's real success is in its comprehensive event development. Analogous to the marathon, the NBA and NFL have pursued similar strategies with their respective All-Star games. The NBA schedules the popular "Jam Session" the week (early February) of their All-Star game, at the game site. At Salt Lake City's gala 1993 event, for example, the NBA occupied both the Salt Palace and the Delta Center with an interactive convention of fun, stars, and sponsor exhibits.

Fans could get autographs, play arcade and amusement park style games, and see exhibits from sponsor companies like Reebok (hold Shaq's shoe) and Starter. AT&T had a "long-shot" display where fans attempted three-pointers, and Miller Brewing Company's Sharps® brand staged a free-throw contest. The idea is to give fans a place to go and concentrate on basketball, NBA style. The NFL pulled a play straight out of the NBA's playbook at their Pro Bowl. They conduct a skills competition where fans come to Aloha Stadium and watch players compete in run-offs, and other contests. The NFL uses its celebrities to capture the personalities of fans and players in a fun atmosphere.

5. Staging events is also an effective method of corporate introduction. Even in China, centuries of tradition and iron-fisted leadership have not discouraged progressive sports marketers. Savvy opportunistic marketing professionals know that one billion consumers live within its borders. To capitalize on the market potential, Volvo, the Swedish car

maker, has entered into a five-year, four-event golfing promotion entitled the Volvo Tour of China. The car manufacturer will subsidize the prize money and explore the flourishing westernized marketplace.

Volvo, through its European and American sponsorships, realizes that sporting events work for distribution, dealer, and consumer business goals. By allying with a high-status sport like golf, Volvo hopes to identify with the emerging upper class in China. Furthermore, Volvo understands the cultural sensitivity required in doing business in China. China had banned boxing for many years and only imported table tennis events from Western programmers and promoters. For both Volvo and the Chinese society, golf is a safe activity from both a spectator and sponsor perspective.

Selling (and Buying) Events

The Super Bowl and the Olympics command an audience's attention. Even these events need aggressive promotion. The NBA, the acknowledged league marketing leader, hired Bill Murray, the great comedian and actor, to promote the league and its image. By using an established figure like Murray, the NBA acknowledges the need to promote itself. Tennis, likewise, feels the need to address its fans. The U.S. Tennis Association (USTA), a nonprofit governing body, addresses the tennis market to maintain its audience and sponsors. The organization sells licensed merchandise and promotes its own events, like the prestigious U.S. Open. By having the organizing committee place its support and manpower behind events and membership drives, the fans will receive better service and access. By fostering an interactive, cooperative approach, sponsors will feel that their needs, i.e., commercial interests, can be met through innovative merchandising and promotional programs, rather than isolated, desultory efforts. The USTA encourages fans/customers to participate in the events and that will make its sponsorship sales efforts more competitive and viable in the contemporary marketplace.

Event partnership goes beyond the simple commercial interests of sponsors and promoters. The Olympics, for example, coordinates municipalities, diplomats, fans, athletes, sponsors, and even federal governments. In 1996, the federal government will help provide 2,000 buses for the Olympics. By gathering and relocating them to Atlanta, the organizing committee will save \$12 to \$14 million.[10] Consequences like that make federal intervention a worthwhile venture. Local government has a more critical role. They issue construction permits, easements, security, and facility access. Local government can even develop outside revenue sources. License-plate sales that commemorate the 1996 Olympic Games will bring almost \$6 million to the event production capacity of the host committee.

Another important detail to note is that the city of Atlanta won the rights to host the Games in 1990. It will take virtually every day of the six years (2,191 total days) allotted to prepare for the seventeen-day event. Whether Atlanta will be better off in terms of city services and public goods will be up to the economists, analysts, and citizens of Georgia. The world will be thrilled, to say the least. From a sponsorship and civic impact perspective, it might be worth the effort to chronicle the Olympic aftermath as well as the prologue.

Representative groups from hopeful Olympic hosts watch the Atlanta development project with keen interest. Potential sites submit bids to the IOC years in advance to gain the prestige, publicity, and money that accrues to the host city. The high stakes world of international sporting events has defined three issues that allocate sites:

1. Facility preparation.
2. Governmental cooperation
3. Money/Financial sources.

In the Winter of 1995, the IOC (headquartered in Lausanne, Switzerland) shortened the list of the 2002 Winter Games finalists to four locations. (See Table 2.) Each host pitched its city as the ideal Winter Games site by showing existing facilities and approved construction for the necessary ones. Each site carefully prepared a cost projection, since revenues can be predicted (based upon past Olympics) with far greater accuracy. The cost projections, can wildly fluctuate, and threaten the Games' potential. These estimates were carefully made seven years in advance. And all for a two-week stint as host to the world's greatest athletic competition.

Table 2.
Possible Hosts for the 2002 Winter Olympics

Hopeful Host	Estimated Cost of Games[11]
Salt Lake City, Utah	$798 million
Quebec, Canada	$567 million
Ostersund, Sweden	$780 million
Sion, Switzerland	$472 million

Quebec's population approaches seven million while Ostersund, by comparison, only has 60,000 residents. Although there is a size disparity, both sites have government-supported financial plans to accommodate the international demands of the Olympics. Both host sites claim to have available hotels, transportation (nearby airport and local metro lines), media facilities, alpine ski sites, and facilities targeted for skating, luge, sponsor hospitality, and the athletes' Olympic Village.

The IOC and the eventual site need the six to seven years of preparatory time to accommodate the Games and maximize revenue opportunities. For the 2002 Games, the IOC made its decision on June 16, 1995, choosing Salt Lake City as the lucky winner. The IOC usually favors the major political powers, because their stability and financial resources allow the committee to meet the enormous needs of the Olympic Games, its broadcasters, sponsors, and other marketing partners. The sentiment to grant the Games to third world countries is strong, but the IOC resists political instability. The Moscow games of 1980, for example, were not a logistical disaster, but a financial one. When Jimmy Carter led a U.S. boycott of the Games, the events became a marketing as well as a competitive afterthought.

More on Event Franchise Expansion

Much discussion has focused on event franchises and the marketing clout that they represent. Franchise extension has its merits because they generally do not need to prove themselves. They get television and sponsor access based upon their heritage, a type of corporate nepotism. *Sports Illustrated,* the most popular American sports magazine (in terms of sales and profitability), has recently taken the event route to increase its exposure and profit potential. The former rigid world of advertising and promotion evenly divided advertising sponsorship expenditures between categories such as cars, apparel, booze, tobacco, etc., and vehicles such as radio, television, and print. Furthermore, the media clutter for outlets was not as cluttered as today.

Today, advertisers and audiences want more from their media buys. By restricting the opportunities to one form of media, i.e., print, contemporary marketing opportunities are being ignored. Coke®, Budweiser®, and Miller® all proved that the name of a flagship brand can be shared to create other franchise products, such as Diet Coke®, Bud Light®, and Miller Genuine Draft®. By shrewdly applying the reputation of a franchise in an acceptable capacity, market potential grows without high introduction awareness costs. For Time Warner to create a show entitled, "Sports Chronicles," recapping a week's activities would be ambiguous. The show would need to define itself across a market. A show dubbed, "The Sports Illustrated Review" would be easily identified by viewers and programmers as a comprehensive sports anthology. The *Sports Illustrated* name represents so much to sports fans, a value that is hard to quantify. With over three million subscribers and many millions more readers, the magazine is poised to have a wide impact on the entire sports media market.

The recent growth in viable and effective outlets has changed the reflexive marketplace and flattened the traditional revenue curves for all industry participants. Given that, *Sports Illustrated* determined that future revenue sources could come from diversification of the product, the *Sports Illustrated* name. In one of its first efforts, *Sports Illustrated* created a sports festival to travel to theme parks (Six Flags®) owned by the Time Warner conglomerate, *Sports Illustrated*'s parent company. If this proves to be popular with fans, the idea can move to other areas of target concentrations like college campuses and shopping malls. This could be sponsor-driven ("Coca-Cola presents the *Sports Illustrated* Campus Sports festival") and integrated into corporate activities, all with the *Sports Illustrated* name attached to it. To further its event identity, the magazine spent the necessary millions to become an official sponsor of the Summer Olympics. Commemorative editions, pins, posters, and merchandise will test the creative powers of licensing and cross-promotions like never before. The exciting result is that *Sports Illustrated* will have a vested interest in the Games, and sports fans should benefit from the formal relationship.

The actual Games coverage, specialized print ad sections, and Atlanta based entertainment opportunities will allow *Sports Illustrated* to become interactive with subscribers and advertisers. Bringing its readers and advertisers together, is the focus of *Sports Illustrated*'s business. The event forays will inevitably lead the magazine into television programming. With fellow Time Warner bedfellows HBO and TVKO having successful sports forays, *Sports Illustrated* can complement its entertainment efforts by bringing premium entertainment specials from text to video.

In fact, *Sports Illustrated* already offers videos on the Swimsuit edition and famous league commemoratives (Super Bowl Champions, Larry Bird, and other legends). By programming and broadcasting under its name, the audience expects the quality of journalism and story access to mirror the industry standards set by the magazine. Television will be the window/interface to interactivity with advertisers and features like coupon redemption and placement. Specialized editions on, for example, running, tennis and golf, can target readers and advertisers. Etonic® may not want to buy a full-page color ad in the *Sports Illustrated* weekly, but they may want to buy in all running related forms of media available under the *Sports Illustrated* umbrella.

The *Sports Illustrated* example represents a franchise's potential to expand. Golf's Skins Game has been an event that has successfully expanded to accommodate both a ladies and a seniors format. In an effective strategy, the Senior Skins Game has found a home during the Super Bowl weekend. ABC knows that sports fans plan to watch television on Super Bowl Sunday, so they program a high-profile event to correspond with the weekend. Combining the event's timing with four of golf's greatest competitors, Ray Floyd, Jack Nicklaus, Arnold Palmer, and Lee Trevino, the Senior Skins Game has firmly etched its place in America's sports calendar. In 1994, the Senior Skins, in fact, had better ratings than three of golf's four major competitions, as shown in Table 3.

Table 3.
The Golf Ratings Bonanza

Event	1994 Rating
Masters	7.0
Senior Skins	4.9
U.S. Open	4.6
PGA	4.4
British Open	3.4

Furthermore, the Senior Skins game has beaten at least one of the four "majors" in the ratings each year of its eight-year existence.[12] The purse that the players compete for totals $540,000, but the audience and sponsor-driven revenue is well worth the price. The Senior Skins game takes the established reputation of four golfers (over thirty-five major titles between them), places it in a friendly, but competitive, environment (Hawaii), and lures an audience. Most importantly, ABC has two holiday franchise events in the Skins concept. The regular Skins Game has a home on Thanksgiving weekend, and the Seniors version has an established place amid the Super Bowl madness. The key point is that the Senior Skins Game does not directly compete *for* the Super Bowl's audience, but exploits it.

Attracting Events and Franchises

Enthusiastic markets that can support franchises, through physical attendance and media market benefits, have teams and events. Franchises bring many things to communities, especially money and publicity. Communities want to be "event friendly" (easy for the leagues and governing bodies to stage events especially in terms of logistics) so they stage rallies and band together to throw support behind efforts to attract (or save) a team. Leagues and franchises, in some respects, know more about teasing than pleasing. They naturally look to get the best possible deal. There is only one New York media market and it is occupied, so the current rage is to find the best stadium deal and maximize profitability through that venue and medium.

As documented, events invigorate local economies. Economic impact estimates for Super Bowl host cities conservatively indicate that the game (and its related events) can generate over $150 million for the host city. The Carolina Panthers' first season area economic impact study (ten home football games) indicates that revenues generated by local business will total $358 million.[13] On a smaller scale, the city of San Jose, California, established a Sports Authority to recruit and help manage events for its positive economic impact. By attracting the 1995 National Junior Olympic Track and Field Championships, for example, San Jose can count on an extra 10,000 people (representing approximately $9 million) going there to eat, drink, and compete.[14]

BUILD IT AND THEY WILL COME (OR STAY)

A new facility is the best way to lure a franchise to either move or stay. The Baltimore Colts' management scorned Metropolitan Stadium and, tempted by the beauty of a domed facility with guaranteed ticket sales, moved overnight to Indianapolis in 1984. The city of Chicago and state of Illinois created the Illinois Sports Authority to finance, build, and manage the "new" Comiskey Park. This was the political response to the White Sox being wooed by the Florida tropics and a modern domed facility in the Tampa-St. Petersburg area. Similar stories follow virtually every franchise in every sport. Basketball and hockey usually share facilities simultaneously, so they can negotiate together with city officials, as in the case of Chicago's United Center.

Oakland, California, is a big league city that lost a significant piece of its identity when the enormously popular Raiders left for the Coliseum in Los Angeles. Managing General Partner Al Davis cited financial opportunity as the main reason. Davis felt that the Oakland-Alameda County Coliseum complex was unwilling to upgrade the structure's commercial seating by adding luxury boxes to meet the future demands of a professional sports tenant. He went to Los Angeles and won millions of dollars from his fellow owners in a celebrated court battle. Unfortunately for Davis, he became unhappy as a Los Angeles resident.

Despite winning a Super Bowl in their inaugural year in Los Angeles (1983), the Raiders did not draw well in the city. When the 49ers or Cowboys came to town, the games were well attended, but week to week, entire sections were consistently empty. Davis had shared the Bay Area with the 49ers and succeeded. Why couldn't he duplicate the success with the Rams? After seven years of Southern California, Davis felt the urge to look elsewhere. How about Oakland? The Oakland Coliseum Commission offered him a larger facility, $50 million in moving expenses, eighty-seven new luxury suites, a Hall of Fame to call his own, and ticket guarantees.

The citizens of Oakland, however, decided that education and social services were more important than sports, and pressured the political powers to remove the coliseum board's proposal. Davis remained in Los Angeles, still angling (like all franchise owners) to get a better stadium deal. As the Rams left for St. Louis, and the domed facility promised them, Davis gained leverage with the NFL and the Southern California political power base. Al Davis appeared to be the real winner in the Rams' exit. The unpredictable Davis fooled everyone and moved back to Oakland.

Venue construction applies to other sports, but for the same purpose: to attract an event's potential economic and financial impact. Callaway County (central Missouri) is building a 200,000 seat NASCAR and Indy-car oval that will be just over one mile in length. The project will cost approximately $75 million, but will host many race events. Through the venue, Callaway County can pursue sponsors, promoters, and fans to come to Missouri and spend their entertainment and travel budgets. Perhaps Callaway County looked at Indianapolis' Brickyard (site of the Indy 500) and decided that the reason it became the source of millions of dollars was simply due to its existence. Its reasoning, in part, was influenced by the success of other venues.

Another sport, bowling, has a new home to call its mecca. The $46 million National Bowling Stadium was built in Reno, Nevada, to be the game's showcase centerpiece. Built exclusively for tournament use, the facility features eighty Brunswick lanes and seats 1,200 fans. Reno's visitors bureau expects this center to attract international bowling events and fans to its town, affectionately referred to as "The Biggest Little City in the World." Reno's civic leadership is smart, because it knows that a professional franchise is unrealistic for its community, but a bowling palace fits its visitor and resident demographics. Nevada Governor Bob Miller said about the new facility:

> Some call a bowling alley a poor man's country club. Looking around this facility, we can see that country clubs are a poor man's bowling alley.

Bowling organizations and promoters are already drooling over the opportunities presented by the 363,000-square-foot facility, and are reserving tournament times well into the future. The bowling destination site has characteristics similar to Halls of Fame. For example, 170,000 visitors visited the Basketball Hall of Fame in Springfield, Massachusetts, to celebrate basketball. Bowling may not be as popular, but the fans drive business for the facilities and the cities.

Event facility construction, franchise attraction, ticket sales, and sponsorships are becoming integrated entities in the sports world. Owners and leagues want cities to commit to facility and revenue projections when awarding expansion franchises, approving moves, or scheduling events. The city of Phoenix and its NBA team, the Suns successfully merged the public and private sector with professional sports. The city owns the land and title to the arena, which it sold to America West Airlines. The Suns, though, both designed it and currently operate it. The city invested $46 million into the facility and receive 70 percent of the revenue, approximately $25 million.[15] This partnership, and the one in North Carolina, represent the emerging model of cooperation between government and sports management in the contemporary sports business marketplace, (unfortunately, sports management and labor cannot cooperate as well), where risks and rewards are divided between the two groups.

Stadium revenue became an issue between the Chicago White Sox and the city of Chicago as they negotiated a new ballpark agreement. The original Comiskey Park was showing its age and a new stadium was necessary for both the fans and management. Courted by St. Petersburg, the White Sox almost left Chicago's South Side. The government got involved and decided that the historic franchise meant millions to the city and its fans. To solve the dilemma, the city of Chicago and the state of Illinois formed the Illinois Sports Authority to bring long-term vision and financing to a new facility. The result is the new and improved Comiskey park, literally built across the street from its predecessor.

Funded primarily through a city hotel tax, the facility has a $14.5 million annual debt payment (twenty-year schedule).[16] The hotel tax covers $12 million of the debt, and the balance is funded through facility-generated revenues. By being partners from the beginning, the White Sox and the city/state negotiated reasonable terms that worked for both interests. The Sports Authority runs the facility and have turned a profit ($7 million in the first two years), showing that the government

The pervasive presence of Nike in college basketball—right next to two-time All-American Jason Kidd, currently a Nike spokesman and an NBA star for the Dallas Mavericks. (Photo by Andy Kuno)

Outfield sign advertising a major American clothes retailer, conveniently placed in the left-center and right-center field gaps. (Photo by Andy Kuno. Used by permission of the San Francisco Giants.)

Tobacco companies cannot advertise through the broadcast media, so stadium signs generate impressions and audience access. (Photo by Andy Kuno. Used by permission of the San Francisco Giants.)

Jeff Atkinson, international track star and 1,500 meter U.S. record holder, is an endorser of Nike and its retailer Foot Locker. Track's international appeal is not matched by U.S. broadcast and sponsor interest. Despite the lack of a domestic market, track and field thrives around the world. (Photo by Bill Leung, Jr./Geek Media)

Beer heavyweight #1, Anheiser-Busch, at the ballpark. Bud sponsors twenty-five out of twenty-eight Major League teams. (Photo by Andy Kuno. Used by permission of the San Francisco Giants.)

Beer heavyweight #2, The Miller Brewing Company, also knows that there are lots of customers at the park.

(Above) Gatorade, an important teammate on every NFL sideline.

Troy Aikman *(left)*, marquee hero, drinking from a Gatorade cup... exactly why the Quaker Oats Company bought the sponsorship. (Photos by Andy Kuno)

Roy Jones, Jr., pound-for-pound the world's best boxer, brings in a large audience for USA.

(Above) Arnold Palmer and Pennzoil... one of the most prestigious endorsement relationships. Palmer's timeless, unrivaled appeal is captured on the side of Pennzoil's signature big rig. (Photo by American Action Sports)

(Left) When you're "The Great One" (Gretzky's nick-name), your name gets used in many places. (Photo by Phil Schaaf.)

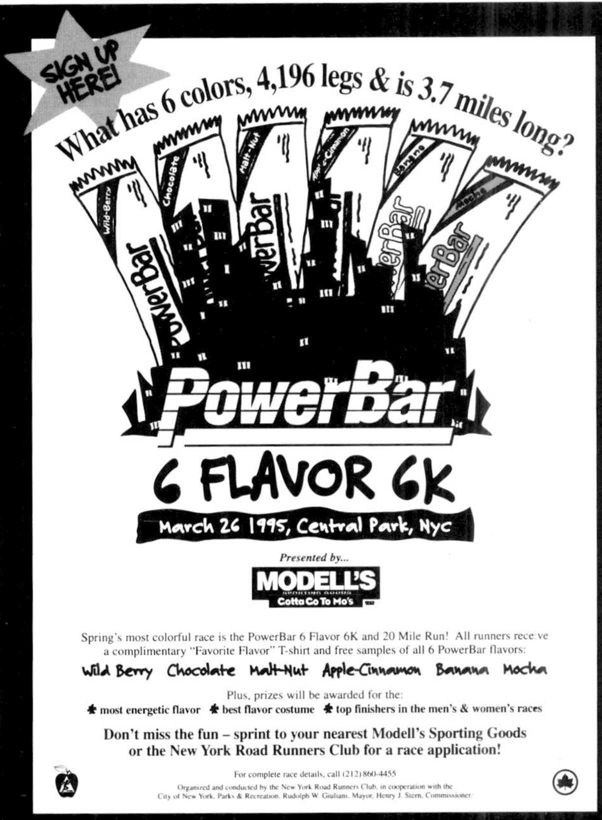

(Above) The Irish National Soccer team toasting their primary sponsor Guinness. The sponsorship was a success, especially after Ireland defeated Italy at a World Cup match at Giants Stadium. (Photo courtesy *Beverage World* magazine)

(Left) A reproduction of PowerBar's successful six flavor, 6k event, held in New York City's Central Park. The event resulted in the identification of the product's retailers with participating athletes, local media, and thousands of consumers.

can be financially responsible and successful. The White Sox's rent schedule minimizes risk and provides incentives for both parties to maximize profits. The White Sox pay no rent for the first 1.2 million fans that come into the park, but pay 35 percent of the gross revenues (tickets, concessions, and parking) to the Sports Authority after that threshold has been attained. The Sports Authority, however, does not sit back and watch the White Sox do all the work. They sell the 100 luxury boxes, starting at $50,000.

Small-Scale Events

Minor league baseball, is, by name, a smaller scale event. That does not mean, however, that it is in any way inferior in terms of entertainment quality. Promotions like the Lethbridge (Alberta, Canada) Mounties' "Pack Your Bags Night," encourage fans to bring travel bags to the games, and at the end of the sixth inning, a winner is drawn (it can be a couple). A waiting limousine takes the fan(s) to the airport for an eventual destination of Toronto, and a weekend of Blue Jays baseball. Alberta has a rich baseball/softball tradition, with such luminaries as Jake James, the famed "Iron Man of Medicine Hat," a Lethbridge resident.[17] Lethbridge's minor league team and its promotions aim to entertain the fans while reinforcing the popularity and history of Canadian baseball.

The Nashville Sounds bring a fan out onto the field between innings to catch three pop-ups. If the fan catches all three of the balls, everyone gets free pizza. As pressure packed as that might sound, nothing compares to the "Beer Batter" designation. If a player earns that dubious distinction, fans line up at the concession stands to purchase a half-price beer—if, and only if, that player (always from the opposing team) strikes out. At the very least, this gimmick always raises fan interest and stadium volume, if not beer sales.

The Las Vegas Stars, naturally, have had an Elvis Night. And the Charleston River Dogs have a mascot, Charlie, who resides in a dog house near right field. But the best promotion undoubtedly belongs to the Chattanooga Lookouts and their unique "Used Car Giveaway Night." On this very special evening, nine used cars are given away to lucky fans, one each inning. The creativity allowed on the minor league level indicates the independence of the leagues governing the teams.

The Memphis Chicks and Toledo Mud Hens do not have to answer to commissioners and corporate sales directors who have complicated exclusivity clauses in their sponsorship agreements.

But the minor leagues are not only about outlandish promotions, they are about the realities of small market entertainment. Their economies cannot successfully support the financial needs of a professional franchise. Professional franchises not only need fans in the stands, they need cable subscribers, merchandise clients, and promotional targets for event sponsors. Sponsors, in turn, need a market size that can support the advertising investment in a team. The Detroit Pistons began its franchise history playing in a Fort Wayne (Indiana) high school gym in 1948. It is unlikely that either the Pistons, or professional basketball, will return to Fort Wayne because the city cannot financially support a team.

Individually Sponsored Tournament Events

The NBA has league sponsors like Gatorade®, Coca-Cola®, the Miller Brewing Company, and Dollar Rent-A-Car, and individual teams like the Los Angeles Lakers have individual team sponsors like GTE. As outlined earlier in this chapter, NASCAR's events are sponsored by a variety of companies all looking to identify with race fans. Similarly, the PGA is a succession of national events with different sponsors and administrators all marketing the same product: championship golf. The Tour has done a fabulous job in developing golf fans and sponsors. Furthermore, the PGA is the most generous organization in professional sports. It is involved with hundreds of charities and raises millions of dollars for causes through its events. All of this is possible because the PGA has perfected client relationships on the sponsorship side of sports entertainment. The list of corporate partners (entitled tournament hosts) shows the PGA's work in promoting golf and the products and services of its sponsors.

In addition to the category sponsors listed in Table 4, other notable PGA tournaments feature the following corporate sponsors: Federal Express, Nestle®, Shell, United, Kmart, Ryder, and Disneyworld.

Table 4.
Some Golf Sponsors Grouped by Category

Electronics	Auto	Financial Services	Communications
Canon	Buick(four events)	Kemper	AT&T
NEC	Mercedes	Deposit Guaranty	MCI
Motorola	Chrysler	Franklin Funds	BellSouth
	Honda	Andersen Consulting	Bell Canadian
	Lincoln-Mercury		Northern Telecom
	Oldsmobile		
	Nissan		

The PGA is fortunate to satisfy the individual company's needs with its focused, regional events. It should be noted that the PGA has official category sponsors, such as Michelob® and O'Douls® Beer that apply to all events.

Full Sail Ale: A Diversified Event Strategy

THE COMPANY

The Full Sail Brewing Company overlooks the spectacular Columbia River gorge in Hood River, Oregon. Its products, Full Sail®'s Ales and Lagers, are enjoyed by sports enthusiasts and participants throughout the West. Combining grass-roots marketing efforts with major sports affiliations, Full Sail is a shining example that smaller breweries (and budgets) can successfully market its products through major (and relatively minor) sporting events and activities.

ITS SPORTS RELATED MARKETS

Full Sail distributes a mix of its beers in the following states: Alaska, California, Colorado, Idaho, Montana, Oregon, Washington, and Wyoming. The brewery emphasizes identification with consumers and activities that would appreciate the association of a hand-crafted beer, but it does not entirely ignore all efforts at appealing to the traditional sports markets. Growing at a fast rate, Full Sail takes advantage of both mass market access opportunities and niche event identification to grow its consumer base.

PROFESSIONAL SPORTS IDENTIFICATION

On a professional sports level, Full Sail has neon signs in the Seattle Kingdome (Mariners and Seahawks), Oakland Coliseum (Golden State Warriors), and Portland's Civic Auditorium (Trailblazers). To Full Sail, it is more important to sell beer at these venues, than simply generating impressions through its signs and billboards. The advertisement does lead to a first taste impression, after which the consumer is engaged. Selling beer not only puts the product in fans' hands, but it gives them advertising tie-in opportunities to pursue in other applications.

For example, Full Sail ran a feature commercial on the Seattle Supersonics' pregame radio program. The spot capitalized on the product being sold at the Tacoma Dome (temporary home for the 1994–1995 season while the Seattle Center gets refurbished). Knowing that the Tacoma Dome was fifty miles away, and that the pregame drive would have good ratings, Full Sail ran the following ad on KJR radio:

"The Full Sail History of Beer"

> 200 million years ago, dinosaurs rule the earth (sound of growling T-Rex).
>
> 65 million years back, due to an acute shortage of beer and sports bars, dinosaurs become extinct. Aww.
>
> 8 million years ago, human-like apes appear, but cannot get cable.
>
> In the Ice Age, civilized humans appear, invent sports bars, and eventually sports.
>
> 6000 B.C.: the first beer is brewed near Iraq. It will become the second most popular beverage worldwide.
>
> 1770 B.C.: the code of Hammurabi dictates that those who water down their beer are put to death. That seems fair.
>
> 1967: Seattle Sonics are created as a good excuse to drink beer.
>
> 1987: Full Sail Brewing Company is founded, and using the code name of Hammurabi as a guiding principle, creates rich ales and lagers from pure barley malt, water, hops, and yeast.

1994: Full Sail brewers introduce their Red Ale, which pretty much concludes the history of civilization.

1995: Thanks to Full Sail, Sonics win it all.

Full Sail: the crowning achievement of 200 million years of struggle.

Full Sail Brewing Company, Hood River, Oregon.

On a Smaller Scale

Away from the professional sports scene, Full Sail diversifies its involvement to include both events and participants. The brewery makes a point to pursue participatory sports teams and clubs like the Foot Bag Club of Portland, the Full Sail Kegelers (bowlers) and the Full Sail Impalers (soccer team). Full Sail also sponsors local events such as the "Hood to Coast" relay race, the Equestrian Festival (the Hood River Memorial Hospital's fundraiser), and is the title sponsor to the Full Sail Gorge Cup, a premier windsurfing series. Hood River is a world famous destination for windsurfing enthusiasts, and the brewery views the Gorge Cup as an excellent opportunity to tie in with one of its town's best local attractions and support the Hood River community.

Involvement with all of these groups and their events furthers Full Sail's commitment to people whose specialized sports interests reflect a capacity to appreciate the quality of Full Sail's beers. Full Sail patiently brews its products and pays attention to its diverse and loyal consumers.

Analysis

It is one thing to discuss public relations campaigns, but the important thing is to identify a strategy that works. For Full Sail and other companies who balance a diverse portfolio of event marketing opportunities, the most important question is always the same: How successful are these efforts in terms of sales? For brewers, success can be quantified through their volume. In 1994 Full Sail brewed 52,000 barrels and in 1995 it brewed 80,000.

Full Sail's success is further punctuated by its brand new multi-million-dollar facility in Hood River. The new brewery can expand to provide an annual capacity of 250,000 barrels of fresh and frothy Full Sail to the Northwest and beyond. Their growth is due to many things:

- Specialized market attention and balance between events and commercial vehicles, i.e., the Sonics and the Foot-Bag Club.
- Excellent distribution.
- Most critically—product quality. One taste will prove that.

A UNIQUE OPPORTUNITY

Courtenay Becker-Day, as an America³ team member, is a participant in one of the most compelling sports stories from 1995. Sporting events tend to identify and support unique and inspirational teams like the 1980 U.S. hockey team, the 1985 Villanova men's basketball team (National Champions), and even the Jamaican Bobsled team, who won the hearts and attention of the international public.

As Becker-Day and her America³ teammates prepared for the America's Cup competition in San Diego, Full Sail recognized a unique sponsorship opportunity with the event's first all-women's sailing team. Becker-Day hails from Oregon, and the circuitous network of sponsorship traveled from Hood River to San Diego as Full Sail pursued an agreement with America³. Full Sail will supply the team with beer and some apparel (which is not to be worn in competition). This is a perfect fit for both the team, its support staff, and Full Sail. Most importantly, the America's Cup trials coincide with Full Sail's expansion into the San Diego market, and the sailing event truly fits the product's image and target consumer. Furthermore, America³ is the best team to identify with from a publicity standpoint, due to the attention focused on the team.

Not only is sailing a natural fit, but the idea of an all women's team appealed to the brewery. Full Sail's corporate philosophy strives to put women into nontraditional roles, and this sponsorship correlates to the same spirit. America³ proves that women can compete in the rigorous environment of competitive sailing, eroding the misperceptions of athletics and gender equality.

6

Understanding the Sponsors

> Exposure to target audiences is nice, but in the competitive soft drink industry, sponsorships have to drive actual product sales in order to justify participation.
>
> —Richard Bishop, Coca-Cola Enterprises

As an experienced sponsor, Richard Bishop has had the opportunity to review, purchase, and reject many sponsorship opportunities. All sponsors have different criteria for analyzing and implementing sponsorship opportunities, but they share the two fundamental objectives that Mr. Bishop mentions:

1. Promotional exposure of a corporate product or service.
2. Using event access as a product sales vehicle.

Sponsorships help Coca-Cola develop the retailer-manufacturer relationship, the staple of its business.

In 1995, companies will spend almost $5 billion on sponsorship purchases. The money to support those sponsorships in media, print, and merchandise campaigns will certainly more than double that figure. Companies pour significant resources into sports entertainment marketing opportunities. R. J. Reynolds spent $4.5 million on NASCAR in 1992. The Winston® Cup competition, after all, has a price. *The Spon-*

sor Factbook reports that a 1995 Milwaukee Brewers scoreboard advertisement can cost $125,000.

In packaging, presenting, and selling sponsorship agreements to corporate interests, event organizers/promoters attempt to accomplish two goals:

1. To finance and profit from the related event.
2. To promote products and services from sponsoring companies.

These two objectives work in unison in all entertainment forms: movies, music events, amusement parks, festivals, and sports. With the abundance of sporting events and programming, the invested billions are easy to identify. Hockey rinks have corporate logos placed on the boards around the rink. Race cars look like neatly stacked, colorful coupons. NBA and Major League Baseball sponsors use rotating billboards near the competitive action. Ticket stubs and game programs have colorful advertisements and redemption coupons. Billboards ring domes, arenas, ballparks, and fields so that fans at the facilities and in the television audience can see them. Television itself continues to schedule more sports programming events, like the Golf Channel, as the audience and advertisers continue to buy the opportunities that the programming presents.

Athletes themselves sell their identities to reap sponsor benefits. Richard Petty, one of the most celebrated stock car racers, went on a farewell tour in 1992 that generated fan enthusiasm and media attention as he retired from competitive racing. His retirement placed him and his famous STP #43 Powder blue stock car on sports pages around the country. Petty did not cheat his public nor did he cheat his sponsors during his farewell to racing. Other athletes feature similar agreements. Greg Norman, perhaps the world's most popular golfer, has an endorsement with Reebok that features his trademark shark logo. Norman's hats, shirts, and shoes are available where Reebok golf merchandise is sold, and will be seen wherever and whenever Norman plays golf.

The variety of opportunities, privileges, and advertising rights for sale are universally referred to as sponsorship. Sponsorship has three basic meanings in the sports industry:

1. *Sponsorship subsidizes an individual athlete's or a group of athletes' training and competition-related expenses.* The sponsor's fee is

not tabulated according to the return on investment, but rather the needs of the athlete(s). The sponsor will receive more exposure relative to the popularity of the participant's sport and his/her position within that athletic discipline. Olympic sports such as skiing, cycling, skating, and track and field are typical beneficiaries of this type of sponsorship. Sponsors assess the constraints of their promotional budgets, prospects of the athlete(s), the sport's popularity, and perhaps most importantly, the relevance of their product to that sport's audience. Those factors are weighed against the price of supporting the training and competition expenses. The conservative cost estimates to train a world class athlete run $40,000 dollars per year.[1] Figure skaters and the athletes who require highly skilled training obviously have higher expenses.

An example of subsidy tie-in sponsorship matches the U.S. Ski Team and Subaru. Subaru uses the name of the team in its advertising in exchange for a fee. Subaru's four-wheel drive product line and target demographics correspond with the image and audience of the U.S. Ski Team. As the prospects of the U.S.'s ski team have improved through the Mahre brothers, Bill Johnson, Cindy Nelson, Tommy Moe, and Picaboo Street, the value of the association has improved dramatically. Unfortunately, not all sponsorships evolve so successfully. It is difficult to justify sponsorships, though worthy in philanthropic terms, on a strictly marketing basis. Intercollegiate swimming programs, for example, are great for the coaches, athletes, and fans. Olympic champions like Matt Biondi, Mark Spitz, and Pablo Morales have developed through the competitions. But subsidizing these programs through sponsorship is more difficult to justify than men's or women's basketball purely on the basis of media exposure.

2. *Event subsidy.* Entire associations hinge upon the identification between events and products. The Nike Tour, golf's minor league system, began as the Hogan Tour, named after the great Ben Hogan's equipment company. A multilevel sponsorship, the Nike Tour involves several key promotional inventory components like entitlement, product display, athlete access, media considerations, and hospitality space. Nike's sponsorship fee provides the seed money to fund the administrative and event needs to make the Tour succeed. Nike receives international media and event exposure through its sponsorship, while establishing an intimacy with young professionals and avid golf fans who enjoy golf at every level. The Nike Tour plays in major cities like Buf-

falo, Cleveland, Philadelphia, and Tallahassee. Several events are televised on The Golf Channel, and its weekly stops are featured on "Inside the PGA Tour," the PGA produced, ESPN programming staple. Nike receives year-round exposure with the PGA, its players, and the fans through the Tour. Furthermore, Nike contributes to the burgeoning golf market, virtually a recession-proof demographic.

Analogous, but even more important than the Nike Tour is a recent case (1992) involving Nike, its top spokesman (Michael Jordan), and high school sports programs in Chicago. Due to budgetary cutbacks, many programs have been jeopardized and some threatened with total suspension, potentially excluding thousands of kids from competitive, supervised sports programs. At the last minute, the necessary $915,000 had been raised through the Students First/Marcus Palmer Foundation. Foot Locker, a major shoe and apparel retailer, contributed $400,000 while Michael Jordan and Nike also donated $100,000 each. The "team effort" raised the money, and play continued for the rest of the year. Not only did Foot Locker, Nike, and Michael Jordan receive the exposure for a charitable deed, but they strengthened their identity with high school students, their sports programs, coaches, and the fans.

3. *Comprehensive sponsorships.* Combining promotional inventory like media time, arena access, licensing privileges, print advertisements, and tickets binds the sponsor and team to each other. The more comprehensive the sponsorship, the more leverage a sponsor has to tie-in the sports property with his trade retailers and consumers. Media exposure is usually a major component in comprehensive sponsorship. An exception are Olympic sponsorships, which have traditionally sold without media time "bundled" into the agreement. That will change, however, as networks, sponsors, and the IOC want to share the risk of the Games, and not create any exposure issues with regards to ambush marketing tactics (which were discussed in chapter 1). An unstated element to the Olympic tie-ins reflects opportunities outside of formal sponsorships. If a company has not purchased worldwide or region specific rights, the company can still pursue the Games identification through an athlete endorsement, and use the athlete in specific media. The Games, though, do discriminate in terms of publicity. Biathlon competitors are not as popular as the gymnasts, skaters, runners, or swimmers. Television dictates exposure, and exposure gives the investment return. Therefore, taking the chance with only an endorse-

ment, or a focused media buy, will not give the sponsor the leverage or the margin of error to reach the audience that the comprehensive sponsorship does (it's a lot like health insurance).

A classic comprehensive sponsorship is Coca-Cola® and the NFL. Pepsi® cannot be found anywhere near the NFL sideline, near the teams, and during NFL retail promotions. Coca-Cola's umbrella sponsorship enables promotions such as the successful "Monsters of the Gridiron" campaign to be executed. The league sponsorship allows the reproduction of logos, likenesses, and players in national media and retail campaigns. Coca-Cola even created its own trading card series based on the "Monsters" campaign.

All three forms of sponsorship accomplish the objective of placing a corporate name in a sporting event. However, there is a vast difference between the beneficiaries. The first two categories are dependent upon sponsorship for survival, whereas the third category uses sponsorship in order to sell products directly. But in all cases, sports advertise products and services. Someone from Buick made the decision to buy the rights to Ben Crenshaw's visor. In 1992, marketing managers from almost 1,400 different companies purchased 4,400 stadiums signs and billboards. These billboards were sold by 105 different professional franchises, and their marketing partners, in forty-four different cities.[2] All of these decisions are calculated attempts to capitalize on the emotional nature of sports, they are not impulsive purchases made by fanatical brand managers who cannot resist the appeal of sponsorship. Diverse companies with different industry emphases and different target consumer groups use sports as a marketing tool. How do sports fit in with so many different corporate marketing strategies? It will help to understand the people within the marketplace who analyze and purchase sponsorships.

Who Makes Sponsorship Decisions?

One certain attribute relates to all sponsors. They want to make money. Their goal is to gain a comparative advantage in their markets. If a sports advertising opportunity will help attain that goal without placing the promotional budget in jeopardy, then the promotion might receive consideration. Sponsors know their business better than the sports rights sales representatives. Proposals need to be positioned to complement current promotional strategies, not necessarily redefine them. *Sponsors want to feel that sports promotions are working for their company's specific goals, not the other way around.*

The motives/objectives of the sponsors need to be identified when submitting a proposal. Companies will buy sports advertising opportunities because their customers are sports fans, not because the sponsors are sports enthusiasts. People do not have job titles that say: "sponsor." The decision makers who either accept/reject the sponsorship opportunities presented are from a variety of sources.

1. *In-house company representatives.* This person can be the sales manager, promotions director, marketing manager, new business development director, or even the chief executive officer. More than likely, the decision to pursue a particular venture has been discussed and analyzed by people from all of the above groups. Frequently, promotions need to be run through all sales channels, thereby necessitating some degree of input from managers at all corresponding levels.

Oftentimes, the financial scope of a promotional investment will determine who presides over the decision-making process. A player appearance at a store opening does not require an executive summit, but purchasing an NFL license or worldwide Olympic sponsorship does. Companies do not make rash, impulsive decisions on partnership programs that require commitment of both financial and labor resources over a great period of time. The $40 million that Kodak spends on its Olympic sponsorship represents more than just money for its employees. It means developing retail and media campaigns that will be effective throughout the life span of the promotion.

Regional promotions with individual teams such as the Buffalo Sabres are made by the managers and personnel that work within that region. Sometimes, sponsorship decisions funnel through larger regional distinction, for example, West Coast, Mid-Atlantic, etc. But sponsorship opportunities frequently go straight to corporate headquarters for review. Companies like M&M Mars, for example, makes national and regional promotional purchases through its headquarters in New Jersey.

2. *Advertising agencies.* Firms such as Leo Burnett and Associates, J. Walter Thompson, BBDO, and Hal Riney and partners work with companies on both a regional and national basis to develop creative and effective campaigns to promote products and services. Many company

representatives defer all decision-making authority on advertising issues to the agencies, especially on media related issues. Agencies will not make the decision to buy a sponsorship, rather how to use the identification through media channels to create the greatest awareness possible. Quaker Oats did not develop the "Be Like Mike" campaign for its Gatorade® brand, its agency did. Of course, Gatorade®'s top management made creative contributions, but they did not develop the campaign from start to finish.

Agencies essentially have two purposes. One is to create an advertising campaign, such as, "Nissan is built for the human race." The second primary agency function is to purchase advertising vehicles for its corporate client. For example, an agency will buy prime time advertising spots for its clients, and place the ads that they developed on the program. Commercials for "Roseanne," "60 Minutes," and the "NBA on NBC" are all bought by the same people. There are so many effective advertising vehicles within the electronic and print media that expertise from a media agency is essential.

Many companies rely upon their agencies to create and place the brand identity within their markets. Coca-Cola worked primarily with the McCann Erickson agency for years. As Coke® has expanded internationally, the hundreds of millions of dollars that it has poured into advertising its brand has recently been diversified through some specialty agencies, including Michael Ovitz's Creative Artists Agency. Agencies have the responsibility to protect a company's budget throughout advertising production and placement, and to help that company have an impact on its revenues. Furthermore, agencies have the responsibility to maintain accounts, and that can be difficult given the finicky needs and expectations of corporate interests.

Agencies primarily conceptualize and coordinate integrated advertising efforts. Historically, they do not pursue traditional stadium promotions and athlete endorsements, because sponsorships are not costs that add to agency billings, only expenses. To motivate an agency to use an athlete or athletic license, the company/client needs to bring it to the agency. Therefore, sports sales representatives usually need to sell the celebrity and/or team to the company first, and have them bring the athlete/sponsorship to the agency. Agencies earn money through total management of campaigns, from conceptualization to placement, not through administration.

Key Questions a Sponsor Asks

- How much merchandise is included in the proposal?
- If there are media considerations (radio and/or television), do they correspond with the target consumers? Will the extra media attract promotional partners, such as retailers?
- How will the sponsorship enhance the key relationships with the company's distributors, retailers, and sales force?
- Does the promotion tie-in or complement other promotional ventures that the company pursues?

Merchandise is a major component to all sponsorships and is the term applied to the tangible elements that companies receive in their sponsorship agreement. Merchandise includes game tickets, ad space, commercial spots, premium event access such as meeting the players, coaches' "chalk-talks," and souvenir items. The packaging of all promotions will vary, but they all contain some form of merchandise agreement. In media purchases, for example, broadcasters will frequently include a significant amount of merchandise for the sponsor(s). The Ford Motor Company is the title sponsor of tennis's Australian Open called The Ford Australian Open. (In fact, Ford is the only title sponsor of any major event in tennis or golf.) Ford is both the title sponsor of the tournament and recipient of courtside stadium logos, and it receives a fixed amount of event tickets and tournament activities. Merchandise is an assumed element given to all sports packages, because if companies are expected to pay the sponsorship fees, they will want to be there to see how the excitement mixes with their products, customer guests, and the fans in the stands.

Media purchases are intended to generate media traffic. Buzz words like audience reach (size of audience), frequency (the number of times the audience is hit with the message), gross ratings points, exclusivity (no competitor's presence allowed in designated forms, i.e., time slots), billboards (the drop-in of a logo around a statistical review), and fixed-position spots (e.g., first commercial at the end of each inning) determine a sponsor's interest. Some buyers call the Super Bowl the "Ego Bowl," because it takes considerable swagger to spend the $1 million per thirty seconds that it requires to advertise. On the other hand, Super Bowl ad buyers will say that it represents an incredible event audience.

One that craves the spectacle as much as the actual action. Ratings companies like A. C. Nielsen use sophisticated techniques to accurately gauge the audience size of all events. Network television, obviously will have a wider potential audience than cable television, but that does not mean it will command higher sponsorship fees. Fees are based upon the audience size and the demographic profile. Golf may not attract the largest audiences, but it certainly does have an affluent following. For that alone, networks justify the higher advertising fees.

All media buyers essentially want to buy the right number of viewers at the best price. If no audience exists, then the event will not be commercially viable. Companies buy time to reach consumers, and/or to attract promotional partners. Frequently, two companies can cooperate on a venture to share costs and promotional benefits. Pepsi Cola and Kroger Grocery Stores, one of America's largest chains, pursue promotions for dual purposes. Pepsi wants Kroger to stock its products, and Kroger wants Pepsi to tell consumers to go to Kroger in order to buy it. If one company will bring media benefits to a promotion, then it can buy the promotional participation of another. ESPN's "Up Close," an intimate sports personality show featuring the top stars of the sporting world, always closes the show by acknowledging travel sponsor Continental Airlines, and shows one of the airline's jets soaring boldly through the sky. Continental's fixed position as the closing ad sponsor justifies (in Continental's view) its agreement with ESPN on ad purchases and tradeouts.

USAGE: APPLYING SPONSORSHIPS TO INFLUENCE CUSTOMERS

When a sponsorship does not include television/media exposure (for example, the Olympics), sponsors ask themselves one simple question: *How can I use this promotion?* The sponsor breaks down the promotional inventory, including merchandise allocations, and decides how to service existing clients while creating programs to expand market operations. For example, a typical NBA sponsorship package to a company like Nestle could include the following:

- *Tickets,* a variety of premium seats, suites, and event accommodation.
- *Access privileges,* team golf tournaments, banquets, charity events, and player events.

• *Arena promotions,* halftime activities, pregame mentions, and fan interactive entertainment like giveaways and sampling opportunities at a specified number of games.

• *Stadium advertising,* the scoreboard, at players' seats, on rotating billboards, etc.

• *Logo and likeness usage rights* in advertising and retail applications.

Knowing that it has these elements at its disposal, Nestle can create and present a variety of ideas to its most important customers, the supermarket chains and retail partners. Retailers handle the companies' products, and those of its competitors, before the consumer makes a purchase decision. Retail merchandisers are responsible for shelf space positioning, store locations, and sales presentation. Consumer product companies deploy field representatives to assist in the merchandise display and presentation, but it is the store operator who ultimately handles the products in his/her store. The esteemed retailer holds a position of power and consumer product companies need to create and maintain favorable working relationships.

The Importance of Retailers

The importance of a retailer cannot be underestimated or accurately defined in a simple phrase. In regards to sports marketing projects, it is critical to understand that sponsors do not always think of the end user in terms of a sponsorship opportunity. Sponsors know that before they get greedy and think of all the consumers who will be influenced by their savvy marketing programs, they must consider the retail partners and their receptiveness to an association. Retailers are really the promotional gatekeepers of the sports marketing industry. Their stores are truly prime pieces of real estate that need to be managed, priced, and sold. If Coca-Cola or Reebok wants to receive attractive end-aisle display privileges, then they will have to pay their vendor dues through retail specific advertising. For example, ads that close by stating, "pick up your two-liter bottle of Coca-Cola® at your participating 7-Eleven stores," indicate that a promotional relationship between 7-Eleven (retailer) and Coca-Cola (vendor) resulted in a specific advertisement.

Product managers want retailers to embrace promotions. If retailers have input and interest in a promotion, then they will have some degree of ownership and interest in its execution and success. By working together, the retailers and vendors attract consumers to stores around the world. Coca-Cola and its largest Northern California retailer, Safeway Stores, pursued a 1990 summer promotion featuring Will Clark, then a star first baseman with the San Francisco Giants. Safeway wanted to capitalize on the popularity of Clark, a charismatic leader of the exciting Giants, the 1989 N.L. Champions. Coca-Cola's responsibility was to sign Clark to an agreement, then produce a commercial and point of sale materials for store displays. In return for the time, money, and effort invested by Coca-Cola, Safeway would do two things:

1. Commit a significant amount of media advertising (which had accumulated through promotional co-op funds) specifically to the campaign.
2. Build and stock high-profile store displays of Coke® in Bay Area stores.

The program was called "Drive Home a Winner," and it worked for Coca-Cola, Safeway, and baseball fans in the Bay Area. The hard work of Coca-Cola, Safeway, and Clark heightened exposure of Coke®, excited the retailer, and gave them a mutually agreed upon promotion to apply to future programs and opportunities. This case reflects the characteristics of a modern, regional sports promotion. Coca-Cola leveraged its relationship with Clark, Major League Baseball, and the Giants to sell more soft drinks to Safeway, its largest customer. Safeway placed the product in its stores and committed advertising support to maximize its potential. By working together, they created consumer excitement and strengthened their working relationship.

Coca-Cola could quite possibly be the king of retail promotions, but the same relationship between manufacturer and retail points-of-sale applies to a variety of products from consumer electronics to automobiles. Cadillac, as a major sponsor of the Senior PGA Tour, uses the Tour to drive customers into its showrooms around the country. The Senior Tour obviously represents Cadillac's key customers and it created a test drive dealer promotion in conjunction with the Tour and its events. The promotion, according to Cadillac insiders, resulted in an extra $90 million in sales over a three-year period and $250 million over five years.[3]

Cadillac uses the Senior Tour as Coca-Cola used Will Clark—to increase dealer foot traffic and consumer activity. Dealerships are franchised investments from independent regional operators. Cadillac, the manufacturer, desperately needs to strengthen its customer promotions to support its sales channels. By encouraging qualified customers (Senior PGA golf fans) to test drive its cars, Cadillac increases its sales. This gives testimony to three facts:

1. The promotional value of golf, as the governing body (PGA) administers and positions it.
2. The quality of Cadillac manufacturing in the marketplace.
3. The abilities of Cadillac's promotional and sales staff to capitalize on the promotion.

The Detroit Pistons developed a unique program with Meijer Grocery Stores, a metropolitan area retail outlet. The Pistons created a "Center Court" sponsorship where manufacturers can buy (for $15,800) guaranteed end-aisle display space for one week.[4] The Pistons will also provide:

- Consumer sweepstakes team promotion—at the display.
- Ten radio spots (sixty seconds each).
- VIP party for twenty-five guests attended by either a coach or team player.

This promotional package is designed specifically to attract the interest of consumer product companies that need promotional programs to introduce new products, or reduce inventories of old ones. A store likes to rotate promotions, to keep its retail image fresh and dynamic. The sponsorship's one week display time gives the Pistons and the Center Court sponsors maximum flexibility in promotional exposure with the team and Meijer Stores.

Other Sponsor Priorities

Certain objectives are shared when companies review sponsorship opportunities.

- Enhance their product's (or service's) image.
- Pursue a target consumer group.
- Leverage the promotion with retailers, to increase volume shipments and store traffic.
- Pick events that can sell more products!

The optimal promotion accomplishes all of the above objectives simultaneously. Nike's extensive Air Jordan® campaign exemplifies a successful strategy where the manufacturer, Nike, enhanced its image, exposure, and sales through an investment in Michael Jordan, the NBA, and their media advertising vehicles. They also created a modern blue print of comprehensive product development through licensing a player's identity and his charisma.

The Issue of Barter and Trade-out

Sponsor agreements frequently are based upon service trade agreements where companies receive association with events through the trade of corporate services. Airlines give free flights in return for commercial time. The promotional exchange sometimes is a combination of money and product, but the concept and principles are consistent. Companies want to integrate products into an events business. Delta Airlines is the title sponsor of the Delta Center, home of the Utah Jazz, and the Jazz fly Delta Airlines.

Sponsors with products, or services, to barter can leverage those with promoters selling the sponsorships. Panasonic, as a 1996 Olympic sponsor, did not want Sony's Jumbotron® used in any Olympic facility. As part of its sponsorship, Panasonic provided a replay board to be placed in Fulton County Stadium (as mentioned in chapter 1), even though they had never before manufactured such an item. Broadcasters and relevant promotional partners barter their own services and business inventory to gain access to sporting events. By positioning their products as a part of the event, and giving their services (which have a significant monetary value), they gain promotional benefits.

Cost of the Promotional Multiplier

In conducting a cost/benefit analysis of a promotion, sponsors have many associated expenses to consider, the multiplier. After purchasing a promotional package or endorsement opportunity companies know that they have only started to use their checkbooks. Eastman Kodak, Anheuser-Busch, and Coca-Cola need to change their packaging processes to attach the Olympic logo that costs them many millions to acquire. In the aforementioned Coke® promotion with Will Clark and Safeway Stores, Coca-Cola assumed the associated display and video production expenses.

Quaker Oats, manufacturer and marketer of Gatorade®, contracted Michael Jordan as a celebrity spokesman. Gatorade®'s expenses only began to tally. Quaker Oats needed to fund the creation and implementation of print and electronic media materials for its eventual "Be Like Mike" campaign. After developing this campaign, Quaker Oats needed to hire a director and film crew to produce the commercials. Then, radio and television time was purchased from networks, in addition to print spaces in journals and magazines. Given the plethora of advertising outlets, Gatorade® contracted the additional services of its media agency in order to make the best placement decisions. Clearly, Quaker Oats has money invested in several resources to assist in the execution of this promotional campaign. Additionally, new labels designed for bottles and packages, as well as product bins for retailers were produced and distributed, requiring extra labor. All of this costs Quaker Oats and the Gatorade® brand many millions of dollars. Of course, the "Be Like Mike" campaign is not extraordinary in its extra costs—all promotions have the same development and execution costs—but it is a well known case that examines the related costs of a major sports promotion.

Through its investment, Gatorade® has an obligation to maximize the potential reach of its promotion relative to its resources. The investment in Mr. Jordan and the NBA requires financial support in regards to marketing materials. Therefore, in evaluating the Michael Jordan advertising campaign, Gatorade®'s management needs to ascertain if the business grew at an acceptable rate relative to the total cost of the entire promotion. The multiplier is nothing more than the added costs of executing a promotion. It includes expenses such as the following:

• Creation of advertising campaigns and related media purchases, from billboards to network spots.

• Creation of supplementary materials for marketing campaign field execution. Packaging point-of-sale materials and premium items for giveaways.

• The time and labor the promotional campaign takes to sell to employees, retailers, and promotional partners.

During the 1992 summer Olympics, a relevant case in the cold cereal aisle took place at local supermarkets. General Mills's Wheaties® featured the world's greatest basketball player, Michael Jordan. Kellogg's Raisin Bran® featured five of his Dream Team teammates, Larry Bird, Karl Malone, Chris Mullin, David Robinson, and John Stockton. In the time that it took to decide whether five "Dream Team" members were equal to or superior to one, millions of dollars of time, research, planning, and marketing execution had already been spent. The lure of international basketball inspired two large manufacturers to invest in expensive licensing promotions, all to sell more cereal. Ultimately, the related costs of advertising and marketing need to be recouped through sales, the focus of every promotion.

The Importance of Timing

A key element to understanding the sponsors' mindset, is to understand that for every sponsorship agreement that companies pursue, there are at least twenty-five opportunities that have been rejected. Buyers of promotional sponsorships have a limited amount of resources and can only devote so many resources to any given program. Companies use vehicles that work for their brand image, target consumers, and also attract the corporate culture.

Timing plays an important role in the successful sale of a sponsorship. Companies commit budgets six to twelve months in advance, and if the budget has been spent, companies will have no flexibility to pursue opportunities that materialize down the line. Therefore, companies need to submit proposals and exploratory discussions well in advance.

No promoter or sponsorship sales agent can ignore a sponsor's timetable in selling a promotion. If a company purchases an opportunity, but does not know how to use the merchandise or cannot afford the multiplier's cost, then the sponsor may not continue the relationship. Short-term sponsorships are not good for anyone, because a failure in the sponsor-client relationship indicates a breakdown where someone's needs, usually the sponsor's, were not met. It is both parties' responsibility to ensure that the sponsorship is mutually beneficial, rather than just a signed contract written by attorneys.

Timing certainly influences the buying and selling of sponsorships. Companies like consistency between promotions, but the one in question needs to differentiate itself to some degree. It also needs to be consistent with outside forces in the industry. Issues like the recession and political drama (Desert Storm War) may preclude a company's promotional participation. Also, promotional displacement is difficult to achieve. Michael Jordan has been an international spokesman for Gatorade® for many years. It would be difficult to convince Gatorade® otherwise. The only realistic manner to sell Gatorade® a new spokesman would be if they had considered it first.

Security and Continuity in Sponsorships

Companies like to maintain long-term identification with promotions, so sponsorships are negotiated on a multiyear basis. In 1995, CBS tore up their billion-dollar agreement with the NCAA, and expanded its coverage of events and rights fee payment. FedEx wants to receive the financial benefits of scale with the Orange Bowl, so a three-year agreement (as opposed to a year-to-year contract) gives both FedEx and the Orange Bowl Committee a sense of continuity in the promotion. Coca-Cola has multiyear, multimillion-dollar deals with the NBA and the NFL for the same reasons. Long-term deals between rights holders and sponsors allow the relationship to develop and expand so that a true codependency is established.

The aforementioned Orange Bowl gives customers and FedEx managers a landmark activity to kick off the new year. Sponsoring the game gives FedEx millions of dollars worth of exposure, estimated at almost $13 million in 1992, and over $15 million in 1995, in just three hours of entertainment.[5] Through its entitlement rights, FedEx has primary access to one of college footballs best games. That access is much more than television exposure. It means hospitality tents, tickets, parties and fun. For the overnight delivery specialist, the game is an absolutely, positively great idea

If FedEx declined to continue the relationship, it would give a competitor an opportunity to walk into a fabulous sponsorship. Furthermore, it would leave a gap in its calendar of activities, and it might even affect employee and customer morale. And in any business, customer relationships drive the maintenance and success of all sponsorships.

Sponsor Service

Service is an important issue to sponsors. As in any business, reliability and dependability make customers happy. If a sponsor needs extra tickets for an event, a privileged introduction to a star athlete, or simply V.I.P. treatment, the event liaison needs to accommodate the request. Service begins the moment that the promotion is presented. In many ways, service is another piece of the proposal. Each time there is interaction between the sponsor and the promotional sales representative, the promotion's attributes are reinforced, packaged, and sold.

Promotional purchases buy more than access to an advertising vehicle. They buy an invisible seat on the bench, sideline, and dugout. Sponsors are teammates, business teammates. When a company purchases a sponsorship opportunity, they buy a relationship with the competition, event, fans, and the administrative organization that orchestrates the event's operations. The integrity of the relationships are a high priority. Because sponsors pay huge amounts of money for promotional access, they need swift delivery of the sponsorship's benefits and merchandise. The sponsor's personal business concerns in terms of retail accounts, inventory management, and the administrative tasks that allow businesses to flourish, preclude companies from managing all sponsorship aspects. Sponsors truly rely on the teams, marketing groups and representatives to work with them on promotions. If Spalding gives away miniature basketballs at a Dallas Mavericks' game, then the Mavericks need to have all of the balls and labor ready and waiting when the doors open. Spalding pays the Mavericks for reliability and execution so that the promotion's potential is maximized.

Sponsors also like continual updates in terms of opportunities. If more tickets, or promotional events develop, sponsors like to have the first chance to buy into the opportunity. Teams and promoters also keep sponsors abreast of other team related issues that occur both on and off the fields/courts. Specialized attention to both business and entertainment affairs helps forge long-lasting relationships between sponsors and promoters.

COPING WITH THE UNEXPECTED

Effective relationships allow companies to react to the unexpected events that have an impact on the sports world. When Dan O'Brien (triathlon participant) failed to qualify for the 1992 Olympic team because of a botched pole vault competition, more than personal disappointment was at stake. Reebok had a $20 million promotional campaign featuring him and Dave Johnson, two of the world's most accomplished decathlon athletes.[6] The two Americans were competitive favorites, and Reebok had hopes to make them fan favorites as well. When Dan O'Brien failed to clear the bar on his third vault at the Olympic qualifying trials, Reebok had to act quickly to salvage its promotional plans. It decided to create humorous commercials featuring the two *not* competing, as opposed to humorous ones emphasizing the competition.

Dan O'Brien gamely conceded to the strategy and participated fully in the Olympics as a spectator, analyst, and product spokesman. Naturally, O'Brien would have liked to compete in the Games, but in the high stakes world of sports marketing campaigns, Reebok needed O'Brien to show his corporate face, and he did. Dave Johnson was the unsung hero of the promotion. He genuinely consoled his teammate and made the necessary adjustments in his schedule to document the new "ending" to the Dan and Dave saga. Johnson eventually won the bronze medal despite a stress fracture in his foot. The ultimate legacy is that Dan and Dave did not win the Gold medal in Barcelona but, with Reebok, won a gold medal for adaptability in history's most publicized track and field promotion.

O. J. Simpson's highly publicized double murder trial put his sponsors on the defense as well. Many had to explain and justify their relationship with O. J. The high stakes of promotional investment and the public's delicate perception demanded a comment. Hertz®, NBC, and O.J.'s other business contractors could never have anticipated the former star's predicament, but they had to answer to their future involvement with the Hall-of-Fame running back. O.J.'s corporate partners all issued diplomatic comments explaining the abrupt ending to formal contractual commitments. The comments were not extraordinary, but the need to make a public statement demonstrates the influential mechanism of celebrity and brand identity.

Sponsor Analysis

The buyer-seller relationship creates two different analytical viewpoints. The seller, obviously, wants to pursue the relationship to make the promotional relationship a dependable annuity. On the other hand, the sponsor has a "bottom-line" approach in reviewing a sponsorship. Coke® and Pepsi® need to know if their Super Bowl commercials and sports retail promotions sell more soda pop. Each day, companies receive the proposals that event promoters produce and mail. Whether the proposals meet the intended objectives usually determines the fate of the sponsorship. Therefore, the evaluation process is critical to the development and longevity of promotional relationships. Answers to the following questions identify the main criteria in evaluating a promotion:

- Do the gains of the relationship justify the expense? Would the money be better spent through another campaign?
- Does the promotion involve key retailers, distributors, and channel personnel? And what degree of enthusiasm do they have through the involvement?
- Did the promotion generate added value, or simply added costs?

In addition to the above questions, companies analyze consumer and retailer feedback. If a company has a Reggie Jackson poster redemption program where consumers send in "proofs of purchase" to receive a poster of Mr. October, and no one sends in coupons, then Mr. October was not the best celebrity vehicle. Or perhaps the promotion was not properly advertised. Consumers, after all, need to have a reason to seek out a brand for consumption.

Companies like to see feedback from consumers. Coca-Cola ran a "Monsters of the Gridiron" NFL promotion where people could telephone (via Sprint®) to participate in the promotion. Millions phoned in, which did not mean that they bought Coca-Cola®, but it did mean that they responded to the promotion. The "Monsters" promotion and the ticket stubs with coupons allowed manufacturers to track consumers' usage. Companies buy the rights to this type of promotion for three purposes:

1. To take advantage of a sponsorship
2. To track consumer response.
3. To evaluate the effectiveness of a sponsorship to drive quantifiable business.

Tracking sales allows companies to truly measure a sponsorship. Fans chanting "pizza . . . pizza . . . pizza" at basketball games often do so because a pizza sponsor such as Pizza Hut will give ticket holders a free pizza if the home team wins a game by a specified number of points. A past promotion with the Golden State Warriors allowed ticket holders to redeem a game ticket stub where the Warriors defeated an opponent by twenty or more points. Pizza Hut can then see how many fans come to its restaurant to redeem the coupon, and in most cases, purchase more product. Programs like this work for all involved parties. Fans are encouraged to remain at the facility and root for the home team. Most importantly, Pizza Hut and the Warriors created a quantifiable consumer promotion within the context of a sporting event.

Promoting Feedback Between Promotional Buyers and Sellers

Promoters and sales agents monitor the success of programs by seeking feedback from the sponsors. It helps the event to solicit their opinions. Promoters and event organizers cannot control competitive outcomes or the degree of excitement created by an event, but they can influence the relationship between the sponsors and the fans. Some helpful questions to ask a sponsor:

- What did, or did not, work with related event promotions? Why?
- What could be changed to make a better fit for the sponsor's goals? Are there changes, or wrinkles, that could deliver the promotion better? For example, would the company benefit from more hospitality access, media benefits, or product sampling capacity?

• From the sponsor's viewpoint, how could the promotion improve?

• Did the event give the sponsor access to its consumers and key business relationships?

These questions do expose the promoter to criticism, and that is exactly the point. For a sponsorship to be an investment, and not just an expense, event promoters and coordinators need to ask for criticism and suggestions. If a sponsor can help shape an event, he will naturally shape it for his future participation. The worst thing that can happen is that a sponsor will say that the event is a horrific investment and not worthy of future participation. It is doubtful that a sponsor would be so critical, but at the very least he could help identify shortcomings that might exist and how they can be reversed. The relationship needs to be an open dialogue between sponsor and promoter. Frequent discussions will serve to make the event more profitable for all involved parties.

Why the Athletes Thank the Sponsors

After every golf tournament, a corporate executive from a large corporation such as Buick, MCI, Miller Brewing Company, or Franklin Funds will present a check to the victorious athlete. The athlete thanks the sponsor, because he/she knows that the sponsor's participation means prize money. The average PGA tournament victor wins $180,000. Some tournaments have $500,000 purses. Money like this encourages loyalty and recognition. In team sports, corporate presentation comes in the form of awards like the Miller Lite® MVP (NFL), or the Rolaids® Relief award (Major League Baseball).

Athletes recognize that sponsorships and broadcast contracts subsidize salaries. As sponsorships increase, salaries rise. Current stars like Frank Thomas, Fred Couples, Michael Andretti, Riddick Bowe, Steffi Graf, and Katarina Witt owe a great deal to their predecessors. Athletes such as Jack Dempsey, Joe Louis, Richard Petty, Billie Jean King, Walter Hagen, Curt Flood, Rafer Johnson, and thousands of other competitors brought the rewards that today's athletes enjoy. As mentioned in chapter 2, Billie Jean King received a clothing certificate for winning her first Wimbledon singles event. Table 1 traces the women's tour prize winnings over twenty-five years demonstrating how sports and corporate sponsorships benefit athletes.

Table 1.
Women's Tennis Association Prize Money[7]

Year	Prize Money	Tour Sponsor
1971	$ 250,000	Virginia Slims®
1976	$ 2,200,000	Virginia Slims®
1981	$ 7,400,000	Avon® and Toyota
1986	$14,200,000	Virginia Slims®
1991	$24,600,000	Kraft General Foods
1993	$33,000,000	Kraft General Foods
1994*	$35,000,000	Kraft General Foods

*The 1994 tour's sixty-two events took place in twenty-two countries.

A Sponsor's Perspective: Great Western Bank in Its Communities

With over thirty-eight billion dollars worth of assets, Great Western Bank is the second largest savings bank in the United States. Based out of the Los Angeles area, they are a full service bank that specializes in checking services and home mortgage financing.

Sports advertising is a key component of the bank's broad marketing strategies, and accounts for almost 20 percent of the marketing budget. In addition to the two tenants of the Great Western Forum, the Los Angeles Lakers and Los Angeles Kings, Great Western Bank currently works with the California Angels, Los Angeles Dodgers, San Francisco Giants, Oakland A's and Golden State Warriors. Great Western also pursues collegiate sports marketing opportunities with UCLA, USC, Cal State Northridge, and the Miami Hurricanes.

David Stepp, former Vice President, Group Marketing Manager of Great Western Bank, discussed the strategy in pursuing sports promotions for a major financial institution and identified relationships as the key element to a successful sports promotion.*

*Mr. Stepp left Great Western in early 1995 to join Union Bank.

PHILOSOPHY

We are in this business for the fan, not the team. Every fan that goes to a game needs a checking account, the core of our business. One day, that fan will need a home loan. How can we get them to come to us? Promoting a team is not the total answer but it fits into our overall scheme of bringing positive community presence to our company.

The team's performance is secondary. The A's, for example, have very loyal fans. The team has done a great job of identifying with their community. Whether they are in first place, or last place, the A's relationship with the community is very important, and something that Great Western does not want to lose. The key is to take the promotion and make it work for both the bank and the community.

For example, we have a program with the Golden State Warriors that raises money for six local high school sports programs. At each Warriors home game, we conduct a silent auction of autographed merchandise, and we have raised some good money for the schools.

Next season, we will make a display wall and take it on a tour to various branches. Our public relations department will put together a series of press releases to go out to the local newspapers, and we might be able to get some publicity for our branches, the Warriors, and our mutual efforts to raise money for high school sports. Our branches are simply businesses within the community that can give something back and create goodwill. In this case, the added value of the Warrior's promotion can help us do exactly that.

STRATEGY

Virtually all of our deals are long-term deals. We try to establish relationship programs with all of our teams and sports buys. We generally look for a three-to-five-year deal with an escape clause at the end of each year. The escape clause allows us to break our deal at the end of any year of the contract by paying a penalty. It is necessary because of the nature of the economy, and the business forces that can potentially affect the banking industry.

But the long-term deals, frankly, give Great Western more leverage. It makes us more valuable to the supplier, because they know that we are committed to working with them to come up with programs that make sense for the bank and the team. Our deal with the A's started as an open ended relationship. One year we bought a stadium billboard as a piece of our deal, and then later on down the line, they call and ask if we want to put an ATM machine in the stadium. ATM's are not cheap, but it is nice as a financial services company to be able to provide an actual service at the ballpark.

Another key issue for us is exclusivity. We have to have it, and we pay for it. Great Western refers to many of its sports sponsorships as fixed position sponsorships. This is a media term which means that we buy specific times where our ads will run during the course of a broadcast. There are no spot buys, and certainly no presence of a competitor. Through these fixed position buys, we achieve the frequency of our message to the audience. So during the course of a game, they will hear "brought to you by Great Western Bank," over and over.

However, exclusivity to Great Western does not mean that the team cannot work with another financial institution at all. We understand that the team needs to make money, and we do not interfere in all forms of promotions, but we protect our median and signage interests. If Bank of America wants to give away a bag with its name on it, fine. Of course, Great Western wants to know about the promotional opportunity in advance, and to have the right of first refusal. That way, there are no surprises when your institution has clients at the game, and all of a sudden, your competitor is visibly present.

Lastly, all sports marketing expenditures have to justify themselves from a media standpoint. As a public company, Great Western has obligations to its shareholders. In considering a proposal, the promotion must generate media to merit our consideration.

The Importance of Relationships

Money does not buy relationships in sports promotion. Furthermore, one cannot expect to make a relationship with a couple of phone calls. The two parties need to agree to certain terms and the concept of exploring other issues over a period of time. By taking the time to work together, the two parties develop the necessary flexibility to try new ideas and better serve each others' purposes. For instance, the Warriors silent auction program has been so successful that we have taken it to the Los Angeles Kings and Lakers. For the Lakers, it is the Magic Johnson Foundation. The Kings have a range of charities, like the Big Brothers, that participate. Due to the relationships with these teams, we had the leverage to run these programs.

In marketing terms, companies do not get added value from media purchases. When a company buys a two-million-dollar media buy, they know exactly what they are getting. There is nothing except the actual advertising time. But with sports, companies get intangibles. Coupons in the season ticket holder mailers, extra ads in the game programs. When Great Western buys into a sports sponsorship, we buy into a relationship. For example, the Warriors will call me up to tell me that they held a chalktalk speech with Chuck Daly, and that they put up our banners and gave us sponsor mention. Then they will say that they are holding another talk, and invite us to bring twenty special guests. Things like that can make a sponsor very happy.

The Case of the Great Western Forum

One interesting relationship is with Dr. Jerry Buss, current owner of the Los Angeles Lakers and the Great Western Forum. It all started years ago when he came to Great Western at a time when he owned both the Lakers and the Kings and said that he was going to start a cable sports network named Prime Ticket. He wanted Great Western to be a charter advertiser. At the time, we made a huge, long-term commitment, which hindsight has proven to be a great investment.

After the Kings were sold, Dr. Buss proposed renaming the Fabulous Forum as the Great Western Forum. Fortunately, the people at Great Western agreed. In essence, it is a big outdoor billboard that generates a lot of media. Every time there is a televised event, the building gets a lot of attention. And any time there is an event there, all of the print ads and publicity enhance our relationship with the Forum.

From our standpoint, the second phase of this particular promotion is to make people aware that The Great Western Forum refers to the bank. We have scoreboard messages and dasher boards [a digital sign as in a bar] inside the facility that refer to the bank itself. We need to reinforce the message that we are a bank. It is not enough to simply put your name on the building.

Our involvement with the Forum allows us to get involved in event sponsorship like the Great Western Bank Rodeo or the Great Western Bank Team Cup Volleyball. We had a college hockey tournament, and that was a success. The Forum arrangement is impossible to quantify. It gives us a tie to two teams that receive tremendous support from the community. The media exposure and traffic that the building receives makes this a successful arrangement. People like the Kings and the Lakers. For that reason, we need to take advantage of our opportunity to talk to the fans.

Analysis

In the services business, it is difficult to quantify sports marketing. It has to make sense from a media standpoint. Every sports promotion purchase must deliver the Gross Ratings Points that we need. In our business, the financial services business, we look at our business as a whole. If the checking account business has grown tremendously, great. Has the Sports marketing contributed to this? Definitely. How much? We do not know.

Sports is not a priority to our company. Great Western's priority is to open more branches and have more loan agents in the field. As a public company, we have an obligation to the shareholders. Great Western Bank needs to keep everyone involved, from potential customers to clients. As long as a sports promotion can help Great Western achieve its goals, it will be considered.

The Future of Sports Marketing in the Services Industry

It takes a long time to bring change to any industry. But all of us in the sports marketing field have an obligation to ensure the future. There are no new athletes for professional leagues if the schools can't have the programs. With respect to the major colleges, those are highly developed businesses in their own right. There are some interesting sponsorship opportunities at the collegiate level, and that will help support their athletics, but there should be concern for the fate of the high schools.

We, the sponsors, should develop a high school sports foundation where I sit down the representatives from Coke and Chevron and devise programs that can work for us and the schools. As a fan, people might not like to see the corporate banners on a high school fence, but without that banner, there might be no fence. A very real danger is negative public perception of commercializing high school sports.

On a professional level, people might be less enchanted with the athletes and the teams. If there is no fan support because the team is alienated, then the sponsorship is not worth anything. If the communities do not support the teams, then maybe they will rally behind the colleges and high schools.

But people love to go to baseball games and basketball games. The heroes are now known as real people, and the entertainment and enjoyment of sports will not go away.

7

The Media and Broadcast Industry

> Monday night, San Francisco's Jerry Rice wore on his nose a plastic CNS Inc. Breathe Right strip, . . . Tuesday, CNS' stock rose 11%.
>
> —Michael Hiestand, *USA Today**

In 1951, the DuMont Network paid $75,000 for the rights to televise the NFL Championship Game between the Cleveland Browns and Los Angeles Rams.[1] This was a landmark investment, for it was the first television broadcast rights sale for championship football. Forty-three years later, the NFL's all-time leading touchdown scorer (Jerry Rice), wore the aforementioned CNS® strip during a Monday Night Football telecast, bringing attention, discussion, and notoriety to an unknown product. The resulting popularity and publicity of the CNS® strip validates the importance of television exposure in sports marketing applications. Seen by millions of viewers, the incomparable Jerry Rice and the unique strip made a great impression on the broadcasters, viewers, and CNS® investors.

No one would ever say that the 11 percent rise in CNS®' stock is 100 percent attributed to Jerry Rice's usage, but it is more than a coincidence. The publicity from the ABC prime time telecast (approximately thirty million viewers), and the newsprint attention in the nation's most widely read newspaper (circulation greater than 1.5 mil-

*Jerry Rice wore the strip on a "Monday Night Football" game in 1994.

lion, with a readership of six million), publicized the product (actually an anti-snoring device).

The broadcast media, i.e., radio and television, has created indelible images of personalities like Olga Korbut, Pele, Franz Klammer, Henry Aaron, Joe Louis, Michael Jordan, Joe Montana, and thousands more. Athletes have become a part of the international culture, immortalized through their exploits analyzed by broadcasters. Television and radio are integral parts of our everyday lives. We all watch and listen for many reasons: to be entertained, informed, distracted, exhilarated, amused, and bewildered. The airwaves serve many purposes, and it makes sense that marketing efforts run through the broadcast channels as well.

Virtually every marketing plan has an electronic media angle. Campbell's hired Nancy Kerrigan in 1994 to be a spokesperson for its soups. She was included in its largest campaign ever: "Never underestimate the power of soup." Campbell's recognized that skating is the highest-rated sporting event among females, its target consumer. Using Kerrigan, a healthy, wholesome, and talented skater ties in sports and soup, two staples of the American culture. Companies use television to tie images together, usually of a brand and an element of competition. The appreciation of sports is a significant part of all cultures, and commercial broadcasts on the radio and television airwaves both celebrate and financially exploit that fact.

Companies spend millions of dollars to put their names in conjunction with the potential excitement of sporting events. General Motors happily spent $12 million on CBS's NCAA Men's Basketball Tournament.[2] The car manufacturer likes the educated, high income demographics of college basketball, and it backs up its interest with a financial investment. And if firms cannot buy spots that interrupt the competition, they will try to place their logos in the action somewhere, on the athletes clothing, on a car, near the court or field, somewhere/anywhere so that the millions at home can see the association of the companies and the action.

The Industry

Television and radio broadcasting is not only about sports entertainment and event revenue maximization. It is a full-circle industry where companies place advertising commitments to many types of programming. Table 1 shows 1993's top advertisers for all types of programming.

Table 1.
Leading Advertisers for 1993[3]

Company	Amount
Procter & Gamble	$624,000,000
General Motors	$454,000,000
Philip Morris	$374,000,000
PepsiCo	$310,000,000

Sports entertainment accounts for a large portion of this budget. By 1992, companies were spending over $1.5 billion annually advertising on sports broadcasts.[4] Furthermore, two of the three most expensive spots in annual advertising are for sporting events, the Super Bowl ($1 million per thirty seconds in 1995) and the NCAA college basketball Championship Game ($400,000 per thirty-second spot in 1994). Both events occur during inclement weather seasons, and attract enthusiastic viewers and advertisers.

Companies advertise via the broadcast networks because it works. At least one television set was on in each home for an average of 7.32 hours per day in 1992. Advertisers know that someone is listening and/or watching. Most importantly, sports deliver a broad based demographic of attentive fans. The advertising fees that networks earn are justifiable because the research substantiates their investment decisions. The Super Bowl, the highest commercial fee in all of television, had an average advertisement recall of 66 percent in sampled viewers (1993), which was almost triple the recall rate for prime time programming on the day after recall (23 percent).

In 1950, there were ninety-eight commercial television stations on the air and only 9 percent, or 3,800,000 households with television sets. By 1993, there were 1,541 commercial television stations broadcasting to 93,100,000 households, or 98 percent of American homes.[5] Additionally, cable television is available in 62 percent of American homes, and the number of pay-cable subscribers has risen from 140,000 homes in 1975 (0.2 percent of American television households), to 25,900,000 (27.8 percent of homes) in 1993.[6] This proliferation of channels, programs, and customers, that is, the viewers, has played right into the hands of sports entertainment and its advertisers.

By 1994, BJK&E Media Group calculated that Americans were watching an average of 179 hours of sports programming annually; events like cycling, skating, skiing, tennis, golf, football, basketball, and baseball on all levels of competition, from the Little League World Series in Williamsport, Pennsylvania (ABC), to the College World Series (ESPN) in Omaha, Nebraska. Despite the saturation of events and multiplication of channels and programming outlets, companies rely on television exposure to advertise their products. Table 2 shows what sports spending stalwarts spent on broadcast advertising in the first six months of 1994 (as reported by *Advertising Age*).

Table 2.
1994 Broadcast Advertising Costs

Company	$ Rank	Amount Spent
Nike	46	$68 million
NordicTrack®	75	$40 million
Reebok	82	$38 million
Gatorade®	160	$22 million

In the time that broadcast interests have aligned themselves with sporting events, the two entities have spread the popularity of existing sports and its competitors, given corporate access to event entertainment, and simultaneously created the huge spiral of wealth within the sports industry. Broadcasting brings expanded dimensions to events that govern social choices, influence consumer behavior, and generate revenue. For example, the 1994 World Cup was an elimination tournament of teams representing twenty-four countries and fifty-two games in a bracketed elimination format. The games were attended by 3.5 million fans, and it generated $4 billion of business activity in the United States, but television generated a worldwide viewership of more than thirty billion people over the course of the tournament. Television multiplied the audience for the World Cup, like it does for every broadcast event, for the sport, its fans, *and* its sponsors.

But the key consumer audience is in the United States, mainly because it is the wealthiest nation, and because the majority of the sponsors, Coca-Cola, McDonald's, Nike, MasterCard, Sprint, and Anheuser-Busch are American companies. It was critical to do well here in the host country. And the results were positive. Nielsen ratings showed that the July 4 U.S.A.-Brazil match received a 10.4 rating, or 27 percent share, almost a full four ratings points higher than the prior highest ratings for soccer. The real test, though, was for the championship game featuring Brazil and Italy. The July 4 game had a natural interest in the home team, but this game was decidedly about the sport, and not about bandwagon nationalism. The World Cup Organizing Committee was proud to report that the game, played at the Rose Bowl (Pasadena, California), had the highest paid attendance in the history of sporting events ($43.5 million), and it captured a 12.4 rating, or 29 percent share, a new standard for a U.S. soccer audience. Table 3 shows a breakdown of the viewing audience.

Table 3.
World Cup Audience Breakdown (Associated Press)

Region	Total Number of Viewers*
Asia	14.8 billion
Eastern Europe	4.6 billion
Latin America	3.9 billion
Western Europe	3.2 billion
Africa	3.1 billion
North America/Caribbean	1.2 billion
Middle East	500 million
Pacific	20 million

*Total number of viewers over the course of the tournament

Television is the main determining factor of league scheduling, for example, night games, so that a larger audience can see the game, and the ads will be priced accordingly. Television influences banner placement and billboards in stadiums. It used to be that the best billboard was next to the scoreboard because fans constantly referred to it. Now, the most expensive logo placement is the one that will be most visible on television. It is the same with logos on clothing items. Tennis players, golfers, and runners all wear logos on areas that are visible during play.

Athletes in these categories receive large endorsement contracts because they are large, charismatic billboards. During the course of competition, the logo generates millions of impressions that companies hope will parlay into sales. It was estimated that the 1991 NASCAR season returned $219 million in paid advertising through the logos on the race cars.[7] Each televised NASCAR event had twenty-six minutes worth of exposure and seventy-seven mentions.

Furthermore, the industry has evolved to the point where analysts supply both the buyers and sellers with relevant information pertaining to broadcast advertising.[8] Some examples are:

What is the wealthiest television audience?	Tennis fans.
What is the poorest (least affluent)?	Baseball fans.
What event is watched by the most women?	Figure skating.
What sport has the oldest audience?	Horse racing.
How many viewers of NFL football are women?	41 percent.
What sport has the youngest audience?	The NBA.
Who is the most recognizable sports personality?	Michael Jordan.

Information like the above goes into the analysis of both packaging (selling) and purchasing a part or parts of the broadcast rights to a sports property. The same sports marketing issues of category exclusivity, permissions rights for merchandising/licensing, and right of first refusal/renewal etc. all apply to the broadcasting of an event. All sports fans have heard the announcement: "all rights to this broadcast, any rebroadcast, or retransmission are the exclusive property of (name your favorite network) and any use without the expressed written consent of (same broadcaster), or the (name of league) is prohibited." Networks pay a lot of money for the rights to say that statement. It indicates their ownership, and networks protect that right.

Protection by leagues and governing bodies regulate the items that can be displayed to avoid individual athletes generating too much money independently. A celebrated case involved Jim McMahon of the Chicago Bears during the 1985 Super Bowl. McMahon wore an Adidas turtleneck underneath his jersey that prominently displayed the logo. Pete Rozelle, the NFL's commissioner implemented legislation not allowing players to wear clothing featuring logos other than that of the NFL and its teams. McMahon responded by wearing an Adidas Headband, and that was disallowed. Finally, on the road to the Super Bowl, McMahon wore a headband simply saying "Rozelle." And, during the Super Bowl, he wore an Adidas headband around his neck. Both individuals made their points, but the underlying force was the persuasive power of television and its reinforcement of commercial images seamlessly embedded in sports entertainment events. Rozelle wanted to protect the league's advertising control, and McMahon wanted to give Adidas, his sponsor, added exposure.

In broadcasting, it is essential to understand that the buyers become sellers. Networks buy the event in order to sell it to a variety of sponsor interests. They also create commercial events such as the Skins Game. In regards to the Event Triangle's broadcast model, the television is the facility for the entertainers and sponsors. The George Foreman-Michael Moorer fight took place before more than 10,000 people at the MGM Grand Hotel in Las Vegas, but five million households with HBO saw the boxing match in the comfort of their homes.

When George Foreman, the forty-five-year-old hero to everyone, knocked out champion Michael Moorer with a crisp right cross, HBO viewers witnessed what could have been the richest punch in the history of pugilism.* Television made it possible for George Foreman to capture the imagination of the world.

Industry Breakdown

The broadcast industry currently has four major players:

1. Radio
2. Network television
3. Cable television
4. Pay cable television

*Foreman eventually fought Axel Schulz of Germany in the Spring of 1995 and retired as champion when Mike Tyson rejected Foreman's offer for a bout, which, experts say, would have been the highest grossing bout of all time.

RADIO

The forerunner to television, radio was the original device that spread the legend of athletes like Babe Ruth, Joe DiMaggio, Red Grange, Jack Dempsey, and other greats from the early twentieth century. Radio was not the largest financial component of sporting events, but more of a publicity tool. The promoters needed the attention, and the print and radio media controlled the information monopoly.

Although that is not the case today, radio still is a productive revenue source for professional sports and the burgeoning sports talk radio industry boasts a total of 130 stations featuring exclusive sports formats. According to the Radio Advertising Bureau, total ad spending on the radio airwaves was a healthy $8.9 billion in 1992. Radio has flexibility, identifiable markets, and effective reach. Even in professional football, where television is king, radio has retained a profitable niche, on both a national and regional level. (See Table 4 for 1994 Radio rights fees.) CBS pays the NFL an average of $1.2 million per annum to broadcast nationally on its affiliated networks. In their own markets, teams combine to earn more than $54 million from radio broadcasting rights.[9]

The radio will always be a place where fans can tune in to follow their teams and/or hear the news of the sports world. Because if a game is not in progress, sports information is on the dial somewhere.

NETWORK TELEVISION

The four major networks are ABC, CBS, NBC, and Fox. Their programming is regulated by federal laws and available to the public without incidental or indiscriminate charges like monthly billing. As Cable television systems and other pieces of the "Information Superhighway's" infrastructure are built and installed, customers will have full access to programming options but they will have to purchase the broadcast packages that include cable companies' programming like ESPN, Lifetime, the Discovery Channel, and TNT.

The major networks air all or part of many major sporting events involving the United States, and/or its athletes, teams, and competitions. These networks pay fees to event owners for the rights to broadcast their events as they take place. For example, NBC paid Notre Dame University $38 million for the five-year national rights to broadcast its games. As an independent school (not associated with a collegiate conference), Notre

Dame could negotiate that deal. The University of Washington does not have the same leverage as a member of the Pac-10 Conference. The conference negotiates on behalf of the ten athletic participants, a six-year $119 million package with ABC and ESPN, which the schools divide evenly.

Table 4.
1994 Team Radio Rights Fees[10]

Team	Radio Station	Annual Fee
Chicago Bears	WGN	4,500,000
San Francisco 49ers	KGO	4,000,000
Dallas Cowboys	KVIL	3,750,000
Washington Redskins	WTEM (AM) WBIG (FM)	3,500,000
New York Giants	WOR	2,800,000
Los Angeles Raiders	KFI	2,600,000
Denver Broncos	KOA	2,500,000
Seattle Seahawks	KIRO	2,500,000
Los Angeles Rams	KMPC	2,400,000
Miami Dolphins	WIOD and WQBA	2,100,000 (combined)
Philadelphia Eagles	WYSP	2,000,000
New York Jets	WFAN	1,600,000
New England Patriots	WBZ	1,600,000
Houston Oilers	KTRH	1,500,000
Kansas City Chiefs	KCFX	1,500,000
Pittsburgh Steelers	WTAE (AM) WVTY (FM)	1,500,000
Detroit Lions	WWJ	1,500,000
Minnesota Vikings	KFAN (AM) KEEY (FM)	1,400,000
Atlanta Falcons	WSB	1,400,000
Buffalo Bills	WBEN	1,200,000
Tampa Bay Buccaneers	WQYK	1,100,000
New Orleans Saints	WQUE	1,000,000
Cincinatti Bengals	WCKY	1,000,000
Green Bay packers	WTMJ	800,000
Indianapolis Colts	WNDE (AM) WFBQ (FM)	800,000

The major networks bid on a number of athletic properties from auto racing to the Olympics. They pay fees to the organizers and go out and sell advertising space and features, such as Fox's McDonald's Game Break (a highlight/update feature), to clients. The networks work with the leagues under federal jurisdiction to provide access to sports entertainment in a fair and equitable manner. In other words, broadcasting laws are consistent with the idea to help local teams present their product in their markets, but not at the expense of profitability. The NFL, for example, will not broadcast a game in its local market if it is not sold out. The idea is to encourage stadium ticket sales. Therefore, if the Cincinnati Bengals game has seats available twenty-four hours before kickoff, the blackout is instituted and the metropolitan Cincinnati area will see a different game in the time slot offered by conference broadcaster NBC.

An application of the blackout rule and its effects indicate the structural limitations of the NFL's broadcasting capacity. In November 1994, the Los Angeles Rams and Los Angles Raiders played to a sellout crowd in Anaheim, thus lifting the blackout rule and allowing the game to be televised in the nation's largest television market. This was the first Ram sellout since November 1992, and it featured an attractive matchup of the two local teams. It was, however, the same day (and same time) as the San Francisco 49er-Dallas Cowboy game 400 miles north at Candlestick Park. Obviously, the 49er game was more attractive to national advertisers and fans alike, but it was unavailable in Los Angeles because of the stringent broadcasting laws that pertain to NFL network broadcasts. The Rams-Raiders game was carried by NBC, and it had to be televised in the local market (1:00 P.M.). Fox, therefore, could not air a 1:00 P.M. game that would compete against the Ram-Raider game on NBC. The "no doubleheader" rule states that one network cannot televise two games in a market where an NFL game is being played. So despite having paid $1.58 billion for the rights to broadcast NFL action, Fox could only broadcast a 10:00 A.M. (Pacific Standard Time) game in the Los Angeles market, which featured the Chicago Bears at the Miami Dolphins. One would think that $1.58 billion would go a little further in influencing league policy, but apparently the NFL has nothing in common with political parties.

The rules intend to protect both the broadcasters and the teams in local markets. This case hurt the financial potential of Fox, and the enthusiasm of football fans. Denied the choice of programming, viewers throughout Southern California could not watch the superior matchup of the two-time defending Super Bowl champion Dallas Cowboys and four-time Super Bowl champion San Francisco 49ers. But misery loves company, and fans in Boston, Green Bay-Milwaukee, Miami, New Orleans, and New York could not get either parts or all of the game due to similar circumstances.*

An overlooked, but equally important component of network television, is the *affiliate* relationship. Affiliates are the stations not owned by the network, but licensed contractors of the affiliated broadcasting network. The exchange gives the network a place to distribute its products such as news and programmed entertainment, and it gives the local station high-profile vehicles, such as the NBA and the NFL to sell. The commercial arrangement divides the inventory for events. For the 1995 NFC Championship game example, Fox had fifty-eight game units of thirty-second commercial segments,[11] and it gave its affiliates a total of ten thirty-second segments to sell.[12] KTVU, the San Francisco affiliate, apparently realized approximately $500,000 for the segments in its own market. Furthermore, KTVU has its own pregame and postgame show opportunities, a lucrative draw. Given the fact that Northern California weather was at a historical worst for the championship game, KTVU had a trapped audience, perfect for sales.

Cable Television

Cable broadcasts to 62 percent of U.S. households and is a niche-oriented service, offering choice to viewers. The cable industry generally bids on a part of a sports property, allowing a major network to fund and carry the majority. For example, ABC, NBC, and Fox carried the bulk of NFL action, but TNT and ESPN divided the late-night Sunday evening game broadcast fights in 1994. TNT aired late night gridiron action in the first half of the season, and ESPN the second. Cable is also the place for second-rate fare, from unknowns in boxing, to the wild world of professional wrestling. Sometimes it can even be quite valuable, as in the case of the World Wrestling Federation, which generates between $15 and $20 million in annual ad revenues.

---

*They couldn't watch the game unless they had a satellite dish, the pay-per-view NFL Season Ticket package (a viewing package for the fans so they can watch the games of their choice, not the games the NFL dictates), or a neighborhood sports bar equipped with one of the above.

Sporting events find valuable places on cable networks such as USA, TNT, and ESPN. The USA Network has consistently broadcast extended coverage of the U.S. Tennis Open and golf's prestigious Masters. This allows total event coverage for events that span several days, such as golf and tennis tournaments. By carrying early action, event fans can see it in its entirety. USA will carry the opening half of a tournament, and the primary network the conclusion. For example, USA will carry the first two days of the Masters (Thursday and Friday), and CBS will broadcast the Saturday and Sunday rounds. This collaboration allows the event to be broadcast in its entirety without impinging upon CBS' regular daytime programming. Furthermore, the networks' partnership enhances the spectacle of the event for the PGA, the Masters host committee, the players, and the sponsors. If Cadillac wants to advertise during CBS' weekend telecast, they might want to take advantage of USA's introductory coverage.

When Jimmy Connors made his memorable and improbable march to the U.S. Open quarterfinals in 1991, tennis fans were able to see it, because of USA's comprehensive coverage. The unexpected, dramatic elements of major sports championships deserve coverage. Through the proliferation of cable systems and channels, fans can enjoy these events from start to finish. Serving sixty-two million households, with 12,500 affiliates, the USA Network brings comprehensive coverage to sports fans and advertisers. Some programming properties of the USA network include:

Tennis: French Open
U.S. Open
Golf: AT&T Pebble Beach Pro-Am
The Players Championship
The Masters
PGA Seniors' Championship
NEC World Series of Golf
1995 Ryder Cup Matches

PAY CABLE TELEVISION

HBO, Showtime, and all pay-per-view (PPV) outlets are penetrating the threshold of consumers and are a legitimate power in sports programming. Pay cable stations either feature a one-time event such as boxing, or a subscription to a host of games and events, i.e., Prime Ticket, HBO, and SportsChannel. Even ESPN and ABC are getting into the picture by offering a college football package of games where individual games are $9.95, and a season ticket of twelve costs $59.95. The industry estimates this venture (ABC and ESPN are both owned by Capital Cities) to have generated $2 million in revenue in 1993 (150,000 buys).[13]

Single events, however, are not the only source of revenues for pay cable broadcasters. Regional cable broadcasters package and sell programming of amateur and professional sorts. Prime Ticket (80 million in revenue)[14] in Southern California reaches approximately four million homes in California, Arizona, Nevada, and Hawaii, and features the Anaheim Mighty Ducks, California Angels, and San Diego Padres.

The Prime Ticket Network was sold to TCI, a large cable conglomerate, because of its ability to sell both subscriptions and advertising, and because they are developing the niche of Spanish language broadcasting, "Prime Ticket La Cadena Deportiva"—the first all-Spanish, total-sports network, currently broadcasting into 900,000 homes in Southern California, a significant market.

Pay cable is the perfect platform for new concepts in sports programming. One new venture that will test this new market is The Golf Channel. The Golf Channel broadcasts approximately twenty-five American and forty international golfing events and shows like "GolfCenter." Priced at a reasonable $6.95 per month, the Golf Channel will bring a new approach to the tradition-laden game of golf. The venture will test new formats, players, tournaments, broadcast styles, and sponsor-driven business. It is quite possibly the forerunner to an all pay-per-view format to all golfing events. Partly owned by the PGA, and with Arnold Palmer as chairman, the Golf Channel is a well-conceived venture designed to increase access to great golfing action for its fans.

Pay-Per-View (PPV)

As the name succinctly states: if you want to watch, you have to pay. This is an emerging industry that will become a significant determinant in the future of all sporting events and cable systems across America and probably around the world. But the future of PPV is dependent upon future governmental legislation and standardized technology.

The legislation will allow promoters to package and price the entertainment, which discriminates against viewers that do not have PPV technology, and/or do not currently pay for it directly, because the networks own the rights. Legislation is certain to come with the digital express, i.e., Information Superhighway. The much ballyhooed Information Superhighway will bring variety and quantity in terms of choices to viewers. It is currently estimated that airwave piracy of sporting events costs the industry $3 billion annually.[15]

But despite the pains, the menu is growing for sports on PPV. Elite boxing matches, such as Holyfield-Foreman, have sold for as much as $39.95, while a Cincinnati Reds game in 1992 could be had for $4.95. If hockey was your sport and you lived in Illinois, a Blackhawks game could be purchased electronically for only $19.95. As digital systems and online services are installed and implemented, this industry will explode and be a significant competitor to traditional event broadcasters.

But the biggest star is championship boxing. Due to the proven popularity of pay-per-view (PPV) for Boxing's super-fights like Bowe versus Holyfield, the four major networks do not even bid on the fights. With PPV, fights can earn more than $100 million, for potentially less than one round (three minutes) of actual action. No network could recoup that kind of investment with commercial interruption and other forms of sponsorship. But cable operatives reap the benefits. Evander Holyfield's matches against Buster Douglas and George Foreman in 1990 and 1991 grossed $85 million dollars combined, and Mike Tyson's two fights against Razor Ruddock grossed $75 million.

Pay-per-view is not always about multimillion-dollar windfalls, however. NBC lost over $50 million with their Triplecast pay-per-view offering for the 1992 Olympics. The viewing benefits (beyond total coverage and access) were not clear to a leery public. But the experiment paved the way for future ventures and gave valuable feedback to the value of an event's revenue producing power. NBC took its financial loss and its humility lumps, but led the vanguard into the ambitious world of pay-cable television and premier sporting events.

Ratings

Ratings are simply the means by which an audience's size is determined. And audience size is the single most important determinant in both pricing and selling units of broadcast advertising. One television ratings point is equal to 954,000 homes with television sets. Whether or not viewers watch or remember the commercials is yet another debate, but the first step is to put the commercial in a place where it can be seen. television has certainly proved itself on that premise.

Perhaps one of the best attributes of television advertising and promotion is the feedback from the investment. Networks are fed results of the audience in less than forty-eight hours after the event. The much hyped Dallas Cowboy-San Francisco 49er regular season clash on Fox (November 13, 1994) lived up to its billing as the 49ers vanquished their demons of the 1990s, the Cowboys, in four thrilling quarters of intense competition. Everyone had their game faces on. The studio team of Terry Bradshaw, Howie Long, Jimmy Johnson, and James Brown analyzed each angle of the game, broke down the matchups, and by the time the game announcers, Pat Summerall and John Madden, chimed in with their own sentiments, fans were tingling with anticipation. But behind the scenes, Fox executives were holding their collective breath, for this was the first *big* game that the network had televised. It was going to be closely watched, and Fox needed a smooth performance to prove its status as a premier sports broadcaster.

The report card is always the ratings, and they were in print less than forty-eight hours later, a 22.3 overnight rating in the twenty-seven broadcast markets that carried the game, and in combination with the other half of the doubleheader (Miami-Chicago), the overnight doubleheader rating was a nineteen, one of the five highest Sunday telecasts since 1986.

The implications of the ratings go beyond the obvious return on investment issues. Often times, networks sell advertising spots, or more accurately, the rates for advertising spots at a guaranteed ratings level. Broadcasters will give sponsors "make-good" assurances. "Make-goods" mean that if an event does not achieve specified ratings, then the broadcaster (either radio or television) will give additional commercial placements to the advertiser (on any combination of mutually agreed upon events) at no additional cost.

The Subsidy Mechanism

Events live and die by broadcast subsidy. By securing rights fees, sports leagues and promoters not only gain the actual financial commitment, but they benefit from the added value of franchise development of the property. Merely by televising an event, the broadcasters bring an audience. The audience is not a directly paying customer, except for cable and/or pay-per-view fees, but they do pay indirectly. The flow of the game is interrupted so that those sponsors can talk to the viewers. During Super Bowl XXVII, for example, the actual playing time of the game was only fifteen minutes and forty-two seconds, whereas commercial time was forty-three minutes and thirty seconds. The other two hours and twenty-three minutes of the broadcast were for huddles, halftime, measurements, penalties, and game administration.[16]

Networks purchase the rights from leagues (NFL), representing organization (IMG), or individual promoters (Don King). After purchasing the entity and the entitlement restrictions and/or corollary agreements that are attached to the sale, the actual broadcast is split up and divided in sections, blocks, or modules defined as commercial inventory. The inventory is then packaged and sold to a collection of advertisers who desperately want to communicate with the solid, consistent, loyal sports audience. When the mechanism is clearly defined and substantiated by past results, the rights fee benchmark has been established and the competitive bidding process begins. If the event is a prestigious one like the Olympics or Super Bowl, then it can be a seller's market.

According to *Mediaweek,* Fox reportedly bought the following from the National Hockey League:

- Five-year rights package for $150,000,000.
- Nine regular season games.
- Nine playoff games.

That would mean that Fox is paying over $1.5 million per game and at normal ad sequences, would need to sell ads in excess of $30,000 in order to break even after the production fees. Fox's sales staff will present packages offering tickets, category exclusivity, and early access to the franchise of hockey, a sport whose popularity is rising. Most importantly, Fox is gambling that hockey's payoff is in the near future. As sponsorships blend in many details, such as licensing, merchandising, and media opportunities, the popularity of the league will soar and the rights fees will be recouped through enthusiastic ad support. Additionally, hockey's core audience of young males fits in with Fox's programming and may enhance ratings for other shows, specials, and sports. Undoubtedly, Fox is looking for efficiencies to develop in its own business strategy, and is hoping that hockey will deliver much more than simple commercial sales opportunities.

Major League Baseball had a four-year, $1.06 billion deal with CBS, netting the league (the team owners) $265 million per annum. When CBS encountered a flat ad market and tough World Series matchups of small market teams (Oakland versus Cincinnati) in a short series (1990 World Series lasted four games), the network lost a significant amount of money. When negotiations began for the next contract, both the league and broadcasters knew that $265 million was not a realistic figure to expect. ABC and NBC offered a straight revenue sharing program amounting to 40 percent of ad receipts. CBS countered with an offer of $120 million in fees plus revenue sharing once a revenue threshold of $150 million was attained.

Perhaps to show their employees, primarily the players, a willingness to embrace the concept of revenue sharing, the owners boldly created The Baseball Network (TBN) in 1994. TBN is a joint venture between ABC, NBC, and Major League baseball to test the waters of a risk/reward scenario with each other. Both sides have the option to rescind the deal if TBN fails to make $330 million in its first two years (a certainty because of the 1994 labor strike), and binds them only for three years of mutual pursuit otherwise. With the broadcast viability of baseball regionalized, including the absence of a veritable cash-cow franchise like the NFL's Monday Night Football, baseball needs to experiment with formats and strategies to position its product for the next generation of viewers and entertainment competitors.*

The sponsor-broadcaster mechanism also works for analysis purposes. The ratings, or audience statistics, are readily available just days after the broadcast. The A. C. Nielsen Company reliably gauges the audience through its aforementioned ratings system. Oftentimes, net-

*The Baseball Network was dissolved in a 1995 announcement made by ABC and NBC, effective at the end of the contract with Major League Baseball.

works will guarantee an audience size to sponsors, and if those ratings are not met, then the broadcaster will refund (normally in advertising trade barter) a percentage back to the paying advertiser.

Rights Fees

These can vary. Simply put, the rights fee is the price paid to broadcast (and rebroadcast) either all or part of the event occurring over a mutually agreed upon time frame. The terms and considerations according to the agreement are added to the contract before it is executed by both parties. For example, Capital Cities, ABC's parent company and 80 percent owner of ESPN, paid $11 million for the domestic rights to the 1994 World Cup. ABC televised eleven of the matches, and ESPN the remaining forty-one.

The NFL debated giving rebates to its broadcast partners as late as early 1993, before Fox television made the blockbuster offer of $1.58 billion for four years. The NBA recently sold the next four years of broadcasting rights to NBC and TNT for a total of $1 billion. Notre Dame sold its gridiron broadcast rights to NBC for $38 million over four years. The NCAA's basketball tournament, featuring the top sixty-four teams, cost CBS $1 billion for seven years. Wimbledon's last contract netted $25 million from partners HBO and NBC. The Olympics are fast approaching the $500 million mark.

But rights fees can go the other way. NBC purchased the Mobil Cotton Bowl in 1992 for $2.75 million (for three years). No small fee; however, CBS, the prior broadcaster, had paid $4.1 million. The World Gymnastics fee plummeted from $2.5 million to a relatively minuscule $300,000 in the same time span, and the fledgling World League of American Football saw its bottom line slashed by 50 percent in 1992 ($26 million to $13 million). The US Olympic Trials, the preeminent track and field event in the United States also suffered a 50 percent reduction in broadcast revenues ($4 million to $2 million), and the esteemed Tour de France endured the unkindest cut of all. It got bumped from a major broadcast network (ABC) to a cable station (ESPN), and saw their rights fee fall from $1 million to zero. The Tour de France still needs to air the race to get all of those billboards, jerseys, and water bottle logos beamed to North America, so they will take nothing for the event, even though this bicycle race has one of the grandest traditions in all of competitive sports.

The general rule is, if no one watches, no one will pay, nor will someone broadcast it. If people will watch it, but not too many, someone will broadcast it, but will not pay to do so. Finally, if an event does draw a large, defined audience, several broadcasters will bid wildly for it.

Once an event has a broadcast slot (e.g., Saturday, 1:00 P.M.), the broadcaster unleashes a sales force on media buying agencies around the country, primarily New York and Los Angeles. The agencies manage enormous budgets for these clients, and want certifiable proof that a certain type of audience, the client's target consumers, will be watching somewhere. Placing these advertisements with an event's audience effectively heightens awareness of a product or service.

The commercial airwaves and sporting events bring audiences and sponsors together. Their popularity cannot be denied:

- Five of the top ten rated shows of all-time are sporting events: Four Super Bowls and the 1994 Winter Olympic figure-skating competition featuring Tonya Harding and Nancy Kerrigan.
- The cable network with the most subscribers is ESPN (CNN is number two).
- The highest ad rates are charged for the Super Bowl ($1 million per thirty seconds for ABC's Super Bowl XXIX in January 1995).
- The most watched event in world history was the 1994 World Cup (thirty billion total viewers).

With captive audiences defined by such great numbers, the financial context of broadcast properties has grown tremendously. For example, in 1992 the rights to televise the sport of football (professional and collegiate competition) cost an aggregate sum of $1.28 billion. CBS shelled out $338 million, ABC, $300 million, and NBC, $233 million, and regional broadcasters accounted for the balance.

Table 5.
The History of Olympic Broadcast Rights

Year	Games	Site	Fees	Network	Broadcast Hours
1960	Summer	Rome	$394,000	CBS	20
	Winter	Squaw Valley	50,000	CBS	15
1964	Summer	Tokyo	1.5 million	NBC	14
	Winter	Innsbruck	$594,000	ABC	17.25
1968	Summer	Mexico City	4.5 million	ABC	43.75
	Winter	Grenoble	2.7 million	ABC	27
1972	Summer	Munich	7.5 million	ABC	62.75
	Winter	Sapporo	6.4 million	NBC	37
1976	Summer	Montreal	25 million	ABC	76.5
	Winter	Innsbruck	10 million	ABC	43.5
1980	Summer	Moscow	87 million	NBC	150 (boycott)
	Winter	Lake Placid	15.5 million	ABC	53.25
1984	Summer	Los Angeles	225 million	ABC	180
	Winter	Sarajevo	91.5 million	ABC	63
1988	Summer	Seoul	300 million	NBC	179.5
	Winter	Calgary	309 million	ABC	94.5
1992	Summer	Barcelona	401 million	NBC	161
	Winter	Albertville	243 million	CBS	116
1994	Winter	Lillehammer	300 million	CBS	120
1996	Summer	Atlanta	456 million	NBC	TBD
1998	Winter	Nagano	375 million	CBS	TBD

*TBD, to be decided

WHAT TABLE 5 MEANS

The Olympics sell the following for the broadcasters:

- Commercial advertising—thirty- and sixty-second spots and billboards.
- Merchandise—event participation, and retail sponsorships.
- Network programming—the new season of Murphy Brown.

The broadcasters learn:

- Event revenue maximization through cable and merchandise sales.
- From past experience, how to do it better the next time—that is why they keep buying the rights years in advance.

The sponsors and public benefit:

- The organizers, the IOC, and the broadcasters refine the process.
- Maximum coverage of desirable events.
- Maximum exposure of best athletes.

The IOC needs to continually enhance and uphold the Olympic franchise. The IOC has the upper hand because they will always retain authority of the Games, whereas the participating networks only retain control (and thus receive the financial benefit) during the duration of their contract. Therefore, the networks always upgrade and contribute to the long-term notoriety and popularity of the Olympic Games, and the organizing committee receives the remuneration in the form of escalating rights fees.

The 1996 Summer Olympics has an international television rights fee goal of $910 million. By 1994, it had more than 80 percent of that goal ($720 million) committed.[17] The IOC and its organizing committees achieve sales success because its event is magical. The 1992 Winter and Summer Games had a total audience of 2.3 billion viewers. In America, ratings for the 1994 games were up 35 percent from the 1992 Games (largely due to the Tonya Harding-Nancy Kerrigan controversy), and as ratings climb, so do the broadcast fees. NBC lost money on its $401 million investment on the 1992 Summer Games, but it was determined that it could make it work in Atlanta, so NBC put its money where the challenge lay ($456 million), and won the broadcast rights through a sealed bidding process.

Television Spreads Popularity

The progressive NBA is already thinking ahead to other markets. They traditionally start the season with two games in Japan. In 1994, for example, the Clippers and Blazers played a two-game series there. As international restrictions erode, broadcasting and merchandising opportunities will grow. The NBA had over seventeen million fans attend games in the 1993–1994 season, but it sold $2.85 billion in licensed goods worldwide (and $3 billion the next year).[18] Efforts like USA Basketball, the marketing arm and creator of the Dream Team pays dividends for the NBA. The league broadcasts its games in 141 countries, and has six foreign marketing offices. They all support the focused, comprehensive licensing and merchandising of all NBA products, from broadcast entertainment to licensed, manufactured goods.

Perhaps the NBA will start a satellite league. The key is, of course, television. No other device can bring the excitement of the games and the charisma of the performers night in and night out like television. As the globalization of the world accelerates, the NBA, NFL, and Major League Baseball all want to be on the vanguard of the financial opportunities that exist. Furthermore, television is cheap. Beaming satellite signals is a lot easier than staging an actual event. It requires less time, money, and patience. Promoters would rather stage the event in an enthusiastic environment, and transport that excitement via telecommunications to new markets. As the markets mature, they invest more resources to increase profitability.

The NCAA's basketball championship is a premier event that has achieved elite event status. "March Madness," the "road to the Final Four," Dick Vitale, and the sixty-four teams that strut and sweat to the championship are a proved commodity. So proven that CBS ripped up its seven-year, $1 billion broadcast agreement with three years to go and paid a record total rights fee of $1.725 billion for the seven-year rights.

Worldwide rights are now negotiated as an element of a property. Wimbledon, the Olympics, and other sports properties command international corporate advertising interests. And sports interests are aggressively pursuing the international expansion of these sports. Fox's NFL package was a mutual interest case. The NFL wants to reintroduce its World League and enhance its global presence whereas Fox needs to sell in all of its markets to maximize its profits. The NFL is thrilled to sell Fox worldwide distribution benefits (where applicable) in the package. The NFL knows that the growth rate of the U.S. television market is relatively flat, and that Fox is the best bet in international markets at the moment.

Television Success Is Critical

Television brings exposure, the fans, and the sponsors. It ties event pieces nicely together. Without the investment from broadcast interests, events remain fragile. Golf ratings fell in 1991, but the three major networks decided to televise seventy-five events in 1992, mainly because they could still sell the ads. Golf is as close to a "recession proof" sport as any. Advertisers covet the game's demographics, and the loyalty of the audience makes up for the fluctuations in media efficiency figures.

The NHL had not had a network television contract for almost two decades. The league's fan base has been traditionally concentrated in the Northeast and Canada, and it has fought image problems with the public over issues like fighting and the perception of low-scoring, dull action. But through the spark provided by Wayne Gretzky, Mark Messier, Jeremy Roenick, and their peers, hockey carved a cable television niche in the eighties. By the 1990–1991 season, the league was earning $17 million from regional SportsChannel broadcasts. But the problem with regional sponsorship acquisitions is that they lack stability, as evidenced by the $5.5 million the league earned the following year. Finally, with new commissioner Gary Bettman (fresh from the NBA), the league secured a long-term commitment from sports-hungry Fox for a four-year $150 million deal. They also had an ongoing relationship with ESPN that was upgraded to add tens of millions of dollars to league coffers.

Conversely, the World League of American Football (WLAF) was created by the NFL in 1991 to export the game of choice in America abroad. ABC was the broadcast partner and they helped subsidize the league with a two-year experimental multimillion-dollar contract.*

Start-up costs such as administrative staffs, coaching staffs, players, and equipment, for the league were huge. When the ratings (far below a two) were poor, the league could not look to television to increase its investment (or interest) in the developing franchise. The league lasted only two years, before it was temporarily suspended. Now, with Rupert Murdoch's Fox Network in the NFL game, the worldwide interests bode well for a resuscitation of the World League concept. Murdoch owns satellite networks in Asia, Europe, and Latin America that will

---

*Teams were based in large European cities and North American ones that did not have NFL franchises, they included the Barcelona Dragons, London Monarchs, Frankfurt Galaxy, Ohio Glory, and the Sacramento Surge.

partner with the NFL in developing football's international potential. Murdoch's blockbuster deal with the NFL (four years for $1.58 billion) included 49 percent of the World League. As an equity partner, Murdoch has more than a casual interest in the international growth of a game he could easily grow to love.

The new World League will only feature European teams. And it has a partner, Murdoch, who will not rely upon American audiences to judge its success or failure. Fox's equity stake is about development and management. While it is buying a premium product for the U.S. market, the NFL, it is buying a highly speculative one, the World League, in the large European market that is exploding with telecommunication advancements. Fox could even subcontract the broadcast rights. Fox's authority and autonomy will allow it to explore new ways to make the proved commodity of football a viable financial vehicle in a mature European marketplace. Television and its persuasiveness will undoubtedly be the critical component in converting European sports fans to the game of American football.

Finally, broadcasting is important, because it is one of the two primary sources (the other is gate receipts) of income for athletic events. The turnstiles are the avenue to gain a finite physical audience. Broadcasting is the mechanism to geometrically expand it. League averages, as reported by *Financial World* for franchise income sources in 1993 are listed in Table 6.

Table 6.
1993 Average Franchise Income

League	Gate (Millions)	Media (millions)
Major League Baseball	$23.8	$27.7
NBA	$16.5	$14.9
NFL	$13.7	$41.3
NHL	$17.2	$ 5.4

Credibility

The NHL's multitiered, long-term contracts with ESPN and Fox lend stability and more importantly, guaranteed financial subsidy to the sport. With this income, teams know that they have a base cash flow with which they can operate their franchises by paying talent, developing players, and pursuing unique marketing tactics. Especially in a sport that seeks mass market appeal, television is the vehicle that can introduce and educate potential markets of fans. Without the television backing, the league did not enjoy the elite status that its rich heritage and exciting entertainment deserved. Mainstream acceptance ties communities and franchises together, in good times and bad, and helps solidify the financial structure of the team: the key objective in franchise management.

Football had a similar history. Teams were located in the East and Midwest, and they played in converted baseball facilities like Yankee Stadium and Wrigley Field. In 1958, when the Championship Game between the Colts and the Giants was broadcast to a national television audience on CBS, a new passion had been created by players like Gifford, Ameche, and Unitas.

Pete Rozelle, the NFL commissioner, knew that the league was at the threshold of significant exposure. He persuaded Congress to give the NFL an antitrust exemption so that he could solicit competitive bids from individual networks, giving the winner exclusivity and commercial viability. With the congressional exemption, Rozelle negotiated a two-year, $9.3 million contract with CBS.[19] By 1964, the popularity of the NFL spawned an upstart challenger, the AFL. The new league's play was not like its counterpart's. AFL games were offensive outbursts highlighted by extraordinary individual heroics from players like Cookie Gilchrist, Darryl Lamonica, Len Dawson, Otis Taylor, and many others. The AFL lacked the history and stability of the established NFL, but they did capture the attention of NBC, who paid an unheard of $42 million to broadcast the so-called other league in 1964. NBC's hunch paid off, for the first Super Bowl was a challenge match played by the top teams in the respective leagues.

Both CBS and NBC televised the first Super Bowl in 1967, and the broadcast reached a total audience of seventy-seven million people. Two years later, the AFL's Jets, led by renegade Joe Namath, beat Unitas' Colts, and the two leagues merged to standardize the game and develop the business franchise of professional football that is now a $5 billion annual business. The Super Bowl has so much credibility that it unquestionably commands the highest commercial rates.

The Rate Card—Supply and Demand

Next to the identity of the unknown soldier, advertising rates can be some of the best kept secrets in America. The same broadcaster will charge different amounts for the same advertising unit. The broadcaster is simply selling air space, costly air space. The basic costs for it are the rights fees plus production fees plus profit margin determined by ratings potential. The Super Bowl is always the most widely reported rate card, with current rates topping out at $1 million per thirty seconds. Advertisers only paid $42,500 for the same spot in 1967, the first Super Bowl, but the league and the networks have nurtured this event to these seemingly ridiculous heights. However, advertisers keep paying. In fact, for the right event, they line up. If there was no market, the rates would drop. Just look at baseball. The Cincinnati Reds and WLWT, their broadcaster, exchanged rights for $5 million in 1993, but settled on $4 million for 1994 and 1995, because the local market for baseball had diminished.[20]

A prime thirty-second spot on NBC's 1992 Summer Olympics (Barcelona) broadcast was $320,000. The Fox network, after spending over $1.5 billion on football, planned to sell its thirty-second spots for $120,000 during the season. As the playoffs neared, a sure-thing showdown between the 49ers and the Cowboys in the NFC Championship game drove advertising rates up to $500,000 per thirty-second unit. Table 7 shows sample 1993 thirty-second spot costs for sporting events. Compare it to Table 8, which shows sample thirty-second spot costs for entertainment television programs.

Table 7.
1993 Sample Thirty-Second Spot Costs for Sporting Events

Programming Event	Network	Cost per ad[21]
Super Bowl XXVII	NBC	$850,000
NCAA Championship Game	CBS	$400,000
NCAA Final Four game	CBS	$350,000
NBA Championship Game	NBC	$350,000
Baseball All-Star Game	CBS	$275,000
NBA All-Star Game	NBC	$200,000

Table 8.
1993 Sample Thirty-Second Spot Costs for Other Entertainment Programs

Programming Event	Network	Cost per ad
Academy Awards	ABC	$600,000
"Seinfeld" season finale	NBC	$350,000
"Home Improvement"	ABC	$305,000
Emmys	ABC	$300,000
"Roseanne"	ABC	$261,100
Miss America Pageant	NBC	$200,000
"60 Minutes"	CBS	$188,700
"Late Show"	CBS	$ 30,000
"Tonight" Show	NBC	$ 30,000

Advertising rates are not always rigid. Just before the 1992 World Series, CBS had to reduce advertising prices or risk carrying excess inventory into the Fall Classic. Advertising spots originally priced at $390,000 were reduced by 50 percent. Playoff spots slated between $150,000 and $175,000 were cut to $75,000. CBS acknowledged that it was going to be in the red, it just did not want to hemorrhage. CBS had purchased the exclusive broadcast rights (four years, over $1 billion) anticipating that the World Series was an undervalued franchise. As the economy dipped, and the competitors represented smaller markets in Oakland, Cincinnati, Toronto, and Atlanta, the worst case scenario appeared. Furthermore, the economy was in a prolonged slump and advertising budgets were slashed in virtually every industry. But CBS, and other broadcasters, know that the market competes efficiently for top commercial dollars, and when the tap is dry, the buying line gets very short and prices drop.

However, spots are not normally sold in single units. Broadcasters and sales agents create season packages, ones selling large blocks of time. The Greenville Braves' AA minor league team sells its "On the Farm" highlights show to the SportsSouth network (potential audience of four million homes in seven states). A typical advertising package sells one thirty-second spot on twenty shows for $4,000. Title sponsorships are available starting at $10,000, and features like "Player of the Week" and "Trivia Quiz" can be had in the $7,500 range.

While minor league baseball shares structural similarities with the rest of professional sports, its relative, Major League Baseball, is smarting from a slow retreat by its best sponsor, Anheuser-Busch. Not only is the Busch family a major league team owner (St. Louis Cardinals), they have a stadium named after them, Busch Stadium. Anheuser-Busch and its family of products are a perfect fit for the national pastime, and it advertises with twenty-five of the twenty-eight Major League teams (all except the Brewers, Expos, and Blue Jays). And its advertising purchases supported that notion, with media buys totaling $100 million in 1988. But by 1993, those buys had decreased to $75 million, with no sign of the slide ending. Baseball was losing valuable ground to other entertainment options such as concerts and other sporting events like hockey and golf. With only so much money to spend and the amount of events increasing, sports institutions are fighting to keep their fans and sponsors. The increase in competition for the advertising dollar forces companies to carefully analyze these investments based on returns, *not* solely impressions and media efficiency responses. This reality, much more than anything else, is giving sponsors the input and leverage into the shaping of sports entertainment and league competition.

Inventory Creation

Broadcasters sell the same entity, the airwaves, in a variety of ways. Advertisers, likewise, buy the same basic product, the audience, in numerous forms. Both buyers and sellers create ways to insert logos, names, mentions, and corporate acknowledgment throughout the scheduled broadcasts. Together, and with the reliable help of their media buying agencies, they derive meaningful ways to tactfully, skillfully, and effectively integrate their names and corporate messages with the games/competitions.

Time: Spots are usually sold in units of thirty seconds. For regular season NFL games in 1993, there were fifty-six units to sell. Fifty-six was the maximum amount that the NFL allowed CBS and NBC to merge with the actual gridiron action.

Billboards: During the broadcast, logos are placed over some graphic or included on a running message board on the screen, for example, Bud Light® halftime statistics or the Southwest Airlines® scoreboard update.

Features: This entails capitalizing on a conditional turn of events to tie-in a sponsor with the relevant action of the game. For example, as a relief pitcher comes into the game, "It's time for a pitching change. And as we wait for (pitcher) to warm up, we remind you that Jiffy Lube®'s fourteen-point service is the best way to keep your car running at its best. There are twenty-two Jiffy Lube® locations serving your car maintenance needs." The "Features" category includes special backdrops, or tagged highlights.

Entitlement: This allows the sponsor to make a corporate name part of the event, for example, the MCI Heritage Classic or the Jeep Eagle Aloha Bowl.

Drop-ins: Much like a billboard, logos are placed onto the screen at a prescribed time. For example, ESPN constantly refers to the Vantage® Score Board to update Senior PGA golf scores.

The Perfect Vehicle

The airwaves find customers. That is the practical consensus among marketing managers. To influence the customers and compel them to commit financial resources to your product and service, they need to be reached. It might be too late to wait if you rely upon packaging or word-of-mouth. Furthermore, retailers might not want to stock a product that has no media advertising support, for who will buy something about which nothing is known?

Companies are bound to the broadcast airwaves. The consumer lurks behind the screen and speakers, and commercial sponsorship does get a message to the listeners. The Johnnie Walker® World Championship is a twenty-eight-man competition in mid December broadcast from Jamaica. The tournament spends $6.5 million to stage the event ($2.7 million just for prize money). United Distillers, the manufacturers of the famed scotch, describes the tournament as a finale for all of international golf. And they served the international golf community in 1995 by broadcasting the event to eighty-three countries.[22] Like tobacco products, hard liquor is banned from many forms of advertising. In the United States there is no paid commercial advertising for hard liquor. Buying the entitlement rights gives the Johnnie Walker® brand millions of impressions via mentions, billboards, signage, and other standard entitlement privileges. Broadcast for a total of four hours (two days of coverage) on ABC, Johnnie Walker® hopes to capitalize on the spirit of the Holiday season with its target consumer: upscale, adult males.

Johnnie Walker® has international business interests and was the beneficiary of a spontaneous endorsement by one of the worlds' top players, Britain's Nick Faldo. After his triumph in the 1992 British Open, Faldo told the world that he was so happy that he was going to buy everyone in Britain a bottle of Johnnie Walker®. The company gladly capitalized on the unexpected act of generosity and offered to redeem British Open ticket stubs for free samples. Faldo's quote made international papers and so did Johnnie Walker®.

Ethics

Networks have been challenged by several cases that can be termed as scandalous, sensationalistic, spurious, and legitimate news, and often times, that refers to the same case. The O. J. Simpson trial and his low-speed chase represent a rather macabre element of the press and society, as do other events such as the Tonya Harding-Jeff Gilloolly debacle, or simply reporting the allegations of the impropriety of sports stars. The fact is, though, that gossip and sensationalism sadly have a place in the sports media, and the public finds this interesting. The networks, therefore, have been on both sides of the fence in ignoring and exploiting an opportunity.

- Pete Rozelle is still criticized for not canceling NFL action the weekend following John F. Kennedy's assassination.
- Franklin Delano Roosevelt wrote then commissioner of baseball Kenesaw Mountain Landis and encouraged the continuation of baseball during WWII, to boost everyone's morale as a positive distraction.
- The devastating earthquake in the San Francisco Bay Area during the 1989 World Series featuring the A's and Giants delayed the competition until the chaos in the affected community had abated.

However, it should be mentioned that the networks have been noble and influential in regards to sensitive issues in our society. Advertisers such as Coca-Cola noted the sacrifices of soldiers in the Gulf War combat and attempted to note the solemn state of our world's affairs. An elaborate campaign for Coke® was planned and millions were spent on Super Bowl advertising (a 3-D campaign). Instead of following through on the campaign, they respectfully took the time to acknowledge the war and its participants, rather than Coca-Cola's latest advertising efforts. In a less-publicized case, CBS pulled $1 million of airline advertising for the 1994 U.S. Open (tennis) following the tragic crash of a USAir airliner in Pittsburgh. Although they may not always make the best decisions, advertisers and networks can recognize their responsibilities in ethical broadcasting.

How Does Television Justify the Fees?

Great question. Quite simply, television works. Americans watch, and they are intrigued and coerced by the commercial messages that they see. Although the actual spending (billions) seems obscene, commercial development through broadcast marketing is the most effective way to communicate to large audiences.

Sometimes networks lose money on a deal, but the event brings a lead-in audience to other important programming, or it fits a demographic of the broadcaster. Wimbledon, for example, is the world's most prestigious tennis tournament. Mutually broadcast by HBO and NBC, the tournament's history and setting provide the most dramatic stage in tennis, the All English Tennis Club. Also, NBC and potential advertisers are aware of tennis's refined, wealthy audience. In fact, one survey by the BJK&E advertising agency determined that the sport of tennis has the most affluent audience on all of broadcast television.

Wimbledon is truly a unique sports property by drawing an elite demographic and having salient, differentiating qualities. Played on grass, and with formal clothing restrictions (players must wear white), the tournament is routinely attended by English royalty, and broadcast back in the early morning hours in America. Dubbed, "Breakfast at Wimbledon," the oldest Grand Slam tennis event has been a staple of NBC Sports' tennis broadcasts.

HBO, a pay cable station, is thrilled to be a part of the telecast. They do not need to woo advertisers annually. They need subscribers. This is a valuable property that they extend into a historical collage of images past and present. Wimbledon is that premium niche sports property that fits its target demographic. HBO cannot afford to carry the entire event, nor can it serve the entire American tennis community (cable only broadcasts to 62 percent of homes), but the broadcaster enjoys the privileges of its minority position. If NBC bails on the project, a new broadcaster may not be so quick to share with HBO, and/or have prior commitments to broadcast partners, such as in the case of ESPN and ABC. Ultimately, the issue of broadcasting Wimbledon will be up to the open market. The question is not; "Will Wimbledon be broadcast? And if so, by whom?" As stated in chapter 1 in regard to the ESPN-Major League Baseball issue, the question for Wimbledon is: "At what price will Wimbledon be broadcast? And who will meet that price?"

Wimbledon's contract went into negotiations as soon as the past agreement expired. At stake were American and foreign rights. In the past, these had been negotiated separately, but as technology, broadcast alliances, and international deregulation takes place, some networks look for everything. International Management Group (IMG), the pre-eminent sports and event marketing management company, handles the negotiations and markets the tournament. Mark McCormack, IMG's founder (Wimbledon promoter), was reportedly looking to negotiate a six-year contract for approximately $210 million. McCormack narrowed the bidding down to Fox, ABC/ESPN, and NBC/HBO, the incumbent rights holders.

Fox, wanting to capitalize on the international appeal of Wimbledon, and its international airwaves, eagerly entered the bidding fray. It wanted satellite rights in Asia and Europe as well. Fox's real interest leveraged the NBC/HBO bid to $25 million annually, but only for U.S. rights. As the sales representative, McCormack had to ponder the revenue streams, efficiencies, and profit centers that accrue to the broadcaster and tournament, as well as the future value of the Wimbledon franchise. Fox bid $120 million for four-year world rights.[23] Wimbledon eventually stayed with NBC. The continuity of its broadcast team, the strength of its affiliates, and the long-term commitment to the event made its bid the best one for Wimbledon and IMG.

Are There Negatives to Broadcast Advertising?

Television and radio have been accused of becoming marketing anachronisms. That the needs of the leading edge marketers are beyond the simplistic formula of reaching an audience through frequency and consistency, i.e., the reinforcement of a message. Event promotion specialists and retail trade managers all want "bang for their buck," or "mileage" out of their marketing pursuits. To some, buying air time is a quantifiable, finite element without tangible longevity. A common complaint is that, "once the ad airs the money is spent and we're not sure what we have to show for it."

Some studies substantiate this argument. A Gallup and Robinson survey determined, for example, that Anheuser-Busch's $7 million investment in nine commercial spots during Super Bowl XXV (Bud Bowl) resulted in only four times the awareness of one thirty-second spot. The study indicates that other advertisers experience similar diminishing returns. This study, however, does not include the retail identification and point of purchase materials of the Bud Bowl. To Anheuser-Busch, the commercials were merely a component of the promotion, not the entire focus, and the media strategy fits in with the rest of the promotion's elements, i.e., the retail and print efforts.

ONE POTENTIAL PROBLEM: SATURATION

The biggest problem in sports broadcasting is the greed cycle. Sports property rights holders naturally want to sell their broadcast interests for the highest amount of money, for example, the 1996 Summer Olympics cost NBC $456 million. The networks, in turn want to recoup their investment, and approach advertisers with pricey promotional packages. There is only a finite amount, albeit a large amount, of advertising money to be spent. Companies like IBM, Coca-Cola, and Chevrolet cannot invest their resources into every viable event.

More and more events look to television and radio to subsidize and carry them, and the competition gets fierce. Programming choices often face a sink or swim scenario, as with the World League of Football (WLAF). The WLAF was subsidized by the NFL, and broadcast on ABC. Saddled with terrible ratings (less than a two average for a combined 1991–1992), ABC slashed its rights fee by almost half after one year, and had little interest in pursuing the venture. Without television's investment in the league for both publicity and subsidy, the league did not get exposure or revenue. It does not take a genius to figure out that exposure and revenue are key elements to generate event interest. Television can be the key interface between the public and the commercial interests that breathe life into an event.

Because of television's commercial power, more and more events are being created to gauge the sports fan's appetite. Of course, this increases the competition for broadcasters and advertisers, but the right formula means profitability. No sport has developed the alternative event formula to its advantage quite like golf. The PGA Tour concludes play in October with the Tour Championship, but non-tour events fill up the airwaves after the season officially ends. With camera-friendly international superstars and exotic vacation areas easily found, golf's superstars are the beneficiaries of the James Bond formula: beautiful places, rich people, and competitive intrigue. No sport brings those three elements together better than golf, which helps to explain its appeal to both fans and sponsors. Table 9 presents a sample of off-season golf events and their networks.

Table 9.
Off-Season Golf Events

Event	Network
The Skins Game	ABC
The Senior Skins Game	ABC
The Franklin Funds Shark Shootout	CBS
The Johnnie Walker® Cup from Jamaica	ABC
The Wendy's Three Tour Challenge	ABC
The Diner's Club Matches	ABC

All of these events are designed to involve key sponsor(s) and tie-in to their business and exposure needs. The conceptual forces behind these concepts know that as winter rolls in to the majority of the United States, a beautiful green golf course in Palm Springs, Arizona, Hawaii, or Florida is a welcome sight. Furthermore, throw in golf's biggest names, Norman, Palmer, Couples, Love III, Irwin, Zoeller, Azinger, Nicklaus, Price, etc., and a revenue-producing event has been created.

But for each extra event, the selling of sponsorships becomes difficult. The NFL, NBA, NHL, the above-mentioned golf tournaments, and Major League Baseball are all competitors. They compete for the same dollars from the same buyers at General Motors, Coca-Cola, Procter & Gamble, Anheuser-Busch, Philip Morris, and their peers. And no network is guaranteed to sell all of its inventory. Circumstances do have an impact on the saturation or availability issue. As the NHL and Major League Baseball went on strike in the Fall of 1994, Fox sold all of its NFL advertising spots by Halloween.[24] Perhaps unrelated, but coincidental, ABC jacked up the Super Bowl advertising spots to $1 million per thirty seconds (that's $33,333.30 per second!) and college football enjoyed its best ratings ever. Certainly, the abrupt ending to baseball, and the delay in hockey's start contributed to football's windfall.

Flexibility in the Marketplace

Sporting events are not the only avenues for commercial advertising. The use of widely accepted and popular athletes (product endorsers) in commercials during other broadcasts is a common occurrence. Sports fans watch other shows, like "60 Minutes," "Cheers," and "The Simpsons," so advertisements are placed on these programs. Sports crosses virtually all major demographic lines in the United States, and with the surfeit of available market data (usually at a price), matches between audiences and products campaigns are made.

Puma, the German shoe manufacturer, reintroduced the "Clydes®," a shoe worn by former Knick star, Walt "Clyde" Frazier. Puma wants to tell old customers that the shoe is back, as well as tell the next generation that there is a stylish shoe from the past that might interest them. To do so, Puma bought $1 million worth of advertising time on shows with different audiences, "Roseanne" and "Beverly Hills 90210." The demographic fit for Puma, and its main man from the seventies, Walt Frazier. Most importantly, Puma sold more "Clydes®."

Don't Forget the Print Media

Long before the airwaves, the print media was the information monopoly. Today, the print media shares its audience with radio and television.

Although it is no longer the primary information mechanism, it still represents a powerful part of the industry with both advertisers and consumers for general sports and individual ones. The National Golf Foundation, for example, has identified six million golfers who are over forty-nine years of age and, more importantly, have an income in the excess of $100,000 annually. This demographic attracts advertisers such as Cadillac, Callaway®, Rolex®, Buick, Johnnie Walker®, and vacation destinations like Palm Springs, Myrtle Beach, and other golf developments. As you can see in Table 10, this healthy industry also attracts U.S. distributed publications.

Table 10.
Golf Publications Distributed in the U.S.

Magazine	Circulation[25]
Golf Digest	1.4 million
Golf	1.2 million
Sports Illustrated's Golf edition	400,000
Golf for Women	277,512
Links	250,000
Golf World	146,410

In addition to these, there are several regional publications that cater to their geographical areas. Golf, as mentioned throughout this book, is virtually a recession-proof sport because golfers will suffer financial setbacks, but they will remain the decision-making powers of the corporate world. Companies pay for this access, because at the executive level, there will be a place for golf.

But the industry is much more than golf. Magazine's like *Sports Illustrated* have over 3 million subscribers and advertising revenues over $300 million. *USA Today* has over six million readers, and a nationally renowned sports section. And in a rank of consumer classifications, sports ranked sixth in total revenues in a 1992 study by *Advertising Age.*

The conclusion is that sports is a profitable venture in all forms of media—radio, television, and printed matter. The media is simply another method by which fans enjoy sports entertainment.

Conclusions?

Conclusions are both obvious and simplistic. Until the "Information Superhighway" evolves and defines an accepted and *used* (usage equals revenue generation) standard of media choice, speculation on the broadcast and media will be just that. Today, as the existing structure of network, cable, and other pay-per-view options thrive, it is obvious that traditional commercial advertising works for sponsors' objectives. Otherwise they would not invest their resources into the medium.

Yes, it can be simply stated. The media, despite its escalating clutter, does indeed process and distribute information to diverse demographics successfully. The rights fee and commercial advertising rates are merely the prices paid for the mechanism.

Case Study: The USA Network in the Sports Market

The USA Network offers premium cable entertainment programming to over sixty-two million households in the United States. Sports has long been a part of the network's historical strategy, and USA has carried events such as Major League Baseball, the NBA, NHL, professional golf, tennis, and college basketball.

USA's current sports lineup primarily consists of professional tennis, golf, wrestling, and boxing. Rob Correa, the Vice President of Programming/Sports Acquisitions discusses in a personal interview, some of the issues in the contemporary cable marketplace that affects sports programming for networks, advertisers, and fans.

PHILOSOPHY

> Our philosophy changes depending upon the property in question. For boxing, it is not to buy into a lot of long-term deals. Boxing is capitalism at its best and its worst. The sport itself is promoter-driven and the quality of the fights can vary greatly. The promoters who sell the fights are looking merely for the best deal, and if they have a great matchup, they will most likely take the bout to pay-per-view or the networks. With boxing, USA goes fight to fight, and we either look for the marquee name, or a great bout featuring two competitive

fighters. USA has been televising boxing since 1981, and we have a show, "USA Tuesday Night Fights," which has evolved from all of our experiences with the sport.

With golf and tennis, it's the spectacle of the event. Compared to boxing, the audiences are different, but their enthusiasm makes the event worthwhile. USA's strategy is to buy properties that are consistent with our customers. With golf, we don't buy just PGA events, we try to buy the most attractive ones. For instance, the Masters is one of the most prestigious sporting events anywhere, and the ratings bear that out.

We bought the rights to the Ryder Cup with the same thought in mind, a prestigious, highly anticipated event with an elite field of athletes. It also helps that the Ryder Cup features some dramatic matchups of the best American and European golfers, something that American golf fans look forward to and enjoy. Knowing that the Ryder Cup and the Masters are on our schedule helps to anchor and focus our schedule. Having those events, we can hype them and refer to them in all of our other events, which promotes the property and the network. So, for example, when we broadcast the Doral-Ryder Open, we can preview the Masters, which occurs one month later.

PROPERTY CRITERIA

There is a simple standard that breaks down the criteria in purchasing a property for USA and it probably applies to other industry broadcasters. Shows can work on many levels, and as a buyer, you will pursue it for four basic reasons:

1. Ratings—the event has a specific amount of viewers.
2. Demographics—the event has a particular audience.
3. Affiliate participation—the cable operators.
4. Public relations vehicle—the broadcast makes the company look good.

As a buyer, each opportunity presents different advantages. Tennis, for example, provides a unique audience and demographic. With golf, USA was the first network to have Thursday and Friday golf coverage and we entered into partnerships with other networks to share costs on the production side, but that's it. We do not sell or package advertising with the weekend broadcaster. The cost division varies between networks, but the issues are usually easy to negotiate and work out.

Affiliate Relationships

Affiliate relationships are akin to licensing agreements. The basic agreement provides 365 days of twenty-four hours of programming to affiliates. Our objective is to give them consistent ratings and low costs to our programming. If we deliver on our end, through programming choices and promotional opportunities, their job is easier.

We give them two minutes of advertising per hour and access to promotional items like tickets and ad copy for their own regional efforts. An important element to affiliate relationships is to give them network-produced promotional spots. This keeps the affiliate's own production costs down and helps them create effective local market cross-promotions. For instance, we will leave time on preproduced "promo" spots for an event and the local affiliate will tag that with its own sponsor messages.

Going for the Ratings

Prestigious events like the Masters or the U.S. Open obviously deliver an audience, but so do non-traditional entertainment events like wrestling. The WWF [World Wrestling Federation] is a great television package. It attracts an audience and works well with affiliates and advertisers. For example, Lawrence Taylor recently announced a one-time bout with the WWF. The press was crawling all over the place, hyping the event.

Wrestling brings out the age-old formula that has worked for sports' most notorious promoters. Don King and old-timers such as Bill Veeck [former baseball owner] have had a knack for capturing the attention of their audience, and they never minded having a good time in the process.

But wrestling is only one example of working in the buyer's market. USA pursues golf events over several months based solely on the event's ability to attract advertisers. At the same time, USA is not so naive as to think we're the only ones making money through golf. Other broadcasters and advertisers are out there in the same market. The real winner is the public, because they get many more golf events.

CABLE'S FUTURE

USA will always try to broadcast sporting events, because sports is essentially a self-promoted product. Newspapers, newscasts, talk radio, and people on the streets are all talking about sports. Teams like the Dallas Cowboys and the Chicago Bulls don't have to pay money to promote their product through traditional advertising channels, everyone knows about them. It is almost a seamless relationship between the public and the event forum.

Years ago, as cable became a significant player in sports entertainment, people said that no one would ever go the games if they were all broadcast. That was an ignorant conclusion, because the exact opposite occurred. Television cannot replace the ballpark experience and it does not try to do it. Television, if anything, has increased the popularity of all sporting events, and driven many more fans to the various facilities, and helped the leagues to expand. And all of the broadcasters are essentially paying to promote sports competition. No wonder the value of franchises and events has increased dramatically.

I think that the television markets will continue to open up, where concepts like local blackouts will no longer apply, and cable will continue to be a major force in expanding consumer choice. In many ways, cable started with sports and movies, and in many ways, that is the way a significant portion of our industry is perceived and will evolve.

8

Licensing and Merchandising

> Dallas Cowboy owner Jerry Jones has been complaining about NFL rules that limit each franchise to a 1/28 share of league licensing deals. As Jones pointed out to the Washington Post last week, merchandise bearing the Cowboy logo generated 28 percent of all NFL Properties revenue in 1993. Still, don't hold your breath waiting for the league's other twenty-seven owners to offer Jones—or anyone else—a bigger slice of the pie. Cleveland Browns owner Art Modell put it this way: "We are twenty-eight fat-cat Republicans that sit around the league meetings and vote Socialist.[1]

NFL Properties, the league's licensing arm, has agreements with 350 manufacturers who produce 2,500 different items bearing the likeness or logo of the league, and/or its teams and players. These contracts produced $3 billion in worldwide merchandise sales in 1994.[2] *Reproducing an image, or portion thereof, of a team, athlete, league, company, or any copyrighted property for a fee to the rights holder of said property is the simple definition of licensing,* a multibillion-dollar source of revenue in the sports industry. Practically stated, licensing uses/attaches a logo or likeness to a variety of merchandise such as hats, shirts, backpacks, sweats, cups, keychains, telephones, clocks, balls, and virtually anything that is packaged. The key is that the license is issued to third party companies who produce, package, distribute, and sell the units in as many places as possible. The licensing agent, for example, the NFL, does not assume the expense or risk of the investment.

The Big Four of Merchandise Sales

The top four sellers of merchandise are listed in Table 1.

Table 1.
Four Biggest Merchandise Sellers

League	Gross sales	Year[3]
Major League Baseball Properties	$3.5 billion	1993
NFL Properties	$3.0 billion	1994
NBA Properties	$2.5 billion	1993
NHL Properties	$1.0 billion	1993

It used to be that a sports fan could only buy a shirt, pennant, hat, or souvenir item at the event facility. Not today. Licensed merchandise is available at virtually every conceivable clothing retailer, department store, and/or specialty shop. Companies like Castrol are even giving away merchandise to customers who buy their products. If you buy a case of Castrol® Motor Oil, you can send away for your free (key concept) NFL hat. Castrol thinks enough of the promotion to pay for both the league licensing rights and the hats.

Although event sites are no longer the only place to buy team souvenirs, they are still a good place for impulse purchases. The Anaheim Mighty Ducks sold over $300,000 worth of licensed merchandise during their first game of play.[4] That averages to more than $18 per fan who attended. But the Ducks' (and all other sports teams') most profitable business comes through its retail sales, which are now in the multibillion-dollar range for all major sports properties.

Retail outlets, like Macy's, WalMart, Foot Locker, and their competitors sell the excitement and delirium attached to sports. The Carolina Panthers were awarded their NFL franchise in October of 1993, and within a week, over one million licensed items featuring their logo were sold locally (almost one item per person—population 1.23 million).[5] The team did not have one player nor did it have an opponent. In fact, the first game was more than two years away, but the fans could proudly display the colors and team wares, all provided by their local department stores and related retail outlets. They were all more than happy to welcome the Panthers to town.

SUCCESS EQUALS SALES

Merchandise sales are a derivative of popularity. The NHL's licensed sales growth (1990 merchandise sales of $150 million), shows that its expansion into the United States' West and South, and its creative designs, i.e., Mighty Ducks and Sharks, are popular with consumers. Furthermore, popular teams in large markets generate the greatest revenues. The Chicago Bulls are the all-time leading merchandise sales leaders. It is no coincidence that the team featured Michael Jordan, the world's most popular athlete.

The Toronto Blue Jays won back-to-back World Series' in 1992 and 1993. They feature exciting players like Joe Carter, Roberto Alomar, and the great Paul Molitor. They are the first franchise in Major League history to draw over four million fans in a single season. Their ballpark, the SkyDome, is the only indoor/outdoor ballpark in baseball, and the team's popularity is supported by merchandise sales figures. The Blue Jays dominated the Canadian market in 1993 by selling almost $60 million worth of goods in Canada.

The Kansas City Chiefs traded for Joe Montana, one of sports' greatest icons, in 1993, and sold out their stadium on the way to the AFC Championship Game that season. The hysteria and interest generated by Montana also led to merchandise success. By midseason in 1994, the Chiefs were second in the league in merchandise sales, their highest historical position in that category.

The trickle down theory of "Reaganomics" may not have worked for everyone in the eighties, but when it comes to the paradigm of successfully merchandising a line of licensed goods, the success has trickled down. In 1991, minor league licensing revenues were a measly $2.5 million.[6] By 1994, as the industry matured, total merchandise sales soared to $40 million.[7] The Cedar Rapid Kernels (a California Angels class A team), chose its name in 1992 strictly for merchandising purposes. The Kernels name change paid off with merchandise sales in excess of $100,000 in each of its first two years. The regional identification between minor league teams' names and their geographic location is a new trend that is not only generating money but is generating local loyalty.

Another calculated minor league merchandise success story is the Rancho Cucamonga Quakes class A team. Located in the Southern

California desert, they devised a marketing strategy to maximize their appeal at the turnstiles and souvenir stands. By naming the team the Quakes, and the playing facility "The Epicenter," management hit the funny bone of the public and opened their wallets at the same time. By midseason in 1993, the Quakes had already sold $500,000 worth of licensed goods. Feedback like that can only help them at the gate.

Table 2 and Table 3 show the top five teams in terms of sales for the NFL and NBA, respectively.

Table 2.
NFL's Top Five Teams in Merchandise Sales

Team	1994 Rank	1993 Rank
Dallas Cowboys	1	1
Kansas City Chiefs	2	9
Miami Dolphins	3	4
Los Angeles Raiders	4	2
San Francisco 49ers	5	3

Table 3.
NBA's Top Five Teams in Merchandise Sales

Team	1994 Rank	1993 Rank
Charlotte Hornets	1	2
Chicago Bulls	2	1
Orlando Magic	3	3
Phoenix Suns	4	4
Seattle SuperSonics	5	15

The Oakland Raiders are an interesting licensing case study. As the first team to feature black in their color scheme, and with a renegade image to boot, the Raiders (both the Oakland and Los Angeles editions) have the third best-selling licensed logo in sports history (trailing the Dallas Cowboys and the Chicago Bulls). The success of the design and its consumer acceptance spawned the change in uniform styles and color schemes to capitalize on the success structure of the Raiders. It is interesting to note that the team had problems selling tickets while in

Los Angeles, but it never had difficulty in peddling merchandise in both its new home and across the country.

To be an "officially licensed" anything, all your manufacturing company needs is to obtain the rights to reproduce the images, likenesses, and logos of the league, team, and/or individual(s). Obtaining the rights can be both expensive and lucrative. It should be noted that to obtain an NFL Players license (the rights to the names of the players such as Boomer Esiason, Dan Marino, and friends), the NFL Players Association (labor union) both sells and manages the agreement. If the company wants to buy the rights to the names of the teams (Bears, 49ers, etc.), and the uniforms, NFL Properties, or the league (management), executes the agreement. Both management and the players' labor organizations, however, will agree that selling a license is good, because the licensees, that is, companies like Starter, Sega, Apex, and Rawlings, pay the investment costs in successfully merchandising the eventual product lines. These costs include:

- Manufacturing costs such as labor and material
- Administrative overhead
- Shipping and distributing
- Promotional fees for marketing campaigns
- Inventory costs

Basically, the licensors get a great deal. It is the conservative approach to profit opportunities, because the licensors (NFL, NBA, NHL, etc.) minimize their risk and do not obscure their main focus, which is event entertainment. The NHL is not a cap and clothing manufacturer. It needs to promote its league and create, maintain, and expand a fan base. It then needs to sell that fan base to broadcasters, fans, and sponsors. Yes, merchandise sales are a profit center for every team, but it is not the primary emphasis of the business. Merchandise sales will always be behind ticket and broadcast sales. Generally speaking, if those two categories are taken care of, merchandise opportunities will follow.

Licensing Magic

When Hot-Shot Video Games (fictitious name) wants to create a game called, "Reggie White: The Play-Stuffer," they have several licensing considerations. The company needs to develop the actual game, which includes writing the software code for graphical display, play options, opponents, and voice enhancement features (costs can go up to $400,000). Then Hot-Shot needs to pay Reggie White his fee (minimum of $100,000 advance plus royalties), and then undertake the packaging, warehousing, and shipping costs. Then it has to obtain the other necessary license, either from NFL Properties, or the Players Association, to feature identifiable teams and/or players, other than White. Next, Hot-Shot has to decide which game platforms it will develop for: Sega®, CD-Rom, Nintendo®, Sony®, 3-DO®, and/or Jaguar®. Depending on which platforms the manufacturer develops, the cartridges add extra costs.

An analyst calculates the revenue streams and forecasts the potential return on investment. The net revenue per platform for an average game is $32 per game sold through, meaning purchased at a retail outlet such as Target Stores. Reggie White's royalty would likely be 4 percent of that, less his advance. Therefore, if 300,000 units sell through, White's royalties would amount to:

300,000	x (.04)(32)	– 100,000	= $28,000.
(Units Sold)	(Royalty)	(Advance)	(Royalty Figure)

The likelihood is that Hot-Shot Video Games would sign Reggie White for a minimum of two years (plus options), gain the exclusive worldwide rights and develop the game on a minimum of three platforms such as CD-Rom, Sega®, and Sony®. White is not the catalyst for the game. The developer seeks a category, and White merely is the celebrity vehicle to differentiate the product. In the competitive video game development field, the sophisticated marketplace will weed out poorly conceived games, and they will fail in spite of a fabulous license. Celebrity licenses help sell products—*if* those products are good.

NASCAR is another ringing cash register in the licensed goods industry. In 1988, NASCAR sold a respectable $60 million in licensed goods. By 1994, they were smoking on the front burner at $600 million in sales, a 1,000 percent growth in 6 years! By 1996, estimated sales are projected to hit the magic mark of $1 billion. NASCAR packages drivers (personalities), race teams, and events in an integrated merchandising program. Its drivers are the best spokesmen and salesmen. Dale Earnhardt once sold $900,000 worth of items on QVC in just two hours.[8]

Collegiate interests have capitalized on the industry. In the early 1980s, shirts, sweats, caps, and other related items were only available at that particular college. In fact, Slippery Rock State used to get many requests for items emblazoned with its unique name. But by 1989, retail sales of licensed merchandise had reached $1 billion. Four years later, sales topped the $2 billion mark. Furthermore, manufacturers are working on ways to enhance their market share in union with the colleges and universities that they supply. Sara Lee, the manufacturer of Champion® sportswear, has entered a pilot program with several universities (University of North Carolina, University of Rochester, and UC Berkeley). Hanes® wear, L'eggs® panty hose, Jogbra®, Playtex® bras, and many other products will put approximately 2 percent of profits back into the women's athletic programs at participating schools.

The program is called the "Sara Lee Collegiate Partnership Program" and it requires that Sara Lee products are sold on appropriate campus sites like the campus store, student unions, concession stands, and/or through the athletic department. This program makes great sense for Sara Lee because it virtually guarantees widespread distribution, excellent public relations, and an identity with its primary consumer group, women. Perhaps most importantly, it is a creative attempt by academic institutions and profit-seeking corporate interests to balance the inequity of funding between men's and women's athletics at the college level.

The entire industry of licensed products is over $60 billion. Sports and Colleges account for over 20 percent of that industry figure. Why is putting a logo, name , or image (Air Jordan®, Shaq, Greg Norman's Shark) so profitable? Obviously, it is an extension of the excitement surrounding the competition. Sports fans are unfailingly loyal, and wearing the colors of their favorite teams is a way to show that faith and devotion. Licensed merchandise conveniently is many things:

Affordable: from pins to golf bags, all budgets are accommodated.

Timely: as gifts, memorials, etc. It's no secret that when a team wins its merchandise sales increase.

Fashionable: it breaks gender barriers and as the scope of the market has grown, the evolution of designs, materials, and creativity has taken a quantum leap.

To consumers, licensed merchandise is simply an extension of being a fan. It's an identifiable way to be a part of our culture and our communities. Teams, leagues, and promoters benefit from this and want to create, and/or host events to capture this profitable source of income. Licensed goods, after all, do not strike, complain, morally degenerate, or detract from the competition. Licensed products are an adjunct. In Atlanta, two years prior to the Olympic Games, $75 million worth of Olympic merchandise had been sold.[9] Major League Baseball estimated that the cancellation of the 1994 playoffs and World Series resulted in a 10 percent reduction in annual revenue, or hundreds of millions of dollars. The games fuel sales, and to keep this auxiliary market flowing green, owners, promoters, and league labor representatives need to keep the balls in play.

Industry Expansion

Licensors, i.e., leagues, teams, and rights holders, are pursuing three main strategies to maximize profitability.

1. *Modifying designs,* changing uniform colors, nostalgia pieces, etc.
2. *Creating new categories,* adding new products, licensees, and sales vehicles.
3. *Expanding markets,* going international.

Design Enhancement

Teams are redesigning their uniforms, bringing back nostalgia with period pieces and playing "Turn Back the Clock" games. One company, Mitchell and Hess, has transformed from a small sporting goods store to a $1.5 million business by selling over 17,000 authentic reproductions of classic baseball jerseys annually.[10] Capitalizing on market trends has not escaped big league franchises either. In 1990, the Chicago White Sox changed their uniforms to a predominantly black color scheme. In their first year, they led the major league merchandise sale figures, topping $80 million in sales.[11] The NFL celebrated its seventy-fifth year of business by designating several Sundays as "Throwback" days, where teams would wear a uniform from their past. Some were classic designs from past eras, such as the old uniforms worn by the New York Jets and Giants, and some were hideous nightmares (Packers, Steelers, and Bears) that should have remained sequestered and unseen.

But the point is to do something different. Change the recipe *and* add more merchandising opportunities for NFL Properties. The San Francisco 49ers created some controversy when their superstitious head coach, George Seifert, petitioned the league to allow the team to continue wearing the replica uniform. Coach Seifert noticed that the team was undefeated in the circa 1955 uniforms, and he wanted to continue playing the hot hand. June Jones, the Falcons' head coach, complained of league favoritism to an elite team, and it took a judgment by commissioner Paul Tagliabue to resolve the whole matter.

Commissioner Tagliabue knows a good story when he sees one, and he also knows that media attention is good for the "Throwback" campaign and the fans. He initially ruled that teams could only wear the uniforms a total of five times (originally each team was required to wear them three times), and then he waived any restrictions for the entire season. The commissioner capitalized on a developing storyline and helped the media, a group always looking for a story, maximize its potential. This experiment was a low-risk way to create another category in the competitive licensing business. And it worked. By late season, the league expected to sell $40 million worth of replica jerseys.[12]

New Products and Markets from Licensees

Coca-Cola is one of the world's leading sports sponsors. As stated earlier, it is involved with sixty-seven sports-related activities in the 195 countries in which it bottles, produces, and distributes its products.[13] The company supports athletics at the local, national, and international level. Coca-Cola also sells items out of a thirty-two page merchandise catalogue that features Coca-Cola merchandise items with the logos of the leagues it sponsors, the NFL, NBA, Major League Baseball, the Olympics, and the World Cup.[14]

Furthermore, the financial power of Coca-Cola has fueled a sports licensing force: the commemorative Olympic Pin. As a primary sponsor of the Olympic Games, Coca-Cola has pursued many angles to exploit the aura of the games. By creating popular collector pins, Coca-Cola has given the fans a desirable item, which the company will both sell and market.[15] As the top sponsor of the 1996 Olympic Games Pin

Society, sales are estimated to approach 50,000,000 for the 1996 Games in Atlanta. (See Table 4 for prior sales of Olympic Pins.)

Table 4.
Prior Sales of Olympic Pins

Year	Site	Number of Pins
1984	Los Angeles	17,000,000
1992	Barcelona	25,000,000
1994	Lillehammer	18,000,000

This example shows the win-win relationship of a successful licensing arrangement. Licensors get promoted to make money. Each licensed sale means a royalty or money earned from licensing the image to third party enterprises, like Starter, Russell Athletic, and other manufacturers. The leagues risk nothing in this relationship. In 1991, Major League Baseball, for example, earned an 8.5 percent royalty on the 3,000 manufactured items.[16]

Sponsors always seek to build an emotional link between their brands and the consumers. The sale of merchandise shows the degree to which fans are bound to their sports teams. More telling is that the number of licenses that exist for the amount of products exemplifies the financial power of sports in other markets. Video games, trading cards, book sales, posters, and other items carve a niche through their use of the athletes or teams. The NFL, J.C. Penney, and Star Kist® tuna entered into a September 1993 cross-promotion where ten million cans of Star Kist had a 10 percent off coupon on NFL licensed merchandise redeemable at J.C. Penney stores. This promotion gives J.C. Penney, Star Kist, and the NFL a redemption tracking rate and an opportunity to use the licensing of America's most popular sport in consumer incentive programs.

INTERNATIONAL EXPANSION

The NBA and NFL play several annual games abroad. Professional tennis players and golfers earn some of the highest endorsement contracts because of their international schedules. Obviously, intercontinental exposure translates into merchandise sales. In Mexico alone, current licensed sales of $20 million are estimated to quintuple to $100 million by 1996—a phenomenal growth! The driving force has been the satellite broadcast market of major sports to the south.[17] Illegal sales are estimated at a minimum of $30 million. The demand is there. NFL Properties even has a special investigation unit researching improprieties. As the leagues increase their efforts to market and distribute goods commensurate with broadcast penetration and team expansion, sales and profits will soar.

One Licensing Offer

NFL Properties sold approximately $3 billion in goods worldwide in 1994. The NFL, after its costly initial World League of American Football venture, recognizes the relative ease in printing, packaging, and shipping goods to retail points of sale around the world. In the NFL's opinion, it is easier to have manufacturers buy a license and sell merchandise abroad, than to fund teams and leagues to generate fan interest and money. Furthermore, to capitalize on nontraditional markets, the league schedules exhibition games in Europe, Asia, and Latin America. Exhibition games are meaningless to most fans here in America, so the NFL exports some overseas. The games feature the most popular teams such as the Cowboys, Bears, Chiefs, and 49ers. It is a calculated move that generates fan interest and market feedback from potential expansion areas.

By sending the teams overseas, the NFL hopes to create defined markets for merchandise sales, future broadcast rights, and, one day, the revised World League. To further its growth, the NFL has made it easy to obtain a license. Much like the PC-Microsoft marriage, NFL Properties has a message machine outlining the licensing guidelines. If one has a product: bean bag chair, toothbrush, cologne, anything, and they want to carry an official NFL license, they can start by dialing the league office and asking for the Properties Division. The message menu tells manufacturer and potential license holders how to pursue an NFL license for their products and brands:

THE NFL'S MESSAGE

> To be considered for a license, you need to send a complete business plan outlining your product, price points, advertising, and marketing plan, and your existing network of distribution channels, as well as a product sample to:
>
> NFL Properties
> 410 Park Ave
> New York, NY 10022
> Attn: New Products Division
>
> If you don't have a sample ready, an artist's drawing or picture will do. It is not necessary to have team identification on the sample. We can imagine what it will look like with a team logo on it.
>
> The terms of our license are as follows:
>
> The royalty rate is 9 percent, and is paid based on the wholesale price of each unit sold. The length of the license is typically two years. There is a minimum guarantee of $20,000 per year, which is due at the beginning of each fiscal year. You must also have product insurance in the amount of $3 million for bodily injury, and $1 million for property damage. All licenses are nonexclusive and are restricted to traditional retail sales only. After you submit your sample, it may take up to eight weeks before we can respond—due to the heavy volume of requests that we receive. Please be patient.
>
> If you are calling about a Super Bowl license, all Super Bowl licensing is handled separately. Send all Super Bowl submissions to: [name] for evaluation. The royalty rate for [the] Super Bowl is 9 percent, and there is an advance due upon signing.
>
> Please don't call us to check on the status of your product. We will get back to you after reviewing your proposal. Thank you for your interest in the NFL. Please remember: follow these instructions, and do not call one of our licensing managers. We appreciate your cooperation and look forward to receiving your material. . . . Thank you.

This is an excellent, informative introduction into a licensing agreement. Obviously, the NFL does a fabulous job of promoting its league and teams. It is the most valuable sports league, with the highest visibility. Furthermore, the players are arguably secondary to the league itself. The NFL relies on its stars to lure and retain fans, but the actual athletes are faceless behind the uniforms, equipment, and team identification. When a potential buyer purchases a license, they are getting thousands of hours of promotional support via media exposure. License holders also buy instant credibility and recognition for their items, such as bed sheets, shorts, ornaments, cologne, sweats, and other licensed merchandise.

However, acquiring rights is not always an easy matter. Leagues often have a limit on the number of licenses granted to a particular category. No license holder would want to have a limitless amount of competitors peddling the same item; it would hurt the licensor from a standpoint of market saturation and the dumping of inventory. If too many competing manufacturers in the trading card category, for instance, flooded the market with NBA cards, then none would hold any real value and the industry's earning potential would be inhibited.

Revenue Division

The most critical issue is the proper division of income. A major source of revenue for companies, athletes, and team owners are trading cards. The trading card industry was almost a $2 billion industry in 1992[18] and the revenues go to three groups: to players, their unions, and the owners. Basically, trading cards subsidize the unions, the thorn in management's side. It is no surprise that the owners keep a keen eye on the card business.

The NHL is a good example. The league and the players' association each receive an 8 percent royalty. The players do not get a dividend, but their union functions because of it. In baseball, players do receive a disbursement, anywhere from $80,000 to $100,000 annually. The NFLPA, the labor arm of the National Football Leagues' players, received a subsidy of $21 million in 1991 from the sale of football cards. License holders, such as Topps, Pro Set, and Upper Deck happily pay the royalties and watch the owners smolder as that money finances the constant legal struggle that is pervasive in virtually every major sports labor-management relationship.[19] The NFLPA's counterpart, the NFL itself, receives a reported 9 percent royalty on its goods.

Licensing as a Promotional Piece

Buick is one of the PGA's most important sponsors. The car manufacturer is the title sponsor of four PGA events: the Buick Open in Michigan, the Buick Classic in New York, the Buick Southern Open in Georgia, and the Buick Invitational in San Diego, California. Obviously, Buick is geographically spread out so that it can maximize its golf related exposure. As an integral part of its strategy, Buick uses its golf alliance in as many promotional forms as possible. In 1994, Buick distributed 150,000 computer disks containing a golf simulation game featuring the Warwick Hills Country Club. The disk also features key information about Buick: pricing, fuel consumption, and key features.

Most importantly, the disk allows the user to select the items, and/or elements for viewing. The results are that more people are test driving Buicks and buying them. Buick advertises the disk in selected computer industry magazines and uses direct mail to reach prospective Buick owners who own computers. Buick's efforts match product advertising with its golf sponsorship. By licensing the PGA name and the Warwick Hills Country Club name, Buick has a marketing tool that its competitors do not.

Sponsorship rights give licensing opportunities to corporate partners. The Portland Trailblazers, Oregon's only professional sports franchise, are extremely popular throughout the state with fans and sponsors alike. Bank of America used its sponsorship to sell more checking accounts and bank services. With the franchise's twenty-fifth year anniversary, the bank developed a strategy capitalizing on the silver anniversary theme. Blazer Checking in 1994–1995 was a sweepstakes that required no customer purchase, but encouraged interested parties to entertain Bank of America's enticing offer of free checking until the year 2000. Bank of America put a time limit on the offer, and waived all monthly fees until December 31, 1999, with no minimum balance required. It was a deal almost too good to be true. Each account also featured some Blazer premiums:

- One hundred seventy-five free Blazers twenty-fifth anniversary commemorative checks.
- Free Blazers checkbook cover.
- Limited edition poster of the Blazers' "Legendary Lineup" (all-time team).
- Ten percent discount on Blazer merchandise at specific retail outlets.
- Sweepstakes entry featuring free Blazer tickets and bank services.

The promotion lent itself to media support, retail identification (posters and displays), and fan involvement. Bank of America created an identification between its primary service, checking, and old and new customers who were fans. Blazer Checking also gives excellent follow-up opportunities on future promotions with the team and/or its players. The bank will have a data base of Blazer-related promotion friendly customers.

Bank of America, as it extends its operations throughout the west, uses its successful sponsorships in new markets to gain credibility, identity, and leverage. The bank knows that sports teams are highly identified in communities, and that means potential customers. Bank of America, headquartered in California, has sponsorships with the Seattle Supersonics, Phoenix Suns, and San Antonio Spurs. All of these deals allow the teams and bank operations divisions, both wholesale and retail, to co-sponsor on specific products such as credit cards and checking accounts. More importantly, the sponsorships allow the bank to extend out into the communities that support the teams and their banks. The relationship with the local team gives the bank an introductory platform with community businesses and citizens. By licensing the basketball team's image, Bank of America can merchandise its services to a widespread part of the community, an effective and proved strategy.

Autographed Memorabilia

Why is sports memorabilia a $4 billion industry? Consider the following:

- Nolan Ryan earned $2 million in 1992 by signing memorabilia for Scoreboard®.[20]
- A Jackie Robinson jersey, stained with his blood and sweat, sold for $66,000.[21]
- Twenty-three golf clubs from past British Open champions Bobby Jones, Willie Park, and others sold for $1,031,101 at a London auction.[22]
- Kareem Abdul Jabbar autographed basketballs cost $150.00 whereas Bill Russell's cost $495.00. Russell historically refused to sign autographs until cash became a part of the deal.

Perhaps the most elusive autograph of all-time has been Bill Russell's. The enigmatic Hall-of-Famer has been lured out of autograph hibernation by financial incentive. At one autograph show, the five-time NBA MVP received a minimum of $295 for his signature, and a maximum of $995.[23] Only 500 autograph tickets were sold, guaranteeing a minimum gross revenue of $150,000. At the same show, Wilt Chamberlain, Russell's on-court foil, and fellow Hall-of-Famer, signed for $75 each. A simple lesson in supply and demand.

The memorabilia craze extends away from the playing field. For example, the home that Mickey Mantle was born and raised in (Commerce, Oklahoma) sold for $60,500 at an auction. The buyer had plans to refurbish the home and move it to either Las Vegas or Branson, Missouri, to be a museum for Mantle's memorabilia.

Macy's, QVC, and other retailers sell autographed merchandise. It is a huge business for fans, athletes, and merchandisers. The obvious business angle has changed the autograph moment between athletes and fans, but the reality in sports is that every aspect of it is truly a business. And the market for anything signed is still maturing. Autograph shows, commemoratives, and catalogues featuring merchandise has evolved beyond the simple collector. The Upper Deck card company has created an Authenticated Division where it packages and authenticates items of its endorsers: Reggie Jackson, Michael Jordan, Joe Montana, Wayne Gretzky, Larry Bird, and others.

Darryl Strawberry, an eight-time All-Star, and all-time Met home run leader (252), reported income from autograph shows and appearances totaling $442,000 during 1989 and 1990. The IRS, much to Strawberry's chagrin, felt that he underestimated that figure by $503,000. Pete Rose befell similar circumstances when the agency fined him $50,000 for failing to report almost $346,000 in memorabilia income. Strawberry eventually pled guilty to income tax evasion charges, was fined, and sentenced.

The macabre reality is that once a celebrity is deceased, the supply of memorabilia relating to the athlete is obviously maximized. Therefore, the value of the merchandise climbs. Furthermore, when an athlete's fortunes turn (either upward or downward) so does the value of his cards, signatures, and related memorabilia. Why? Because this fickle market is solely determined by individual buyers and sellers. It is *not* the stock market, where extensive evaluation and complicated theories like the Capital Asset Pricing Model are applied. In memorabilia, there really aren't institutional buyers, (although a large retailer might be analogous to one), simply small retailers and collectors. These buyers and sellers determine the market for autographs and related memorabilia.

Merchandising

Licenses are attractive because a logo or likeness can help volume sales at retail locations. Reebok, the number two shoe and apparel manufacturer, recognizes that football is the most popular sport in America, and it sees the international potential being pursued by both the league and its broadcasters. An NFL license would give Reebok a stepping stone into its international retailers with brand identity. Additionally, Reebok can negotiate with teams to supply them with jerseys and those sideline hats that are worn by design, not by random interest. By buying into an NFL license, the buyer is guaranteed exposure, exposure, and more exposure. Every game is televised. Every play is analyzed and replayed. Reebok can see its logo being stitched onto uniforms and into homes around the world.

Reebok sees the $3 billion annual sales figures. It knows that sales of replica jerseys are up 75 percent in 1994 over 1992 figures. Reebok looks at its manufacturing and distribution capacity. It knows that in its premier spokesman, Emmitt Smith, it has an effective advertising vehicle. The ingredients are all identifiable. This deal can be done. If Reebok can squeeze onto the NFL sidelines with jackets and apparel, it feels that it can become a successful player in both manufacturing and distributing licensed products. The production, distribution, and advertising of this activity is the nuts and bolts to *merchandising* the product line. Getting the rights and turning that into a retail venture is the merchandising venture, and the ultimate goal of the investment in the project.

Distributing, promoting, and selling product brands through retail points of sale shape many sports marketing activities. Foot Locker, perhaps America's most important athletic footwear and clothing store is tightly aligned with the NBA. Foot Locker's primary goal is to generate consumer traffic at its stores. Stocking the latest and greatest in licensed goods and shoes, Foot Locker promotes these products aggressively. The retail chain spent over $8 million during the 1994–1995

NBA season in a comprehensive promotional campaign involving over 1,400 of its stores.[24] The campaign included:

- Distribution and collection of NBA All-Star Game ballots.
- All-Star merchandise and sweepstakes.
- Million Dollar Shot (a three-point attempt) contest. Contest winner shot for the big bucks live on TNT's NBA All-Star Saturday Night broadcast.
- Sold an NBA All-Star Action video for $4.99, specially produced by NBA Entertainment. Video only available at Foot Locker.
- Mexico and Canada locations included.
- Merchandise incentive opportunities, such as discounts and giveaways of products like Spalding basketballs, Huffy backboards, and other officially licensed products.

Foot Locker supported the campaign with a season-long run of paid advertisements on TNT, one of the NBA's two broadcasters, and fifteen regional spot buys. Print advertisements ran in related media (*USA Today*) as well. Eight million dollars were spent quickly to support a comprehensive sweepstakes. The approach was both sound and innovative. Foot Locker's emphasis was to generate store traffic via an NBA promotion. By having promotion specific items for sale (video and licensed merchandise) and use (All-Star ballots and sweepstakes entries), the retailer was able to track promotion-specific sales and gauge the results of its efforts. Obviously, Foot Locker has many more marketing campaigns and consumer-driven attractions, but its investment and interest in the NBA's fan base is a sponsorship created specifically to capitalize and develop opportunities for merchandising licensed products.

This NBA-Foot Locker promotion even went down under to Australia. Due to the forward-thinking league, and the presence of Australian personalities such as Luc Longley, the NBA enjoys great popularity in Australia. Foot Locker sent 20,000 ballots for storewide distribution and expected the ballots to last six weeks. Its estimations were off by thirty-two days, as all 20,000 were cast in just ten days. Forty thousand more were sent in early December to meet the demand.

Licensing in Promotions

Sports licenses are an effective way to create incentives for consumers to buy a product. Castrol® motor oil uses its license with the NFL in a similar fashion. Emblazoned on each case of oil, its core product, is an offer for a free NFL hat of the consumers choice. The hat is an incentive to buy the oil. Knowing the demographics of its customers and NFL fans makes this a smart merchandising match. The hat itself probably costs Castrol less than $1.00, and small cash rebates for similar amounts are not nearly as exciting as free "gifts" like an NFL hat, so the incentive offer makes sense from a marketing perspective. It is the event triangle manipulating its interdependent parts: Football fans (sports audience) use the motor oil purchase (sponsor involvement) to get their free hat (event access).

Similarly, *Sports Illustrated* sales promotions matching up various forms of media use the triangle in the same manner. Every sports fan has seen the ads offering free videos of Michael Jordan, Larry Bird, "Blooper" highlights of funny/embarrassing moments, or your favorite NFL team that come to you free, when you buy your annual subscription to *Sports Illustrated.* This is an extremely effective concept and has helped make up for the lost revenue in the magazine industry, for example, *Sports Illustrated* has lost 900 pages ($35 million) in advertising revenue between 1989–1993.[25] *Sports Illustrated* still is the number one sports magazine in the United States with a circulation of 3,400,000 copies. But advertising emphases have shifted from simple buys of space on the pages and airwaves of our various forms of media to a more sophisticated promotion-driven event. Hence, the exciting commercials featuring sports highlights, enthusiastic fans, and, of course, the toll-free phone number with polite operators standing by, waiting for *your* call.

Credit card companies featuring favorite NFL teams is another creative application of a sports license. General Motors is entering an agreement with the PGA to make its co-sponsored credit card, the GM MasterCard®, the official credit card of the PGA. General Motors is buying the right to promote the card within the PGA, and especially among its players and facilities, the Tournament Players Championship (TPC) courses. This sponsorship makes sense. Credit cards are convenience items used for many travel and business functions. By licensing the PGA's name, images, and affiliations, General Motors captures a wealthy demographic in a sophisticated setting.

LICENSING EQUALS NAME RECOGNITION AND ENDORSEMENTS

Ozzie Smith has a custom Rawlings glove. Karl Malone, an official Spalding basketball. Michael Jordan's name adorns shoes, shirts, basketballs, and baseball bats. Names sell products. Jordan's journey into baseball was a valiant effort on his part to pursue the national pastime. His bat is still available for little leaguers and adult collectors. His name means recognition. Wilson, Jordan's sporting goods endorser, wants to capitalize on his popularity, and they produce a line of bats bearing his name.

Endorsements are simply a form of licensing. Companies contract the rights to use a player's image, name, and relevant biography in mutually agreed upon forms of advertising over a negotiated period of time. Michael Jordan and Nike, Shaquille O'Neal and Reebok, Steffi Graf and Adidas, and anywhere companies place an athlete's identifiable traits are forms of licensing. And companies pay heavily for the right to associate a product with an athlete's characteristics.

Virtually anything can be licensed, from Barney the Dinosaur and the Mighty Morphin Power Rangers to Shaquille O'Neal and Richard Petty. By purchasing the rights to use an image, a company acknowledges that the public's perception of that individual's abilities is worth a nominal price. Furthermore, the merchandising of items featuring athletes and teams helps to reinforce the public image of the athletes and leagues. This makes the public walking billboards when they wear the clothes and hats featuring these images.

SALES EFFORTS BY THE HOME TEAM

The Charlotte Hornets are one of the most popular and successful NBA teams. In spite of no history, no past championships, nor any hereditary ties to the NBA's past, the Hornets have been embraced by their fans and basketball fans across America. The Hornets' licensing efforts include twenty-seven separate retail outlets within a thirteen-mile radius from their arena. The Hornets' catchy teal colors and logo are successful with all NBA fans (Hornets merchandise is the most popular in the

NBA), and more importantly, the home town fans, as evidenced by the twenty-seven separate outlets.

The Chicago Cubs play the majority of their games on national cable television station WGN. Furthermore, their popularity is enhanced by their tradition (lovable losers), their ballpark (historic Wrigley Field), the announcer (the venerable Harry Caray), and exciting stars like Mark Grace and Sammy Sosa. The Cubs, owned by the Tribune Co. (WGN), aired a television show entitled, "A Cubs Gift for You." This home shopping foray gave the Cubs fans throughout WGN's broadcast areas a chance to buy some Cubs' merchandise. The television show was an impulse buyer's dream. There was a chance to buy items found in the Cubs' three stores, merchandise catalogue, and at Wrigley Field. In addition to sales, this venture increased the Cubs' integrated licensing efforts.

9

Sporting Goods and Lifestyle Marketing

> When I was a kid growing up in Evansville (Indiana), we didn't have a major league team, . . . but they had a AAA team, and I used to work over there a little bit. We didn't collect the players' autographs, but we used to use their gloves, bats and balls and just have a great time. For a kid, that was the ultimate—getting to play with professional equipment on that beautiful field.
>
> —Don Mattingly, New York Yankees[1]

Don Mattingly's baseball career began long before his Evansville, Indiana, experience. His first field of dreams was on a little league diamond, an international institution enjoyed by millions of players, parents, coaches, and equipment manufacturers. Founded in 1939 (three teams donated $35 for uniforms), Little League has grown into the largest sports organization for children in the world. Over 2,600,000 participants from sixty-one countries form 180,000 teams.[2] All of the teams and players need gloves, hats, shoes, bats, and balls. The visibility from the professional ranks and baseball industry keeps manufacturers like Mizuno, Rawlings, H&B, SSK, Reebok, Nike, Russell, and Wilson integrating their baseball equation of the majors, minors, schools, softball, and organized leagues. Manufacturers obviously market their products in conjunction with major league sports franchises (and their players) to capitalize on the athletes who may never sign a professional contract, but who can play with professional equipment.

Marketing for sporting goods manufacturers utilizes the appeal of sports teams and events with the public. The idea is to provide the catalyst that allows the individual athlete to pursue his athletic interests.

"Just Do It."	"Life is short. Play hard."
Nike	Reebok

These two popular slogans define more than well-known marketing campaigns. They attempt to capture the essence of the competitive spirit that motivates all people (professional athletes and simple enthusiasts) to lace up their shoes and participate in sports. More accurately, Nike and Reebok's memorable calling cards exhort people to enjoy sports from a more realistic place than one's couch. Of course, it is in their interests to inspire the average person to get off the couch and use one of their products to find that healthy elixir.

When individuals talk about "sports marketing," they often exclude the individual's participation, or, more plainly stated: the equipment. The emotional and physical enjoyment of playing sports and pursuing athletic hobbies obviously has consumer implications. Rock climbing, tennis, golfing, jogging, fishing, aerobics, softball, bowling, "roller-blading," and skiing have manufacturers and destinations that invest billions into attracting the same consumers that New York teams such as the Knicks, Rangers, Yankees, and Giants pursue. Fitness activities are walking to the neighborhood park to play pickup basketball, and/or climbing aboard an airplane to go to Park City, Utah, for a weekend skiing trip. Much like spectator sports opportunities, participatory sports activities are consumer decisions that tilt the balance of the industry. Baseball proponents bemoan the rapid appeal of the in-line skating ("roller-blading") craze, for it diminishes little league sign-ups (kids are signing up for roller hockey leagues), and the sale of gloves, bats, and balls.

Consumer goods like backboards, skateboards, snow skis, water skis, basketballs, footballs, fitness trainers, cross trainers, swim goggles, rowing machines, mountain bikes, soccer cleats, baseball spikes, volleyballs, fishing poles, golf clubs, archery sets, tennis rackets, shoes, sweats, and jock straps are all components of the sporting goods industry. Thousands of items are produced and shipped to a variety of stores that display and sell merchandise to both serious participants and intrigued neophytes. In one study, conducted by *American Sports Data,* skiers who ski less than twelve times per year actually purchase one-half of all skis sold. To the manufacturers, it is about getting new products on the shelves and into the hands of all users. Whether or not the buyer actually uses it is another matter entirely.

The "Weekend Warriors" (a term for people obsessed with maximizing their time away from work) of the nineties have shoes for basketball, running shoes for jogging, golf spikes for the links, tennis shoes for tennis, and a cross-trainer for walking the dog—a multiplicity of styles, brands, and categories. In the fifties, there may have been four different categories of athletic shoes manufactured and sold to the mass market: a cleated shoe for soccer and football, basketball shoe (Converse's Chuck Taylors®), and running shoes (for both sprinters and distance runners). Of course, there were tennis shoes and golf shoes, but they were not available on every retailer's shelves. The industry's specialization has diminished as the benefits of scale (the more product you buy, the less expensive it is) accrue to the large retailers.

One only needs to look at the old photos of competition. The 1972 USA Olympic men's basketball team, for example, all wore the canvas Converse shoes that technologically had no comparative gadgetry, such as Rebok's Pump®, but they were on the players' feet. Jim Ryun's best miles, and Jesse Owens' best sprints, were not run with sophisticated lightweight equipment, they were run by superior athletes in fabulous condition. And although their exploits certainly inspired millions of athletes to exercise, they did not do it with a corporate calling card. Bonnie Blair's Mizuno racing outfits, Andre Agassi's Nikes and John Daly's Reeboks are all a part of the presentation and training. Reebok even made a shoe, the PreSeason®, for training purposes that was promoted through a campaign with spokesmen Emmitt Smith and Frank Thomas.

Of course, modern equipment and training techniques do help athletes achieve results, and they also motivate and inspire average sports fans to pursue their own physical fitness activities. The recent in-line skating phenomenon illustrates the integration of modern technology with athletic endeavors. Rollerblading as it is commonly called, does not divide the marketplace, it expands it. Over $300 million worth of wholesale shipments in the fledgling industry attract both men and women to fitness activities and leagues.[3] Fitness companies practice what they preach as well. Nike's World Campus in Beaverton, Oregon, has restaurants, childcare centers, dry cleaning services, and fitness facilities. Employees are encouraged to exercise as part of their daily activities. Nike wants to do more than sell a healthy image, it wants to convey the spirit to and through its employees.

Today's athletes have better equipment and training. The industry's development indicates that the bygone era's (subjectively defined as the time before 1984) marketing and product classifications were simple and underdeveloped. Virtually every sport today has a shoe with spokesmen and spokeswomen. Furthermore, all equipment are focal points for competitive advantage and commercial development.

Contemporary companies like Nike, Converse, Adidas, Wilson, Hind, Asics, Spalding, and Reebok have best exploited the marketplace through creative and effective use of athletes, images, and marketing tactics. Converse, the original shoe of choice in professional basketball, had Julius Erving endorse its Superstar® basketball shoe in the late 1970s and early 1980s. The company, however, never built and promoted a shoe bearing his name. Puma created perhaps the first true player's shoe with Walt Frazier's "Clydes,"® but the manufacturer faded from the mass market basketball scene in the late 1970s, and so did the nineties prototype advertising and retail merchandising campaign. Adidas' famous tennis shoe the Stan Smith® evolved through the tennis channels, but was not mass marketed. The popularity and explosive growth to the shoe industry can be connected to the efforts of one company and its main spokesman: Michael Jordan and Nike.

In the mid-1980s, Nike gambled on a strategy where they developed a basketball line emphasizing one player in a national campaign. The investment in Michael Jordan paid off as shoe sales zoomed (along with Jordan's popularity). Nike not only became the dominant shoe and apparel company in the sports world, they helped define an industry standard where an athlete's personality and expression of performance defined a product and its marketing. The proof is truly in the financial return for Nike and Jordan. With over ten different models carrying the Jordan name, Nike has racked up great sales, such as the $200 million in 1992.[4]

Nike also applied the strategy to the unique case of Bo Jackson, the first two-sport star to capture the imagination of America. But it all goes back to Nike's investment in Jordan, and Jordan's inimitable talents that resulted in such product-fan identification. Nike controls 54 percent of the basketball category, the most lucrative and prestigious international shoe category. In bottom-line terms, 54 percent of the basketball market is an estimated $453,600,000 in revenue. Jordan's return in 1995 certainly helped Nike maintain and increase its position.

Today, Reebok, Fila, Converse, and LA Gear have personalized shoes with athletes like Shaquille O'Neal, Shawn Kemp, Jamaal Mashburn, and Karl Malone. The campaigns all identify the charisma and competitive excitement of the athletes, with the technological benefits of their shoes. Based upon the appeal of the player, and the fans' enthusiasm to identify with his/her talents, signature shoes generate certifiable consumer activity. Active or retired, the Air Jordan® is the best selling shoe.

This branding of athlete-product is not exclusive to the court sports. Golf equipment companies pursue similar signature series clubs and apparel. For years, Jack Nicklaus put his name on MacGregor® clubs until he started his own club company. His peers, Arnold Palmer and Gary Player have similar equipment companies that bear their names and designs. Other players like Tom Watson (Ram), Davis Love (Tommy Armour), Fred Couples (Lynx), Greg Norman (Cobra), and Chi Chi Rodriguez (Callaway) have high-profile promotions in which their names are either on clubs, or identified with them through endorsements. But does the public recognize the association? Table 1 lists five golfers, their club brands, and what percentage of the public recognizes this association.

Table 1.
Five Golfers, Their Clubs, and the Public's Recognition[5]

Athlete	Club Brand	Public Recognition (%)
Greg Norman	Cobra	57
John Daly	Wilson	53
Fred Couples	Lynx	49
Tom Watson	Ram	40
Nick Faldo	Mizuno	15

Golfing fans are noted for their demographics exclusivity. The above figures indicate that endorsements and equipment branding are not necessarily an automatic association. The industry, however, supports the product-athlete endorsement because it is great exposure and sport identification. All manufacturers want to be a part of the success for the world's best players and the fun for the rest of the playing (and paying) public.

Industry Context

Reebok's 1993 worldwide advertisement spending eclipsed $100 million, and Nike's $270 million. The two shoe giants spend this money to create new product categories and support old ones. Neither of the two leaders wants to go the way of Adidas in the early 1980s. Adidas neglected to support its products with progressive advertising and consumer attention. It subsequently lost its position as an international market leader in all categories except soccer.

The aggressive marketing campaigns exist because the market is lucrative; the 1994 shoe market is valued at $12 billion.[6] The entire Sporting Goods Industry sold $34.2 billion worth of merchandise in 1993,[7] and outdoor equipment sales have climbed to $8 billion annually.[8] Treadmill sales for home gymnasiums account for more than $500 million dollars of business, and golf equipment is a comprehensive $2.85 billion industry.[9] With figures like these, it is no wonder that Nike, Reebok, Wilson, Rawlings, and Spalding pursue creative marketing strategies to increase their market share. And those creative strategies have a price tag as well.

Over forty-two million people exercise at least 100 times per year.[10] Fitness and health are a byproduct of several factors:

- Medical developments and health awareness.
- Access through facilities and leisure time.
- Product availability.
- Sports marketing.

Drinking and smoking are on a decline. In fact, the federal government estimates that substance abuse and addiction costs the United States $77 billion in health care costs and services. Excessive indulgences concerning vice are now taboo for many advertisers and promoters in addition to fans. Virginia Slims and the Women's Tennis Association (WTA) severed their long-term entitlement packages (Philip Morris and a "seniors" women's tennis program surfaced following the separation from the WTA). Furthermore, pressure from political action groups around the world threatens all forms of tobacco, liquor, and even beer advertising. But although citizens are learning the merits of a balanced diet and exercise, the future of physical fitness is not without its real threats. Computer and video game popularity are activities that now replace traditional sports games for many children. And while these games feature popular sports and athletes, they don't require bats, balls, gloves, and teammates.

But the biggest potential risk to all of athletics is funding for school programs. As mentioned in chapter 2, Michael Jordan and Nike spearheaded a venture to save some Chicago area programs. Furthermore, coaches, athletic directors, parents, and the athletes themselves are creating fundraisers to keep their athletic departments intact. The volunteers and benefactors to little leagues, Pop Warner teams, and high school and grammar school programs are heroes who give future generations a competitive chance to experience the education of competition.

Sports marketing also has a definitive impact on our fitness behavior. The NBA's popularity not only helps its league, license buyers, and sponsors generate revenues, it also motivates participants. Table 2 shows the National Sporting Goods Association's report on basketball's popularity.

Table 2.
Sales as a Popularity Index

Year	Number of Players	Income from Ball Sales
1988	23.1 million	$60.3 million
1992	28.2 million	$73.2 million

The growth in three on three tournaments and regional leagues feeds into the NBA campaign to lure more fans. In regards to sporting goods manufacturers, it is the hard core enthusiasts who also buy the basketball shoes and licensed goods. But sports' popularity is not exclusive to the "Michael Jordan effect": where everything he does, everyone mimics. Professional hockey's expansion into California and the sun belt has had its own effects beyond the Kings, Sharks, and Mighty Ducks merchandise sales. Roller hockey and in-line skating has taken these areas by storm and challenged Little League for the hearts, minds, and dollars of young fans. In-line skating does not require the organization of baseball, nor does it require the number of competitors. Furthermore, children can skate on their own time. The outgrowth of leagues has been a modern day grass-roots phenomenon, and proof that professional sports influences fans of all ages to participate in fitness activities.

Another derivative of exposure and opportunity is volleyball. The California Beach Volleyball Association, for instance, reports that 3,000 fans gather to watch a typical beachside event. More importantly, the amount of players doubled in the period between 1989 and 1992 to 1.4 million. Statistics like these excite sporting goods companies and sponsors; hence, the proliferation of events. Sponsors provide the funding to stage events, and fans respond through their attendance and consumer behavior. Oakley® and Revo® sunglasses are a player's staple, and the exposure through volleyball has transferred their use to other markets like Major League Baseball and skiing. Volleyball hit the mass market through its players at the beach. Its success in marketing products through the events is due to creative and effective strategy, and colorful characters. There is even a retail store in Milwaukee, Wisconsin, devoted exclusively to volleyball, indicating that the popularity of a sport can even overcome the weather when consumer interest exists.

The sporting goods industry manipulates the Event Triangle like all other consumer product companies. As a function of the games, the equipment featured in the events, whether it is uniforms, shoes, hats, gloves, bats, or balls, are one big interactive billboard. (See Table 3.) As spectators stay riveted to the action, they cannot help notice the inanimate objects that are integral parts of the competition.

Table 3.
Some Sports' Official Ball Manufacturers

Sport	Official Ball Manufacturer
NFL	Wilson
NBA	Spalding
Major League Baseball	Rawlings
U.S. Open (tennis)	Wilson
1994 World Cup	Adidas
NCAA Football Championships	Rawlings
NCAA Basketball Championship	Rawlings

The "official" anything designation has nothing to do with a governing body's objective decision of structural superiority. The above companies do make fabulous products. When was the last time a ball went flat during a game? Companies also pay for the rights to have their ball used in the highly publicized games and competitions. In the case of college sports, the individual schools have the freedom to choose any ball for their teams. Bowl games also have the same freedom to choose a ball, and/or pursue a sponsorship from a manufacturer. But if the event is an NCAA sponsored game, such as the sixty-four team NCAA Basketball Championship, Rawlings' balls are used exclusively.

Exclusivity in the sporting goods industry trickles down to other qualified products. The NFL, for example only allows three different shoe manufacturers to supply cleated shoes to league players: Apex (recently bought by Converse), Nike, and Reebok. NFL jerseys were manufactured by five different companies in 1994: Apex, Champion, Russell, Starter, and Wilson. In all cases, the logos are displayed directly on the jerseys. Logos are painted on shoes if players put tape over the identifying marks.

A Prominent Company in the Marketplace

Reebok International, Ltd. is the world's second largest shoe maker. Reebok's success is not tied to a growing industry, but to its effective marketing within it. (See Table 4.) Currently, Reebok conducts business in 140 countries. It exports an American image to countries like Thailand, South Korea, China, and the Philippines. It also has an apparel business that accounts for almost $500 million of its revenue. Reebok's goal is to have that figure reach $1 billion by 1999.

Table 4.
Reebok's 1994 Revenue within Different Sports Industries

1994 Category	Industry	Reebok
Tennis	$305 million	$ 55 million
Basketball	$840 million	$150 million
Walking	$560 million	$112 million
Running	$800 million	$148 million
Soccer	$204 million	$ 11 million
Women's fitness	$520 million	$112 million

Reebok's top three spokesmen, Shaquille O'Neal, Emmitt Smith, and Frank Thomas are arguably three of the most popular athletes in all of sports, and Reebok has developed campaigns emphasizing their star appeal and Reebok's extensive lines. Reebok's industry contribution is category creation like the Blacktop® basketball shoes and the PreSeason® cross-training shoe.

Reebok has a history of innovation. They made their first successful venture catering to the female fitness market in the mid-1980s. Seen worn on national television by the then red-hot Cybill Shepherd (star of "Moonlighting"), sales took off. Women have always been a primary audience for Reebok (55 percent of its market in 1991). Reebok also targets the fitness category and has led product innovations and introductions into the step aerobics and the slide workout apparatus. Reebok produces its own fitness videos, featuring its own products and concepts. Whether or not these products become industry standards is up to the marketplace. Reebok's intent is to continue to bring these products to the marketplace for the consumers to judge.

An Integrated Strategy

As an apparel, fitness, and shoe conglomerate, Reebok (and Nike) uses an integrated strategy to promote all of its products in the separate markets. Furthermore, Reebok also does brand imaging within those categories to promote the Reebok name and product identity. Reebok buys advertising time on diverse shows and mainstream sports markets. In 1994, for example, Reebok created "The Reebok Eliminator" cycling program, and bought time and entitlement rights to TNT's NBA broadcasts and created the "Reebok Halftime Report."

As a large company, Reebok commits resources to its endeavors. It signed Jimmy Connors to a two-year endorsement contract for the legend to promote the company's Hard Court® shoe and apparel line. The company, through its two-year deal, indicated that it does not want to make a hasty judgment on Connors' impact. Reebok is acknowledging the benefits of the learning curve, and to the notion that the second year of a promotional arrangement can yield benefits not available in the first. But it realizes that programs like this cost money, and it earmarked $10 million to the Hard Court® marketing program.[11]

Reebok also played a part in the NBA's export campaign. In 1993,

Converse sent stars Larry Johnson (Charlotte Hornets) and Kevin Johnson (Phoenix Suns) on an old-fashioned European barnstorming trip. They visited Barcelona, Madrid, Rome, and other cities promoting the NBA and Converse. Reebok sent Shaquille O'Neal to Asia in 1994 for similar purposes. Sending its top spokesman establishes an identity for Reebok in a foreign country and demand for products bearing his name. Since the shoes are manufactured in the Orient, Japan is a critical market, and Reebok sent its top spokesman in order to substantiate that the shoe manufacturer is willing to pay the price to put its best foot forward. And, in Shaq's case, it's a very big foot.

All of Reebok's efforts aim to provide technologically superior products that will increase its market share. While it has a variety of product categories and sponsorship agreements, the company manages to keep its identity within all of these categories. Nike, Reebok's main competitor, manages to achieve the same results, and from the sidelines, it is a fascinating case to observe and apply educationally.

Home Fitness

The fitness boom has many roots and byproducts. From step aerobics to Jim Fixx's *Complete Book of Running,* personal fitness has become a major part of many peoples' lives. Education, marketing efforts, and simple vanity have contributed to the growing consciousness of physical fitness. Furthermore, many have discovered that fitness corresponds to productivity and health. As a result, many companies have large workout facilities at their offices, and insurance companies offer incentives for active people. The health and fitness phenomenon has had many effects in terms of consumer products. Products like the Health Rider®, NordicTrack®, and Soloflex® are home fitness products that accommodate the busy lifestyle for people on the go.

The companies that make these products do not have to educate the public about fitness. Instead, the companies merely have to convince the health consumer that their product will help him achieve his desired level of fitness within the busy framework of his life. The Soloflex® machine is, perhaps, the best example of the home exercise equipment phenomenon. Beginning in 1978, the Soloflex® was the first home weight-lifting machine, and the basic design has stayed the same since then. Not only is the Soloflex® the oldest muscle machine, it is still the best known.[12]

The machine tapped into the home exercise market and defined the industry. Working primarily through well-crafted media campaigns, the Soloflex® uses video brochures and infomercials to educate interested parties about how to use it. The company attempted to display its machine at retail locations, but it did not work, because the sales staff could not adequately demonstrate the product. It sat there lifelessly. But with the installation of VCR machines in virtually every home, Soloflex® took off by using video brochures to show off the machine's attributes and demonstrate individual exercises and entire workouts.

Soloflex® also exploits the cable broadcast infomercial opportunities. Through the use of buying cheap time, Soloflex® gets to reinforce its message and image as a reliable, effective exercise tool to the public. The competition in the home health business has stiffened, with other products using the same media driven strategy that Soloflex® defined and perfected.

International Dimensions

The globalization of sports entertainment, and its heroes and activities, has created billion-dollar franchises such as the World Cup, the Olympics, and basketball. From a sporting goods standpoint, the world is much more than an event advertising platform, it is a manufacturing and distribution chess game that concentrates production and packaging in the Far East (Korea, China, and Indonesia) and marketing and distribution in North America and Europe. The European shoe market is worth almost $6 billion and Adidas' last international stronghold.[13] North America is a $12 billion market, and is dominated by Nike and Reebok.[14] The most interesting battle is for third place and LA Gear, Converse, Fila, and Adidas are all legitimate contenders with great products and innovative marketing programs such as the Larry Johnson-"Grandma" electronic and print media campaigns.

The production issue though is as much political as it is financial. Off-shore labor sourcing is a common practice in many markets. And the fact that a pair of shoes stitched and boxed in the Far East, then shipped to Milwaukee or Munich is far cheaper than manufacturing them near the eventual retail destination has been proved for many manufacturers. Cost considerations are nothing new for manufacturers, but jobs are a concern for government agencies. Currently, the tariffs for "off-shore" production are not prohibitive for Nike and Reebok.

Furthermore, the cost savings allow the companies to expand into other categories and emphasize image and retail advertising. But the impact goes beyond the political ramifications. It forces a competitor, such as Adidas, to shift its production from Western Europe to elsewhere, and that takes time and money. In the international chess game, the leaders are still a few moves ahead of the pack. Converse, Fila, LA Gear, and Adidas are all jostling to gain market share and shelf space. Meanwhile, Nike and Reebok are investing millions into events like the Goodwill Games, the World Cup, and the World Championships of Track and Field.

And as sports entertainment (broadcasting and events) expands and penetrates into new markets around the globe, the impact of the fitness and health industries grows. European and Latin markets are easily accessed by events like the World Cup and the Olympics. The distribution network, furthermore, allows images to come across the television one day, and have the shelves stocked with goods the next day. Nike, Reebok, and Converse have sent their barnstorming spokesmen into Asia and Europe. More significantly, they have pursued endorsements with key personalities from Brazil, like Romario and Bebeto (famous soccer players from the 1994 World Cup Champions), in order to replicate their successful American marketing programs abroad. Reebok's work with baseball player Juan Gonzalez in America and Latin America links the two markets through one star.

How about Those Retailers?

The large, powerful retailer power brokers are the well-known companies and mass merchants like Foot Locker, Champs, Big 5, Copelands, Modell's, Kmart, Sports Authority, Target, Gander Mountain, and Wal-Mart. Sports retailers work with vendors to generate foot traffic and store business. They broker the stars and images that the leagues and games create. An $80 billion industry,[15] the business of sporting goods manufacturers parallels grocery stores and the packaged goods producers. Shoes, skis, hats, and bats are consumer products just like soap, soda, and cookies. In the grocery relationships, most products have a shelf life, or perishability factor, that obviously would not apply to a pair of shoes.

But in many ways, shoes and gloves are equally as perishable because of fads, trends, and competitive success. There are very few heroes like Larry Bird or Michael Jordan, whose popularity endures regardless of their playing status. Their products certainly have longevity, but a player like Ickey Woods can go from NFL star as a dancing fullback for the Cincinnati Bengals to premature retirement due to a knee injury. Products based on his personality or performance carry more risk. Additionally, there are regional implications for promotional vehicles. Wayne Gretzky's Ultra Wheels® are popular in-line skates throughout North America, but a Mark Grace glove model may not be a big seller outside of Illinois.

One Retailer's Brief Biography

Foot Locker promotes itself as "The World's most Complete Athletic Footwear Store." A division of the Kinney Shoe Corporation, Foot Locker has 1,800 locations in the United States, Australia, Canada, Mexico, Hong Kong, and Europe. Foot Locker merchandises brand-name footwear and apparel in virtually every shoe category, including basketball, running, tennis, soccer, aerobics, and football. Teaming up with the NBA, NFL, and Major League baseball, Foot Locker has twelve months of popular sports promotions, and millions of shoe customers. With international retail sites, they are one of the most important partners for vendor promotions.

Statistics as a Yardstick of Success

Tennis, a sport with elitist origins, has long featured great champions like Fred Perry, Don Budge, Helen Wills Moody, Althea Gibson, and Jack Kramer. With international events and starched outfits and personalities, the sport maintained its appeal to the wealthy and privileged. Tennis gained great popularity in the seventies by capitalizing on the international appeal of personalities such as Bjorn Borg, Ilie Nastase, Margaret Court, Arthur Ashe, Virginia Wade, Guillermo Vilas,

Chris Evert, Rod Laver, Billie Jean King, and Jimmy Connors. Television, of course, bridged the gap between the average sports fan who popularized the sport and the country club settings, i.e., Forest Hills and Wimbledon, of tennis' past. The French Open, for example, was restricted to French Clubs prior to 1925, became an Open Championship in 1968 (an elimination event), and an event exclusively for contract professionals in 1972. "Bridging the gap" between the elite and the general masses means popularity and participants—which increases the number of players and the amount of equipment being used.

In spite of its popularity with international audiences and sponsors, the game has suffered several setbacks in terms of player relations, e.g., Monica Seles being stabbed by a manic disciple of court rival Steffi Graf, Jennifer Capriati's highly publicized drug associations, the retirements of Jimmy Connors, John McEnroe, and Martina Navratilova, etc. The list of negative elements has hurt the game and its sponsor-driven pursuits. If its fortunes reverse through the inspiring play of a charismatic star like Andre Agassi, who won Wimbledon in 1992, the U.S. Open in 1994, and the Australian Open in 1995, then the sport may rebound.

But people aren't playing as much tennis any more. Nothing underlines that more than the equipment sales. Consumers put their money where the sports interests are.[16] In 1993 racket sales fell 25 percent ($112 million) and ball sales fell 15 percent ($100 million) in 1993.

Pete Sampras, one of the two best players in the world reportedly rode on a flight with baseball star Barry Bonds. Bonds was swamped by autograph seekers, Sampras was not. The fallout from other activities hurts tennis off the court—in department stores and sporting goods sales. Industry luminaries are concerned that tennis' reputation needs to be salvaged, and they are introducing urban youth clinics and seniors divisions for both men and women (Borg, Evert, etc.). But the sports following can be gauged through its sales figures.

Maintaining the Games for Everyone

As David Stepp mentioned in the feature interview from chapter 6, sport marketing people need to ensure the future of the games, and he is not talking about the Dodgers or the Yankees. He is talking about the high schoolers and little leaguers who depend on sports for social and physical development. Stepp noted that without the participation of these athletes, there would not be professional athletes.

Nike, a sports marketing leader, and one of America's most successful companies, has taken the initiative to give children and teenagers priority in sports participation. Realizing that budgetary and social constraints prohibit deserving enthusiasts from pursuing athletics, Nike created the "P.L.A.Y" program. "P.L.A.Y." stands for "Participate in the Lives of America's Youth," and Nike has made the program a national movement. To support the project, Nike assists communities and organizations such as the Boys and Girls Club of America with the construction of facilities and the publicized participation of such athletes as Kirby Puckett, Michael Jordan, Charles Barkley, Jackie Joyner-Kersee, Gabrielle Reece, and Ken Griffey, Jr.

The program is a $10 million campaign that is designed "to insure the rights of kids to play." Nike founder and C.E.O. Phil Knight stated, "There is a crisis in America right now. Kid's sports and fitness programs are being axed from schools and the country's playgrounds aren't safe anymore. Access to play should be a kid's inalienable right. Nike wants to lead the charge to guarantee these rights." Michael Jordan, Nike's most visible spokesman (and co-chair of P.L.A.Y.) said about the issue, "Sports can be a great avenue for kids to stand up to the difficult pressures they deal with and are vital to their development. I wouldn't have wanted to grow up without sports."

Nike's efforts inspired its own manifesto, dubbed "A kid's Bill of Rights."

1. Right to participate.
2. Right to have fun.
3. Freedom of choice.
4. Right to easy access and clean facilities.
5. Right to safety.
6. Right to parental involvement.
7. Right to quality programs.
8. Right to equal access for boys and girls.
9. Right to have in-the-know coaches.
10. Right to have a voice.

This program is not about rhetoric, either. Nike puts its resources and spokespeople behind the program. Based on the need for children to play sports, Nike encouraged Michael Jordan and Jackie Joyner-Kersee to support the concept. They readily agreed to be ambassadors, and have contributed money and time to endorse the program's principles and objectives. More importantly, Nike has committed resources over time to support the programs at the grass-roots level.

Nike emphasizes its relationship with the Boys and Girls Clubs of America, a nonprofit organization that assists more than two million youths in America, Puerto Rico, and the Virgin Islands. The Boys and Girls Clubs work primarily in urban areas (1,566 communities) with underprivileged children (66 percent from families with incomes below $15,000). Nike has donated a grant of $1 million from the "Just Do It" fund to help the Clubs support the development and maintenance of other sports programs. To publicize the association, Nike has spent $650,000 in a national ad campaign. Most importantly, Nike ties its Nike Tour golf events into the process by raising money through events in the communities, i.e., thirty events raised $150,000.

Nike and its promotional partners, i.e., Foot Locker, have found that they can influence the most importance audience—children who want to play sports—through major events. When the 1995 NBA All-Star Game came to Phoenix, Charles Barkley, Foot Locker, and Nike joined together to construct a P.L.A.Y. court at the I.G. Homes Boys and Girls Club in Phoenix. The court was constructed out of 4,000 recycled Nike shoes, 1,000 of which were collected at a Foot Locker/Nike Reuse-A-Shoe promotion. People who turned in shoes received a free ticket voucher to the Foot Locker Slam Fest, and all proceeds from the "Fest" went to the P.L.A.Y. court project. The All-Star promotion galvanized sports celebrities and events to target children's groups and their needs, a partnership that should be applauded and supported.

The Reuse-A-Shoe program is one that deserves applause. By recycling its shoes, Nike addresses the needs of waste disposal, promotional cooperation, and community activity. The results are high performance surfaces that can be used for basketball, volleyball and soccer. Through the Reuse-A-Shoe program, playgrounds in Atlanta, Brooklyn, Memphis, Minneapolis, Phoenix, Portland, and other cities will be constructed and, more importantly, played upon. P.L.A.Y. and its objectives are exemplary in both conceptualization and execution.

10

Endorsements

> By having Jerry Rice be a product spokesman, we attach our brands to the excitement of his performance. When one of the greatest football players ever promotes our products, it generates consumer response, which is the rationale for pursuing any endorsement opportunity.
>
> —John Carthum, Nabisco, Inc.

After nine years as the top receiver in the NFL, Jerry Rice closed out the 1993 season on the precipice of sports immortality. By that time, he had scored 124 career touchdowns placing him second to Jim Brown on the all-time list of leaders. Jerry needed only three more trips to the end zone to break Brown's seemingly unreachable record. The fans, media, and world would have to wait for his historic moment, but not Nabisco. They shrewdly anticipated the hysteria and hype that would follow Rice as he approached this landmark feat, and made advanced plans to capitalize on the promotional opportunity once he eclipsed Brown's long-standing record.

The essence of endorsement pursuits is inherent in this example—*timing*. Occasionally, the performance of an individual rises above the competition and transcends the team and sport. When an athlete or performer taps into that magical element that creates legends, he or she becomes a prime candidate to endorse products and services. Disney has long captured exultant performers in the afterglow of excellence in performance. Memorable spots featuring Joe Montana, Emmitt Smith,

Michael Jordan, Jerry Rice with teammate Steve Young, and Nancy Kerrigan are meant to capitalize on the spontaneous exhilaration of accomplishment. At the same time, the athlete knows that public opinion and memory can fade quickly, so he wants to exploit the opportunity of association when he can maximize his benefit.

From Nabisco's perspective in the Rice example, it knew that all eyes were going to be on number 80 when that ball was teed and kicked off to start the 1994 season. Furthermore, every pregame show would discuss, predict, and reflect upon Jerry Rice's career and his impact upon the league. Rice has always been the best by any standard. By the beginning of his historic season, he had won MVP awards, adorned the cover of *Sports Illustrated* multiple times, and been to eight consecutive Pro Bowls. Michael Irvin, star receiver for the Dallas Cowboys, once said: "They call Michael Jordan, Jesus in tennis shoes. Jerry Rice is Jesus in cleats."[1]

No matter what any one calls Jerry Rice, there can be no doubt about who sat atop the NFL's touchdown heap once he scored touchdown number 127. It provided one of those rare moments in sports when an athlete earned an association with a numeric achievement. Al Geiberger will forever be known as "Mr. 59," for his historic golf round. Hank Aaron for his 755 career home runs, Joe DiMaggio for his fifty-six-game hitting streak, Wilt Chamberlain for the 100 points he scored in one evening's work, Glenn Cunningham and Roger Bannister for breaking the four-minute mile barrier, and so on.

When Fox, ABC, and every highlight film available put his name, numbers, and highlights on display, Nabisco was poised to capitalize with its retailers and consumers. Retailers liked the association, because everyone wants to be home to a winner, and the consumers were continuously reminded of Rice's accomplishment and encouraged to participate in the spectacle of his achievement. Nabisco knew it could tie-in to his ongoing assault on the record books in future years and add to the promotional value of its association. Nabisco realized the uniqueness of the opportunity to work with the most prolific scorer in the history of the NFL, the most popular sports property in America, and that motivated its enthusiastic participation.

In many ways, endorsements are merely the commercial result of three simultaneous events:

1. Athletic accomplishment.
2. Public recognition of the spectacle.
3. Opportunistic marketing on behalf of a company.

Timing as the Endorsement Catalyst

The fundamental objective of football is to score points, and that means touchdowns. No one has ever done it with the efficiency, grace, and style of Jerry Rice. Having passed Steve Largent to become the all-time touchdown scoring wide receiver in 1992, Jerry Rice has laid claim to being one of the greatest athletes of his era. Table 1 lists Jerry Rice's various accomplishments.

Of the thousands of athletes who have put on a helmet, jersey, padding, and other accouterments of the NFL gridiron battle, no one has reached the statistical heights of Jerry Rice. In Nabisco's rationale, a relationship with Jerry Rice brings that elite quality to its marketing arsenal. His notoriety enhances the visibility of the products to cast a lasting bond between target consumers and brands.

In 1994, Nabisco built into that image to capture identity with its brands, consumers, and retailers. Regardless of the 49ers' team performance (the 49ers eventually won the Super Bowl), Jerry Rice had already elevated his name and career beyond that direct association in the eyes of football fans.

That is the added-value of an endorsement. The tie-in between the product or service and celebrity focuses on the individual whose performance has made him a standout among his peers. Rice only needs to score touchdowns, which is hard enough. Nabisco's responsibility is to make its relationship work to its advantage. Being a multibillion-dollar company with extensive marketing experience, they should be able to do just that, regardless of what *Barbarians at the Gate* implied.

What Were the Results?

Nabisco placed an advertisement through its participating Long's Drug Stores newsprint inserts at the start of the promotion. It also placed attractive point-of-purchase displays at the Long's retail locations. The point-of-sale materials featured take-one pads for the consumers to enter sweepstakes to win Jerry Rice autographed footballs and other premium items. On September 5, 1994, the first game of the season, Rice scored the three touchdowns that he needed to break the record.

Table 1.
Some Notable Achievements Prior to the 1994 Season

Awards and Achievements

First round draft choice 1985.
1985 NFC Rookie of the Year.
1985 All Rookie Team.
1986–1987 *Sports Illustrated* Player of the Year.
1987 NFL MVP.
Super Bowl XXIII MVP.
1993 Associated Press Offensive Player of the Year.
Pro Bowl: 1987–1994.
All-Pro: 1986–1993.
All-Madden: Perennial.

NFL Records

Most touchdown receptions in one game: 5.
Most touchdown receptions in one postseason game: 3.
Most career postseason touchdown receptions: 13.
Most career postseason receptions.
Most touchdowns in one season: 22.
Most touchdown receptions in a career: 118.

Touchdowns Scored

Receiving: 118
Rushing: 6
Total: 124

Not only was it the first game of the season, it was ABC's "Monday Night Football" season opener. The spectacular fashion (two long passes and an "end-around" run) in which Rice broke Brown's record put three exclamation marks next to his significant record. National television and the exciting nature of the game only helped Nabisco's promotional efforts. Nabisco ran an advertisement the following week, and ultimately received over 25,000 consumer responses from the Northern California market.

Endorsement Structure in the Marketplace

The Nabisco illustration is not unique. In fact, it is the same set of objectives and constraints characteristic to all endorsements. When Gatorade® hired Michael Jordan as a spokesman, they had to devise a concept that would capitalize upon the popularity and magic of the world's greatest basketball player. Its "Be Like Mike" campaign did just that. It put the dream of equaling Jordan's greatness into everyone's imagination, which is just where it belongs. What person hasn't fantasized about his acrobatic ability and intensity? By creating a mental bridge to Jordan, Gatorade® links his audience and its product. By having a celebrity endorsement, you assume the responsibility of his/her performance and seek to take the unique perceptions and associations of his/her characteristics and build them into an identifiable consumer behavior.

Gatorade® has an 87 percent share of the $1.2 billion sports beverage market and is looking to expand sales in overseas markets.[2] Who better than Michael Jordan, arguably the most popular and revered athlete ever, to bring identity to a drink? But Gatorade® needed to translate Jordan's greatness in a commercial way. With its comprehensive "Be Like Mike" campaign, it did just that. Gatorade® took a well-known figure, placed him in a believable scenario, i.e., playing playground basketball, and built a multiyear campaign around that concept. Even after Jordan unexpectedly retired from the Bulls, Gatorade® confirmed its commitment to him as international spokesman—an endorsement of the endorser, if you will. And when Jordan came back to the Chicago Bulls, Gatorade® developed new advertisements.

Gatorade® clearly did something correct in hiring a high-profile spokesperson, because when Coca-Cola and Pepsi rolled out national campaigns for their sports beverages, PowerAde® and All-Sport®, respectively, they enlisted the services of their own spokesmen, Deion Sanders and Shaquille O'Neal. Both Coca-Cola and Pepsi realize that competing with Gatorade® means that they are competing with Michael Jordan, and that they also need to tap into the charismatic identity of a celebrity. By choosing to work with two-sport star Deion Sanders and the multi-talented Shaquille O'Neal, both manufacturers acknowledge the need to identify with a unique athlete with wide appeal. Both companies committed to campaigns worth approximately $30 million and with the same purpose, to gain a foothold in the billion-dollar sports beverage drink category.[3] In endorsements, imitation can be the highest form of flattery. Coca-Cola and Pepsi obviously know a great deal about beverage promotion. By following Gatorade®'s advertising example, they validate the importance and value of a celebrity endorsement in product marketing.

Another contemporary case involves Right Guard® Deodorant. Gillette, Right Guard®'s manufacturer, took famous tough-guy personalities, Charles Barkley, Hulk Hogan, and Marvelous Marvin Hagler, and created a humorous advertising campaign that showed the three gentlemen in refined, sophisticated settings using polysyllabic words and affecting a demeanor bordering on supercilious, i.e., Charles Barkley on a fox hunt expedition. No one who followed sports would ever dispute the competitiveness and toughness that these celebrities attained in their respective disciplines. In fact, they were the benchmarks for hard-nosed, down and dirty play in their professions, achieving both notoriety and success in the process. Gillette's strategy was to stretch the public's attention and create awareness for one of its franchise brands—Right Guard® Deodorant—through the placement of well-known personalities in uncharacteristic settings.

Its strategy was to focus on both television and print media that targeted males 18-34. The campaign worked, because Gillette contracted the perfect personalities (at the height of their popularity) for the theme of the campaign, and they placed them in the proper advertising mediums.

General Mills has also made timely endorsements a cornerstone element in the promotion of its Wheaties® cereal. Wheaties® boxes have long featured champions from many sports such as Mary Lou Retton, Walter Payton, Joe Montana, Michael Jordan, Pete Rose, and even the entire 1980 US Hockey team. General Mills obviously believes in the promotional value of honoring athletes at peak moments in their careers. Furthermore, consumers respond to General Mills' campaign, which reinforces its commitment to this type of promotion. The consumer product company's objective is always the same, build brand awareness around the positive attributes of the product so that it influences consumer behavior, i.e., sales/market share.

Opportunity

William "The Refrigerator" Perry, Mary Lou Retton, Mark Spitz, the Jamaican bobsled team, and Nancy Kerrigan are people whose notoriety raised the spectacle of their performance and who benefited from it financially in terms of endorsements. Endorsements certainly work for the athletes. The lucky few get big money to increase their fame and following. It's a dream job for those who can acquire it. But most importantly, endorsements work for the corporate world. Consumers buy products featuring their favorite athletes' names and likenesses. Look at any sporting goods store and you will see shoes, hats, shirts, ball, rackets, clubs, just about everything endorsed by a variety of celebrities. Need a weight-lifting glove? Lee Haney, the multiple world champion body builder, has got just the one for you. Buying a basketball? How can you resist Wilson's Michael Jordan model? If you're mad at him for playing musical sports, Larry Bird and Karl Malone have Spalding versions on the same shelf.

Consumer product companies are always looking for that next certifiable, identifiable star, because the impact that individual has in his public sphere of influence. The recognition and loyalty of his fans means sales in terms of cereal, video games, chewing gum, shoes, hardware, and just about anything. The concept is always the same. Integrate a personality into a product's image, accentuating the association, and build a comparative advantage over your competition. Companies look for successful personalities with exciting, accepted public images. Michael Stich, following his 1991 Wimbledon singles victory, reportedly increased his endorsement earnings 600 percent to almost $6 million.[4] Stich broke through the ranks of distinguished athletes, to the level of international champion through his victory. PepsiCola® seized the initiative with Shaquille O'Neal, and not for his affable disposition. They want to exploit his popularity, charisma, and high profile to win over consumers around the world.

Endorsement Statistics

Tables 2, 3, and 4 list the top endorsement earners from 1974, 1990, and 1993, respectively:

Table 2.
1974 Top Endorsement Earners

Athlete	Sport	Endorsement Earnings
Arnold Palmer	Golf	$1.8 million
Pelé	Soccer	$1.5 million
Emerson Fittipaldi	Auto Racing	$600,000
Eddie Merck	Cycling	$500,000
Stan Smith	Tennis	$400,000
Rod Laver	Tennis	$400,000
Billie Jean King	Tennis	$300,000
Hank Aaron	Baseball	$200,000
Tom Seaver	Baseball	$100,000

Table 3.
1990 Top Endorsement Earners

Athlete	Sport	Endorsement Earnings
Jack Nicklaus	Golf	$8 million
Arnold Palmer	Golf	$8 million
Greg Norman	Golf	$7 million
Michael Jordan	Basketball	$6 million
Boris Becker	Tennis	$6 million
Steffi Graf	Tennis	$5 million
Andre Agassi	Tennis	$4 million
Ivan Lendl	Tennis	$4 million
Stefan Edberg	Tennis	$4 million
Gabriela Sabitini	Tennis	$4 million

Table 4.
1993 Top Endorsement Earners

Athlete	Sport	Endorsement Earnings
Michael Jordan	Basketball	$32 million
Shaquille O'Neal	Basketball	$11.9 million
Arnold Palmer	Golf	$11 million
Jack Nicklaus	Golf	$10 million
Jim Courier	Tennis	$9 million
Andre Agassi	Tennis	$8 million
Steffi Graf	Tennis	$7 million
Greg Norman	Golf	$7 million
Joe Montana	Football	$6.5 million
Pete Sampras	Tennis	$6 million

Endorsement Trends

For the beneficiaries, the trends are obvious:

1. From the athlete's standpoint, accomplishment is the catalyst to reward. Michael Jordan's three consecutive championships, two MVP awards, and Dream Team association certainly were contributing factors to his meteoric rise to the endorsement pinnacle. Notice between 1990 and 1993 his endorsement earnings jumped by more than 500 percent. All of Jordan's hard work paid off financially and in historical terms.

2. Enduring personalities whose legends have defined their sports, i.e., Montana, Nicklaus, and Palmer, will always have a place in this elite club. Personalities whose accomplishments have defined eras will always identify with the generation corresponding to their careers, and therefore, they will always have endorsements.

3. International sports give athletes greater opportunities to earn money away from their events. Tennis, auto racing, golf, and the Olympics are sports marketing standards on any continent. These sports bring entertainment to the world while producing opportunities for the athletes. As marketing efforts go worldwide, it makes sense to identify with the appropriate celebrities. Kodak's involvement with the Olympics is an integral element to its worldwide marketing strategy, and they

need to enhance that association. Their long-term use of Edwin Moses, one of the world's greatest hurdlers, reinforced Kodak's Olympic commitment. Most importantly, the endorsement was emphasized in Asian and European markets where track and field enjoys greater popularity relative to America. Large companies enjoy the benefits of "spotting" promotional tie-ins to the most appropriate markets (region-specific, not national, but tightly targeted and defined), mainly because they can afford to.

Types of Endorsements

Association. Take the product, place it in the athlete's hand, and take his/her picture. This is the old-fashioned model. Crude, but effective. Simple, although uninspired. These are usually found in print ads or billboards for regional advertising purposes. Companies normally will not invest the millions of necessary dollars in any promotion that is not tied to a sophisticated, comprehensive campaign. This category is also characterized by logo placement, either on an athlete, golf bag, or automobile. What does it cost to put a logo on a NASCAR vehicle? Essentially the driver's uniform, sponsors are asked for up to $1 million for the hood and side panel, between $100,000 and $200,000 for the frontside panel, and anywhere from $150,000 to $450,000 for the rear side panel.[5] Of course, a lot depends on the driver and the racing team, but it is big money to buy that type of exposure, regardless of where your driver finishes.

Leverage. Use a spokesman to gain access and leverage with a team, league, or sport. This is exemplified by the modern sneaker endorsement deal. Coach Mike Kryzewski of Duke will receive $15 million from Nike for seven years.[6] For this, Duke's players will wear Nike shoes for their practices and games. Coach Kryzewski will also use the shoes in his camps, and wear Nike apparel whenever he can. After all, he has been handsomely compensated. All that Coach Kryzewski has done to earn this contract is guide his exemplary collegiate program to seven Final Four spots in the last nine years (1985–1994), including two championships.[7]

Pelé (real name Edson Arantes do Nascimento), the most popular soccer player in the world's history, capitalized on the 1994 World Cup with $30 million in endorsements to coincide with the competition.

Having played for the Brazilian National team (three-time World Cup Champion team member: 1958, 1962, and 1970), and the New York Cosmos (1975–1977) of the North American Soccer League (NASL), Pelé was in a position to profit in both continents. Working with MasterCard, Pizza Hut, Umbro, and scores of other companies and organizations, Pelé had the leverage to be in great demand. More than a great player, Pelé has become the ambassador for sportsmanship in his sport, and the 1994 World Cup presented a tremendous opportunity for him and the companies he represented.

Credibility. Introduce a product to gain a market in terms of customers and distribution. First Team Sports was founded by two sales representatives in the sporting goods industry. They had watched Rollerblades achieve widespread acceptance and profitability and decided to enter the market. But how do they introduce a product that retailers will shelve and customers will buy? The answer was simple—the Great One. First Team Sports contracted Wayne Gretzky, gave him $100,000, stock options, and royalties based upon sales.[8] By 1992, they had $27 million in sales, and almost 20 percent of the markets. Next? It signed Katarina Witt and Brett Hull. Their skates, the Ultra Wheels®, is an example of a proactive organization willing to invest in the marketing tools and resources that will sell its products. In this case, First Team budgeted this endorsement expense into its cost of goods sold to position and sell its skates.

Personality fit. Use a celebrity's image to identify with target demographics. This is a personality, not product, "fit." John Madden's True Value® Hardware campaign, Jack Nicklaus' Lincoln Continental® endorsements, and Arnold Palmer's Pennzoil® tractor commercials are prime examples of a celebrity being popular among a specific consumer group. As markets emerge, i.e., Latin America and Asia, identifiable personalities will receive opportunities there. Boxing's Julio Caesar Chavez has signed deals with a video game manufacturer and Pepsi® because he is a legitimate Latin star, and that market has considerable maturity, potential, and power both in the U.S. and abroad. Ditto for Texas Rangers' star Juan Gonzalez. Reebok has signed the home run hitter to be a significant product spokesman in both domestic and foreign markets. As television brings more and more sporting events to the world, cross-cultural alliances like these will be important.

Product fit. Use the athlete's reputation directly with equipment like shoes, ball, gloves, and other items used by athletes in competition and training. Nike, Reebok, Spalding, and Wilson are the most direct examples. It is overwhelmingly obvious why a shoe company that makes basketball shoes would want basketball players to wear its shoes. But a subtle feature of the product category is sales potential in terms of consumer use. Football is the most popular (watched) sport in America, but the average American can't wear a football shoe on the street, or to the library. However, a basketball shoe or a tennis shoe can be worn anywhere. Virtually every NBA player receives some form of compensation for wearing a particular shoe, but few baseball players, football players, golfers, and skiers receive significant compensation for the shoes that they wear.

Another example in this category occurs in auto racing. Dale Earnhardt won the Winston Cup in 1993, an honor bestowed upon the best finishes in NASCAR races. In the process, he used 1,500 tires. The sticker price for these tires is normally $271 each, but Dale wears the Goodyear logo—saving him several hundreds of thousands of dollars in tire costs.

Competitive response. Good old-fashioned market share competition. Titleist®, long the predominant choice of ball played on every golf tour, always has a separate contest at each tournament for the players using its ball. For example, if a golfer won a tournament while using a Titleist®, he/she would receive a cash bonus from the ball manufacturer. Cash bonuses obviously corresponded to tournament results. This system certainly worked for Titleist®, much to the chagrin of Dunlop, manufacturers of Maxfli® balls. Dunlop knew that the golf equipment industry is a billion-dollar business, and it wanted to become a player in every golfer's bag. To gain notoriety, Dunlop signed Seve Ballesteros, Jack Nicklaus, Greg Norman, Arnold Palmer, Curtis Strange, and Ian Woosnam, among others.[9] This make an impression with consumers. Titleist®'s response: they recently signed two-time U.S. Open champ Curtis Strange away from its upstart competitor. The burgeoning golf market, over twenty-three million players (more than one half of this group is in their twenties and thirties), is an annuity waiting to happen for the successful marketer.[10] Golfers rarely buy new clubs, but balls are almost mandatory purchases with each round.

Assumed risk. A newer, widespread category is where an athlete will assume the financial risk/reward scenario in exchange for his/her participation in a commercial venture. Quarterbacks Boomer Esiason and Warren Moon traded their fees for the opportunity to sell advertising time on their own radio shows. They reasoned that they had the contacts, presence, and help to sell the time and profit in terms of remuneration and experience.[11] The athletes do not make the sales calls themselves, but lend their names and support to the efforts of the personalized sales staff members. By controlling some of the advertising time, the athletes can bring some financial results to all of those off-season golf tournaments that they attend. It makes sense for the athletes to pursue this relationship. It gives both the radio stations and the athletes incentive to improve the commitment and quality of the product. In this situation, both the fans and the sponsors benefit from the entrepreneurial spirit of these two great quarterbacks.

Equity positions. In exchange for his product endorsement, Greg Norman was allowed to buy 12 percent of Cobra Golf for $1.2 million in 1991. Three years later, his investment grew more than tenfold.[12] Senior golfer Chi Chi Rodriguez got 75,000 shares of Callaway in 1992. The stock split twice and his holdings are worth more than $10 million—almost double his career earnings on the regular and senior tour. Fred Couples received $5 million in Ashworth stock, and in the Wayne Gretzky Ultra Wheels® example, he received equity in the consumer product company. This strategy gives the athlete more incentive to support the product and the marketing of it and reduces the strain on direct-cash payments.

Buyers and Sellers

Just like sponsorships and almost every other type of commercial enterprise, there are two differing views pushing the financial broom of endorsements. There's the buyer, and there are lots of sellers. Both the buyers and the sellers pursue three similar goals:

1. *Profits.* For the athlete that means money, in the form of cash payments, royalties, and/or stock opportunities. For the company, the objective is to enhance business operations in terms of both image and sales.
2. *Legitimacy.* The product plateaus at the same level of excellence as the celebrity. As Michael Jordan says; "You better eat your

Wheaties®!" Jordan and his fellow athletes get more than money from endorsements, they get prestige. All athletes are highly competitive individuals who like to win any contest, whether it be a championship event, game of cards, or the endorsement game, especially when it means money—just ask them. At the same time, by paying the big bucks to get a Jordan, Gretzky, Madden, etc., companies are paying the price to be the best.

3. *Transference.* The manufacturer of the product wants the excitement and enthusiastic response at the point-of-sale from the very same fans that yell and cheer during the game. The athlete, meanwhile, wants to use his influence to his commercial advantage. Who wouldn't?

SELLING AN ENDORSEMENT

The seller's objective is relatively simple from a conceptual standpoint, sell the celebrity vehicle to the best company in terms of prestige and established marketplace, i.e., Coca-Cola, Nabisco, Pepsi, for the highest possible price. Athletes are not accustomed to receiving a scanty fee for effort, and if you want effort you had better be prepared to pay for it. The second goal is to get the best possible visibility for your client. Troy Aikman is not going to want to exclusively endorse Snickers® bars in the Dallas area for $10,000 when he knows that he could potentially do the same for a Nestle candy product in a national campaign for twenty times that amount.

Visibility is important in terms of legitimacy, because if a personality is featured in another advertisement, it means that the association is simultaneously being reinforced elsewhere. Some people say that Michael Jordan is spread too thin. But he has thirty million ways he can disprove that. Jordan and his representation are opportunistic. He, like any smart property, diversifies and categorizes his endorsements. There is only one official shoe of the NFL and that is manufactured by Apex. There is only one official shoe of Michael Jordan, and that is manufactured by Nike. Jordan's other product endorsements, McDonald's, Gatorade®, Hanes®, Wheaties®, and Electronic Arts' video games do not jeopardize each others' profitability.*

---

*An argument could be made in regards to a Nike-Hanes conflict, but if there was one, either company would have done something about it. Hanes, the textile giant, is a subsidiary of Sara Lee, and the apparel lines that Jordan endorses for them do not conflict with his Nike products.

The fact that Jordan has several business relationships, including videos and books that detail his life and career, only proves his popularity and viability as a product spokesman. Consumer product companies want to tap into that element. They do not intend to make the personality more famous, that is merely a byproduct of the relationship. It is the sponsor's objective to have the athlete help the product sell and sell some more. The athlete who has reached this plateau of recognition and notoriety charges a premium for her services. All of the charisma and glitz that you get with a celebrity has a price tag, and the market will determine it. Golf legend Jack Nicklaus is past his prime in terms of competitive success, but he is right in the middle of it in terms of endorsement profitability. This gentleman is still a great player, but most importantly, he is more popular than ever. Put his name on shirts, balls, or golf courses and it brings the credibility of their athletic achievements to those particular products. More importantly, his social grace and professional demeanor appeals to a key demographic.

In fact, the degree of visibility is a major issue with athletes. Players nowadays want more than just the financial rewards. They want advertising emphasis. After an All-American collegiate career at Kentucky, Jamaal Mashburn was chosen by the Dallas Mavericks as the fourth pick in the 1993 NBA draft. Big, strong, fast, and tough, Mashburn was destined to become an impact player in the NBA. His ambition, though, extended beyond the hardwood. He wanted to be successful in the endorsement arena. He signed a five-year, $6 million contract with Fila® Sportswear to endorse a signature line of shoes and apparel.[13] His deal was not simply slap a name on a shoe and ship it to retail locations. Fila committed to a $15 million media campaign to be conducted in fifteen U.S. markets, not just in Dallas and the Southwest.[14] Mashburn had never played in an NBA game, but he had tremendous ability, personality, and dedication. Fila sized up the market, knew what types of commitments other marquee players were getting, and placed its investments with Mashburn.

Mashburn probably learned from the example set by Shaquille O'Neal, who signed on with companies intent on making him a star. His deal with Reebok calls for a minimum of $3 million annually, plus royalties. Furthermore, it stipulates that Reebok must spend at least $50 million in related advertising in the first three years of the relationship.[15] In this case, it's the proverbial tail wagging the dog. Shaq was smart in knowing that he was helping Reebok do more than just sell shoes, and that he deserved a positive benefit of image enhancement. After $50 million in promotions, Shaq will be known wherever television sets are plugged in, turned on, and tuned in by viewers.

ONE MAN'S EARNINGS PORTFOLIO

Shaquille O'Neal is not only one of the greatest impact players to come into the NBA, he is undoubtedly the best marketed. After playing only one season, Shaquille's annual income is in excess of $15 million. Furthermore, like any wise investor, Shaq is diversified. In addition to his basketball earnings, his movies, records, and equity-oriented consumer product endorsements make Shaq a multifaceted marketing force. With a long-range strategy toward cross-promotions and heavy royalties, Shaq is willing to invest his own resources, i.e., time and confidence in payoff/future value of investment return, into his off-court ventures.

Revenue Source	1993 Estimated Earnings
Basketball Salary	$ 3,300,000
Reebok	$ 3,000,000
Pepsi	$ 2,200,000
Merchandise Interests	$ 3,000,000
Video Games, and Toys	$ 1,100,000
Books, Movies, and Records	$ 2,000,000
Other Sporting Goods	$ 600,000
Total:	$15,200,000

Of course, an athlete of Shaquille's stature does not explode onto the sports scene too often, nor do other athletes enjoy this type of business traffic. Shaq definitely benefited from the international appeal of basketball and the example Michael Jordan set, that a basketball player can be a successful international product spokesman. But athletes and business people alike must respect the success and notoriety (precociousness, too) of Shaquille. This attention and opportunity would not have been possible if Shaq did not have the ability to handle it so skillfully.

Shaquille pursued a similar relationship with Pepsi. He received $12 million over five years with stipulations regarding Pepsi's direct advertising expenditures on their promotional agreement.[16] These deals worked out for both Pepsi and Reebok in a related manner. After analyzing their prized investment, they combined on a successful cross-promotion featuring product redemption coupons for Reebok shoes with Pepsi® liter purchases in the Summer of 1993. This type of program targets the same consumer for two different consumer needs. Rather than confuse or clutter the market, it brings operating efficiency (outside of the logistics) to an athlete's endorsement profile. Look for many more cross-promotional ventures to be pursued among endorsement buyers and sponsors as marketing tools, because they work for the corporate interests, the agents whose investments shape the industry.

Lastly, a seller has to look objectively at the circumstances surrounding the athlete in question, and set the endorsement potential accordingly. The figure-skating gold medal winner has an endorsement potential advantage over the successful biathlon competitor, or lugist. Figure skating is characterized by a high degree of personal expression, pageantry, and drama of the performance (recently both on *and* off the ice). This allows the audience to identify with the sport and personalities and ultimately manifests into tremendous opportunities for the skaters as the endorsement bucks go where the greatest impact can be felt. As always, those are the high-exposure/visibility sports with a worldwide emphasis like basketball, tennis, and auto racing.

Factors in Endorsement Opportunities

- Exposure of sport.
- Established presence of athlete within that sport.
- Feasibility of tie-in to consumer product in question, i.e., Chris Evert and Nuprin® is plausible. Evert and Craftsman® tools is not a likely match.

Another germane issue is that a player may be in a popular sport, but is not visible as a personality outside of his uniform. Football players, except quarterbacks, rarely get endorsement opportunities. Lawrence Taylor, the greatest defensive player in the history of the NFL, played for a successful team in the biggest media market, and still did not get significant national endorsements. Thurman Thomas, Barry Sanders, and several other fabulous, popular athletes do not get the same recognition from advertisers. It always seems to go to the quarterback. Why?

One successful venture, "The Quarterback Club," identifies the popularity of quarterbacks and the value they represent. The "Quarterback Club" features eleven of the most popular signal callers in the NFL—Jim Kelly, Troy Aikman, Randall Cunningham, Boomer Esiason, and Warren Moon to name a few, and they pursue a variety of opportunities. The Club has worked with Domino's Pizza, video game manufacturers, and trading card companies. In one deal, each featured quarterback received approximately $500,000 for five years to be included in a special card set from NFL Properties.

Quarterbacks receive the most attention and compensation (of the twenty-eight NFL teams, quarterbacks are the highest paid on fourteen) from fans, owners, and marketing executives. Quarterbacks have the camera focused on them for each play. Furthermore, they are also mentioned as the play develops. The skill position player, on the other hand, does not have his name tied to the action each moment. When announcers recount the action, they don't say, "Mark Stepnoski hikes the ball to Troy Aikman."* They say, "Aikman takes the snap and fades back to pass. . . ." What happens next is up to Aikman and his teammates. But, for better or worse, the quarterback is always one-half of the action on each play, and the exposure can make or break him in terms of recognition and endorsements.

Obviously, there are exceptions. Emmitt Smith, and O. J. Simpson before him, have been able to break the quarterback's endorsement grasp, but many of their peers have not. From the sponsor's perspective, they want the big-name, high-impact star who is certain to command a high amount of media attention. In the sport of football, that person is almost always the quarterback, unless the other player does something so extraordinary, he is able to capture the spotlight, i.e., Jerry Rice's touchdown record.

The elements of the endorsement contract are similar to any other sponsorship agreement. The basic contract is comprised of terms and conditions with considerations that mitigate the conditions of the binding agreement. The contract will state the payment, duration, and rights of the license or agreement between the personality and his or her contracting authority. Key elements are time commitments for promotional purposes, geographical uses, photo and press issues, appearances, and forms of

---

*Stepnoski left the Cowboys following the 1994 season.

media the athlete's likeness can appear in, i.e., print or electronic media. The more ways that the company wants in terms of access and usage of the player's image and time, the higher the endorsement's price tag.

Buyers

The lucky buyer/seeker of a celebrity endorsement recognizes the issues that influence his/her decision to pursue this endorsement. The first things to be determined are the overall marketing goals of the company, and/or brand in question:

- Exposure?
- Market share?
- Retail/channel marketing development?
- Internal purposes, i.e. incentive or reward?
- Target audience/demographics?
- All of the above?

Determining marketing goals is a difficult task in itself, but once they are identified, the company needs to see how a celebrity would fit in with those goals. In the case of Gatorade®, the domestic (U.S.) market had matured to $1 billion, and because Coca-Cola and Pepsi were lining up products, Powerade® and All-Sport® respectively, Gatorade® was looking to maintain as much domestic market share and expand overseas.[17] Who would instantly be recognized and bring legitimacy to a product. The answer, obviously, was there's no one quite like Mike.

Next, the company needs to ponder what advantages come with a relationship. McDonald's has a license to use logos and uniforms in promotions, so when they film Pete Stoyanovich and Chip Lohmiller for its "through the uprights" advertisement (a continuation on the hamburger chain's H-O-R-S-E theme featuring Larry Bird and Michael Jordan), it can film the kickers in their uniforms. This is an important issue, because the uniform is the first thing that brings recognition to the viewer. Lohmiller and Stoyanovic in their street clothes or gym shorts would not have done that for McDonald's, but put them in their jerseys, and they look like football players.

In the Lohmiller-Stoyanovich example, the NFL license is a built-in advantage for McDonald's and the two place-kickers. Because of the license, the athletes can better market themselves, and McDonald's can take advantage of its prepaid privileges of its relationship to the NFL. So everyone wins, the kickers literally kick for cash, the fast food giant expands on a theme established by Larry Bird and Michael Jordan, and the league integrates its personalities and teams into a high-profile promotion.

CAVEAT EMPTOR

Yes, buyer beware. Ask Pepsi how it felt in regard to its Mike Tyson endorsement after his much publicized private life overshadowed the excitement and appeal of his athletic exploits. Advertisers pay the premium for endorsement services because they feel a personality can deliver an audience, and heighten a particular brand's image. Companies that invest hundreds of millions of dollars in positive image enhancements are not interested in negative associations. No sponsor wants the smoking gun of scandal or potentially unscrupulous characteristics to be tied to its precious brand names. The most obvious case involves the O. J. Simpson double murder trial and the over-publicized attention to his personal and public life.

O. J. maintained an identity with the public after his playing career largely through his endorsements. When his life unraveled before the public, so did his endorsement contracts. Companies issue vague statements wishing the individual well in his pursuits, thank him for his services, and move on in a hurry. In fact, morality clauses are elements of many endorsement contracts these days. The salesperson is essentially peddling a perishable entity. If Schick sponsors the Chicago Blackhawks, it identifies with the entire team. If they have an exclusive agreement with Jeremy Roenick, their biggest star, then its risk is concentrated on the health and fortune of that one individual. If he gets hurt, or is plagued by unsettling issues in his private life, then it gives his sponsors cause for concern, which is not a harbinger for mutually pursued endorsements.

Volatile personalities bring the unexpected. Jose Canseco carrying a gun in his car did not endear him to anyone. Canseco is certainly entitled to his character flaws, it just makes him a risky endorser. The public does not demand a goody-two shoes. They embrace irreverent characters, i.e., Charles Barkley, but they want to trust their celebrities.

Arnold Palmer, Wayne Gretzky, Michael Jordan, and Joe Namath are all individuals who have the trust and admiration of the public, and they continue to profit from it.

Another potentially troublesome area is the unexpected. This is best illustrated by the "Dan and Dave" saga. By not making the 1992 Olympic Team, Dan O'Brien stunned the world. Instead of a world's greatest athlete showdown in Barcelona, Reebok had a uniquely challenging set of circumstances facing them. With $20 million invested, Reebok could not scuttle the program. Instead, they adapted and altered the emphasis and did a great improvisational job in the face of a minor disaster.

What It Means and What It Costs

It is indisputably linked that with endorsements, you get what you pay for. If you want Michael Jordan, the most popular athlete ever, it will cost you. On the other hand, football player Wesley Walls would do a backflip for the money that Jordan is offered in endorsement agreements. By paying the endorsement premium, a company does the following.

- Identifies with a certifiable winner.
- Parlays the excitement of the athlete into a brand's image.
- Provides an opportunity to integrate marketing strategies into relevant forms of media.

The best place to air an advertisement featuring Shaquille O'Neal is during a basketball game first, and other sports contests second. Reebok spent over $3 million in paid advertisement during Super Bowl XXVII, featuring M. Shaq Diesel himself.[18] By placing the celebrity in an appropriate medium, the company is reinforcing several images, that of the player, his/her place, and the brand's place as a key part of the activity. The audience wants to see the athlete perform, and they will certainly accept them in a commercial application.

Capitalizing on Unique Attributes

Bo Jackson mesmerized the established American sports world by successfully playing and excelling in both football and baseball in the late

1980s and early 1990s. His unique status as a "can-do" individual put him in the elite echelon of sports personalities and endorsers. The public embraced Jackson's improbable heroics and stayed with him through his celebrated hip replacement surgery in 1992. Nike, his signature sponsor, always stayed with Bo, recognizing a successful story line. What athlete has not coped with adversity? Bo's persistence only cemented his popularity with America. Nike, in fact, used the Bo Jackson experience to its advantage in its relationship with Deion Sanders, another two-sport star.

Los Angeles Dodgers' pitcher, Chan Ho Park, signed with telecommunications giant Sprint to target the Korean American market. Park is the first Major League player to have been born in Korea. The fact that he is also an exciting, top prospect enhances his legitimacy as a spokesman. Most importantly, Park demonstrates that despite the questions on the integrity of the game, it is still an effective marketing tool and executives will use its stars and/or images to sell the products. Park presents a unique opportunity to address a market segment, and Sprint believes that the added-value of his profile and identity in America will work for Korean-Americans looking to make long distance purchasing decisions. The ads featuring Park will have him speaking with his mother in Korean, a familiar theme in any language. Even baseball players need to call home to their moms.*

Endorsement Tie-ins

The greatest advantage to endorsements is the complementary advertising opportunities that they offer. By placing famous personalities in an acceptable, legitimate environment, the company synergizes its efforts to reach an audience. The memorable Reebok network advertisement featuring Shaquille O'Neal, Bill Russell, Wilt Chamberlain, Kareem Adbul-Jabbar, and Bill Walton emphasized the historical significance of the league and its promising future. Shaq, as great as he is,

---

*Unfortunately, Park's play did not live up to his promotional promise and he was demoted to the minors in 1995. On the other hand, Park's appeal was made up by Hideo Nomo, the second Japanese-born Major League Baseball player. With his unique windup and fastball, Nomo took the fans and the league by storm, eventually becoming the starter for the National League in his first All-Star game in June 1995.

could learn from those other gentleman. The McDonald's H-O-R-S-E contest with Larry Bird and Michael Jordan is noteworthy not only for its creativity, but for complementing McDonald's NBA marketing commitments. McDonald's has a large commitment to NBA broadcast interests. It makes sense to use the basketball celebrities during the telecasts. McDonald's brings the fun and good-natured competition among friends to the Big Mac®. It reinforces the image of the league and the actual product. Yes, that Big Mac® and french fries are important to two legendary athletes, so why not to everyone?

Reinforcing an association between a product, endorser, and sport shows the sponsor's commitment to the three key groups:

- Fans
- Athletes
- The sport itself

Money drives the entire relationship. Companies forecast the return of promotional investments and respond to the opportunities that can best enhance their business operations. Joe Montana, Reggie Jackson, Ted Williams, Michael Jordan, Mickey Mantle, and Wayne Gretzky talking about card collecting is a strong endorsement of Upper Deck's primary objective: enthuse and motivate a consumer response. By appealing to a representative cross-section of fans, Upper Deck shows that collecting is fun for people of all ages.

The Reality of Endorsements

Endorsements work for companies, otherwise the industry would not be expanding. There are three basic characteristics of the endorsement business climate.

1. They are expensive, and potentially risky. Athletes want to pay for nothing and get compensated for everything. They are pampered, handsomely rewarded, and perhaps, overpaid, but they do need to be remunerated for their promotional services. Companies learn this and pay the costs, knowing that there are risks involved, i.e., Mike Tyson and Pepsi.

2. Only the most popular athletes get the deals. There were twelve Dream Team members, but Clyde Drexler, Christian Laettner, and the majority of their teammates did not participate in the international endorsement world. Perhaps it is their choice not to aggressively pursue all outside business opportunities, but most endorsement deals are only for a select few.

3. Endorsements favor the high visibility sports. Basketball, football, tennis, golf, auto racing, and big-time Olympic stars generally are the endorsement elite. In golf, baseball, and basketball, the athletes' expressions and nuances are a part of the competition. The fans can identify with these personalities, and that is the first and most critical step in the endorsement progression—identification. Once that happens, companies wait for the timing to correspond with promotional needs, and that is how endorsements are born.

The future of endorsements will always be bright. They may someday wane in popularity, but they will never go entirely out of fashion. As long as there are gifted athletes who capture the public's attention, companies will line up to contract their promotional services, and in the process, continue the evolution of celebrity endorsements.

11

Sports Marketing Buyers and Sellers

> Sports marketing is a team effort. When you can successfully associate your client with a sporting event consistent with their brand personality, target audience, geography and timing, everyone wins.
>
> —Lisa Marie Smith, Goldberg Moser O'Neill

> You work your butt off, so a bunch of total strangers can come and have a great time.
>
> —Joe Carroll, Sports Marketing Operations Specialist

As an agency promotions director, Lisa Smith recommends and develops sponsor strategies in many markets, including the sports advertising industry. On the other hand, Joe Carroll shapes and executes the directives of clients like Smith. To Smith, sports advertising is one of many commercial opportunities for the variety of clients that she represents. Her position, like many other promotional buyers, requires that she weigh the merits of all available sponsorships for her client's demographics and product needs. Joe Carroll, meanwhile, wants his event to fulfill and exceed the expectations and needs of Smith and other sponsors. Individually, each has a vision for the event and its promotional outcome. And the work of both contributes to the evolution of sports entertainment.

The targeted focus of this book, i.e., sports marketing, does not mean to exclude the value of other advertising outlets such as news talk formats, network programming, print opportunities, children's markets, etc. Promotional buyers and representatives are certainly aware of the availability to invest promotional budgets in mediums outside of the sports industry. Once buyers make a decision to purchase a sports advertising vehicle, their next moves trigger the promotional cycle of sponsor publicity and commercial placement, which expands the sports industry. Press releases, retail promotions, related advertising through appropriate channels, and targeted consumer programs all involve the sponsor with the sports property.

Sports marketing at its essence is role playing, and every job is clearly defined. The athletes compete and entertain. The promoting organization, whether it be a league (NBA), team (Dallas Cowboys), or governing body (International Olympic Committee), publicizes, packages, and sells the entertainment. It quantifies the value through sponsorships, broadcasting rights fees, and licensing partners. It also coordinates and presents the entertainment in the appropriate venues (facilities) and markets (broadcast areas).

If this book has brought forth any idea about sports marketing, the primary one would be that the industry *evolves* through the buyers and suppliers of sports advertising and promotions. In 1954, Wilson Sporting Goods paid golf legend Arnold Palmer $2,000 per month to be a product spokesman.[1] Forty-one years later, both Palmer and Wilson have learned from their experiences and apply different criteria to their promotional relationships. Sponsors integrate promotional inventory into media and retail campaigns that are judged by the sales success of the brands and services attached to the promotion. The Bud Bowl, an oft-cited example, has been highly successful for Anheuser-Busch and the NFL. As a buyer of sports advertising, Anheuser-Busch gains leverage with the leagues, broadcasters, and audience. The brewery has learned through its promotional investment of ways to improve the promotion's reach and success with its consumers and retailers.

The Fans Are the Focus

The fans certainly know what to do. They either show up, tune in, or stay away. Most importantly, they know that there is a cost attached to sports entertainment and they are willing to pay that price. As stated throughout this book, the fans' enthusiasm and loyalty provides a captive audience for corporate sponsors. Together, fans and sponsors structurally support and expand the sports marketplace. If you include participants and spectators, the annual sports market's sales value has been estimated at $179 billion.[2] The money flows through all of the known sources: ticket sales, broadcast contracts, labor contracts (both administrative and athletic talent), and merchandise sales.

Sponsorship is the corporate acknowledgment of the fans' devotion. Sponsors buy into the teams, leagues, and athletes. Their interest drives up broadcast and labor contracts. But they do so for the return on investment. If there was a more effective advertising vehicle available, they would use it. Sponsors may be sports fans as individuals, but when they represent their companies, they purchase sports advertising opportunities for calculated purposes.

The Sales Equation: Locating a Buyer

This book started by defining sports marketing as a sales process. Throughout the first ten chapters, the book has focused on the buyers, or sponsors, and what they do with their sponsorships and promotional access. The focus needs to shift to the seller's role. Sellers have a difficult task to excite and maintain sponsor involvement, their event subsidy.

Sellers need to generate leads, locate the buyers, send proposals, present opportunities, sell the sponsorships, and integrate the resulting promotions. That all sounds like a simple procedure, but in reality, sponsorship sales are difficult. The process is more investment opportunity than purchase for consumption purposes.

Throughout the sales process, remember the creed: *My event is a favorable opportunity for (name of company) to identify with its audience. Most importantly, this event will help sell the products and services of (same company) through my event vehicle.*

To push a sponsor's product through the sales channel, the seller needs to give the sponsor a participatory role. A team, league, or property tries to work the sponsor into the ticket holders, listening audience, and communities. Central to the sales issue is determining the proper sales contact.

FINDING THE BUYER (A CHECKLIST)

• Determine promotional fit from sponsorship to company, i.e., media or stadium promotion. What are you selling?

• Determine contact's identity and decision-making capacity. Phone company and ask who is in charge of placing advertisements, or in charge of reviewing event promotion proposals.

• Send pertinent introductory information regarding sponsorship.

• Discuss feasibility of sponsor's interest with corporate contact.

• Establish a meeting time.

• Define available promotional inventory for sale, and relevant price ranges.

• Determine budgetary possibilities and trade-out possibilities.

• Outline a timetable for discussion and decisions.

This process will not necessarily sell a high-priced sponsorship, but it will narrow the process by which promotional sales agents qualify leads and package, present, and sell sponsorships.

QUESTIONS THE SELLERS NEED TO ASK THEMSELVES?

• Who is the buyer? Is this a person, a committee, or an agency representing the firm?

• Are there obvious conflicts, i.e., exclusivity? For example, can the Sacramento Kings approach or sell billboard space to Shell, Exxon or Chevron in their facility, Arco Arena.

• Does the sponsorship fit a sponsor's demographics? If so, are there sufficient vehicles (radio, television, print, etc.) to satisfy the sponsor's needs?

• Can the expenditure be justified through involvement? What kind of features can your sponsorship bring to the company and its markets? Will it identifiably move more product?

• What combination of opportunities will customize a sponsorship to make it irresistible?

• Will the sponsor be able to see the obvious benefit of participation?

BEING A BUYER*

This is a position of power and authority. It is also one of great responsibility. Sponsorship decisions cannot be based on personal enthusiasm, or interest, but on return. Buyers want to maximize "the bang for their buck." They do that by acquiring the rights to the necessary advertising inventory, i.e., radio/television time, print considerations, and merchandise considerations, and by effectively placing it within the markets.

Being a buyer also requires intuitive skills. Buyers need to weigh the needs of consistency in alliance with the importance of rotating new advertising vehicles. It takes years to build significant relationships between sponsors and rights holders. The Wimbledon broadcast, for example, stayed with NBC and HBO, despite an aggressive offer from Fox. The consistency and reliability of that relationship obviously has significant value. On the other hand, properties can be bought at a premium, as in the Fox-NFL example, despite a long-term relationship (CBS-NFL).

Working in the Sports Marketplace

THE SUPPLY SIDE

Working from the event manager's position is not necessarily a limiting position. Working for a professional sports team provides exposure to the variety of sponsors, media partners, and communities with whom they work. There are, however, a finite amount of positions with professional teams. If you want to be employed as a marketing representative of a Major League Baseball team, then there are twenty-eight potential employers. But, as one can easily imagine, not too many opportunities become available.

The best idea is to start in the minor leagues of any sport. The Continental Basketball Association and the Nike Tour need publicists and marketing representatives. These organizations do not have the same administrative layers that would delay introduction and exposure. Another great place to begin a career in the sports marketplace is through volunteering at a local event. Road races, golf tournaments, and

---

*See chapter 6 for greater detail.

charity events need competent individuals who enjoy the exposure to high-profile events. Perhaps the best place to gain experience is working for an actual sponsor such as Coca-Cola or ABC in the sports related division.

THE BUYERS' SIDE

Sports are fun and exciting for everyone in the industry, but to be involved, one does not need to be employed by a team or league one can work for a broadcaster or sponsor. CBS, Coca-Cola, and their industry competitors are involved in the sports entertainment industry. In fact, these and similar organizations have greater exposure to a wider variety of events and promotional considerations than individually focused teams and event operators. By working for an organization that partners with sports properties, ownership is a temporary position. ABC, as a buyer from the NFL, owns Monday Night Football, and they sell the product to advertisers and viewers. The NFL, though, still courts the broadcaster and works with them for its objectives.

An association with many properties enables sponsors and promotional partners to learn about selling to sport's end users—the audience/consumers. It also gives exposure to new concepts of integrating the principles of the Event Triangle with events and fans. This observation of promotional execution assists in the development of sports entertainment and access in all sports.

Furthermore, the development of the sports industries opens up sports entertainment to more consumers and advertisers. One encouraging development is the participation of females in the sports business market. (See Table 1.) Both from the sponsor/buyer side and the seller/provider one, sports are for all people. By opening them up to all cultures and groups, the sports market grows for both the teams and advertisers.

While this study breaks down a television audience, it measures the variety of sports against one another. Furthermore, it identifies that sports' demographics are not as skewed as some advertising analysts would think.

Table 1.
Percentage of Female Sports Viewers

Sport	Total Viewers	% Female[3]
Pro Basketball	57,808,000	43.1
Pro Baseball	67,851,000	42.9
Pro Football	91,535,000	41.4
College Football	65,715,000	39.7
Pro Tennis	23,641,000	39.0
College Basketball	49,254,000	38.8
Pro Boxing	25,503,000	38.1
Pro Hockey	19,341,000	4.9
Pro Golf	33,067,000	31.5
Fishing Shows	18,486,000	31.0
Wrestling	16,563,000	28.1
Auto Racing	25,715,000	27.8

Threatening the Buyer-Seller Relationship

> It's just a few hundred folks trying to figure out how to divide two billion dollars.
>
> President Bill Clinton, discussing the baseball strike (February 6, 1995)

When leagues falter due to labor-management strife, the entire Event Triangle cycle breaks down. (No events equals no fans which equals no sponsors.)

The effects are detrimental to all. Without the 1994 World Series, $18.3 million worth of ticket revenue was lost.[4] One hundred million dollars worth of television advertisements was lost.[5] Furthermore, merchandisers selling World Series memorabilia have no products to peddle. Rawlings, the official baseball manufacturer only produced 20 percent of its normal allotment of fall classic commemorative balls.

Cities do not get the exposure, or millions, that come from hosting a World Series event. The concessionaires, security guards, and the commensurate mass mobilization of resources (jobs) do not take place. Simply put, an identifiable amount of event-driven money is not injected into the economy. Yes, the money goes somewhere. Some advertisers/sponsors will spend it elsewhere, on other sports, advertising outlets, or consumer rebate programs. Some companies will save the sponsorship money, and add it to its "bottom line." Fans will do the same, either spend it elsewhere or save it. But it will not be tracked and defined in a focused, finite time span in the sports entertainment industry.

After thirty-three days of the strike, the *USA Today* estimated that the owners had lost $280.5 million in revenues, and players, $150,173,300. If the baseball strike cost millions, what about the United States' boycott of the 1980 Summer Olympics in Moscow? Fabulous athletes like Renaldo Nehemiah, Carl Lewis, and Mary Decker missed a chance to make their mark in Moscow. Furthermore, the broadcasters, retailers, merchandisers, and fans missed out as well.

But its not just the athletes, owners, fans, and cities. Publicly held companies and their investors take the hit as well. Due to the 1994 strikes in both baseball and hockey, Topps, a trading card manufacturer, saw net third quarter income fall 68 percent over the prior year. It also discontinued its shareholder dividend. This negative reality indicates that when the sports machine is turned off, the ripple effects hit many groups beyond the owners, players, sponsors, and fans. The bickering groups' misguided selfishness has negative financial consequences for all levels of the business community, from small subcontractors to institutional portfolio investors.

Sports labor strikes now even involve the office of the president. It is absurd that baseball was on his agenda, right next to issues affecting the International Monetary Fund, federal budget, interest rates, education, and national security. But there it was, because baseball is both the "National Pastime" and a major player in the multibillion-dollar sports entertainment industry. Sports, woven into the culture, receive special consideration because of its financial implications.

The losers are the fans, the leagues, the employees, and the business advertising interests (broadcasters and sponsors) that know how to package sports entertainment in an acceptable, profitable fashion. The NHL (1994–1995) eventually came to terms with its players and instituted a forty-eight game schedule. That resolution, however, did not make up for the thirty-three games that each club missed, nor the revenue to the line employees who staff the facilities, ticket offices, and merchandise booths of the teams. The agreement, furthermore, did not reconcile the basic differences between the players and the owners and bring the the two sides closer together in terms of understanding and consensual growth. Rather, the two sides are arguably farther apart than ever. Not a harbinger for optimal labor relations. Baseball's solution was worse. There was no agreement, just a court-ordered injunction.

Sports Marketing Profile: Robin Carr-Locke

Robin Carr-Locke is currently a public relations manager at Nike, overseeing publicity for women's sports, women's fitness, grass-roots marketing and P.L.A.Y. (Participate in the Lives of America's Youth). Like most industry veterans, she got her start in professional sports at the proverbial "bottom." Beginning as an administrative assistant with the San Francisco Giants, Robin was promoted twice in her ten years with the club, eventually becoming Director of Communications/Publicity Manager.

A casualty of baseball's 1994 strike, Robin immediately found a job at Nike. Her experiences in professional sports as an administrator, and as a woman, are compelling to anyone in the sports industry.

WHY SPORTS?

My dad was a sports writer, primarily covering tennis. He would often take me along and that gave me a chance to see sports from a perspective other than the television set. Looking back, I saw some great matches and how the athlete's image gets filtered by the media.

When in college, I saw a woman at a Virginia Slims tournament handing out press releases, gathering statistics and being an intermediary between the media and the players. I found out that she was a public relations representative, and I checked my school catalog for a "PR" major. That would be my first real step towards a sports career.

In leaving school, I knew I wanted to break into sports, but couldn't get my foot in the door right away. I took a job at an agency to get general experience while attempting to get interviews with sports teams. I finally landed an informal one with the San Francisco Giants [1985]. The actual interview depressed me, because as most people find out, there are limited openings in sports. I was told to be patient and wait for an available opportunity.

SERENDIPITY

About six months later, I'm at a Giants game, and the guy I interviewed with [Duffy Jennings] saw me and told me of an opening with the team. I called him the next day, set up another interview, and two days later landed a job with a major league baseball team!

The job itself was very "entry level" in terms of its tasks, but I didn't care, I finally made it into sports . Unfortunately, the mood at the Giants' office was tempered by the fact that the club lost 100 games for the first time in franchise history. They went into the last game at 62–99, and lost in the final innings. That typified the year for the team—a lot of frustration on the field. But I look back on my first year in sports as a success. I learned so much from the environment and the people I worked with, even if my job wasn't the most glamorous.

I didn't mind the down-time and the monotony of some of the actual work, because the club always promised me that they would promote me. And in 1988, I became the assistant Public Relations Director, assuming more responsibilities, like helping edit *Giants* magazine, setting up interviews, and doing more game day work—traveling with the team, doing stat work, and coordinating interviews between the media and the players.

Two year later, the Giants decided that they needed to get more visibility for their community programs. The club was being overshadowed by the Oakland A's, whose community work was not really different than the Giants', but much better publicized. They asked me to write a proposal addressing the matter, and they promoted me to become Director of Communications.

OWNERSHIP DICTATES IMAGE

At the time, the Giants were owned by Bob Lurie, and he developed a "family" atmosphere. He trusted those on his staff, and he gave them security and responsibility. But the club was a bit behind in terms of cutting-edge appeal, and our approach to community relations reflected that.

Corey Busch and Al Rosen, my bosses, called me in and asked for a proposal on steps to upgrade our community profile. My job was to develop a proactive outlook. I appreciated the opportunity and faith in my abilities. We ultimately developed some unique programs like Project Open Hand, where Dusty Baker, the team's manager, handed out meals. Even better was the Until There's A Cure Day—the first AIDS benefit in professional sports.

I'd been lobbying for the AIDS benefit for years, and it was hard to sell at first. The former Giants regime was worried that the cause had nothing to do with baseball, and for that reason, it wouldn't be a successful association for the team. But Bob Lurie sold the team after the 1992 season, and the new ownership, led by Peter Magowan, was looking for exactly these types of community activities. Seeing the Until There's A Cure Day was tremendously gratifying.

In retrospect, it was a true collaborative effort, especially on Dusty Baker's behalf. His own experiences as a player, and his beliefs about helping others inspires him to pursue things like Open Hand and Until There's A Cure. It's no knock on other managers when I say that Dusty is the best. His sincere interest in community projects made them successful.

A Unique Promotion

One idea that is a good look at sports, its personalities, and the risk of public perception was the new Giants uniform unveiling [in 1994]. I had an idea to do it at the Up and Down Club—a hip nightclub in San Francisco's south of Market region. The club was owned by supermodel Christy Turlington and her sister, and I thought that it would be a great opportunity to move away from the sports bars, baseball's safe haven.

At first, the idea was not received enthusiastically, but I called Barry Bond's agent, and said that Christy was in, when in fact I hadn't confirmed her participation! Then I called Christy's people and said Barry would do it if she'd do it! As it turned out, we got lucky. Christy donated her time for free, Barry and Willie Mays were great, and the Giants got some great press. It was a win-win [situation] for the club, Christy, and the Giants.

But it was not easy. My point of view was to push the team and its image. But there was a lot of resistance to ideas like the Christy Turlington one. Baseball is great because of its traditions, but I found that some of the traditional perceptions inhibited the league from pursuing creative ideas.

Being a Woman

I never felt that I was a feminist until I worked in baseball. I was naive in 1985, because I had hoped that a lot of issues that I eventually confronted were taken care of in the sixties.

Baseball has a reputation of resisting minority groups, which is not accurate. It's important to remember that it is hard for *anyone* to get into a front office position—man or woman.

There are only so many positions in sports organizations, and they are rarely vacated. In analyzing the issue, there really is not that much turnover in the industry. That alone makes its hard to get in the position to be hired, regardless of gender.

Having said that, I can also say that it was hard being a woman working in baseball. I dreaded Pittsburgh. It always seemed that a security guard, or bus driver, would either try to kick me off the bus, or out of the locker room. I definitely stood out, because there aren't that many women roaming around with the kind of freedom my job gave me. And in the eyes of the security people in some of the cities we visited, I had to be either a groupie, or a girlfriend of one of the player's wives. The reality was that I did often have to prove myself for no reason other than being female aroused somebody's suspicion.

One time, a security guard [in Pittsburgh] wouldn't let me into the locker room, even though my job was to be the liaison between Dusty [Baker] and the press after a game. The guard didn't want to let me in, and we exchanged words before I finally got past him. Dusty overheard a part of it and asked me what had transpired. When I told him, he was surprised. He asked me; "Because you're a woman? You're kidding . . . that still happens? That's ridiculous. I'll make sure to say something to him later." And this type of thing was as recent as the Summer of 1994.

With the players, there was an unwritten approval period. Each Spring and in September, when we had the roster call-ups to forty players, I'd have to break the tension and gain their trust. Since there are new faces all the time, it took some people some time to get used to me. And, of course, there will be some good natured teasing. But when Will Clark or Matt Williams, two big stars would say hello, that meant that I belonged to the new players.

But the bottom line was that no matter how long I was there, the questioning of my presence was constant. One day it would be a flight attendant. The next day someone at the park. People do not realize how important it was to me to be accepted.

I had to distinguish between kidding and insensitivity. I couldn't tattle on people every time something happened. Before I got my first promotion, Duffy Jennings, one of my bosses, asked Al Rosen [the general manager], Roger Craig [the manager at the time], and Mike Murphy [the clubhouse manager] if it would be OK for me to be exposed to the team. Management was concerned if there would be a problem with me being there, and wanted to make sure that things would be smooth from the start. It's nice that they cared enough to ask, but it also indicates the sensitivity to women in baseball.

In looking back, I don't regret anything. The coaches, players, and management always treated me well. I just wanted to do my job, and the Giants—to their credit—gave me the opportunity.

The Strike

In 1993, the Giants had a great year. They signed Barry Bonds and won 103 games. As 1994 approached, I looked forward to my tenth year with the club. With the strike looming, I thought that an experienced public relations person would be a valuable asset in the eyes of management. No one wanted to prepare for a strike, but I felt, if anything, there would be even more work. All of it "damage control."

The strike hit August 12, and we had a golf tournament on the 15th. On the afternoon of the 16th, fifty-five people got called in during the afternoon. All fifty-five were laid off, four days after the strike.

I was definitely hurt. After ten years, who wouldn't be? But I soon realized that it was a simple business decision, and I had to assume the professional consequences of industry turmoil. That's the hard thing about baseball, and most sports. We, as fans, expect them to always be successful and available. For all of those years that I earned a paycheck, I knew that the work I did was for the Giants, but I always felt a part of the national pastime. The strike really put the issue of a baseball job as a livelihood into focus.

The Aftermath

The team said that I could get my job back when the strike was settled, but I didn't want to go back. I had a chance to start over. I had started to interview with local companies when Nike called about an opening. I had spoken with them a year before, but I wasn't interested in leaving the Bay Area. This time, though, I was ready and eager. So I brought information packets with me and video highlights of things that I had worked on to the interview. I even brought a second interview suit in case they wanted to talk to me the next day. I put pressure on them, because I was about to accept another job, and I told them that. They asked me back the next day, and in twenty-four hours, I had a new job.

WHO REALLY LOST IN THE STRIKE

Things with the Giants hadn't really changed. My boss, Bob Rose, was fabulous throughout the strike. He always called me to assure me that my job would be there once the strike settled, and that I was in the team's plans. But I went in unannounced one day and cleaned out my office. I don't think the team was expecting me to leave, and it was hard to go, but once you're laid off, some feelings of loyalty are affected.

During the strike, the media always mentioned the hot dog vendors and ballpark concessionaires, but no one ever mentioned the staff that worked long hours, made long trips, and gave a lot to the team. Ironically, the public relations people in baseball, who know the media so well, seemed to avoid publicizing their hurt over being a casualty of the strike.

LOOKING BACK

My own experience with the Giants is emblematic of the changing face of sports ownership. With Bob Lurie, it was more family than business, and the team needed more of a business approach that Peter Magowan brought with him.

Because of the strike, a lot of marketing people lost their jobs, and the owners and players lost millions. It's sad, because I have so many feelings for baseball. Today, I'm dealing with many athletes—both men and women—and I'm enjoying my exposure to other sports. I'm also working with P.L.A.Y., Nike's comprehensive outreach program. In looking at baseball, they need an agreement. It seems like they still have a lot of work to repair the relationship between players, fans, and teams. I hope that they get it back, because it's a shame that it took the hits that it did.

GENERAL COMMENTS ON SPORTS EMPLOYMENT

When you work in sports, it's long hours, the unexpected (like earthquakes during a World Series) and paying your dues. A lot of people get in and get a start, but don't last long because they have unrealistic expectations. People who make it have the necessary patience to get through the seemingly endless series of monotonous tasks and restricted access to being promoted.

There's no place for whiners, either. If you really love it, you'll assimilate to the culture of sports. It seems that young interns and people coming in are a bit more impatient than when I started. The bottom line is that if you put up with some of the negative things and persist, you'll achieve your goals. It sounds corny, but it's been true for me.

12

Future Issues in Sports Marketing

> Sports sometimes seem to be an inflated balloon. Maybe it needs to be deflated a bit. . . . At the very least, we all need to have a sense of humor about it.
>
> —Chris Friden, House O' Dreams Productions

How can one have a sense of humor when baseball players do more litigating than hitting and pitching? Is it possible, from a marketing standpoint, to look beyond the financial dimensions of staging sporting events and consumer-product promotions dependent upon them? This book has explored and defined the links between sponsors, events, and fans—the Event Triangle model.

Management operates franchises in sports that can sell from $750,000 (Arena Football) to $192 million (NFL). Promoters for pay-per-view bouts are earning in excess of $50 million for one fight. Broadcasters buy and sell sports properties for billions of dollars. The rapid integration of sports entertainment and corporate involvement has developed the sports industry of today. Issues like pay-per-view television, integrated marketing strategies, facility licensing, and some new ones like virtual entertainment, federal intervention and supervision, equity endorsement contracts, cross-promotions, and corporate event control will continue to evolve and influence the Event Triangle of tomorrow. Athlete salaries reflect this.*

*There is no data readily available, but managment's income has also risen.

Table 1.
Comparison of the Average Sports Salaries of 1980 and 1994

Sport	Year	Average Salary[1]
Baseball	1980	$ 144,000
	1994	$1,200,000
Basketball	1980	$ 180,000
	1994	$1,400,000
Football	1980	$ 79,000
	1994	$ 737,000

The Main Issue

The main issue in sports is greed. Specifically, if greed will damage both the image of competition, and the competition itself. Major League Baseball generates almost $2 billion annually. The owners and players cannot agree how to divide it. Notre Dame has no conference affiliation, i.e., Pac-10, ACC, Big 8, and it left its NCAA cohorts in the broadcast rights dust by negotiating its own $38 million agreement with NBC for the exclusive broadcast rights from 1991 to 1995.[2] This may be a dangerous precedent of the "rich getting richer," as other college programs do not get the broadcast funding that Notre Dame receives. This is a capitalistic society and neither Notre Dame nor NBC can be blamed for the relationship. Notre Dame is one of the unquestioned kings of college sports, one of the few institutions that can claim a national following. NBC's shrewd investment provides a cash windfall that Knute Rockne, the Four Horseman, and their minions never imagined.

But for every Notre Dame, there are ten Slippery Rocks or St. Cloud States that do not participate in the financial boon of college sports. Sports programs are no longer student body privileges, but cash gains or losses. Other men's and women's programs are either subsidized or jeopardized by the animal of commercialism in college sports. The tilting balance of power is reflected through competitive investments in college sports programs. ABC has a $210 million contract with the CFA, college football's governing body,[3] and CBS has over $2 billion committed to college sports programs through the year 2000. Education is not the emphasis for the contracts. It is audience attraction.

College sports traditionally have strong demographics of enthusiastic, educated, and wealthy consumers. The commercial viability of a minority of college programs clearly outweighs the interest in sustaining athletic opportunities for all students. For some, the morality of the revenue distribution issue is appalling. For others, it is not. In both amateur and professional sports, it is secondary to profitability.

Revenue distribution, for example, fuels the problems in baseball. Small market teams are forced to compete for the same pool of talent, players, coaches, scouts and administrators, with less revenue. The New York Yankees earned over $39 million more than the Pittsburgh Pirates in 1993 media revenues alone.[4] How can that fail to influence the comparative ability of the clubs to both play the game and market the action? Teams need competitors to survive, and they need to share revenues to some extent. The solution to revenue distribution will not easily be found, but the road of risks makes it a compelling story.

Associated financial risk defines the future of sports entertainment. Mega deals, like Coca-Cola's $250 million five-year NFL commitment and their $285 million worldwide NBA sponsorship are more like mergers than advertising purchases.[5] By investing significant money into a sports property, Coca-Cola and its advertising brethren really take short-term equity positions in the property. Broadcasters are complicit in the equation. The interdependency of fan, sponsor, and sports promoter interests consolidates the promotional focus of sports entertainment for both short- and long-term survival.

Legislation

It has been documented in this book, and throughout all forms of media and government, that professional sports and the federal government are creeping towards formal laws that will apply to the rules of the game.* As the baseball strike dragged on, and a variety of opinions consulted as to its economic and social impact, a growing sentiment against the two sides developed. The court of public opinion could not side with either the owners or the players. Both groups were viewed as wealthy, petulant combatants led by intransigent lawyers. Worsening matters for both sides

*They are already involved, i.e., baseball's anti-trust exemption.

were studies that showed how much money was lost to municipalities and auxiliary employees (concessionaires, ushers, maintenance, etc.).

A study conducted by a national Mayors representative group showed that for every game held at Atlanta's Fulton County Stadium, $3 million dollars flows into Atlanta. For a game at Shea Stadium (New York), $2 million worth of economic activity, $62,000 in taxes, and 850 jobs are generated. In Baltimore, at the beautiful structure known as Orioles Park at Camden Yards, one game amounts to $1.2 million in revenue and 2,000 jobs to the city of Baltimore.

Given these financial implications, public opinion will tilt toward the third party of city employees, concessionaires, security agents, and other ballpark beneficiaries. In the past, taking sides in labor stoppage issues in major league sports had been difficult. That is no longer the case. Support can galvanize for these third-party victims and give Congress an excuse to wade further into the high-profile professional sports industry.

The Future of Broadcast Interests

The future landscape of all forms of broadcast entertainment, including sports, can be summed up in one word: *choice*. Steps are being taken to dismantle the federal and regional bureaucratic agencies that legislate the rules of access and opportunity on the airwaves. The NFL and NCAA have pay-per-view packages. Professional boxing and wrestling have had enormous success in the pay-per-view format. The early market feedback for pay-per-view is that it can be profitable if the combination of star-power and legitimacy are delivered.

The future is also comprised of alliances that make sense for broadcasters and rights holders. Fox's networking communication service, Delphi Internet, is developing interactive ways to capitalize on its NFL association. Fox wants to cross-platform its NFL television relationship/package with other video, television programming, and related media interests. Between Fox's diverse media capacity and the NFL's range of products and services, i.e., NFL Films, NFL Properties, etc., Fox can tie-in to promote its coverage, the entertainment of the gridiron, merchandise opportunities, its sponsors' promotions, and any potential money-making ideas that work between the two profit-seeking organizations.

Another alliance that is beyond the beginning stage is tele-shopping. Sports merchandise is regularly featured on both QVC and the Home Shopping Network and, with forethought, the opportunities to cash in on the immediacy and passions of sports are a new revenue source soon to become an income statement force. QVC's direct marketing division, QDirect, produced a joint venture with ESPN called "Stadium Stand." It aired in conjunction with three World Cup broadcasts and solicited orders for merchandise and related memorabilia. The effort produced 7,000 calls and an estimated $200,000. Not huge numbers, but encouraging. As time and experience develop this property, consumer activity will certainly increase and add to the growing $4 billion memorabilia and collectible industry.

The current television industry is in a state of rapid change, and sports is a good place to test, probe, and qualify new limits and opportunities. This means that experimentation and test projects are hitting the airwaves to test and define the waters of profitability. But in sports, it all comes down to legitimacy. Jimmy Connors, for example, helped CBS and USA have the highest pre-Final round ratings in the history of the U.S. Open tennis tournament. His surprising charge to the semifinals brought viewers in droves (a 5.9 rating) to their television sets.

However, when he took on Martina Navratilova in a pay-per-view exhibition, the public decided not to pay. Both stars were great, but there was no real drama or believable hype to capture viewer interest. When Bobby Riggs insulted his way into a match with Billie Jean King almost twenty years earlier, he created enough hype to attract network television coverage and the Astrodome as a venue. Connors versus Navratilova was a $24.95 venture in curiosity. The venture's break-even goal was 1 percent of the cable operative homes to purchase, or 190,000, and it fell short. A creative effort, but not financially successful.

Both the legitimacy and interest of an event need to be determined before the PPV route is pursued. Boxing, the most successful PPV event, has taken its own share of lumps. The Evander Holyfield-Larry Holmes bout in June 1991 lost $2.75 million for TVKO, the Time Warner boxing PPV division. That one blow cut the schedule from ten events to six, and also forced the layoff of ten employees.[6] Ouch! Dire consequences indeed for the wrong attraction on the PPV venue.

WHAT PAY-PER-VIEW HAS DEMONSTRATED

Pay-per-view (PPV) is a significant part of television's immediate future. It will encourage consumer choice and finance more sporting events. Due to complicated broadcast restrictions imposed by the government, leagues, conferences, and the other controllers of broadcast rights, the market is slowly maturing. But there are some encouraging facts.

Viewers will pay for the right event. The technology is not hard to grasp. Cable operators and promoters have the channels to promote and distribute entertainment. The critical matter is the proper event. The George Foreman-Evander "Real Deal" Holyfield 1991 bout grossed a staggering $55 million for one night of action. Viewers were willing to pay the $35.95 necessary to see the action. Wrestlemania VI, (who says that wrestling is not a sport?) earned $20 million at $29.95 a pop.[7]

Most encouraging is that the revenues for the PPV category have skyrocketed from $216 million in 1991 (boxing accounted for 62 percent) to $377 million in 1993.[8] PPV has quickly gained consumer acceptance as an appropriate, logical medium for boxing events, and not for blockbuster heavyweight bouts.[9] Julio Caesar Chavez fought an over the hill Hector "Macho" Camacho and enticed 800,000 subscribers at $25 each for a whopping $20,000,000.

NBC'S TRIPLECAST DISSECTED[10]

NBC's Summer Olympic games' attempt at the pay-per-view market was bold both in its conception and execution. The venture gambled that viewers were ready to commit their time and financial resources to total Olympic broadcast coverage. The results were not financially fruitful. The feedback, however, helped shape the immediate future of pay-per-view for events and their audience. Cost to fans were $125 for a fifteen-day subscription or $29.95 for a one-day price (later discounted to $19.95). NBC's regular (free) programming consisted of 161 hours of televised events while the Triplecast televised for 1,080 hours. NBC/Cablevision's promotional cost was $40,000,000.

Table 2.
Alliance of Advertising Specialists and Their Goals for the NBC Olympic Triplecast

Firm	Specialty
DDB Needham	Image and awareness.
NW Ayer	Holiday theme advertising.
Della Femina McNamee	Sports advertising.
Saatchi & Saatchi	Marketing services and holiday promotions.
Communications Diversified	Sports sales promotions.

Optimistic estimates: Ten percent addressable homes equals 2,200,000 homes.

Two million non-addressable homes, i.e., the service delivered via basic cable services like SportsChannel America, in which NBC and Cablevision have an interest.

Results: Two hundred fifty thousand homes ordered Triplecast.

- Estimates range from $40-60 million in losses for NBC, $50 million for Cablevision.
- Pushed PPV format into over 22 million homes.
- Pioneering effort, bold in scope and dimension.

The successes and failures show the sensitivity of the market to price and product. Clearly, the Olympic Triplecast case shows that no amount of promotion, or advertising, will coerce viewers into an expensive simulcast or test experiment.

When the promoters find a sponsor who can work with cable operators, at home viewers, and the event participants, then the commercial interests that have shaped the evolution of sports on network television, will be the driving force of PPV. This also pertains to the other menu-driven opportunities offered on the future "Information Superhighway," the cultural express delivery service.

The NFL's pay-per-view venture gives access to football fans for virtually any game. This flexibility circumvents all network regulations regarding blackout rules and allows fans to choose their favorite contests. Called "Season Ticket," the venture had 210,000 residential sign-ups, and 5,000 bars (commercial enterprise). The success of the program, slated for the last five weeks ($49.95) of the 1994 season, had NFL sources estimating 300,000 DirecTV purchases for the 1995 season ticket price of $139.00. That is $41,700,000 of revenue for the NFL—and they owe it all to the power of television, technological development, and the allure of sports entertainment.[11]

Infomercials as an Advertising Strategy

The Alien Wedge®, Health Rider®, Nordic Track®, and thousands of other products sell through the television medium. These products use similar techniques, catchy graphics, persuasive presentation, and celebrity endorsers. The Health Rider® features noted health buffs Covert Bailey and Greer Childers. The Alien Wedge® infomercial stars Mike Schmidt and Jim Plunkett, two venerable stars and golf fans. The Quik Cook BBQ® is a portable grill pitched by football star Dick Butkus. Three years and 600,000 Quick Cook®s later proves the effectiveness of infomercials and credible celebrity spokesmen. The use of a personality heightens consumer perception of reliability and dependability—two integral components to a purchasing decision.

Ethical Issues

Distilled alcohol (gin, scotch, whiskey, etc.) and tobacco companies (chewing and smoking) cannot advertise on either the radio or television. Federal legislation prohibits it. Events like the Winston Cup (NASCAR), or the Johnnie Walker Championships (golf) circumvent the exposure issues via event entitlement. Philip Morris and R. J. Reynolds, two large tobacco manufacturers are constantly being sued by consumer groups, former smokers, and even the state of Florida (to make up for healthcare costs attributed to smoking). The issue of smoking rights will not go away. Like gun control and abortion, tobacco laws are influenced by powerful lobbyists and contested legal disputes.

The antismoking campaign is not solely an American fad. France passed a law in late 1990 (which took effect in 1991) that placed heavy restrictions on tobacco and alcohol advertising. The French did not merely pass laws that had loopholes. They even canceled the French Grand Prix (July 4, 1993) auto race because of tobacco's indirect, but prevalent, involvement. French broadcasters have received a lot of pressure from both the courts and antismoking groups because of racing's rolling billboard status. French television negotiated a compromise so that they could legally broadcast races and the indirect tobacco advertising, originating from other countries. The cigarette industry, an $8 billion annual business, had invested almost $80 million in racing advertising, but that revenue is lost.[12]

Facilities and Their Franchises in the Next Century

Facility management and ownership have dominated many sections of this book because of their financial consequences to the teams. As mentioned, their luxury suites, atmospherics, and leveraged sponsorships have an impact on the bottom line of all teams. The old relationship of municipal ownership and operation control are virtually extinct. The revenues that they generate are the core of the struggle between the tenants (teams) and the city suppliers.

Since one professional game can bring millions to a community, i.e., $3 million at Atlanta's Fulton County Stadium, cities across the country are negotiating at a disadvantage with their professional franchises. Since the precedent has been set that franchise movement does not ruin a company's finances, teams have the negotiating leverage with their cities. The financial windfall and prestige of being a professional sports town are advantages that mayors and governmental representatives have recognized. And this recognition has brought a new era of cooperation and consensus.

Cooperative efforts are wooing franchises and their millions. St. Louis's successful bid for the Rams was due to the persistent political machinations led by Senator Eagleton. He spearheaded the operation that built the facility, scouted practice facilities, negotiated the lease, and galvanized the public. Perhaps he witnessed the job done by the Carolina Panthers and their ownership. St. Louis lost out in 1993 to Charlotte's (and Jacksonville's) well-conceived strategy.

Charlotte became the 29th NFL franchise through coordination and cooperation. Team owner Jerry Richardson, his staff, and the government came together to carry out the entire operation. Attracting a team and building a facility are expensive endeavors. One of the Panthers' ideas, personal seat licensing will probably be a facility/franchise standard in all of sports in the near future. The biggest concern in franchise movement and expansion is the facility. Teams used to play in converted facilities, or multipurpose municipal venues. That may have been fine for the early stages of professional sports, but not in the image conscious, demanding era we live in today.

The Panthers needed a modern facility and more critically, the financing to build it. The Panthers and their consultants devised a permanent seat licensing concept upon which the viability of the facility and franchise hinged. Their seat sales strategy priced permanent seat rights at values between $600 and $5,400 and they rolled out the plan to the public amid great fanfare (they spent $1 million on the campaign), and ultimately raised $100 million toward their new home's construction.[13] The team sold the rights to 42,000 seats on the first day alone in an impressive display of community support.* This rights strategy will likely be the cornerstone to future facility construction issues. In the past, the cities sought public funding (taxation and bond issues), but met significant resistance from political pressure groups. This permanent seat licensing issue offers a compromise, where fans who want a piece of ownership in the franchise can get that through the facility.

Other facility certainties are entitlement procedures. Wrigley Field may never be renamed "Old Style Field," but the majority of parks and auditoriums are otherwise overlooking free money if they do not seek this form of sponsorship. Changing signs and official releases and press guide mentions cost essentially very little, and the obvious financial gain can help the facility owner. As more and more event sites take on corporate nicknames, the unique value will diminish, but the media traffic and enormous billboard presence will certainly remain.

---

*Al Davis said the personal seat licensing program generated $150 million for the Panthers at his news conference announcing the Raiders' return to Oakland.

Some Basic Conclusions

Sports as an industry is a restricted one, but there are ways to get involved with events and promotional vehicles to make any individual an insider in terms of the structural demands of event marketing and publicity.

Clairvoyance in sports marketing is not usually a risky venture. The beneficiaries (fans, sponsors, and property rights holders) of sports entertainment continue to pay the ticket prices, labor and event costs, cable payments, and sponsorship fees that perpetuate the games. But as the poor attendance for the 1995 baseball season shows, fans can become disillusioned, at least in the short-run. For the sports fans (consumers), we will get more choices in sports entertainment via pay-per-view and broadcast television. Sports property controllers will lose a degree of their control, not to the players, but to the sponsors and event packagers, i.e., broadcasters. This group pays to participate and profit, and they will ultimately determine the ways in which sports are presented to the fans.

People laughed when ESPN launched its first show. But ESPN proved that there is a market for the twenty-four-hour sports fans. Leagues continue to expand and franchise values skyrocket because the expansion of sports has been popular with fans and sponsors, as the new markets and financial results testify.

Creating Opportunity in the Sports Marketplace

The House O' Dreams production company opened its doors for business in 1993 with the idea to create and produce the first college sports review program emphasizing the average odd-ball fan's point of view. Based in Berkeley, California, House O' Dreams was created by Chris Friden and Steve Whyte, two Cal grads who knew that they could present sports without the prohibitive confusion of clichés and uninspired aphorisms.

Now approaching their third year of operation, House O' Dreams has produced over eighty episodes of their "Bear Territory" program. Bringing the best of college basketball and football to its audience, House O' Dreams has expanded into reporting other events. House O' Dreams has brought its delightfully skewed perspective, to Dream Team II, the NBA All-Star Game Weekend, and the San Francisco 49ers'

Super Bowl XXIX victory parade. Its best assignment, though was a trip to the Seattle scene for the 1995 NCAA Final Four. Chris and Steve discuss several key elements to their business.

PHILOSOPHY

Chris: We're the average fan. We try to be as much of an outsider as possible. In talking to athletes or coaches we don't like the programmed responses or clichés that the media routinely generates. It's like there is an agreement to ask the same questions, and provide the same answers, every time. Sports sometimes seem to be an inflated balloon. Maybe it needs to be deflated a bit. . . . At the very least, we all need to have a sense of humor about it. You'll notice that Comedy Central and MTV have guys that do interviews on the street—looking for the comedy angle. The only difference is that these efforts, by MTV and other networks try to be cool and hip.

We, on the other hand, position ourselves as idiots. Our show is a different take. Dan Cortez, who does a great job, is at an event and he is pretty cool. He belongs there. We go, get kicked out, or have some random run-in with security or an official and act like we don't understand it. It's a different approach. Dan Cortez is there, but still cool, so he cannot deflate the scene as much as we do. By going a step further, we bring a more ridiculous angle to the game. But we're still huge sports fans. And that comes across.

Steve: We complain about being the outsiders, but at the same time, it provides a lot of material to do our show. We are always looking to get a reaction, because so much of the sports scene (from a journalist's point of view) can be pretty programmed. Sometimes we forget that our show is, to some extent, getting abused by the system.

We want to present the fan's view, not the objective sportswriter. We want to be biased. Our show is based on major University of California sporting events. We start the show with highlights set to music, and throw in a non-revenue sport like lacrosse, and then we do a studio bit where we sit in our living room and basically act like idiots and try to poke fun at the show. Then we finish with a fantasy type piece, like a take-off on *It's a Wonderful Life.* For the lack of a better comparison, the *Wayne's World* analogy applies. We film out of our living room because we can't afford to film it anywhere else. A big part of our show is to have fun on location, and we try to do something that pertains to the city we're in.

We like the human aspect of it. What gets lost is that athletes and coaches are just people. When we ask a normal question, that any other human would ask, like "How does it feel to score a lot of points and listen to people go nuts?" it takes everyone by surprise. You go to a press conference, and it's the exact same thing every time. The players don't even think of their answers. There could be one piece of videotape containing the pregame and postgame press conferences. The game is to get a reaction—and watch the regular media look at us as if we're crazy to buck the system.

Chris: We interviewed the Dream Team at Oakland, and they were harder to approach. Once they realized that we were there to have fun in reporting their team, they all were receptive and pretty open. Shaq and Derrick Coleman were great, but the system around the players was uptight. The system, not the players, is the barrier. The system creates and insulates the image. There can be no deviation, no frivolity. It seems so ridiculous that they have a narrow definition of professional from the media's standpoint. I listen to some journalists, and their really simple, dumb questions—to which they know that they are going to get a really simple, dumb answer—and I think to myself "you are a professional, and that is the best question you can ask?" It seems that the uncreative system we have is almost unprofessional, because it does not develop the interview.

I mean how many times can you ask, "How do you feel about the win?, " and fool the sports fans out there like there's any emotion.

GETTING STARTED

Steve: The financials have been the biggest problems from the start. We got a media pass and got a slot on public access television. Public access television is getting backed up, but we managed to get a spot here in Berkeley. The good news is that it was free to broadcast, but we could not seek any sponsors—there is no advertising on public access. This was 1993, and we picked an evening slot, figuring that a late evening audience would react better to us (Thursdays at 10:00 P.M.). At first, the public broadcasting people didn't want to give us a regular slot, because they deal with a lot of flakes, but we convinced them that we were dedicated. The main problem was equipment and editing needs. So we went to the credit card industry, took out ten cards, and got our equipment, and a bad case of debt. But we did shoot and produce thirty-six shows on public access television.

C. W. Nevius of the *Chronicle* wrote an article about us that year, and the people at SportsChannel read it, and gave us a slot. Now we had a commercial vehicle, because they gave us advertising time. We were also talking to some other broadcasters, but SportsChannel gave us a good opportunity to broadcast on their network and use some of their equipment. We divide the advertising time in a traditional barter agreement.

Costs

Steve: The fixed costs are equipment and editing. Salaries are only a dream at this point. The basic quality video camera costs about $15,000. We spend about $500 a week on tape for our footage, and editing expenses generally are between $500-$1,000. You also need mikes and lights, and there are licensing fees for using other people's music, which we do in our highlights segments. The estimated start-up costs are between $20,000-$25,000. We spent $30,000 our first year, and $50,000 the next.

Chris: We're a "tweener." We're regional. The big companies that want to work with us need that national reach. So now, we're at the stage where we have to really talk companies into our show. This might not bring in new clients, but it makes us more convicted in what we do. The reality is that we don't want to have to sell our show, but for it to be on the air, and as much fun as we want to make it, we need the sponsors.

The Future

Chris: Things look good in terms of recognition. We've done a few assignments, like the Dream Team and the 49er Super Bowl victory parade and NBA All-Star weekend in Phoenix for Prime Network (based out of Houston). They have a show, "Prime Cuts Plus," that we have contributed to.

Then, they had us going to Seattle for the Final Four. PowerBar wants us to do a national show, so that the exposure is higher. Steve had a great idea to drive the 49er helmet car to Miami for the Super Bowl. Our angle was going to be that they left the helmet car* behind,

*The "helmet car" is usually seen at all stadiums. They usually are used to remove injured players or in other activities requiring an automobile onfield.

and we were such diehard fans that we wanted to bring it to them. We were going to call local radio stations—and get a lot of publicity. PowerBar liked the idea, and were ready to go finance the project, but there were too many restrictions.

We ultimately want to do a college road show on a national basis, and are looking for a broadcaster and, of course, sponsors.

THE REALITY OF BEING AN OUTSIDER

Chris: Whenever I begin to think we've made it in terms of credibility, something happens that proves that I'm still an outsider. A while ago at a Stanford basketball game, I'm in the press room before the game to grab a drink and I'm at the drink cooler when a security guard, the self-appointed safety monitor of the potentially dangerous environment of the press room, yells across the room:

"Put that back!"

I couldn't believe that someone would yell like that in a press room and I really couldn't believe that he was yelling at me, so I asked, "You talking to me?"

Apparently he was, because he jumped all over me, "Put that back right now."

I still couldn't understand him. "Why?" I asked.

"You just put that down right now," he repeated. "Those are reserved for the press and media."

At least now I understood his point of view. "But I am part of the media," I told him.

"Yeah right," he countered, "you don't even have a press pass."

At this point, all of the writers are watching this whole scene. And I produce my press pass, and the rest of the press were mumbling, "wooooo." He could have been polite, but he tried to embarrass me. He should have realized that while he feels defensive about his outsider status, I enjoy it."

Chris and Steve's message is important to both journalists and sports marketers. In their case, they use sports as a platform to present their comedic interpretation of the players, fans, and even society. They also demonstrate that there are many ways to enjoy and analyze competitive action.

One Subjective Suggestion/Solution to Managing Sports' Woes: "The Sponsor Cartel"

The average salary in Major League Baseball and the NBA is over $1 million per year. Ten golfers earned over $1 million between 1990 and 1994 in non-tour sponsor events, i.e., the Skins Game. Athletes and promoters earn money, as do the sponsors and broadcasters. But for the sponsors, the work is more difficult. They need to capture the appeal of sports and package it into the products and services. This requires more than simply writing a check to a broadcaster or promotions company. Sponsor promotions involve decision makers and their subordinates—retailers and wholesalers. Companies need to keep taking the pulse of the sports audience to assess the potential of their sponsorships. To trace the solution to sports labor-management woes, and identify the answers, one needs to look only as far as the fan-sponsor relationship.

Fans support the sports profit cycle. As a group, they attend events, watch them, and lionize the competitors. Furthermore, like trained seals, fans are persuaded by the advertising mechanisms that accompany the events. Our purchasing habits persist as we buy billions of dollars worth of merchandise and equipment that reflect an emotional and monetary commitment to sports entertainment. When athletes go on strike or owners relocate their franchises, fans vow to gather and boycott teams and advertisers. That is not the solution. We should not boycott teams or stop buying merchandise. Fans need representation. After all, the owners and players have high-priced representative clout. Why shouldn't the millions, and billions, who truly support the sports entertainment juggernaut?

Who can represent the fans so that teams don't go on strike? Is it possible to influence the teams so that they play? A group does exist that can influence the sports authority figures (labor and management) to cooperate. They can influence both sides to manage their entertainment assets judiciously. The group? *The sponsors.*

If the marketing titans at Coca-Cola, Anheuser-Busch, Nike, Philip Morris, Reebok, General Motors, ABC, CBS, NBC, TNT, etc., consulted one another to represent the fans, i.e., their consumers, they could get the warring factions to compromise sensibly. If this "Sponsor Cartel" told Major League Baseball or the NHL, that it would pull its advertising from those sports and place it into other events on behalf of the fans, it would produce two effects:

1. *Publicity*—these companies would generate attention and emotional recognition from the fans on their behalf.

2. *Attention*—sports labor and management would finally consider the critical nature of the fan-sponsor equation.

Labor and management would stop pointing the accusatory finger and appreciate their customers (the fans and sponsors). Take away the advertising and broadcaster support, and the money that is being disputed will be invested elsewhere. When CBS purchased the television broadcast rights from Major League Baseball for $1.06 billion, the owners did not take the extra revenue (profit) and turn it over to the consumers (fans) in the form of reduced ticket prices, concessions, etc. They spent it on labor, i.e., the players. More free agent signings, higher salaries, and higher financial risks, which increases the costs of event production and presentation. Fans have to accept management's decisions. Fans cannot ask for binding arbitration, or a new cost settlement on professional sports spectating. If the "Sponsor Cartel" massages the bickering sides in sports entertainment toward honest negotiation, rather than prevarication, then one goal will be achieved: "Keep 'em playing so that everybody can do business." If the cartel encourages the sides to nurture their fan base, it will enhance the reliability of sponsorships and increase their value. Furthermore, for the owners, the cartel's intervention will increase the value of the franchises and marketing efforts, i.e., television and radio contracts. Most importantly, the "Sponsor Cartel" will be a consumer activist organization that will help the fans. Currently, fans lack a voice in the muddled process of labor disputes in professional sports. The solution to representation might be in the sponsors' hands. They can successfully intervene on behalf of their customers (the fans) to take the athletes out of the court rooms and back into competition!

Finally, one must remember that the competition of tomorrow provides the sports marketing opportunities of today.

Notes

Introduction

1. J. Berry, "The Drive with a Difference." *Business Week* (February 6, 1995): special advertising section.
2. Associated Press, "Final Four Puts Seattle in Spotlight." *Oregonian* (March 28, 1995): D1.
3. E. de Lisser, "Pepsi to Spend Millions to Put Name on Arena." *Wall Street Journal* (March 3, 1995): B1.
4. P. Hersh, "Without a Slip-up." *Chicago Tribune* (June 1, 1995: Sec. 5): 1.
5. NPD Group, Inc.
6. Staff, "Short Putts." *USA Today* (November 23, 1994): 3C.
7. T. Lefton. "Universal Inks NFL." *Brandweek* (October 10, 1994): 8.

Chapter 1. Defining Sports Marketing

1. J. Abraham, "Sports Careers National Conference." *Sports Careers* (September 1992): 7.
2. *1995 Information Please Sports Almanac,* p. 553.
3. Ibid., p. 554.
4. M. Mandel, M. Landler, and R. Grover, "The Entertainment Economy," *Businessweek* (March 14, 1994): 60.
5. International Events Group.
6. Sporting Goods Manufacturers Association.
7. Joyce Julius and Associates.
8. J. Flint, "Super Bowl XXVIII Moving towards a Sellout." *Broadcasting & Cable* (December 20, 1993): 7.

9. K. Allen, "Trading Card Revenue a Major Stumbling Block." *USA Today* (December 11, 1992): 4C.

10. Anonymous, "ESPN Buys Out its Contract with Baseball," *San Francisco Examiner* (October 25, 1992): 1D.

11. Comte and Chakravarty, "How High Can David Stern Jump?" *Forbes* (June 7, 1993): 42.

12. S. McClellan, "NBA-NBC deal. . . ." *Broadcasting & Cable* (May 3, 1993): 14.

13. G. Strauss, "Adidas Shoe to Shoe with Nike." *USA Today* (April 3, 1992): 1C.

14. International Events Group.

15. K. Hammonds, "It's One Sharp Ad, but Where's the Blade?" *Businessweek* (March 5, 1990): 30.

16. King, Nevins, Zimmerman, et al. *75 Seasons* (Atlanta: Turner Publishing, Inc., 1994), pp. 30–33.

17. Associated Press, "NFL Broadcast Earnings twice Ticket Sales." *San Francisco Chronicle* (August 7, 1992): E2.

18. Ibid.

19. M. Ozanian, "Squeeze Play." *Financial World* (October 27, 1992): 24.

20. J. Mandese, "How Fox Deal Aids NFL Global Aim," *Advertising Age* (January 3, 1994): 4.

21. D. D'Alessandro, "Event Marketing Winners: Olympics." *Brandweek* (July 12, 1992): 16.

Chapter 2: The Event Triangle

1. Gary Voet, *The Sacramento Bee* (November 25, 1994): p. F12.

2. S. Jenkins, "Billie Jean King." *Sports Illustrated* (September 19, 1994): 60.

3. Women's Tennis Association.

4. D. Garber, "Event Strategy Takes Hold as Brands Vie to Seal Bond." *Brandweek* (January 24, 1994): 17

5. R. Nance, "$4 billion to be Generated." *USA Today* (February 18, 1993): 9C.

6. M. Starr, "We Was Robbed," *Newsweek* (August 22, 1994): 49.

7. Milwaukee Bucks Management.

8. King, Nevins, Zimmerman, et al. *75 Seasons* (Atlanta: Turner Publishing, Inc., 1994), p. 299.

9. Pro Football Hall of Fame.

10. K. Cassino, "An Advertising Atlas." *American Demographics* (August 1994): 45.

11. R. Thurow, "Sponsors Belly Up to NFL's Big Table." *Wall Street Journal* (January 27, 1995): B12.

12. International Events Group.

13. *Beverage World.*

14. Interview with Exxon employees.

15. N.T. Kate, "Make It an Event," *American Demographics* (November 1992): 42.

16. Ibid.

17. P. Nowell, "How NASCAR Victories Translate Into Car Sales." *San Francisco Chronicle* (June 4, 1992): B2.

18. International Events Group.

19. M. Stachura, "The Quickest Green at This Year's U.S. Open." *Golf Digest* (June 1995): 16.

20. *Amusement Business* (January 1995).

21. Anonymous. "Late News." *Amusement Business* (January 9–15, 1995): 2.

22. G. Prince and A. Wolf, "Bud Tries to Bowl Super Viewers Over." *Beverage World* (December 31, 1991): 3.

23. N. Cope, "Boxing Today." *Business London* (August 1990): 80.

24. E. Thomas, Jr. "Atlanta Olympics: Every Minute Counts." *Wall Street Journal* (July 15, 1994): B1.

25. D. Ketchum, "Phoenix in Super Bowl Rotation." *The Phoenix Gazzette* (May 26, 1993): C6.

26. SkyDome Public Relations Department.

27. M. Antonen. "Florida Dome Still Needs Home Team." *USA Today* (March 31, 1992): 2C.

28. Ibid.

29. S. Jenkins. "Billie Jean King." *Sports Illustrated* (September 19, 1994): 60.

30. Hanley and Millard. "The King Reins." *Golf World* (July 24, 1992): 62.

31. Ibid.

32. H. Hersch. "Pele." *Sports Illustrated* (September 19, 1994): 122.

33. Prior to Jordan's comeback game, the highest-rated regular season game had been a CBS telecast of a 1987 LA Lakers-Boston Celtics matchup, featuring the ongoing celebration of the Larry Bird-Magic Johnson competition. The Celtics-Lakers rivalry conveniently attracted bi-coastal media markets, an enviable situation for advertisers.

34. S. Donnelly. "Importing the Glitz." *Time* (December 20, 1993): 69.

35. J. Waldrop. "Football Fever." *American Demographics* (January 1993): 69; Several authors. "By the Numbers." *USA Today* (January 31, 1994): 5B; S. Wollenberg. "Super Bowl Is the Place to Advertise." *Peninsula Times Tribune* (January 24, 1993): D1; Anonymous. "Super Recall for Ads." *Marketing News* (March 1, 1993): B5; J. Mandese. "Super Bowl '94." *Advertising Age* (February 8, 1993): 34; L. Herberg. "Hoping to Be in the Stands." *Arizona Republic* (March 23, 1993): A5; D. Garber. "Event Strategy Holds as Brands Vie to Seal Bond." *Brandweek* (January 24, 1994): 17.

36. D. Garber, "Event Strategy Takes Hold as Brands Vie to Seal Bond." *Brandweek* (January 24, 1994): 17.

Chapter 3: Big League Sports

1. A. Wolff and R. O'Brien. "Greg Norman's Grand Gambit." *Sports Illustrated* (November 28, 1994): 9.

2. O. Dixon. "Tennis." *USA Today* (November 23, 1994): 11c.

3. E. M. Swift. "Another Gusher for Jones." *Sports Illustrated* (December 12, 1994): 44.

4. M. Meserole. "Who's Who." *Please Sports Almanac* (New York: Houghton Mifflin, 1995): 502.

5. M. K. Ozanian. "The $11 Billion Pastime." *Financial World* (May 10, 1994): 57.

6. Wire services. "German Reaction." *San Francisco Examiner* (July 12, 1994): C6.

7. Fox Broadcast during January 15, 1995, NFC Championship Game.

8. World Cup Organizing Committee.

9. Anonymous. "Basketball Crazy." *Register Guard* (August 19, 1994): 2E.

10. "Top 20 Markets." *Advertising Age* (August 2, 1993): M3.

11. New York Times Wire Services. "Ticket Sales a Snag for Rams' Move Plan." *San Francisco Chronicle* (December 12, 1994): D4.

12. Wire Reports. "NFL Price of Admission." *USA Today* (September 14, 1994): 6C.

13. Associated Press. "Big St. Louis Welcome for Rams." *San Francisco Chronicle* (January 18, 1995): B1.

14. Associated Press. "Rams' New Worry." *San Francisco Chronicle* (December 26, 1994): B5.

15. SportsCenter, ESPN, January 17, 1995.

16. T. Verducci, "Marvin Miller." *Sports Illustrated* (September 19, 1994): 65.

17. Associated Press. "Last Strike Cost Owners a Bundle." *San Francisco Chronicle* (December 26, 1994): B9.

18. H. Bodley. "Unflappable Mediator Usery Will Work Until Job Is Done." *USA Today* (November 11, 1994): 7C.

19. Associated Press. "NY Radio Station Sues Yanks for 'Sham.' " *San Francisco Chronicle* (March 18, 1995): B4.

20. J. Ryan. "Selling an Invisible Product: Baseball." *San Francisco Chronicle* (December 8, 1994): B1.

21. G. Boeck. "History Haunts Hapless Clippers." *USA Today* (November 22, 1994): 6C.

22. Comte and Chakravty. "How High Can David Stern Jump?" *Forbes* (June 7, 1993): 42.

23. M. Starr. "We Was Robbed." *Newsweek* (August 22, 1994): 52.

24. *Financial World.*

25. *The Wall Street Journal Index—General News 1993,* p. 2094.

26. S. Mehta. "Small Sports-Equipment Makers Set Own Game Plan." *Wall Street Journal* (November 22, 1994): B2.

27. W. Carlsen, "Giants Dedicate Game to Aids Battle." *San Francisco Chronicle* (August 1, 1994): A15.

Chapter 4: Turning Sporting Events into Sponsorships and Sponsorships into Promotions

1. G. Khemouch. "NBC Nets Miller in NBA Hoopla." *Brandweek* (February 22, 1993): 1.

2. R. Thurow. "Winter Olympics '94." *Wall Street Journal* (February 22, 1994): A18.

3. M. McCarthy. "Big Mac Sprints for Fox Uprights." *Brandweek* (June 27, 1994): 1.

4. J. Jensen. "Soccers' Empty Cup." *Advertising Age* (June 6, 1994): 1.

5. M. Hiskey. "Olympic Sponsor Scores." *Atlanta Constitution* (March 16, 1994): A1.

6. Associated Press. "City Won't Name Stadium after Beer." *San Francisco Chronicle* (April 2, 1994): C1.

7. W. Bulkeley. "Sponsoring Sports Gains." *Wall Street Journal* (June 24, 1994): B1.

8. M. Hiskey. "Olympic Sponsor Scores." *Atlanta Constitution* (March 16, 1994): A1.

9. E. Underwood. "Farah Suits Up with ESPN's NFL." *Brandweek* (August 8, 1994): 8.

10. J. Pelline. "A Feeding Frenzy Over Sharks Gear." *San Francisco Chronicle* (May 5, 1994): D1.

11. J. Zbar, "Winn-Dixie Gears NFL Promotion to Store Brands." *Advertising Age* (October 11, 1993): 27.

12. Anonymous. "World Cup Pay Off." *San Francisco Chronicle* (June 16, 1994): D2.

13. K. Benezra and M. Grimm. "Wendy's Eyes Heisman Title." *Brandweek* (April 25, 1994): 4.

14. Light and Tilsner. "Go Buy Some Peanuts and Coke and Stuff." *Businessweek* (October 18, 1993): 6.

15. E. Norton. "Pro Volleyball Sponsors Enjoy the Beach Life." *Wall Street Journal* (September 1, 1993): B1.

16. J. E. Vader. "Major League Fun Found in Minors," *The Oregonian* (August 21, 1994): C1.

17. M. Landler. "It's Not Just the Fans on the Edge of Their Seats." *Businessweek* (April 13, 1992): 40.

18. J. Jensen. "High School Olympics Seek Big Time Sponsors." *Advertising Age* (December 6, 1993): 1.

19. Staff. "Teenage Research Unlimited." *Advertising Age* (August 23, 1992): S-1.

20. P. Weisz. "Pharmative Pumps Up NFLers." *Brandweek* (August 22, 1994): 18.

21. J. Flinn. "Predator Pricey, but Efficient." *San Francisco Examiner* (June 24, 1994): B1.

22. Grimm and Benezin. "Coke to Stage Olympic Fan Fest." *Brandweek* (June 6, 1994): 3.

Chapter 5: Event Marketing to Scale

1 From *Beverage World* article by Greg W. Prince, "Planet Guinness."

2. International Events Group.

3. J. P. Dawson. *New York Times* (June 24, 1938): 22.

4. Ibid.

5. J. Cox. "Olympic Strategy Has Its Rewards." *USA Today* (February 21, 1994): B1.

6. Atlanta Committee for the Olympic Games.

7. Associated Press. "San Jose SaberCats Join Arena Football." *San Francisco Chronicle* (December 9, 1994): E8.

8. J. Jensen. "IndyCar-ABC Pact Offers Primer for Shared-Risk Deal." *Advertising Age* (May 24, 1993): 28.

9. K. Fitzgerald and J. Jensen. "Marathons Keep Pace with Sponsors' Needs." *Advertising Age* (November 1, 1993): 34.

10. E. Thomas, Jr. "Atlanta Olympics: Every Minute Counts." *Wall Street Journal* (July 15, 1994): B1.

11. International Olympic Committee.

12. P. Sullivan. "Senior Skins a Super Bowl Alternative." *San Francisco Chronicle* (January 28, 1995): B2.

13. J. Jensen. "How Charlotte Snared Panthers." *Advertising Age* (November 15, 1993): 31.

14. D. Sylvester. "San Jose Hits Big with Little Sports." *San Francisco Chronicle* (January 10, 1994): A17.

15. Anonymous. "Jerry Colangelo's Palace in the Sun." *Industry Week* (April 6, 1992): 72.

16. Illinois Sports Authority.

17. Lethbridge Lore, Lethbridge, Alberta.

Chapter 6: Understanding the Sponsors

1. F. Anderson. "To Go for the Gold, You Gotta Have the Green." *Businessweek* (February 17, 1992): 137.

2. Ernst and Young. *The Name of the Game* (New York: Wiley & Sons, 1994), p. 125.

3. J. Cortez. "PGA Tour = $90 Million in Sales: Cadillac." *Advertising Age* (March 22, 1993): 28.

4. *Regional Sports Report.* (January 1995): 4.

5. Joyce Julius and Associates.

6. J. Berry. "Brandweek Skewers 1992." *Brandweek* (January 4, 1993): 11.

7. D. Smith. "WTA to Set New Course Amid Change." *USA Today* (November 11, 1993): 1C.

Chapter 7: The Media and Broadcast Industry

1. King, Nevins, Zimmerman, et al. *75 Seasons* (Atlanta: Turner Publishing, 1994), p. 104.

2. R. Sandomir. *New York Times* (March 18, 1994):16D.

3. M. Staimer. "TV Ad Giants." *USA Today* (March 25, 1994): B1.

4. M. Roarty. "All Signs Indicate It's a Winning Combination." *Sporting News* (May 11, 1992): p. 9.

5. Nielsen Media Research.

6. A.C. Nielsen. *TV & Cable Fact Book,* and National Cable Television Association.

7. N. T. Kate. "Make It an Event." *American Demographics* (November 1992): 42.

8. M. Hiestand. *USA Today* (November 9, 1994): 3C.

9. D. Petrozello. "Radio Rights for Football Inch Up." *Broadcasting & Cable* (August 15, 1994): 32.

10. Ibid., 33.

11. D. Enrico. "Advertisers Bet on 49ers-Cowboys Showdown." *USA Today* (January 13, 1995): B1.

12. J. Carman. "KTVU the Real Winner in 49er-Dallas Matchup." *San Francisco Chronicle* (January 14, 1995): E1.

13. M. Freeman. "College Pay Pack." *Mediaweek* (September 26, 1994): 10.

14. R. Brown. "Chicago Bars Sued over Signal Theft." *Broadcasting* (November 23, 1992): 28.

15. J. Mandese. "Super Slow Bowl." *Advertising Age* (February 18, 1993): 34.

16. R. Martzke. *USA Today* (November 15, 1994): 3C.

17. C. Heuton. "Settling for Prime." *Mediaweek* (September 5, 1994): 14.

18. J. Jensen. "NBA's Golden Touch." *Advertising Age* (October 17, 1994): 46.

19. King, Nevins, Zimmerman, et al. *75 Seasons* (Atlanta: Turner Publishing, Inc. 1994), p. 200.

20. S. McClellan. "Reds Cut . . ." *Broadcasting & Cable* (November 22, 1993): 27.

21. J. Mandese. *Advertising Age* (March 1, 1993): 46; J. Mandese. "Event TV." *Advertising Age* (June 14, 1993): 3. Leo Burnett (January 30, 1995), reprinted in *USA Today*, 5B.

22. "Inside the Ropes." *Golf Digest* (December 1994): 151.

23. D. Batchelder. "Court Chatter." *Tennis* (December 1992): 18.

24. K. Goldman. "Loss of Baseball, Hockey Curbs Gains at ESPN." *Wall Street Journal* (November 1, 1994): B1.

25. Audit Bureau of Circulations; magazines.

Chapter 8: Licensing and Merchandising

1. The preceeding excerpt is from *Sports Illustrated* (October 31, 1994). © 1994, Time Inc. A. Wolff and R. O'Brien. All rights reserved.

2. Sporting Goods Manufacturers Association.

3. J. Pelline. "A Feeding Frenzy over Sharks Gear." *San Francisco Chronicle* (May 5, 1994): D1. and S.G.M.A.

4. L. Deckard. "Mighty per Caps for Mighty Ducks' Season Opening." *Amusement Business* (October 18, 1993): 1.

5. J. Jensen, ""How Charlotte Snared the Panthers." *Advertising Age* (November 15, 1993): 31.

6. M. Starr. "We Was Robbed." *Newsweek* (August 22, 1994): 53.

7. Ibid.

8. C. Roush. "Red Necks, White Socks and Blue Chip Sponsors." *Businessweek* (August 15, 1994): 74.

9. *Marketing News*, (September 27, 1993)

10. *Nations's Business* (October 1991): 13.

11. S. Lubove. "Going, Going, Sold." *Forbes* (October 14, 1991): 180.

12. M. Hiestand. "Check Out These Items for Christmas." *USA Today* (November 22, 1994): 3C.

13. *Beverage World* (Fall 1993): 124.

14. C. Mitchell. *Atlanta Constitution* (May 26, 1994 p. 3.

15. J. Riley and S. Ward. "Pinning Hopes on Olympics." *USA Today* (November 14, 1994): C1.

16. S. Lubove. "Going, Going, Sold." *Forbes* (October 14, 1991 p. 180.

17. E. Malkin. "US Sports Teams Tackle Sales in Mexico." *Advertising Age* (September 13, 1993): 12.

18. Anonymous. *Sporting Goods Business* (July 23, 1993): 24.

19. C. Mortensen. "The NFL's War behind the Trading Cards." *Sporting News* (April 6, 1992): 34.

20. F. Meeks. "Mound Merchant." *Forbes* (April 13, 1992): 20.

21. D. Seideman. "And a Fan Gets a Souvenir." *Time* (December 6, 1993): 24.

22. M. Jaffe. "Sold . . . ," *Sports Illustrated* (July 29, 1991): 76.

23. Anonymous. "Chamberlain, Russell at Autograph Session." *San Francisco Chronicle* (January 19, 1995): D8.

24. J. Jensen. "NBA's Golden Touch." *Advertising Age* (October 17, 1994): 46.

25. C. W. Nevius. "SI No Longer Write." *San Francisco Chronicle* (October 22, 1994): B5.

Chapter 9: Sporting Goods and Lifestyle Marketing

1. Reprinted from "Sign Language, Atheletes & Autographs." Masters Press (1994).

2. T. Parker. "Williamsport . . ." *American Demographics* (November 1992): 36.

3. Sporting Goods Marketing Association.

4. *Sporting Goods Intelligence.*

5. Golf Digest Research Resource Center (December 1994).

6. J. Flinn. "Predator Pricey, but Efficient." *San Francisco Examiner* (June 24, 1994): B1.

7. *Wall Street Journal Index,* General News 1994.

8. D. Rosato. "Take a Gander at Sports-Gear Retailer." *USA Today* (November 11, 1994): 4B.

9. C. Stogel. "Golf Channel Eyes Integrated Ad Pacts." *Brandweek* (January 16, 1995 p. 14.

10. Anonymous. "Poll: Fitness Buffs Declining." *Discount Store News* (August 2, 1993): 4.

11. D. Silverman, "Connors Doubles with Reebok." *Footwear News* (September 6, 1993): 21.

12. Interview with former marketing director, Solutlex.

13. Wentz and Mussey. "Louis-Dreyfus Sets Sights on Adidas." *Advertising Age* (February 8, 1993): 3.

14. J. Flinn. "Predator Pricey, but Efficient." *San Francisco Examiner* (June 24, 1994): B1.

15. E. Neuborne. "Sports Authority: Winner or Loser," *USA Today* (January 10, 1995): 4B.

16. P. Jacobus, "Fewer Are Asking, Tennis Anyone?" *San Francisco Chronicle* (August 17, 1994): A1.

Chapter 10: Endorsements

1. The preceding excerpt is from *Sports Illustrated* (September 7, 1992): 24. Copyright © 1992, Time, Inc. P. King. "Catch the Risings Stars." All rights reserved.
2. G. Prince. "Dream Team III." *Beverage World* (January 1995): 25.
3. K. Tyrer. "Finally, a Challenge." *Adweek* (April 4, 1994): 4.
4. D. Mussey. "Wimbledon Win Raises Stich's Endorsement Profile." *Advertising Age* (July 15, 1991): 16.
5. Gossage McFarland Sports Marketing, Harrisburg, N.C.
6. E. Comte. "Rich as Coaches." *Forbes*, (May 24, 1993): 18.
7. J. Curtis. "NCAA Championship Game." *San Francisco Chronicle* (April 4, 1994): B4.
8. E. Comte, "Blade Runner." *Forbes* (October 12, 1992): 114.
9. J. Bartlett, "The Golf Bag." *Forbes* (September 27, 1993): S18.
10. M. Rosenberg. "Hot Products '89." *Adweek* (October (June 89): 42.
11. J. Jensen. "Star Athletes Go Extra Mile." *Advertising Age* (November 22, 1993): 28.
12. T. Bonk. "Money Talk." *Los Angeles Times* (November 13, 1994): C12.
13. P. Sloan. "Mashburn Heads for NBA, Big Fila Deal." *Advertising Age* (June 14, 1993): 4.
14. Ibid.
15. R. Lane. "Prepackaged Celebrity." *Forbes* (December 20, 1993): 86.
16. M. Magiera. "Summer Brings King Size Shaq Attack for Pepsi." *Advertising Age* (May 3, 1993): 3.
17. J. Liesse. "Gatorade Growth Seen Outside U.S." *Advertising Age* (November 15, 1993): 46.
18. M. Grimm. "Reebok Court King Shaq.' *Brandweek* (November 29, 1993): 5.

Chapter 11: Sports Marketing Buyers and Sellers

1. *Forbes* (December 19, 1994): 238.
2. J. Burnett and A. Menon. "Sports Marketing: A New Ballgame with New Rules." *Journal of Advertising Research* (September–November 1993): 21.
3. American Sports Data/Sports Media Index Report.
4. "The Book of Baseball Records." Reprinted in *USA Today* (November 26, 1994): B1.
5. D. Jones. "World Series Cash Players Count Losses." *USA Today* (November 26, 1994): B1.

Chapter 12: Future Issues in Sports Marketing

1. Michan and Contavespi. "Compounded Interest Are Our Favorite Words." *Forbes* (December 19, 1994): 244; M. Starr. "We Was Robbed." *Newsweek* (August 22, 1994): 52.

2. D. Langendorf. "Effects of Irish TV Deal Still Not Clear." *The Dallas Times Herald* (June 2, 1990): C3.

3. Ibid.

4. "Baseball Rankings." *Financial World* (May 10, 1994): 52.

5. Benezra and Grimm. "Coke Nets $285 Million NBA Pact." *Brandweek* (February 14, 1994): 4.

6. R. Sandomir. "Fix It Time." *Sports Year in Review 1991-1992,* p. 499.

7. J. McBride. "Boxing Is Medium's Undisputed Champ." *Variety* (July 22, 1991): 42.

8. S. Moshavi. "Ruddock-Page Bout Goes to Pay TV." *Broadcasting* (January 13, 1992): 82.

9. J. Cooper. "Waiting for the Technological Godot." *Broadcasting & Cable* (November 29, 1993): 57.

10. R. Sandomir. "Triplecast + Tyson = Trouble." *1991–92 Year in Review,* p. 499; *Newsweek* (January 13, 1992): 44; M. Gelman, "1992 Oly's: PPV's Biggest Test." *Variety* (July 22, 1991): 45; and J. Liesse. "Recent Growing Pains Can't Stop PPV Gains." *Advertising Age* (August 24, 1992): S1.

11. R. Martzke. "Company Dishing Up Games." *USA Today* (November 22, 1994): 3C.

12. B. Crumley. "French Adjusting to Tobacco Ad Ban." *Advertising Age* (January 18, 1993): I-6.

13. J. Jensen. "How Charlotte Snared Panthers." *Advertising Age* (November 15, 1993): 31.

Glossary

These terms are defined in the context of practical uses in the sports marketing industry. This list, and its definitions, are by no means exhaustive. Like the dynamic industry they describe, the terms constantly evolve.

Added-Value (or, Value Added). This is a term that all sales interests frequently use to position their sponsorship opportunity. The concept implies that the buyer will indeed receive more in actual value than they pay.

Definitive added-value situations arise when positive developments occur. For example, NBC's and TNT's advertisers (and the Chicago Bulls' sponsors) experienced tremendous added-value when Michael Jordan returned to the NBA. Obviously, added-value is desirable, if not always obvious. And if it really exists, companies can be certain that it will be reflected in rising sponsorship/advertising fees.

Ambush Marketing. This term applies to companies that identify with sporting events and the activities without paying the tariff of sponsorship. VISA, for example, is the official credit card of the Olympics. In 1994, American Express purchased advertising time from CBS, the American broadcaster, for the games. American Express cleverly created ads saying that you didn't need a visa (i.e., a travel permit) to travel to Lillehammer, you just needed an American Express card. VISA was ambushed because the International Olympic Committee and United States Olympic Committee did not control the inventory of CBS' time. The Olympics have since created a sponsor protection service.

ANCILLARY MARKETS. Also known as alternative profit centers. These develop away from the main entertainment, but capitalize upon the excitement of the athlete(s) and competition. Trading cards and all licensed merchandise are growing (billions and billions) at such a rapid rate that they cannot be truly considered just ancillary markets. Their financial power makes them primary revenue sources in the minds of property rights holders.

ARENA ENTITLEMENT. Selling the rights to a facility's name. The Fabulous Forum turned into the Great Western Forum because the bank's marketing department believed that it would generate media traffic. PepsiCo will invest $68 million into the Pepsi Arena in Denver because it knows that it can sell significant amounts of its products on site in addition to generating media traffic. Over time this will prove to be an excellent investment for Pepsi.

Many examples exist in the arena entitlement category. A short list includes Arco Arena, America West Arena, Target Center, Great Western Forum, and the United Center.

BARNSTORMING. The old way that event promoters (and athletes) made money. Much like air shows and circuses, the show hit the road and traveled to fairgrounds, abandoned fields, and stadiums to entertain fans that had only heard of many sports heroes through the media. The Harlem Globetrotters, it should be mentioned, are still the longest-standing barnstorming act in America.

Babe Ruth and his Bustin' Babes (the team's name) traveled to rural areas to bring his legend and the game of baseball to the masses. Early twentieth century golf matches were nothing more than exhibitions, and as television and a cohesive audience developed, advertisers brought a degree of subsidy to sports. As leagues developed, barnstorming opportunities declined.

Red Grange, it should be noted, is also one of the great barnstorming athletes in the history of America. He attracted great crowds and brought a high-degree of notoriety and interest to professional football.

Billboards and Billboard Drop-ins. These are commercial enhancements to broadcasts, both visual and verbal. The most common billboard is a drop in of a logo for a section of the program. Announcements leading into NBC's Domino's Halftime Report, or Fox's Levi's Dockers® Halftimes are accompanied by billboard drop-ins to promote the event. Other billboards accompany announcements and changes in the action. For example, when a relief pitcher enters a game, an announcer might say It's time for a change, and when your car needs a change, bring it to Jiffy Lube. . . ."

Broadcast Rights Fees. As the title suggests, the fees that networks and stations pay to carry a part of or all of the action. The NFL is divided among ABC, NBC, Fox, ESPN, and TNT. But all of the respective parties have explicitly defined boundaries of which games and which times, they can broadcast. For example, Fox paid $1.58 billion for the four year broadcast rights to the NFL and NBC paid $456 million to broadcast the 1996 Summer Olympics in the United States.

Virtually every event has a broadcast rights fee. The Chicago Marathon will be cheaper than tennis' US Open, and the property holder will negotiate to earn the most amount of money possible. Rights can pertain to international borders and rebroadcasts and other restrictions. The fee is usually determined based upon the audience and the ability to sell advertising. For that reason, unlikely events like professional wrestling can do very well while historic ones like the Tour de France may suffer.

Bye Week. The NFL uses this to extend the season and enhance its broadcast package. One more week of action, hype, and highlights can be packaged and sold to advertisers to generate more revenue for the networks, and more exposure for the league. The bye week rotates so that entire divisions will not play during designated weeks. When each division does this (the players still practice), it extends the sixteen-week season into seventeen weeks.

Category Sponsorship. An event promoter, or rights holder, parcels out the event's inventory in sponsor categories. The PGA has an official non-alcoholic beer, O'Douls. The Olympics has an official fast-food sponsor, McDonald's. The property rights holder creates a valuable premium through distinct designations such as these.

Co-Branding. A bank, for example, will sell checking accounts to customers with the team's logo. Bank of America has offered "Blazer Banking"—a program that is developed because of a sponsorship between the Blazers and the bank. Sports teams' logos on VISA credit cards is another good example of co-branding.

ENTITLEMENT. Buying the name, or inclusion, in the name of an event, or property. Examples are numerous: the MCI Heritage Classic, Shell's Wonderful World of Golf, The Great Western Forum, The Nabisco Dinah Shore, The French Open presented by Perrier.

John Hancock paid the Sun Bowl committee a reported $150,000 to drop the Sun name reference to sharpen the Hancock association. In other words, people still referred to the game as the "Sun Bowl," and not the "John Hancock Sun Bowl," and the people at Hancock wanted to reduce the margin of error. Sponsors pay primarily for entitlement privileges to gain visibility and media exposure. Along with expensive entitlement packages, sponsors receive tickets, hospitality privileges, and all sorts of advertising in publications and billboards related to the event. Entitlement privileges have spread to categories such as the presenting sponsor (the Heisman Trophy, presented by Wendy's), or halftime sponsor, etc.

EQUITY. Many companies like to build value into brands and trademarks through sponsorships and endorsements. Air Jordan®, or Greg Norman's Shark logo are recognized, and sold, worldwide. These brands have tremendous commercial power as the combined result of the corporate investment and competitive excitement. Other brands, such as PowerBar®, have significant brand equity through exposure, recognition, and event usage.

EVENT ACCESS. A byproduct of a sponsorship. If Coca-Cola® needs extra tickets to the Super Bowl, or festivities around the event, its request will most likely receive special consideration from the NFL. Sponsors also receive invitations to other events like coaches chalk talks, and special field passes before games. Tents are placed at golf tournaments for the specific purpose of entertaining clients and providing access that most fans ordinarily cannot receive.

EVENT PRODUCT INCLUSION. Sponsors like to see their products on the bench, or wherever applicable. Gatorade® jugs, cups, and towels are featured on benches in virtually every sport. Gatorade® pays for that distinction. Goodyear tires in racing, and Spalding basketballs in the NBA are other examples. Companies know that consumers of all ages will see what the athletic heroes use and they will buy those products. Remember that big putter that Jack Nicklaus used to win the 1986 Masters? Millions went out and bought the putter, even if they couldn't compete at Augusta National.

EVENT TRIANGLE. The simplistic model that illustrates the interdependence of events, sponsors, and fans. The Triangle demonstrates how each group leverages the others to its own benefit. The premise of the "Event Triangle" is that fans seek the event entertainment through sponsors and promoters, sponsors seek the audience through the event, and the event solicits both the audience and the sponsors. The result is$179 billion in annual business.

EXCLUSIVITY. Having product category privileges in a defined manner. The Olympics are famous for selling high priced sponsorships (up to $40 million). The IOC can do this by guaranteeing exclusivity. This means that Coca-Cola® will be the only soft drink sponsor to associate with the games, use the logo on packaging, and all forms of advertising, etc. Exclusivity allows Rawlings to say that they are the official ball of Major League Baseball. Exclusivity, however, has created the *ambush marketing* phenomenon where companies pursue methods to identify with parts of an event without paying the property rights holder. Exclusivity gives a participating sponsor another promotional angle to build identity with a property. Exclusivity is also a standard part of an endorsement agreement. Reebok, for example, would not allow Shaquille O'Neal to endorse any Nike product.

EXIT MENTION. At the conclusion of a game, the broadcasters will thank the participating sponsors. For example, "the NBA on NBC was brought to you by Miller Genuine Draft® . . . Get out of the old and into the Cold."

FIXED POSITION ADVERTISING. Many advertisers insist on being the first advertiser after a break, or before the game. This is another premium that broadcasters package to their advertisers.

FRANCHISE. A word that has two different sports marketing definitions. The first one is that of a team in a league. The Cincinnati Bengals are an NFL franchise. The Toronto Raptors are a new NBA expansion franchise that will play its first game in 1995. The other meaning is that of a name, or event, that grows in sponsor-related value. The Skins Game is an event where the franchise of the name, format, and promoters has been established. More importantly, it continues to grown in stature and value. Electronic Arts' John Madden Football is another valuable franchise, because there is brand recognition and identifiable profits. As the franchise of a product or event increases, so does the fee of promotional access.

INVENTORY. This is the concept that separates and categorizes the opportunities that property rights holders use to formulate levels of sponsorships. Signage (billboard space), logo/image rights, print and electronic media, tickets, special events,and entitlement privileges are all inventory elements. The key for a promoter is to define all of the inventory that has value. The goal for the promotional buyer is to purchase the necessary elements to create a successful promotion, or message, consistent with the product or service and its trade and consumer markets.

LEVERAGE. A term that applies to a sponsor's strategy in using a promotion in the markets. Companies use their identification rights, endorsement ties, and sponsorship agreements to involve key retail accounts, or distributors. To realize a return on their sponsorship investment, companies seek ways to meet objectives, and engage consumer audience. Gatorade®, for example, might have a new product to roll out, and they might want to sample it at an NBA arena, or All-Star site. In this example, Gatorade® leverages its sponsorship privileges to gain audience access. On the other hand, properties leverage their audience access to attract and involve sponsors.

LICENSING. Paying a fee to a league, team, entity, or individual to reproduce the image, name, and/or logo on either consumer product packaging or merchandise for sale. Starter® owns an NFL license. Nike licenses Michael Jordan's name and image. Kodak, as an Olympic sponsor, licenses the famous five-ring logo to place on specially marked packages. Licensing applies to video games, clothing items, credit cards, trading cards, equipment, and just about anything for sale. It is a big business for suppliers, contractors, retailers, and promotional partners. The NFL, NBA, and Major League Baseball annually sell billions ($9 billion combined in 1994) in licensed merchandise.

MAKE GOODS. If a telecast does not deliver contractually specified ratings, then the broadcaster is obligated to give the advertising company more commercial time on other broadcasts. This is done to minimize an advertiser's risk. If CBS sells Buick commercial time during a golf broadcast and sells the spots based upon a minimum 3.0 rating, and the actual rating is 2.5, they will give Buick a portion of advertising time during other broadcasts to make up for the prices charged for the original spots that were sold.

MERCHANDISE REDEMPTION. A simple concept used by consumer product companies to drive retail sales. Based upon the simple concept of consumer incentive, merchandise offers are a proven lure. Castrol Motor Oil has an NFL license, and they offer consumers a free NFL hat with every case purchased. The consumer receives a free logo hat after they have bought the oil and sent in the proof of purchase seal. Castrol also gets a nice consumer database from the promotion.

RATE CARD. The fees for commercial advertising time on radio or television for an event. Broadcasters try to sell multiple commercial units, or spots, to category sponsors, i.e. beer, soda, fast food, or automotive. The prices are derived on the audience, both the quantity of viewers and the quality. Upscale events like golf, for example, will command higher advertising fees than wrestling. Units are usually sold in multiples of 30 seconds: 30, 60, or 90.

REVENUE SHARING. A boon for the NFL, and bane for Major League Baseball. Revenue sharing means exactly what it implies; teams share revenue. This can be an even split, or one based on percentages. Baseball teams share a skewed percentage of the gate receipts (home team gets more) and national broadcast contract income (divided equally). They do not divide local broadcast revenues, and that leads to revenue disparities among the large and small market teams. The NFL evenly divides national television revenues, providing over $30 million per team. They also equally divide licensing income, but not regional radio and preseason game broadcast revenue. The argument on revenue sharing usually pits the small market teams, i.e. Milwaukee, vs. the large market ones, i.e., New York. The question centers around the benefits of economic socialism to the fans and the leagues. The benefits are obvious in terms of financial solvency, but what team wants to give up its revenue to subsidize its competitor? The problem is that in a sixteen-game NFL season versus the 162-game baseball season, national television coverage applies to *all* footfall games, but only a very few baseball games. Therefore, dividing revenue on local baseball broadcasts is a thorny issue for major league owners and players.

STRATEGIC MARKETING OBJECTIVES. A buzz-phrase that means nothing more than "goals." The phrase is used in this book, and in reality, probably too often. However, the formal approach probably helps companies commit to sponsorships and to promotions that evolve from event identification.

"VENUS FLYTRAP" APPROACH. Trying to position a product, or a company, in a place so that free publicity and athlete access is probable. For example, putting a product display, i.e., video game booth, in a hotel lobby housing teams and/or event participants. The lobby will have many celebrities and media walking through. Maybe they will stop by the booth.

Name Index